Praise for *Social Cognition: Development, Neuroscience and Autism*

"The volume is an important collection of chapters at the cutting edge of developmental social neuroscience. In addition to several well known figures, the international array of authors includes some rising stars whose work points to the future of the field. This exciting synthesis of social cognition and developmental neuroscience will provide stimulating reading for a wide variety of researchers and students of typical and atypical human development."

Professor Mark H Johnson, Director of the Centre for
Brain & Cognitive Development, University of London

"A landmark for a new era in social cognition research, Striano and Reid have gathered together an outstanding collection of contributions to point the way to a truly interdisciplinary social cognitive developmental neuroscience. Coherently organized and thoughtfully edited, this volume represents the latest in research and theory on social cognition in the brain and on how it changes through typical and atypical development. The quality and range of the chapters will make the volume an invaluable reference for researchers and students alike."

Professor Chris Moore, Dalhousie University

"The new discipline of social neuroscience has made remarkable strides in the last decade. This book is an important and highly readable collection of essays in the field. It should help dissolve the barrier between what C P Snow called 'The two cultures' – science and humanities – long separated by a gap he regarded as unbridgeable."

VS Ramachandran MD

"The last 10 years have witnessed an explosion in our understanding of the neural and developmental factors that underlie social interactions in humans. This impressive volume skilfully weaves together the various threads that have driven this revolution forward to produce a work of significant importance.

Striano and Reid have managed to bring together most of the world's top experts in social cognitive neurosciences through 21 neatly written and interrelated chapters. It is refreshing to see that the majority of authors are European-based, thereby providing not just a European perspective on this vibrant discipline, but underscoring the centrality of European research in this endeavour.

As a whole, this collection provides both an erudite and gripping glimpse into what makes us who we are as individuals within a society. While there are several other works on the foundations of social cognition, Section 4 of the current volume on social cognition in children with autism and other developmental disorders makes the work stand out as a unique contribution. It should be essential reading for students of human behaviour and practitioners alike who wish to catch up with the latest developments in our understanding of the social brain."

Professor Denis Mareschal, Centre for Brain and Cognitive Development,
Birkbeck University of London

Social Cognition
Development, Neuroscience, and Autism

Edited by
Tricia Striano
and Vincent Reid

A John Wiley & Sons, Ltd., Publication

This edition first published 2009
© 2009 Blackwell Publishing Ltd

Blackwell Publishing was acquired by John Wiley & Sons in February 2007. Blackwell's publishing program has been merged with Wiley's global Scientific, Technical, and Medical business to form Wiley-Blackwell.

Registered Office
John Wiley & Sons Ltd, The Atrium, Southern Gate, Chichester, West Sussex, PO19 8SQ, United Kingdom

Editorial Offices
350 Main Street, Malden, MA 02148-5020, USA
9600 Garsington Road, Oxford, OX4 2DQ, UK
The Atrium, Southern Gate, Chichester, West Sussex, PO19 8SQ, UK

For details of our global editorial offices, for customer services, and for information about how to apply for permission to reuse the copyright material in this book please see our website at www.wiley.com/wiley-blackwell.

The right of Tricia Striano and Vincent Reid to be identified as the author of the editorial material in this work has been asserted in accordance with the Copyright, Designs and Patents Act 1988.

Library of Congress Cataloging-in-Publication Data

Social cognition : development, neuroscience, and autism / edited by Tricia Striano and Vincent Reid.
    p. ; cm.
  "This edited volume stems from questions and issues that were explored by contributors of the European Science Foundation Exploratory Workshop on Person Perception, held in Leipzig, Germany, in June, 2005. Developmental advances were also presented at the European Developmental Psychology Conference, Dual-Symposium on Person Perception During Infancy in Tenerife in August, 2005."–ECIP summary.
  Includes bibliographical references and index.
    ISBN 978-1-4051-6217-3 (hardcover : alk. paper)   1. Social perception in children.
2. Cognition in children.   3. Cognition in infants.   4. Autism–Pathophysiology.   5. Cognitive neuroscience.   I. Striano, Tricia.   II. Reid, Vincent.
    [DNLM: 1. Cognition.   2. Adolescent.   3. Autistic Disorder–psychology.   4. Child.
5. Infant.   WS 105.5.C7 S6775 2009]

  BF723.S6S58 2009
  155.4'13–dc22

                                                                          2008009665

A catalogue record for this book is available from the British Library.

Set in 10.5 on 13 point Minion by SNP Best-set Typesetter Ltd., Hong Kong
Printed in Singapore by Fabulous Printers Pte Ltd

1   2009

Contents

List of Figures and Tables

Figures

Tables

List of Contributors

Professor Simon Baron-Cohen
Autism Research Centre
Department of Experimental
    Psychology
University of Cambridge
Douglas House
18b Trumpington Road
Cambridge, CB2 8AH
UK

Professor Harold Bekkering
Nijmegen Institute for Cognition and
    Information
Radboud University Nijmegen –
Dept. of Cognitive Psychology
P.O. Box 9104, 6500 HE Nijmegen,
The Netherlands

Sarah-Jayne Blakemore, Ph.D.
UCL Institute of Cognitive Neuroscience
17 Queen Square
London WC1N 3AR
UK

Marcel Brass, Ph.D.
Department of Experimental
    Psychology
Ghent University
Henri Dunantlaan 2
9000 Gent
Belgium

Jon Brock, Ph.D.
Macquarie Centre for Cognitive Science
Macquarie University
Sydney, NSW 2109
Australia

Beatrice de Gelder, Ph.D.
Cognitive and affective neuroscience lab
Tilburg University
PO Box 90153 5000 LE
Tilburg
The Netherlands

Professor Daniel C. Dennett
Center for Cognitive Studies
11 Miner Hall
Tufts University
Medford, MA, 02155-7059
USA

Shiri Einav, Ph.D.
Department of Experimental
    Psychology
University of Oxford
South Parks Road
Oxford OX1 3UD
UK

Professor Birgit Elsner
Prof. Dr. Birgit Elsner
Abteilung Entwicklungspsychologie

Universität Potsdam
Karl-Liebknecht-Str. 24-25
D-14476 Golm
Germany

Elena Geangu, Ph.D.
Romanian Academy of Sciences
M. Kogalniceanu Street, 8
3400, Cluj-Napoca, CJ
Romania

Gustaf Gredebäck, Ph.D.
The Cognitive Developmental Research
  Unit
Department of Psychology
University of Oslo
Postboks 1094 Blindern
0317 Oslo
Norway

Julie Grèzes, Ph.D.
Laboratoire de Neurosciences
  Cognitives
UMR 742 INSERM
Département d'Etudes
  Cognitives
Ecole Normale Supérieure
29 Rue d'Ulm – 75005 Paris
France

Richard Griffin, D.Phil.
Center for Cognitive Studies
11 Miner Hall
Tufts University
Medford, MA 02155-7059
USA

Tobias Grossmann, Ph.D.
Centre for Brain and Cognitive
  Development
Birkbeck College
Malet Street
London WC1E 7HX
UK

Professor Petra Hauf
Department of Psychology
St. Francis Xavier University
P.O. Box 5000
Antigonish, Nova Scotia
Canada, B2G 2W5

Jessica A. Hobson, Ph.D.
Developmental Psychopathology
  Research Unit
Tavistock Clinic and Department
  of Psychiatry and Behavioural
  Sciences
University College London
120 Belsize Lane
London NW3 5BA
UK

Professor R. Peter Hobson
Developmental Psychopathology
  Research Unit
Tavistock Clinic and Department of
  Psychiatry and Behavioural Sciences
University College London
120 Belsize Lane
London NW3 5BA
UK

Stephanie Hoehl
Max Planck Institute for Human
  Cognitive and Brain Sciences
Stephanstrasse 1a
04303 Leipzig
Germany

Marco Iacoboni, M. D., Ph.D.
Director, Transcranial Magnetic
  Stimulation Lab
Ahmanson-Lovelace Brain Mapping
  Center
David Geffin School of Medicine at
  UCLA
California
USA

Robert M. Joseph, Ph.D.
Department of Anatomy and
  Neurobiology
Boston University School of Medicine
715 Albany Street, L-814
Boston, MA 02118-2526
USA

Ildikó Király, Ph.D.
Department of Cognitive Psychology
Eötvös Lorand University
Budapest
Hungary

Professor Charles A. Nelson
Children's Hospital Boston
Developmental Medicine Center
Laboratories of Cognitive Neuroscience
1 Autumn Street
Boston, MA 02115-5365
USA

Pines Nuku
Nijmegen Institute for Cognition and
  Information
Radboud University Nijmegen –
Dept. of Cognitive Psychology
P.O. Box 9104, 6500 HE Nijmegen
The Netherlands

Vincent M. Reid, Ph.D.
Department of Psychology
Durham University
Sciences Site
South Road
Durham DH1 3LE
UK

Deborah M. Riby, Ph.D.
School of Psychology
Newcastle University
Ridley Building 1
Framlington Place
Newcastle-upon-Tyne
NE1 7RU
UK

Professor Philippe Rochat
Department of Psychology
318 Psychology Building
532 Kilgo Circle
Emory University
Atlanta, GA 30322
USA

Stephanie Spengler
Max Planck Institute for Human
  Cognitive and Brain Sciences
Stephanstrasse 1a
04303 Leipzig
Germany

Tricia Striano, Ph.D.
Department of Psychology
Hunter College
695 Park Avenue
New York, NY 10065
USA

Professor Helen Tager-Flusberg
Department of Anatomy and
  Neurobiology
Boston University School of
  Medicine
715 Albany Street, L-814
Boston, MA 02118-2526
USA

Amrisha Vaish
Department of Developmental and
  Comparative Psychology
Max Planck Institute for Evolutionary
  Anthropology
Deutscher Platz 6
D-04103 Leipzig
Germany

Professor Claes von Hofsten
Department of Psychology
Uppsala University
Box 1225, S-75142 Uppsala
Sweden

Abbreviations

1PP	first-person perspective
3PP	third-person perspective
ACC	anterior cingulate cortex
AD	adult-directed [speech]
ADOS-G	Autism Diagnostic Observation Schedule – General
aFMC	anterior fronto-medial cortex
AMG	amygdala
ANOVA	analysis of variance
AOI	area of interest
AS	Asperger syndrome
ASC	Autism Spectrum Conditions
ASD	Autism Spectrum Disorder
BAN	basic affiliative need
BOLD	blood oxygenation level dependent
DS	difference score
DSM	Diagnostic and Statistical Manual
DTI	diffusion tensor imaging
EDD	eye-direction detector
EEG	electroencephalogram/electroencephalographic
EM	enactive mind
ERP	event-related potential (*also* event-related brain potential)
FFA	face-processing area/fusiform area
fMRI	functional magnetic resonance imaging
GM	grey matter
HA	human-agent [condition]
ID	infant-direct [speech]
ID	intentionality director
IOR	inhibition of response

IPLP	intermodal preferential looking paradigm
MA	mental age
MANOVA	multivariate analysis of variance
MEG	magnetoencephalography
MM	mechanical-motion [condition]
MPFC	medial prefrontal cortex
MNS	mirror neuron system
MRI	magnetic resonance imaging
ms	millisecond
Nc	negative component
NIRS	near infrared spectroscopy
OFC	orbitofrontal cortex
PAR	parietal
PET	positron emission tomography
PFC	prefrontal cortex
PLD	point light display
PM	premotor
RT	reaction time
SAM	shared attention mechanism
SLI	specific language impairment
SM	systemizing mechanism
SOA	stimulus onset asynchrony
SP	self-propelled [condition]
SQ	systemizing quotient
STS	superior temporal sulcus
TEC	Theory of Event Coding
TED	the emotion detector
TESS	the emphathizing system
TMS	transcranial magnetic stimulation
TOM	theory of mind
TOMM	theory-of-mind mechanism
TPJ	temporo-parietal junction
VSTH	very simple theory [of mind]
WM	white matter

Editors' Preface

Social cognition is a highly complex field of study. The questions that it involves are at the heart of what it means to be human – to relate to other people, to communicate with them, to learn from them. Researchers are attracted to the field for different reasons. Many developmentalists are concerned with the actual point in time that skills such as face, voice, and body processing are acquired. What types of experiences if any are needed for a newborn or 30-day-old infant to discriminate between people and objects? How does the infant learn whom and what to attend to in order to learn language or to imitate? How do these developments prepare the infant to relate to other people?

As developmentalists we generally address the "when" question, with not very much emphasis on the "how" or the "why." As neuroscientists we have the tools to address mechanisms of social cognitive processes. What is happening in the brain when someone looks at us with an angry or a happy emotional expression? How do these neural processes affect our behavior, and how does our behavior in turn affect neural processing? With the emergence of neuroimaging techniques we are able not only to identify the speed at which information is processed, but also to identify the neural structures and networks that are responsible.

Some years ago, we learned the value of merging our own fields of expertise (Striano: developmental psychology; Reid: developmental cognitive neuroscience) in a highly collaborative and interdisciplinary way. With the use of both electrophysiological and behavioral methods, we found that we were better able to address questions about the ways young infants processed relatively complex social and cognitive information. With these additional tools we were able to speculate better about how these neural processes might interact with early infant behavior or the lack thereof. In many cases we found that results from behavioral development and brain development did not merge. In some cases, measures of infant brain activity seemed to precede behavioral changes and overt responses.

As we obtained answers to some fundamental questions on the nature of early social cognition, we were inspired by many colleagues in our respective fields of both behavioral development and neuroscience. In 2004 we brought many of them together at the workshop "Person Perception during Infancy: Integrating Development and Comparative Psychology, Cognitive Neuroscience, Psychology of Language and Communication," funded by the European Science Foundation. At this mini conference we explored the way that humans understood and processed other people. Our goal was to bring together colleagues from two fields who generally work in isolation, but who were in truth addressing similar questions that complemented each other. At the Person Perception workshop we explored the neural structures and processes that guide complex social cognitive abilities such as those skills required to understand someone's intention or goal. In addition, we explored the neural processes and structures that guide imitation, language, and theory of mind. When we turned to the issue of development, it was clear that many fundamental issues were not resolved. Could our understanding of the early development of social cognition be guided by what we already knew from a vast research on adult brain and social cognitive behaviours? In addition, we took the chance to integrate experts from the field of autism. How could our knowledge of brain and behavioral development help us to understand the mechanisms of autism? In turn, how could our understanding of autism inform adult cognitive neuroscience and early infant development?

This workshop was soon followed by two organized symposia at the European Conference on Developmental Psychology in Tenerife, "Actions, Goals and Intentions" and "Actions, Intentions and Agency." Here we brought together several scientists who reported on some of the fundamental components of what it is to be a social individual. It was clear that there was a synergy through all presenters, from those who were investigating complex cognitive functions, such as predicting goals, through to those who were analysing eye movements and gaze direction. Many of these presentations were eventually published in a special issue of the *European Journal of Developmental Psychology* that we guest edited in 2007. Others have been included in this volume, particularly those that have lessons for related disciplines, such as adult cognitive neuroscience or developmental psychopathology.

This volume also includes several chapters from top researchers who inspired much of our work and whose research provides the basis not only for present understandings of key issues, but has also shown the way forward for the future of social cognition research.

We owe many thanks to all those people who inspired us to put this volume together and who provided the various means along the way. We are grateful to the European Science Foundation and the Alexander von Humboldt Foundation for the support that allowed us to bring these top researchers together.

At Wiley-Blackwell, Elizabeth Ann Johnston has been a wonderful source of support and guidance. Without her help, this volume would not be in its present shape or form.

Just like the inspiration that we have received and given to each other with our diverse backgrounds and expertise, we hope that this volume will inspire students and scientists who research and study social cognition via neuroscience, development, and autism. In sum, we hope that this volume will highlight the benefits of learning about and integrating (or at least being cognisant of) diverse fields. We think this interdisciplinary approach is the key to answering the most fundamental questions of social cognition, many of which have not yet been addressed in any shape or form. This unique volume shows us the way forward in what is unquestionably one of the most dynamic and evolving interdisciplinary fields.

Tricia Striano and Vincent Reid

Part One
Research and Social Cognition

Chapter 1

Social Cognition at the Crossroads: Perspectives on Understanding Others

Tricia Striano and Vincent Reid

Social cognition involves our ability to predict, monitor, and interpret the behaviors and mental states of other people. Given the importance of social cognition in interaction and survival, it is no surprise that humans have evolved to infer the meaning of others' behavior with such adeptness. As adults we can take a quick glance at other people's faces or listen only briefly to their vocal cues, and gain information that is critical to understanding their actual mental state and even their future behavior. There are also aspects of human behavior and cognition that appear unique. These behaviors include prolonged eye-to-eye contact, socially elicited smiling, and intersubjectivity or shared experience between individuals via turn taking, timing, and sharing of affect and expressions (Rochat & Striano, 1999).

With a range of new techniques we are now better able to probe the ways that humans understand others. But these new techniques have also led to some problems. Interest in social cognition from multiple disciplines since the mid-1990s has created an overall field that currently lacks cohesion. Each subdiscipline appears to be following its own path, with little reference to related issues or topics investigated in alternative ways. For instance, the majority of developmental psychologists in this field are focusing on how infants develop an understanding of others' minds. For example, they may try to determine when infants start to understand the intentions of others or they may investigate transitions in social and cognitive behavior that are presumed to relate to advances in understanding others. For the most part, paradigms utilized arc entirely behavioral and are often difficult to relate to the data from other fields. Comparatively, cognitive neuroscientists are investigating complex aspects of social cognition, such as empathy processing, embodiment, and the precise role of the human mirror neuron system. Again, because of differences in methodology, sometimes these results are difficult to place in a wider context of issues, such as the role of development in complex social-cognitive skills or relations between atypical development such as autism and typical social information processing. In research on autism and related disorders, not only are the paradigms and tests developed unique to the field, but also the questions at hand are often different. In sum, if these disciplines were a trio of musicians, they might all be keeping the same beat but they would be playing different melodies.

Despite the rapid attainment of knowledge in multiple fields related to understanding others, one critical factor for further increased knowledge is the integration of multiple methodologies from different disciplines. In this chapter we will outline how integration of these techniques and perspectives can shed light on seemingly complex aspects of the human mind. Through using case examples of specific research we highlight the advances that can be made when we integrate separate fields of research.

Developing an Understanding of Others

Despite the importance of human social cognition and the behaviors that comprise it, we still know relatively little about its ontogenetic course. We argue that this is for two primary reasons. The first reason is the way that social cognition throughout development has been traditionally studied. Many researchers have focused on major transition periods that occur at around 9 and 18 months of age. In this chapter we do not deny that radical changes occur in the ways that infants and children understand other people at certain times in development. We do, however, want to point out that social cognition – understanding and relating to other people – is a protracted process that begins very early in development. A second reason for our limited understanding of the development of social cognition is that we have had limited paradigms to assess it in preverbal infants. This has been changing. We suggest and hope to demonstrate in this chapter that an interdisciplinary research approach is necessary to understand the ontogenetic pathways that give rise to normal and also to atypical human social cognitive functioning.

The Development of Joint Attention:
A Case Study of Multiple Methodologies

We briefly begin our chapter at the developmental transition, the 9-month transition, which has received so much attention and research since the mid-1990s. There is no denying that something changes by the end of the first postnatal year. By around 9 months of age, infants become much more active in some ways. They move around independently and easily coordinate their attention in triadic ways; that is, between people and objects in the world. It is almost as if the infant's need to gather information from other people directly corresponds to the ability to seek and use this information from other people. This transition is nicely summed up in the following paragraph:

Six month old infants interact dyadically with objects, grasping and manipulating them, and they interact dyadically with other people, expressing emotions back and forth in a turn taking sequence. But at around 9 months to 12 months of age, infants begin to engage in interactions that are triadic in the sense that they involve the referential triangle of child, adult, and some outside entity to which they share attention. (Tomasello, 1999, p. 302)

There is no denying that early in development infants are more likely to engage in dyadic interactions with other people and that, later in development, these interactions become more triadic in nature (D'Entremont, Hains, & Muir, 1997; Nadel & Tremblay-Leveau, 1999). Our own research also supports this view. In one study, we had infants of 3, 6, and 9 months old interacting with an adult stranger, as is shown with the 3-month-old in Figure 1.1 (Striano & Stahl, 2005). We manipulated the social interaction between infant and adult in several ways across studies, but highlight three interactive conditions here to make our point. In one condition, the *joint-attention* condition, the adult coordinated attention between the infant and a toy by the infant's side. She did this by shifting her gaze between the infant and the toy while talking about the toy in a positive tone of voice. In another condition, the *look-away* condition, the adult looked away at the toy while vocalizing in a positive

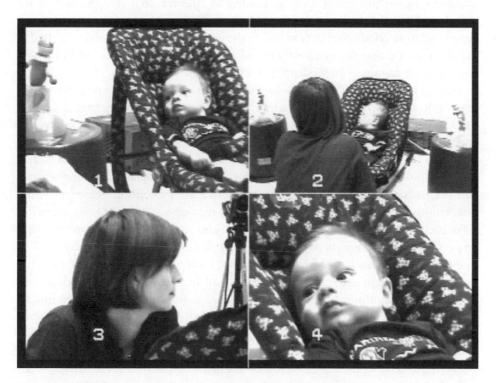

Figure 1.1. Demonstration of triadic interaction in early development
Note: Figure shows 3-month-old following eye gaze viewed from four cameras.
Source: Striano & Stahl (2005).

way, but not by shifting her attention back and forth. We compared these conditions to a normal *dyadic* (face-to-face) interaction in which the adult talked to the infant and did not look at the object. In sum, we found that at all ages infants could discriminate among these three interactive conditions. However, the way that infants discriminated these types of interactions varied according to age. At 3 months of age, infants preferred dyadic interaction, whereas, at the older ages, infants preferred (or at least looked more at the adult during) joint-attention interactions (Striano, 2004; Striano & Stahl, 2005). Why? We think that the demands placed on the 6- and 9-month-olds are very different from demands placed on a 3-month-old. At older ages, infants are capable of manipulating objects and moving around, whereas at younger ages this is much harder without assistance (Campos & Sternberg, 1981). Simply put, triadic interactions are more useful and functional for the older infant. In the same way that we are capable of skydiving or rock climbing, but choose to fly a kite or take a walk to the local pub, the 3–5-month-old infant is highly capable of triadic interactions, although he may simply not require these for effective interaction, survival, or general satisfaction. Social interactions between infants and adults start out primarily dyadic (Stern, 1985; van Wulffen Palthe & Hopkins, 1993). This changes when the need for triadic interactions becomes more important – as infants begin to interact with unfamiliar objects and situations and as they must become sensitive to cues directed at them. But, as we will show later, this is not to imply that infants are not capable of detecting and benefiting from triadic interaction before the end of the first postnatal year. It also may be the case that the systematic use of triadic social skills does not imply any new social or cognitive understanding on the part of the infant.

Did the human infant really develop some new sort of awareness or understanding of others when he was engaging in triadic interactions? Or were triadic interactions merely a different form of social interaction? Possibly the underlying reason and drive for social interaction was the same at 9 months as it was for the infant at 3 months (see also Striano, 2004). We addressed this question in a study of 7- and 10-month-old infants. We tested infants in two phases of social interaction with an adult experimenter (Striano & Rochat, 1999). In a joint-attention phase (or triadic interaction), we measured infants' social responses on a battery of joint-attention tasks such as gaze following, point following, and social referencing. In the other phase of the study, infants participated in a still-face procedure. We expected to find that infants who scored high on triadic or joint-attention skills would use the most re-engagement attempts with the adult during the still-face procedure. For instance, when smiling did not work to re-engage the social partner, the infants might try to clap or then to vocalize to accomplish their goal. These predictions were confirmed. Infants who were engaging in the most triadic behaviors tended to be the same infants who were especially skilled in dyadic responding. This research showed that there seemed to be some link between dyadic and triadic social skills. Maybe it was not the case that the more frequent use of triadic behaviors by the end of the first year meant that infants suddenly understood their social partners differently. But the question still remained (and we think it still does): what did infants understand about the motives and intentions that guided the adult's behavior (Yazbek & D'Entremont, 2006)?

Sensitivity to Dyadic and Triadic Cues

By at least 3 months of age, infants are sensitive to the relevance of dyadic social cues directed at them, with dyadic interactions remaining the primary means of interaction with others. They become upset when communication is not directed at them (Striano, 2004) and even distinguish between an interaction that is directed at them and relevant and an interaction that is directed at them and irrelevant. When do infants become sensitive to the relevance of social cues that refer to objects and events in the world? To address this question, we had 3-, 6-, and 9-month-olds interact with a female adult (Striano & Stahl, 2005). These conditions are shown in Figure 1.2. In one condition, a *joint-attention* condition, the adult talked and smiled and alternated visual attention between the infant and an object. In an *alternating* condition, the adult coordinated visual attention but without smiling or vocalizing. In an *affect-only* condition, she looked at the infant and then up to the ceiling before looking at the object. This condition was to control for the amount of eye contact and positive affect directed toward the infant. In other words, we were controlling for the amount of social cues directed at the infant but making these cues irrelevant by inserting a break in interpersonal contact before the adult looked away at the object. In an *ignore* condition she looked only at the object while taking and providing positive affect. In this study, we found that, by 3 months of age, infants already discriminated among these conditions. In fact, we found little evidence of

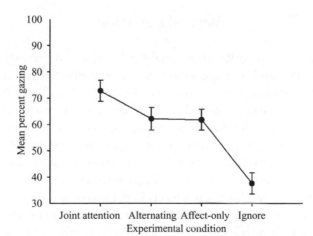

Figure 1.2. Gazing time as a function of joint-attention, alternating, affect-only, and ignore conditions

Note: Results are collapsed for 3-, 6-, and 9-month-old infants.

Source: Striano & Stahl (2005).

developmental transitions in this study. This was the first demonstration that infants could detect triadic or joint-attention interactions by 3 months of age. Just as infants are attuned to the relevance of dyadic social cues, they were also sensitive to the relevance of triadic social information. Two primary questions arose out of these findings. The first question concerned the development of this sensitivity to triadic attention, and the second question concerned the possible function of this sensitivity.

To find out when in ontogeny infants were sensitive to the relevance of triadic social cues, we tested a group of 1-month-old infants (Striano, Stahl, Cleveland, & Hoehl, 2007). In a first study, we compared infants in just two conditions, the joint-attention condition and the look-away condition. These conditions were similar to those described above with the 3-, 6-, and 9-month-olds (see Figure 1.1). One difference, however, was that these conditions were presented for a longer duration of time so that we could be sure that infants had sufficient time to detect the condition differences. In this study, we found that, even at 1 month of age, infants could discriminate between someone coordinating attention and someone just looking away and talking. Then we compared infants in the joint-attention condition and the affect condition – where the amount of social information provided was the same but the adult broke contact for a second by looking away from the infant. This time, 1-month-old infants did not discriminate between these conditions. As in the prior studies, at 1 month of age, it did not matter if this person was providing relevant or contingent, meaningful information. At 1 month, infants are likely to be sensitive to the presence of faces and social cues directed at them, but not necessarily to the more subtle cues such as timing or contingency. One possibility is that further social experience is necessary.

Beyond Detection

A sensitivity to joint attention is essential for learning. For example, it has been shown that, by 18 months of age, infants use others' gaze toward objects to learn labels (see, e.g., Baldwin, 1993; Baldwin & Moses, 1996). In order fully to benefit from joint attention, an infant must have developed an ability to integrate a number of social and cognitive skills. When do infants use triadic social cues to gain information about new things? The function of joint attention for the infant in terms of gaining knowledge about the external world remains poorly understood. Few studies have addressed the issue of how triadic interaction involving adult, infant, and object facilitates learning about objects in the surrounding world. While many studies indicate that infants modify their own behavior according to the social signals they receive, little is known about the influence of the social partner's behavior on infants' processing of the surrounding world. Some research has shown that maternal behavior during mother–infant play sessions is related to 4-month-old infants' ability to recognize and discern a familiar from a novel stimulus. Specifically, infants whose mothers were less involved during toy play (for example,

vocalization, visual encouragement of attention) exhibited higher novelty preference – the type of visual preference that is associated with superior information
processing (Miceli, Whitman, Borkowski, Brautgart-Rieker, & Mitchell, 1998).
Itakura (2001) tested older infants (9–13-month-olds) to assess whether social and
non-social events led to differential behavior on subsequent visual preference tasks.
In this study, infants observed either the mother point to one of two line drawings
(social event) or saw one of the line drawings blink (non-social event). In both
conditions infants looked longer at the stimulus-enhanced drawing (that is, the one
that was pointed at or the one that blinked). However, when the line drawings were
presented again alone (without pointing or blinking), only the infants who were in
the social condition showed a significant difference in their preference for the
drawing that had been pointed at versus the one at which the mother had not
pointed. Thus, looking behavior was influenced by the preceding social and non-
social events.

In our recent research we have started to address the issue of how cues provided
by adult social partners are beneficial to infants in these contexts. Recently, we
examined the effects of differing social cues on object processing in 9- and 12-
month-old infants (Striano, Chen, Cleveland, & Bradshaw, 2006). In a within-
subject design, an adult experimenter spoke to the infants about a novel object in
two conditions. In the *joint-attention* condition, the experimenter spoke to the
infant about the toy while alternating gaze between the toy and the infant. The
object-only condition was identical, except that the experimenter looked to the toy
and to a spot on the ceiling, but never to the infant. In test trials, infants viewed
the toy used in the social interaction along with a novel toy. Twelve-month-old
infants looked to the novel toy equally following both conditions. In contrast, 9-
month-olds looked to the novel toy significantly longer following the joint-attention condition relative to the object-only condition. This can be seen in Figure 1.3.
These results suggest that joint-attention interactions significantly aided object
processing in the 9-month-old infants (a), but not in the 12-month-old infants (b).
This indicates that, by 12 months of age, infants learned about the object as long
as some social cue was provided, whether it was directed only at the object (that is,
object only) or both to the infant and the object (that is, joint attention). In subsequent studies, using similar paradigms (see Cleveland & Striano, 2007; Cleveland,
Schug, & Striano, 2007), we were able to show that by 7 months of age infants
benefited from joint-attention interactions. Learning about objects was enhanced
when infants viewed novel toys in the context of a joint-attention social cue. In a
series of studies, we tested infants as young as 4 months of age. We found that 4-
and 5-month-old infants did not benefit from joint-attention interactions (Cleveland & Striano, 2007; Cleveland et al., 2007). This is interesting, given that, by 3
months of age, infants are already sensitive to joint-attention cues. However, when
we observed their behavior in the types of paradigms described above, we found
that they do not seem to learn anything more. As we will see next, however, taking
a cognitive neuroscience approach and investigating event-related potentials have
revealed something very different.

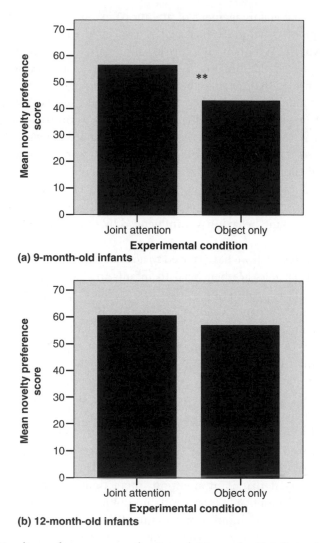

Figure 1.3. Novelty preference scores, for 9- and 12-month-old infants, following joint-attention and non-joint-attention (object-only) interactions
Source: Striano, Chen, Cleveland, & Bradshaw (2006).

Autism and Attending to Others

Work with very young infants shows that the ability to discriminate relevant triadic interactions from irrelevant triadic interactions is clearly an essential step in social-cognitive learning. Given the abundance of information that is always around infants, it is necessary that they are able to pick up on the cues that are most essential for effective learning. Persons with autism provide a clear example of what happens when parsing of relevant information is not possible for some reason (Klin & Volkmar, 1993). Individuals with autism are often reported to attend to irrelevant information in the environment. Imagine yourself at a dinner event. When you sit down at the dinner table, you will probably be attending to subtle social information. Indeed, you may very well be attending to social information (an eye gaze, the nod of your host, or seemingly universal language cues, "Bon appetit!") just in the hope that it will give you essential information about something that is non-social (that is, when to begin to eat). But the mere fact that we attend to these social cues implies that we constantly keep others in mind, and do not want to make the wrong impression. Now imagine being at the dinner table without having others in mind. You will probably pay attention to what is most interesting: if you are hungry, it will be the duck and potato, and, maybe, if you are not, it is the spoons on the table that produce novel sounds every time you bang them against your plate. These are much more pleasing and easy to control and manipulate than the voices of others. You can make the sounds stop and start as you please – if only you could do the same to the people talking around you. We use this example to illustrate the importance of using triadic social cues to gain information. It is one thing to detect these cues, and another to use them effectively. Understanding the drive to interact with others will be a key factor in establishing the origins of human social cognition and those factors that make it go awry somehow, as in the case of autism.

Joint Attention: A Fresh Look with New Methods and Perspectives

In parallel to research investigating joint attention, much research has been conducted into properties of infant electrophysiological responses to cognitive tasks. Most often these responses have been measured with event-related potentials (ERPs – also referred to as event-related brain potentials), the electrical brain activity that is time-locked to the onset of a stimulus (Rugg & Coles, 1995). Since 2000, knowledge of how the functional brain develops has increased dramatically (Johnson, 2005). One component of the infant ERP that is well mapped in terms of cognitive properties is the mid-latency *negative component*, or Nc. The Nc occurs approximately 300–700 milliseconds after stimulus onset, is most prominent at fronto-central electrodes, and is thought to relate to the development of memory and attentional processes during the first twelve postnatal months (Webb, Long, & Nelson, 2005). We have recently developed a new ERP paradigm that is instrumental in understanding the influence of social cues in early neural processing. Before turning to this paradigm, we review one of our first studies that led to it.

In an initial ERP study (Reid, Striano, Kaufman, & Johnson, 2004), we questioned how infants at 4 months processed objects that were cued by eye gaze. In this paradigm, infants viewed an adult's face on screen, with the eyes oriented forward. The eyes then gazed toward an object. Then the infants viewed the objects a second time, to which we time-locked our ERP measure. The infant ERP exhibited an enhanced positive slow wave for the uncued objects relative to the cued objects.

As the positive slow wave has been related to context updating in face-processing studies (e.g. de Haan & Nelson, 1999), the cued object was thus processed and more familiar to the infant than the uncued object. This study reveals in infants both a sensitivity to the detection of triadic cues as well as the functional use of this information by 4 months of age. This study involved the presentation of gaze on screen. It therefore assumed that the social relevance of gaze would be transferred to the infant, even though the gazing adult was virtual.

In a second study involving a live interaction between infant and adult experimenter (Striano, Reid, & Hoehl, 2006), infants interacted with an adult in two conditions. In the *joint-attention* condition, the adult looked at the infant and then at the computer screen, which then displayed an object. In the *non-joint-attention* condition the adult looked only at the computer screen while talking and vocalizing. An example of the set-up can be seen on Figure 1.4. For a trial to be included, infants needed to look at the adult and then to the object presented on the screen. We measured ERPs when infants were looking at the object presented on the screen. We predicted an enhanced Nc for objects that infants viewed in the context of joint attention compared to non-joint-attention contexts. Our results confirmed these predictions. We found that, at 9 months of age, the infant brain responded

Figure 1.4.   ERP joint-attention procedure
Note: E = experimenter; I = infant.
Source: Striano, Reid, & Hoehl (2006).

differently toward objects that had been cued by joint attention versus non- joint-attention contexts. We found an enhanced negative component – which is an index of attention peaking around 600 ms after stimulus onset – for the joint attention condition. These results demonstrated the validity of this new interaction paradigm to understand how the infant brain processes information as a function of social cues. As ERPs can provide a more sensitive measure of the way that infants process information when compared to behavioral paradigms, could we also find signs that much younger infants were gaining something from joint-attention interactions? Recall that behavioral work had shown that, at 4 and 5 months of age, infants did not learn anything more about objects when they were presented in a joint-attention context. In a recent study, we asked whether 5-month-old infants processed objects more fully as a function of joint-attention contexts. In this study, infants interacted with an adult in two different ways. In one condition, the joint-attention condition, the adult looked at the infant's face and then to the object on the computer monitor and back to the infant. In the other condition, the non-joint-attention condition, the adult looked at the infant's chest and then at the object on the computer monitor and then back at the infant's chest. This way we were able to control for movement cues and facial information. What differed across conditions was that there was direct eye contact in the joint-attention condition but not in the non-joint-attention condition. Following an interaction phase in which infants saw objects in these two conditions, they were then presented with the objects. As in the prior study, we measured how the 5-month-olds' infant brains processed information as a function of social interaction. We found an enhanced Nc, about 400 ms after stimulus onset, when objects were presented in the context of joint-attention interaction when compared to those in the non-joint-attention condition (Parise, Reid, Stets, & Striano, forthcoming). These results paralleled what we had found with the 9-month-olds. What is important to recall is that, at 5 months of age, in the behavioral studies (Cleveland et al., 2007) we did not see evidence that infants used joint-attention cues to learn about objects. When we used a more sensitive measure, however, and in particular when we assessed how the brain was processing information in joint-attention contexts, the picture was different. The sensitivity to joint-attention cues was more than mere sensitivity to detection of differences in the social interaction; rather it was functional – at the neural level. These results are important, because they suggest that measures of neural activity can give us information about development that analyzing behavior alone cannot. This is important, not only for understanding the relation between brain and behavioral development across typical ontogeny, but especially for the early identification of infants who may be at risk of later social cognitive impairments such as autism. For example, we predict that an infant whose brain is not manifesting enhanced processing of relevant social information may be at risk of a range of impairments that are indexed through social-cognitive measures. We predict that these infants would have difficulty in parsing social information, in detecting the relevance of information, and in using these cues to interact and learn efficiently.

Conclusion

The attainment of adult social cognition is a long process, and one that does not contain abrupt changes in ability. It is not as if an infant wakes up one day and begins to understand the internal mental states of other people. Over the first months of postnatal development, infants detect social cues provided by others. They learn that some of these social cues are more relevant than others and then use these cues to learn efficiently.

We have been able to show that, by 3 months of age, infants are sensitive to relevant dyadic as well as triadic social cues. Earlier in development, at 1 month of age, this is not the case. Further research is needed better to understand why this is the case. One possibility is that maturation and social experience are critical factors. Another alternative is that the paradigms that we have used are not sufficient to address whether young infants detect and interpret differences in social situations.

While our work has shown that even young infants are sensitive to some types of social cues, we were unable to explain why at times behavioral measures and neural processes did not tell us the same story. Why is it that 5-month-old infants failed to manifest behavioral signs that joint-attention cues aided in learning, while at the same time their ERPs showed signs of enhanced processing following joint attention? Is this a matter of measurement sensitivity? Or is the enhanced brain processing indexing some pre-manifestation of later behavioral signs? We hate to end our chapter with posing more questions than we have addressed, but that is the current state of affairs in early social-cognitive research. We have come a long way, but have much further to go before we can begin to put the pieces together.

Understanding the process of social-cognitive development will be important in understanding what makes it fail to develop in some cases – such as in the case of autism. This is no easy feat, but we hope to have demonstrated in this chapter that, in order to understand development, we need to study development. We must also be open to using multiple measures to address our questions and to use an interdisciplinary approach. The approach we have used in our own research is far from fully interdisciplinary, but we hope that an acknowledgment of our limitations, as well as an openness to new techniques and to various expertise from fields of neuroscience and psychopathology, will help as we tackle some of the most fundamental questions within the field of the development of human social cognition.

References

Baldwin, D. A. (1993). Infants' ability to consult the speaker for clues to word reference. *Journal of Child Language*, 20, 395–418.

Baldwin, D. A., & Moses, L. J. (1996). The ontogeny of social information gathering. *Child Development*, 67, 1915–1939.

Campos, J., & Sternberg, C. (1981). Perception, appraisal, and emotion: The onset of social referencing. In M. Lamb & L. Sherrod (Eds.), *Infant Social Cognition: Empirical and Theoretical Considerations* (pp. 273–314). Hillsdale, NJ: Lawrence Erlbaum.

Cleveland, A., Schug, M., & Striano, T. (2007). Joint attention and object learning in 5- and 7-month-old infants. *Infant and Child Development*, 16, 295–306.

Cleveland, A., & Striano, T. (2007). The effects of joint attention on object processing in 4- and 9-month-old infants. *Infant Behavior and Development*, 30(3), 499–504.

de Haan, M., & Nelson, C. A. (1999). Brain activity differentiates face and object processing in 6-month-old infants. *Developmental Psychology*, 35(4), 1113–1121.

D'Entremont, B., Hains, S. M. J., & Muir, D. W. (1997). A demonstration of gaze following in 3- to 6-month-olds. *Infant Behavior and Development*, 20, 569–572.

Itakura, S. (2001). Attention to repeated events in human infants (*Homo sapiens*): Effects of joint visual attention versus stimulus change. *Animal Cognition*, 4, 281–284.

Johnson, M. H. (2005). *Developmental Cognitive Neuroscience* (2nd edn.). Oxford: Blackwell.

Klin, A., & Volkmar, F. R. (1993). The development of individuals with autism: Some implications for the theory of mind hypothesis. In S. Baron-Cohen, H. Tager-Flusberg, & D. Cohen (Eds.), *Understanding Other Minds: Perspectives from Autism* (pp. 317–34). Oxford: Oxford University Press.

Miceli, P. J., Whitman, T. L., Borkowski, J. G., Brautgart-Rieker, J., & Mitchell, D. W. (1998). Individual differences in infant information processing: The role of temperamental and maternal factors. *Infant Behavior and Development*, 21, 119–136.

Nadel, J., & Tremblay-Leveau, H. (1999). Early interpersonal timing and the perception of social contingencies. In P. Rochat (Ed.), *Early Social Cognition: Understanding Ohers in the First Months of Life* (pp. 189–215). Mahwah, NJ: Lawrence Erlbaum.

Parise, E., Reid, V. M., Stets, M., & Striano, T. (forthcoming). Direct eye contact influences the neural processing of objects in 5-month-old infants. *Social Neuroscience*.

Reid, V. M., Striano, T., Kaufman, J., & Johnson, M. H. (2004). Eye gaze cueing facilitates neural processing of objects in 4-month-old infants. *NeuroReport*, 15(16), 2553–2555.

Rochat, P., & Striano, T. (1999). Emerging self-exploration by 2 month-old infants. *Developmental Science*, 2, 206–218.

Rugg, M. D., & Coles, M. G. H. (1995). *Electrophysiology of the Mind: Event-Related Brain Potentials and Cognition*. Oxford University Press: London.

Stern, D. (1985). *The Interpersonal World of the Infant*. New York: Basic Books.

Striano, T. (2004). Direction of regard and the still-face effect in the first year: Does intention matter? *Child Development*, 75(2), 468–479.

Striano, T., Chen, X., Cleveland, A., & Bradshaw, S. (2006). Joint attention social cues influence infant learning. *European Journal of Developmental Psychology*, 3, 289–299.

Striano, T., Reid, V. M., & Hoehl, S. (2006). Neural mechanisms of joint attention in infancy. *European Journal of Neuroscience*, 23, 2819–2823.

Striano, T., & Rochat, P. (1999). Developmental link between dyadic and triadic social competence in infancy. *British Journal of Developmental Psychology*, 17, 551–562.

Striano, T., & Stahl, D. (2005). Sensitivity to triadic attention in early infancy. *Developmental Science*, 4, 333–443.

Striano, T., Stahl, D., Cleveland, A., & Hoehl, S. (2007). Sensitivity to triadic attention between 6 weeks and 3 months of age. *Infant Behavior and Development*, 30(3), 529–534.

Tomasello, M. (1999). Social cognition before the revolution. In P. Rochat (Ed.), *Early Social Cognition: Understanding Others in the Frst Months of Life*. Mahwah, NJ: Lawrence Erlbaum.

van Wulffen Palthe, T., & Hopkins, B. (1993). A longitudinal study of neural maturation and early mother–infant interaction: A research note. *Journal of Child Psychology and Psychiatry and Allied Disciplines*, 34, 1031–1041.

Webb, S. J., Long, J. D., & Nelson, C. A. (2005). A longitudinal investigation of visual event-related potentials in the first year of life. *Developmental Science*, 8, 605–616.

Yazbek, A., & D'Entremont, B. (2006). A longitudinal investigation of the still-face effect at 6 months and joint attention at 12 months. *British Journal of Developmental Psychology*, 24, 589–601.

Chapter 2

Research Methodology and Social Cognition

Vincent Reid and Elena Geangu

Introduction

This chapter provides a general overview of key methodologies used in social-cognitive research, together with practical and theoretical implications of using these methodologies. The first section of the chapter outlines behavioral techniques, and the second outlines the techniques designed to investigate the neural correlates and mechanisms characteristic of social information processing. These two categories of techniques are not regarded as mutually exclusive; rather they are complementary. Behavioral techniques and cognitive neuroscience techniques are limited both in terms of explanatory power and in terms of the aspects of information processing (social and non-social) they can access.

In terms of behavioral techniques, we have emphasized habituation and visual preference paradigms. One reason for this choice is their popularity for research investigating infant and toddler social-cognitive development. Another reason is represented by the limitations that these techniques impose, which are often forgotten by researchers in the interpretation of their data. Although seen by many scientists as indexing mental representations and memory, habituation techniques are limited in differentiating stimuli for very important aspects of infant information processing such as novelty versus familiarity preference. The visual preference paradigm has proved useful for the assessment of visual attention and discrimination of stimuli in the domains of face perception, preverbal communication, and word learning. Along with its more complex version – the interactive intermodal preferential looking paradigm – it has the advantage of being suitable for longitudinal studies, matching the developmental characteristics of both infants and toddlers.

As there are a multitude of techniques for assessing aspects of brain function, we have focused on two types that broadly cover electrophysiological approaches and haemodynamic approaches. These are electroencephalogram (EEG) and event-related potential (ERP – also referred to as event-related brain potential), and functional magnetic resonance imaging (fMRI). We highlight the spatial and temporal parameters of each technique before outlining the processes that occur to transform the data from the initial raw signals through to when statistics are ready to be performed. We then outline their application to special populations, such as infants or children with autism.

Finally, it should be noted that this chapter is designed as a general introduction to these techniques and is not an exhaustive guide. Rather, it is constructed as á brief overview for those who are not familiar with the methodologies of different disciplines. For any person investigating social cognition within one field, it is likely that the techniques outlined here will provide a rough guide to understanding the basic thrust of findings from disciplines other than his or her own.

Behavioral Techniques

Habituation

Habituation is one of the most commonly used methods in early developmental research for the study of perception, memory, and cognition. We say that an infant habituates when, after repeated presentation with the same stimulus, his or her responsiveness to that stimulus substantially decreases. The origins of this method lie in the work of Pavlov (1927) and Sokolov (1963). According to their work, there is an orienting response from an individual to the slightest change in the environment. This is based on the notion that repeated presentations of the same stimulus lead to the formation of a representation of that stimulus. Subsequently, any new stimulus, based on a comparison with the formed representation, can be detected as being new, therefore eliciting more responsiveness from the subject. Continued presentation of the same stimulus leads to decreased levels of novelty associated with the repeated presentation of the stimulus, resulting in habituation or decreased interest. At the neurological level the hippocampus and other hippocampal-related cortical areas, like the entorhinal cortex, may be involved in habituation (Nelson, 1995).

The theory of habituation was translated for the first time into an experimental method for infant studies by Fantz (1964). It was then developed further by Horowitz, Paden, Bhana, & Self (1972) and Laub (1972). Although looking time is considered the most common measure of habituation, haptic manipulation, galvanic skin resistance, and heart-rate changes are also used (Sirois & Mareschal, 2002).

At the practical level, the habituation method unfolds along two main phases. In the first phase, called the habituation phase, several presentations of a stimulus or a pair of stimuli are produced. Each presentation starts when the infant looks at a stimulus and ends when the infant looks away for a predetermined time (for example, 1–2 minutes). In this phase, for the first two or three presentations of the stimuli the 50 percent decrement criterion (Dannemiller, 1984) is computed or the average responsiveness of the subject. This average responsiveness then serves as a baseline. In the subsequent two or three presentations of this first phase, the responsiveness of the infant is averaged again. If this value falls below 50 percent of the baseline measurement, it is considered that the subject has habituated to the stimulus. In the second phase of the experiment, the infant is presented with stimulus or stimuli that are considered as being different from the ones presented in the first phase. If the infant has habituated to the first-phase stimuli, and he or she was not simply bored by it, the responsiveness should increase significantly.

Although widely used, the habituation methodology is not without weaknesses. Several issues must be considered when planning a study based on a habituation methodology.

One of them is related to the intermediate or optimal level of stimulation principle (Berlyne, 1963; Cohen, 1969). According to this principle, infants, as any other organism, prefer an intermediate level of stimulation called the optimal level. If the level of stimulation is too low, the organism will seek to increase it; if it is too high, it will seek to decrease it. The applicability of this principle is usually age dependent, as it seems that younger infants prefer more simple stimuli. Therefore, when a young infant is presented with new and complex stimuli, his or her responsiveness will decrease, not because of the habituation, but mainly because of lack of interest for that stimulus. It seems that, in general, in the case of complex stimuli, infants seem first to prefer (for example, look longer at) familiar stimuli; only subsequently do they prefer to look longer at novel stimuli. Therefore, one important aspect that must be controlled is the underlying factor of responsiveness: familiarity or novelty.

Special care should also be used when applying the 50 percent decrement criterion. Formal models show that an infant could achieve this criterion simply by chance as a consequence of random variation. The risk for falsely assuming that an infant has reach the 50 percent decrement criterion increases when the mean response levels are low and the variances are high (Thomas & Gilmore, 2004). In the post-habituation phase these infants can potentially be identified by the spontaneous regression effect – namely, if they reach the habituation criterion simply by chance because of random variation in their response, their response in the post-habituation phase will be above the habituation criterion level (Berthenthal, Haith, & Campos, 1983).

In order to use the habituation method efficiently in infant studies, special care should be spent on controlling for the critical points presented above: familiarity versus novelty preference, false habituators, and spontaneous regression.

The visual preference paradigm

Sometimes used in combination with the habituation technique, the visual preference method or the preferential looking method was also developed in the early 1950s and 1960s by Berlyne (1958) and Fantz, Ordy, & Udelf (1962) among others. It is assumed that preferential looking reflects the infants' natural preference for some stimuli over others. This experimental paradigm has proved to be very useful for the assessment of visual attention and discrimination for stimuli in the domains of face perception, preverbal communication, and word learning.

The task requires the presentation of two or more stimuli to the subject. Each stimulus can be presented for a fixed number of trials. A trial starts when the infant visually fixates the stimulus presentation location. The trial lasts as long as the subject visually attends to the stimulus. The end of the test trial is often determined by some standardized criteria, such as a threshold of 2 seconds or more of looking away from the stimulus. The average looking time for each stimulus is then computed. If the subject looks significantly longer to one stimulus than to the others, it is assumed that he or she prefers to perceive and process that kind of information. The stimuli categories can be presented either simultaneously or successively. When simultaneous presentation is selected, the test trials are preceded by a side preference phase. In this phase, in the absence of any stimuli, the subject's looking time to the right side and to the left side of the stimuli presentation display is measured. If the infant looks longer to the right side than to the left side, we can say that he or she manifests a preference for looking to that side regardless of the characteristics of the stimuli. In order to avoid this natural side preference influencing the experimental results, the stimuli are presented on both sides counterbalanced across subjects or as a within-subject design, depending on the number of trials and stimuli that have been used.

The stimuli used in this kind of methodology can be either simple, based on a single perceptual modality, or more complex, involving characteristics presented via complementary sensory domains (for example, a visual and auditory presentation). The discovery that infants are able to map one-to-one auditory and visual cues (Spelke, 1979) advanced the use of a new variation of the classic visual preference method, the intermodal preferential looking paradigm (IPLP). In this method, the subject is presented simultaneously with two visual stimuli – with each one displayed on a different video monitor – and an auditory stimulus. The auditory stimulus matches only one of the visual stimuli. The total amount of time the infant spends looking to either the matching or the non-matching visual display is then computed, and the preference established. It was shown that, very early in development, infants look systematically longer to the visual stimulus that matches the auditory stimulus (Spelke, 1979).

As well as the habituation method, the visual preference paradigm has the advantage of imposing minimal response demands on the participant. This aspect makes the method suitable for use with very young infants, even newborns, given their limited response abilities. Sometimes the research questions are targeted to more complex phenomena, such as how social factors are involved in word learning. In these cases, simple visual preference methods are no longer appropriate, as they do not allow the assessment and manipulation of social cues (Rocroi, 2000). To solve this weakness of the classic visual preference method or the more complex IPLP, an interactive variation was developed and tested for its utility by Hollich, Hirsh-Pasek, and Golinkoff in 1998 – the interactive intermodal preferential looking paradigm (interactive IPLP).

The interactive IPLP unfolds along two main phases. The first phase contains the experimental manipulation of the social cues. Usually, while the infant is seated in the parent's lap, the experimenter plays in front of him or her with two toys (each one positioned either to the right or to the left) and labels one of them. During labelling, the experimenter uses one of the interactive social cues (for example, gazing at the object, touching, pointing, or handling the target object). In the second test phase, the subject is presented simultaneously with the two toys and the experimenter requests the target object. The subject's response is usually coded in terms of looking either to the left object or to the right object (Rocroi, 2000). The interactive aspect of this method, as well as the fact that it can involve combinations of multiple sources of information (for example, social, semantic, syntactic, prosodic, and so on) also makes it suitable for older ages (up to 24 months of age (Hirsh-Pasek & Golinkoff, 1991)), allowing employment in longitudinal designs if desired (Rocroi, 2000).

Habituation and visual preference methods both share common limitations in terms of the type of data that they provide. For example, few data points for each individual are obtained, therefore providing mainly group data. Usually these paradigms produce a yes–no answer to the research questions, such as whether an ability is present at a given age or not. This can make it difficult to establish a functional relationship between a specific stimulus variable and the subject's measured response (Aslin & Fiser, 2005). In the area of behavioral methods, one solution for this problem might be the use of multiple stimulus-response paradigms that afford the acquisition of many data points from each subject. This may help clarify the relation between different characteristics of the independent variable and the subject's response (Aslin & Fiser, 2005).

For the case of autism, the behavioral methodologies have been selectively utilized given their parameters and the special characteristics of autism. For example, the habituation paradigm is encountered less, one of the reasons being the age of the autistic participants. Usually the diagnosis is established no sooner than the age of 3, whereas the habituation methodology is more appropriate for younger ages. The IPLP (Spelke, 1979) and the interactive IPLP (Hollich et al., 1998) have been successfully used with autistic populations as variations of the preferential looking methodology. Walker-Andrews, Haviland, Hufhan, and Toci (1994) used the IPLP for the study of intermodal integration of visual and auditory sensorial information about objects by those with autism who had a chronological age between 2 years 4 months and 20 years 8 months. The procedure they used was similar to the one described at the beginning of this chapter for typically developing subjects. In the same vein, Loveland, Tunali-Kotoski, Chen, Brelsford, Ortegon, and Pearson (1995) used a modified version of the IPLP for the study of the integration of visual and auditory information about emotions in those with autism, choosing to present the stimuli in a sequential manner.

Technological advances have allowed the further development of the preferential looking paradigm, so that a more accurate assessment of the in-depth processing or preferential allocation of attentional resources for certain stimuli can be conducted. In this respect, infrared eye-tracking devices paired with preferential looking methodological principles have been developed. These allow the investigation of several aspects of social information processing by children diagnosed with autism, such as face processing (van der Geest, Kemner, Verbaten, & van Engeland, 2002). Eye tracking provides far finer tuned information on where in a visual scene an individual is looking (see, for example, von Hofsten & Gredebäck, Chapter 16, this volume).

One unique behavioral approach for the study of social-behavior characteristics in infants who were later diagnosed with autism is the use of *post hoc* semistructured observational methods. Examples include the assessment of video recordings of early birthday celebrations, filmed by parents, where the behavior of infants later diagnosed with autism can be assessed for several critical aspects of social cognition, such as eye contact and joint attention (e.g. Adrien et al., 1991; Dawson, Osterling, Meltzoff, & Kuhl, 2000; Osterling & Dawson, 1994). Other than these, stimulus-response paradigms are used for the study of social cognition in atypically developing individuals such as those diagnosed with autism (see, e.g., the review of Dawson, Webb, & McPartland, 2005, for examples on face processing).

Cognitive Neuroscience Techniques

Data derived from cognitive neuroscience techniques do not simply serve to falsify theoretical accounts of cognitive processes that are based on behavioral evidence. Rather, neural systems and mechanisms actively refine cognitive models of information processing. In other words, the investigation of brain-based developmental data can aid in refining cognitive theory or in taking it into completely different directions. For example, the application of neuroimaging techniques to developing populations has already revealed unexpected issues in developmental research that force rethinking of prevailing views (see, e.g., a review by Casey, Tottenham, Liston, & Durston, 2005). This is despite the recent historical nature of the application of such techniques to developmental issues.

There are a multitude of techniques in the cognitive neurosciences, from fMRI, a widely used technique for generating maps of human brain activity, through to transcranial magnetic stimulation (TMS), a technique that overstimulates the activity of a specific part of the brain, effectively suppressing its functionality for a short period of time. Multiple other approaches are also taken, some of which are mentioned throughout this volume. For example, data from near infrared spectroscopy (NIRS) is raised by Iacoboni (Chapter 3, this volume). However, it is not possible to outline the theory and processes involved in data collection, editing, and analysis of all different neuroimaging techniques. We thus present an overview of some electrophysiological approaches and of fMRI. This is not only due to space constraints, but also because these techniques are the most utilized neuroimaging methods in developmental and autism research. Other cognitive neuroscience approaches, such as positron emission tomography and magnetoencephalography, are virtually unheard of with these populations.

Electrophysiological approaches

Behavioral data provide a rich source of information on what infants can discriminate, categorize, and learn. However, the neural mechanisms that underlie infants' extensively described behavior are often unexplored. One class of electrophysiological measurement of brain activity, which is derived from an EEG, is the ERP. This technique relies on the non-invasive and painless recording of brain electrical activity measured by electrodes placed on the scalp. An ERP can be defined as the resultant electrophysiological response derived from the onset of a stimulus.

ERPs are particularly popular for measuring functional brain activation in infants as it is a technique that is relatively easy to record and does not have ethical issues surrounding its use. For example, it is less sensitive to behavior created by movement than other techniques, such as fMRI, and thus it is better suited for studying alert infants, who by their nature move constantly. As fMRI requires a motionless participant, it is often coupled with sedation techniques with children and infant participants. Positron emission tomography (PET) requires the injection of a mildly radioactive substance into the participant and is therefore an invasive procedure. Neuroimaging techniques other than EEG are consequently more likely to be restricted to clinical populations throughout infancy and childhood.

The primary advantage of ERP research over other forms of brain-based methodology is that it provides an excellent temporal resolution for viewing elicited processing, even in the order of milliseconds. Another advantage is that it is relatively inexpensive when compared to other methods of assessing brain function. However, spatial resolution is highly diminished when compared with haemodynamic measures of brain activity, such as fMRI. This is due to the fact that (1) electromagnetic fields summate algebraically so that multiple neuronal generators cannot be disentangled from each other, and (2) the positioning of the electrodes means that they do not sample all activity generated by the brain. Many deep structures are not measurable, although exactly how much or little is open to debate. Further, there is additional spatial smearing due to the resistive properties of meninges, cerebrospinal fluid, skull, and scalp.

One aspect of ERPs that makes them particularly attractive for developmental researchers is the fact that they do not require an overt behavioral or verbal response in sensitively designed passive paradigms. They consequently permit the study of phenomena that may be difficult to investigate with behavior methods alone (see, for example, the descriptions of research into the development of joint attention in Striano & Reid, Chapter 1, this volume). A detailed discussion of the functional specifics of key ERP components found across development is beyond the scope of this chapter (useful reviews are: de Haan, Johnson, & Halit, 2003; Nelson & Monk, 2001). In this section, we aim to outline how testing is done and the practical outcome of designing and using this technique.

Data transformation

The typical process of obtaining an ERP requires recording the EEG with indexed points in time ("triggers"), around which segmentation of the EEG occurs. An epoch is extracted from the EEG that constitutes a baseline before the stimulus and a post-stimulus period of an indeterminate length, dependent on the specific experimental paradigm. As exogenous noise is a problem that is frequently encountered during the acquisition of EEG. After data collection the offline data are usually subjected to high-pass and low-pass filters. High-pass filters can alleviate problems with slow wave drifts throughout data acquisition. Low-pass filters can remove high frequency noise derived from electrical appliances. Common examples are 0.1–35 Hz or 0.3–20 Hz. During data collection, the amplifier augments the obtained biological signals differentially, with every channel measured relative to a reference electrode. The difference between the two electrodes is then amplified, thereby providing a voltage measure for each channel that is relative rather than absolute in nature. The recording reference electrode is often located at the vertex electrode, which is located at the topmost part of the head. The reason for using this location for the recording reference is that it is close to other recording sites and it can be affected by ambient noise in a similar manner to the other channels. As EEG data are always relative – in the sense that the resulting data are a comparison between one electrode and another – data are often referenced after data collection to an electrode that is considered to be more suitable for reasons such as reliability and replication. Common final reference locations include the linked mastoids (behind the ear) or the average reference of all electrodes. At this stage data are typically edited, such that artifacts are removed. With adult data, this procedure is most often performed by a simple algorithm, with parameters set to detect eye blinks, eye movement, and muscle artifacts. With infants, data are typically edited trial by trial in order to ensure that those trials that are included are valid, with the infant attending to the stimuli. The removal of trials with artifacts can be performed at the same time. The remaining individual EEG segments are then averaged together to create one ERP for each condition. It is at this stage that assessment of the ERP can be made. Once the data have been collected from all participants, a grand average is performed where the individual averages of the participants are merged together to form an average of the overall effects. (See Figure 2.1 for an example of a visually induced ERP from an infant.)

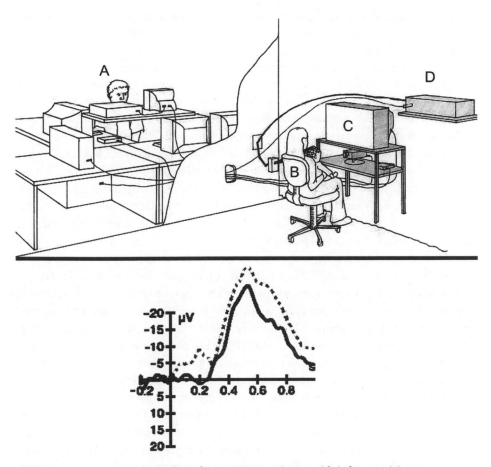

Figure 2.1. Experimental paradigm for an ERP experiment with infant participants
Note: Upper panel: the overall paradigm of a standard visual ERP experiment involving an infant participant. Note that shaded areas are occluded from the participant's view. A = experimenter monitoring data acquisition and stimuli presentation; B = infant, sitting on mother's lap; C = stimulus presentation monitor; D = EEG amplifier. Lower panel: the resulting visual ERP derived from an infant at 9 months of age, comprising a 200 ms baseline and a 1,000 ms epoch. Key components of the ERP include the early Pb component (200 ms) and the large negative component (Nc), peaking in both conditions at about 550 ms.
Source: Vincent Reid, previously unpublished.

ERPs with infants

Because of infants' limited attentional capacity and restricted behavioral repertoire, certain considerations are necessary when designing an ERP experiment for this population. Generally infants are not tested under the same conditions as adults. This is because infants do not benefit from instructions, and it becomes difficult directly to compare adult and infant data. It is possible to apply tasks used with adults to infants if the number of conditions and trials are reduced, and the complexity of the stimuli reduced or the attractiveness of the stimuli increased. However, it is possible if passive paradigms are used for both populations. The resulting data from these two populations on the same paradigm will almost certainly bear no resemblance to each other. This is probably due to age-related changes to the neural systems, such as synaptic density, myelination, and skull thickness. These factors – and many more – influence the morphology and the timing of components of the ERP such as latencies and amplitudes. For example, infants' reduced synaptic efficiency results in greater slow wave activity rather than the peaked activity that is typical of adult ERPs, thereby explaining why the infant ERP does not show as many well-defined amplitude peaks when compared to adult data on the same task. (For an overview of important considerations when designing and interpreting ERP experiments in developmental populations, see DeBoer, Scott, and Nelson, 2007).

Standard visual paradigms usually feature the participant located in a sound-proofed and electrically shielded room, free from any color in order to minimize distractions (see Figure 2.1). Infants are usually placed on their parent's lap. With infants, it is advisable to have the session video-recorded in order to detect and remove those periods of the EEG where the infant does not attend to the screen. As infants have a reduced attention span when compared to older populations, stimuli should be as attractive as possible – for example, using color photographs rather than black and white. There are certain techniques that can greatly alter infant drop-out rates. For example, should the infant become fussy, a short break should take place, with some brief interaction between infant and experimenter. Such interaction could include blowing bubbles or reading a short story. The difficulty here is that too much interaction can lead to the child refusing to continue, whereas too little can lead to fussiness. As with all things, at this point experimenter judgment and experience make all the difference between usable data and an invalid participant. Once the experimenter reinitiates the presentation of the stimuli, the stimuli are initially novel and thereby maintain infant attention. Generally an experiment with an infant will finish when the infant no longer yields meaningful data because of excessive movements or a lack of interest in the stimuli.

Oscillations and time-frequency analysis of EEG

As with all fields, EEG research is constantly evolving and changing. Since the mid-1990s the investigation of event-related oscillations has produced some interesting results and potentially provides new methodological advances. Event-related oscillations are bursts of EEG that occur within specific frequency bands. Two key distinctions appear within oscillation research: evoked and induced oscillations. Evoked gamma oscillations are precisely phase locked to the stimulus onset, as it is an evoked response to the stimulus. Evoked oscillations are often referred to as transient evoked responses. This is because they appear in the data at the same latency and phase in each trial of the same stimulus, unlike other forms of oscillatory activity. Induced oscillations, unlike evoked oscillations, are produced with a different latency for each stimulus presentation. The induced oscillation therefore has a loose temporal relationship to the stimulus. When standard evoked response averaging techniques are applied to the dataset, the induced oscillation is effectively edited from the final data. This is due to its loose relationship with the stimulus. In order to detect these oscillations, time-frequency analysis of single trials is followed by the averaging of the summed powers across trials. Detection of induced oscillations will occur provided that the signal-to-noise ratio is high enough and that the latency variation between and within trials does not exceed the duration of the wavelet that was utilized in the time-frequency decomposition.

One particular advantage of investigating time-frequency relations is that it is possible to investigate changes over time to the perception of dynamic stimuli, such as film clips. For example, Reid, Csibra, Belsky, and Johnson (2007) showed 8-month-old infants movies of complete and incomplete goal-directed actions. They found that infants at this age could discriminate the two conditions at the behavioral level, and this was also manifested in their gamma frequency oscillatory activity in left frontal regions of the electrode array. The ability to present movies to infants allows those in the field to ask new questions that were previously impossible to address, given past technical constraints. For example, it is difficult to know when to place a trigger for segmentation of an epoch when using ERP (a process known as time locking) when viewing dynamic stimuli, such as a movie of someone dancing. This issue is partially resolved by investigating oscillatory activity.

EEG, ERP, and autism

When compared with the long history of EEG, the assessment of social-cognitive skills of children with autism utilizing EEG and its derivatives is a relatively new endeavor. Despite the mildly unpleasant nature of EEG, many research articles note that research with EEG is not difficult when compared with other experimental methodologies. Indeed, Dawson, Carver, Meltzoff, Panagiotides, and McPartland (2002) noted: "we found that such a method is ideal for testing hypotheses regarding brain function in young, normally developed infants and children with autism" (p. 701). Investigation of a sample of articles reveals that this is broadly true, with drop-out rates at approximately 50 percent for children with autism, which is comparable with infant testing in many experimental paradigms when utilising ERP techniques. However, this is only the case once participants have been adjusted for experimental conditions via desensitization procedures.

One way to increase compliance in EEG is to provide a series of training sessions that desensitize the participants in terms of their reaction to the novelty of the EEG and the experimental situation. Each lab has its own unique desensitization process, but this generally involves watching videos of other children wearing an EEG cap, seeing researchers wearing electrodes and displaying positive affective cues, and having the EEG cap placed on the child with autism during a practice session (or practice sessions), with no data collected. For cap-based EEG systems, it is not uncommon for children with autism to take the cap (without electrodes) home with them to practice wearing it before the experimental session. Some desensitization procedures feature the child in a mock experimental room over multiple sessions to ensure familiarity with the unusual environment that is encountered during the actual testing session. Many of these activities are designed to habituate the child to the necessary interactions needed with his or her head, as children with autism are known to be highly sensitive to head contact. The end result of these labor-intensive activities is an acceptable drop-out rate for the resulting study. Other than these methodological issues, general experimental paradigms are usually the same as those for infant studies, whereby the number of conditions are limited because of the attention span of the examined population.

fMRI and MRI

fMRI is the most widely used technique for examining spatial properties of human brain activity. The rapid adoption of this technique is startling, given that the concept was realized only in 1990 (see Logothesis, 2003). The activation signal that is measured with fMRI is based on indirectly measuring changes in the concentration of deoxyhaemoglobin. This arises from an increase in blood oxygenation in the vicinity of neuronal firing. The exact mechanisms of this blood oxygenation level dependent (BOLD) contrast are highly complex. Many aspects of the relation between BOLD and neuron activity are still unknown because of the relatively recent evolution of the technique (see, e.g., Logothesis, 2002, 2003). The signal that is obtained is related both to the underlying physiology in terms of processing the event of interest and to the physics of imaging the brain. Multiple parameters and techniques can be used for the analysis of fMRI. Such techniques include high-speed magnetic resonance imaging (MRI), and echo-planar imaging.

Many experiments are still performed by using extended periods of "on" versus "off" activations. This is known as a block design paradigm. More recently, event-related fMRI has been championed. One example is Zacks et al. (2001). In this study, the neural activity of participants was examined while they viewed everyday activities such as ironing a shirt or playing a saxophone. Following presentation of the stimuli, each individual participant was presented with the stimuli again. In this condition the participant was required to segment the action in the sequences they had seen by indicating when boundaries occurred in the ongoing behavior. The data were segmented based upon each individual's indication of action boundaries. It was found that transient changes in the BOLD signal from 1 to 5 seconds after the perceived action boundary occurred in fMRI data bilaterally in the posterior cortex, and in a small region in the right frontal cortex.

fMRI data processing

One of the most commonly used analysis operations requires the transformation of data via data pre-processing, temporal linear modeling, and activation thresholding. These steps are designed to reduce artifacts and to maximize the possibility of analysing "real" data as opposed to noise. These processes will be briefly outlined here for the non-expert, but for a fuller explanation see, for example, Jezzard, Matthews, and Smith (2001). A simple type of fMRI experiment usually consists of stimuli and non-stimuli (rest) phases. Often the goal of fMRI is to compare neural activation during stimuli and non-stimuli periods. These periods are usually collected many times over, in excess of 100 per condition in most cases. This recording of activation, usually referred to as a volume, is comprised of individual cubed elements called *voxels*. A voxel can be thought of as a location in space as measured across time.

Once data have been obtained, they are transformed by reconstructing the raw "k-space" data into images that resemble brains. As the MRI collects each slice of the brain individually in each volume, it often gets acquired with minor variation in times. It therefore becomes necessary to modify the data so that all voxels within one volume appear to be uniformly acquired. Each volume is now transformed via translation so that the image of the brain within each volume is aligned with that in every other volume. This process is known as motion correction.

Prior to analysis, data are finally subjected to two other aspects of modification. Volumes are often spatially smeared together to reduce noise. Activation levels between each volume can be adjusted so that the mean activation is represented, thereby hopefully removing changes in volume intensity over time. Following this point, data can be assessed via normal statistical processes.

fMRI, developing populations, and autism

Little is known about the impact of fMRI on the early stages of brain development (see de Haan & Thomas, 2002). This has lead to a small number of studies in this area, including those conducted by experimental physicists or those with clinical populations (e.g. Seghier et al., 2004). One attempt to overcome ethical dilemmas has been substantially to reduce the power of the magnet when compared with that used for adults (e.g., with fetuses 0.5 t (Fulford et al., 2003)). Other problems accrue with developmental populations because of movement and consequent smearing. Some periods in development are more conducive to investigation than others. For example, in investigations of fetal development, fetuses are investigated at around 38 weeks of pregnancy, as at this time the head is engaged with the cervix for birth, which means that the fetus's head is kept relatively still (e.g. Fulford et al., 2003, 2004). This may also serve to explain the lack of studies with typically developing infants aged 6–24 months. After this date it may be possible to rationalize with them and provide incentives for them to remain still in the scanner. However, whatever the procedural difficulties, given that it is unknown what effect fMRI could have on the developing brain, it is at this stage premature to state that this technology is a widely accepted technique for use with these delicate populations.

The use of fMRI when investigating social-cognitive capacities of children with autism is an area of research that has flourished since 2000, although the dominant area of investigation remains that surrounding the issue of face perception, with emphasis on the function of the fusiform gyrus, the amygdale, and functionally related areas. In general, children with autism tend to be older than 10 years of age, which is older in age than children in studies utilizing electrophysiological techniques. For example, Gomot et al. (2006) tested children with autism aged from 10 to 15 years. Surprisingly, little research refers to difficulties in their methodology in testing children with autism when compared to testing typically developing children. Even more surprising in fMRI literature is the complete lack of diagnostic criteria included in some published works. The authors of this chapter are not experts in testing with autism; however, our discussions with colleagues in this field reveal the following. Children with autism who successfully participate in electrophysiological or fMRI studies are typically very high functioning. Further, drop-out rates are often high and are often not reported, unless prompted during the peer review process. This creates the unusual situation where it can appear that all children with autism successfully participate in studies, whereas many studies with typically developed adults have an expected drop-out rate. Despite these caveats, the value of investigating neural systems with fMRI is unquestionable, as new and important information can be gained via this technique that is not available from other methods of investigation.

There are also methodological issues with investigating between subject measures with fMRI, such as a comparison of children with autism and typically developing children. This issue is due to a normal set of fMRI data typically containing many data points (for example, 70,000 image voxels for a single subject). When comparisons of fMRI data are made between individuals or between groups, this becomes statistically complex, as multiple comparisons markedly inflate the risk of falsely identifying individual voxels as significantly different between groups simply by chance.

Diffusion tensor imaging

Perhaps more than in many other fields, the technology and application of MRI techniques are in constant evolution. One recent development that is particularly promising in terms of resolving aspects of brain connectivity that are difficult to investigate is diffusion tensor imaging (DTI). This process relies on the physics of diffusion. Diffusion is the process by which matter is transported from one part of a system to another, owing to random molecular motions. This phenomenon is known as Brownian Motion, in reference to the nineteenth-century botanist who discovered this form of motion. When MRI is being used, white matter in the brain appears homogenous. However, as the mobility of water within white matter is restricted by the axons that are oriented along the fiber tracts, through using the principles of diffusion, it is possible to investigate the organization of fiber tracts – and therefore connectivity – within the brain. DTI can therefore assess connectivity between disparate regions of the brain and help to resolve issues of functional significance found within fMRI results (see Devlin et al., 2006, for an excellent example).

Summary

Using habituation and preferential-looking paradigms, we can investigate how infants and toddlers process social stimuli via their observable behavior. Based on how much the infants look at a certain stimulus or category of stimuli, we can make inferences related to attention, memory, and the processing of those stimuli. This way it is decided, for example, if humans are biased towards processing certain types of social stimuli from birth (for example, using the preferential-looking paradigm), if they form a mental representation of a social stimulus, and how (for example, using habituation paradigms). As has been observed, "external" behavior is used to make inferences related to "internal" processing aspects. Sometimes erroneous conclusions may be drawn. This is simply due to the fact that it is hard to attribute the right explanation to a certain behavior, especially when the same behavior may have two or multiple explanations, depending on the context and the characteristics of the stimulus. For example, looking more to a certain stimulus may be interpreted as a sign that the stimulus is completely new or that it is already known to the subject. Even when the research is strictly controlled, results obtained using behavioral paradigms are hard to interpret. In this respect, cognitive neuroscience techniques can assist in validating the behavioral results. This group of techniques offers information about the structural and dynamic aspects of brain activity that we assume are related to social information processing. Putting together behavioral and brain-activity aspects, we can have more accurate explanations on how social information processing happens and how it develops. For example, using a visual ERP procedure following a habituation experiment, we can say more accurately whether the subject's response represents a novelty or a familiarity preference. The resulting ERP can be assessed on the amplitude of the Nc component of the infant ERP, which has been correlated with the allocation of attention to stimuli (see Striano & Reid, Chapter 1, this volume, for a more detailed discussion of the properties of the Nc).

Overall it must be said that both behavioral and brain-based techniques and their disciplines are immensely important for understanding social cognition. It would be wrong to consider one superior to the other. Rather we should conclude that one is more appropriate for studying key aspects of social-cognitive development than the other, but that this depends on the quality of the experimental design, the level of care taken with analysis, and the issue in question. As with all things, the correct question matched with the appropriate methodology will determine the usefulness of the results.

References

Adrien, J. L., Faure, M., Perrot, A., Hameury, L., Garreau, B., Barthelemy, C., & Sauvage, D. (1991). Autism and family home movies: Preliminary findings. *Journal of Autism & Developmental Disorders*, 21, 43–49.

Aslin, R. N., & Fiser, J. (2005). Methodological challenges for understanding cognitive development in infants. *Trends in Cognitive Sciences*, 9(3), 92–98.

Berlyne, D. E. (1958). The influence of the albedo and complexity of stimuli on visual fixation in the human infant. *British Journal of Psychology*, 49, 315–318.

Berlyne, D. E. (1963). Motivational problems raised by exploratory and epistemic behavior. In S. Koch (Ed.), *Psychology: A Study of Science. Vol. 5. The Process Areas, the Person, and Some Applied Fields: Their Place in Psychology and Science.* New York: McGraw-Hill.

Bertenthal, B. I., Haith, M. M., & Campos, J. J. (1983). The partial-lag design: A method for controlling spontaneous regression in the infant-control habituation paradigm. *Infant Behavior and Development*, 6, 331–338.

Casey, B. J., Tottenham, N., Liston, C., & Durston, S. (2005). Imaging the developing brain: What have we learned about cognitive development. *Trends in Cognitive Sciences*, 9, 122–128.

Cohen, L. B. (1969). Observing responses, visual preferences, and habituation to visual stimuli in infants. *Journal of Experimental Child Psychology*, 7, 419–433.

Dannemiller, J. L. (1984). Infant habituation criteria. I. A Monte Carlo study of the 50% decrement criterion. *Infant Behavior and Development*, 7, 147–166.

Dawson, G., Carver, L., Meltzoff, A. N., Panagiotides, H., & McPartland, J. (2002). Neural correlates of face recognition in young children with autism spectrum disorder, developmental delay, and typical development. *Child Development*, 73, 700–717.

Dawson, G., Osterling, J., Meltzoff, A., & Kuhl, P. (2000). Case study of the development of an infant with autism from birth to two years of age. *Journal of Applied Developmental Psychology*, 21, 299–313.

Dawson, G., Webb, S. J., & McPartland, J. (2005). Understanding the nature of face processing impairment in autism: Insights from behavioral and electrophysiological studies. *Developmental Neuropsychology*, 27(3), 403–424.

DeBoer, T., Scott, L. S., & Nelson, C. A. (2007). Methods for acquiring and analysing infant event-related potentials. In M. de Haan (Ed.). *Infant EEG and Event-Related Potentials* (pp. 5–37). London: Psychology Press.

de Haan, M., Johnson, M. H., & Halit, H. (2003). Development of face-sensitive event-related potentials during infancy: A review. *International Journal of Psychophysiology*, 51, 45–58.

de Haan, M., & Thomas, K. M. (2002). Applications of ERP and fMRI techniques to developmental science. *Developmental Science*, 5(3), 335–343.

Devlin, J. T., Sillery, E. S., Hall, D. A., Hobden, P., Behrens, T. E. J., Nunes, R. G., Clare, S., Matthews, P. M., Moore, D. R., & Johansen-Berg, H. (2006). Reliable identification of the auditory thalamus using multi-modal structural analyses. *NeuroImage*, 30(4), 1112–1120.

Fantz, R. L. (1964). Visual experience in infants: Decreased attention to familiar patterns relative to novel ones. *Science*, 146, 668–670.

Fantz, R. L., Ordy, J. M., & Udelf, M. S. (1962). Maturation of pattern vision in infants during the first six months. *Journal of Comparative and Physiological Psychology*, 55, 907–917.

Fulford, J., Vadeyar, S. H., Dodampahala, S. H., Moore, R. J., Young, P., Baker, P. N., James, D. K., & Gowland, P. A. (2003). Fetal brain activity in response to a visual stimulus. *Human Brain Mapping*, 20, 239–245.

Fulford, J., Vadeyar, S. H., Dodampahala, S. H., Ong, A., Moore, R. J., Baker, P. N., James, D. K., & Gowland, P. (2004). Fetal brain activity and hemodynamic response to a vibroacoustic stimulus. *Human Brain Mapping*, 22, 116–121.

Gomot, M., Bernard, F. A., Davis, M. H., Belmonte, M. K., Ashwin, C., Bullmore, E. T., & Baron-Cohen, S. (2006). Change detection in children with autism: An auditory event-related fMRI study. *NeuroImage*, 29, 475–484.

Hirsh-Pasek, K., & Golinkoff, R. (1991). Language comprehension: A new look at some old themes. In N. Krasnegor, D. Rumbaugh, M. Studdert-Kennedy, & R. Schiefelbusch (Eds.), *Biological and Behavioral Aspects of Language Acquisition*. Hillsdale, NJ: Lawrence Erlbaum.

Hollich, G. J., Hirsh-Pasek, K., & Golinkoff, R. M. (1998). Introducing the 3-D Intermodal Preferential Looking Paradigm: A new method to answer an age-old question. *Advances in Infancy Research*, 12, 355–374.

Horowitz, F. D., Paden, L., Bhana, K., & Self, P. (1972). An infant control procedure for studying infant visual fixations. *Developmental Psychology*, 7, 90.

Jezzard, P., Matthews, P., & Smith. S. (Eds). (2001). *Functional MRI: An Introduction to Methods*. Oxford: Oxford University Press.

Laub, K. W. (1972). Habituation of visual fixation in infants 8 and 9 weeks of age. Unpublished Master's thesis, University of Kansas, Lawrence.

Logothesis, N. K. (2002). The neural basis of the blood-oxygen-level-dependent functional magnetic resonance imaging signal. *Philosophical Transactions of the Royal Society of London B, Biological Sciences*, 357(1424), 1003–1007.

Logothesis, N. K. (2003). The underpinnings of the BOLD functional magnetic resonance imaging signal. *Journal of Neuroscience*, 23(10), 3963–3971.

Loveland, K. A., Tunali-Kotoski, B., Chen, R., Brelsford, K. A., Ortegon, J., & Pearson, D. A. (1995). Intermodal perception of affect in persons with autism or Down syndrome. *Development and Psychopathology*, 9, 579–593.

Nelson, C. A. (1995). The ontogeny of human memory: A cognitive neuroscience perspective. *Developmental Psychology*, 31, 723–738.

Nelson, C. A., & Monk, C. S. (2001). The use of event-related potentials in the study of cognitive development. In C. A. Nelson & M. Luciana (Eds.), *The Handbook of Developmental Cognitive Neuroscience* (pp. 125–136). Cambridge, MA: MIT Press.

Osterling, J., & Dawson, G. (1994). Early recognition of children with autism: A study of first birthday home videotapes. *Journal of Autism & Developmental Disorders*, 24, 247–257.

Pavlov, I. P. (1927). *Conditioned Reflexes: An Investigation of the Physiological Activity of the Cerebral Cortex*, trans. and ed. G. V. Anrep. Oxford: Oxford University Press.

Reid, V. M., Csibra, G., Belsky, J., & Johnson, M. H. (2007). Neural correlates of the perception of goal-directed action in infants. *Acta Psychologica*, 124, 129–138.

Rocroi, C. (2000). The Interactive Intermodal Preferential Looking Paradigm. *Monographs of the Society for Research in Child Development*, 65(3), 30–40.

Seghier, M. L., Lazeyras, F., Zimine S., Maier, S. E., Hanquinet, S., Delavelle, J., Volpe, J. J., & Huppi, P. S. (2004). Combination of event-related fMRI and diffusion tensor imaging in an infant with perinatal stroke. *NeuroImage*, 21, 463–472.

Sirois, S., & Mareschal, D. (2002). Models of habituation in infancy. *Trends in Cognitive Sciences*, 6, 293–298.

Sokolov, E. N. (1963). *Perception and the Conditioned Reflex*. Oxford: Pergamon Press.

Spelke, E. S. (1979). Exploring audible and visual events in infancy. In A. D. Pick (Ed.), *Perception and its Development: A Tribute to E. J. Gibson*. New York: Wiley.

Thomas, H., & Gilmore, R. O. (2004). Habituation assessment in infancy. *Psychological Methods*, 9, 70–92.

van Der Geest, J. N., Kemner, C., Verbaten, M. N., & van Engeland, H. (2002). Gaze behavior of children with pervasive developmental disorder toward human faces: A fixation time study. *Journal of Child Psychology and Psychiatry*, 43(5), 669–678.

Walker-Andrews, A. S., Haviland, J. M., Hufhan, L., & Toci, L. (1994). Brief report: Preferential looking in intermodal perception by children with autism. *Journal of Autism and Developmental Disorders*, 24, 99–107.

Zacks, J. M., Braver, T. S., Sheridan, M. A., Donaldson, D. I., Snyder, A. Z., Ollinger, J. M., Buckner, R. L., & Raichle, M. E. (2001). Human brain activity time-locked to perceptual event boundaries, *Nature Neuroscience*, 4(6), 651–655.

Part Two
Cognitive Neuroscience

Editors' Introduction

Since the mid-1990s the investigation of social cognition has expanded in many directions, with work conducted in almost all areas of the arts and sciences from philosophy through to anthropology or psychology. The volume of productivity within any discipline, however, has unquestionably been the most intense within the cognitive neurosciences. In this section we present key issues within social cognition. Many of the chapters have clear and obvious implications for our understanding of development or social information processing in autism.

One reason for the wealth of new research in the area of cognitive neuroscience is the discovery of functional networks related to the detection and processing of conspecifics. Marco Iacoboni opens this section of the volume by presenting new work that outlines developmental aspects of the human mirror system. He does this by investigating its functional characteristics in adolescence. He pushes this research into new areas by linking it with empathy and emotion simulation. Another aspect of this system, imitation, is investigated by Marcel Brass and Stephanie Spengler. Their emphasis, however, is clearly different from that of Iacoboni. The key question for Brass and Spengler is how we inhibit imitative responses when we observe others performing actions. Their conclusions on inhibition and its relation to the theory of mind link directly with the developmental aspects of this volume. Issues such as intentionality have become a hallmark of recent exploration into the social brain. Grèzes and de Gelder address higher-order social-cognitive processes, such as the understanding of intentions, including deceit, and the processing of emotional content within gestural information. The assessment of non-verbal behavior allows linkages with key issues in developmental science, particularly with non-verbal infants and their understanding of intentionality (see Hauf, Chapter 9, this volume, and Reid & Striano, Chapter 11, this volume). Sarah-Jayne Blakemore also raises issues for developmental research in her chapter. She outlines new work on complex components of understanding others, including cheating, fairness, justice, and bargaining. With an emphasis on development, her focus on adolescent processing of these aspects of social behavior results in a unique perspective on social information processing within the cognitive neurosciences. Finally, Pines Nuku and Harold Bekkering outline some new empirical data that also focus on the understanding of intentions. The emphasis is specifically on the effect of eye gaze on information processing. This is then conjoined with work on grasping actions. These new data link to joint attention and its corresponding issues in development and for autism, suggesting that there are synergies that have yet to be tapped for those in development or autism research in terms of the relations between joint attention, hand actions, and attention. In so doing, Nuku and Bekkering provide cohesion to this section as well as highlighting some of the lessons that cognitive neuroscience and adult research have for aligned disciplines, such as the developmental sciences.

This section on cognitive neuroscience demonstrates the importance of integrating different disciplines for further advancement of our understanding of social cognition. At this stage it is possible that cognitive neuroscience as a discipline has the ability to offer more to other disciplines than it will receive. It is, however, interesting to note that, in order to address key issues, particularly in terms of the parameters of intentionality, goals, imitation, and their corresponding functional brain activity, cognitive neuroscience is choosing to take a developmental approach to solve unanswered questions. Whether this remains the case in future years is yet to be seen.

Chapter 3

Do Adolescents Simulate? Developmental Studies of the Human Mirror Neuron System

Marco Iacoboni

The Discovery of Mirror Neurons

In the mid-1990s, a group of neurophysiologists who were investigating the neural mechanisms for the motor control of grasping discovered a special class of neurons in the ventral premotor cortex of the monkey. As expected, these neurons fired when the monkey performed grasping actions and other kinds of object-oriented actions, such as holding, manipulating, tearing, and so on. These neurons, however, also had quite peculiar physiological properties. These cells also fired when the monkey, completely still, observed somebody else performing grasping actions and other object-oriented actions. The firing of these cells almost implied that – while looking at someone else's actions – the monkey was looking at its own actions reflected by a mirror. The neurophysiologists who discovered these cells called them "mirror neurons" (di Pellegrino, Fadiga, Fogassi, Gallese, & Rizzolatti, 1992; Gallese, Fadiga, Fogassi, & Rizzolatti, 1996; Rizzolatti, Fadiga, Gallese, & Fogassi, 1996).

A series of experiments since the mid-1990s have revealed that mirror neurons can implement a fairly abstract coding of the actions of other people. For instance, mirror neurons can use prior information on the presence or absence of an object behind a screen to distinguish between a hidden grasping action and a hidden pantomime of grasping, even though these two actions are visually identical, given that the screen occludes the view of the final part of the two actions (Umiltà et al. 2001). Mirror neurons also fire at the sound associated with an action, such as breaking a peanut, even when the action is not seen at all (Kohler et al. 2002). Mirror neurons also code the same grasping action differently when it is associated with different intentions. In an experiment in which the presence or absence of a container indicated whether the experimenter was going to place a piece of food in the container or eat it, mirror neurons discharged differently – at the time of the observed grasping action – for the two intentions (Fogassi et al., 2005). This suggests that these cells are able to predict the outcome of observed actions while the actions unfold. Note that the cells that discharged while the monkey observed a grasping action for, say, eating were also the cells that fired when the monkey grasped the piece of food in order to eat it itself. Thus, the coding of the intentions of other people is performed by using the same cells that code the intention of the monkey when the animal is achieving its own goal.

Mirror neurons also code actions performed with the mouth. There are two main kinds of mouth actions that are coded by these cells: ingestive actions, such as biting a banana or drinking juice, and communicative actions, such as lip-smacking, a protrusion of the lips that is a facial communicative gesture with a positive social significance (Ferrari, Gallese, Rizzolatti, & Fogassi, 2003).

Mirror neurons have been identified in two main cortical areas of the monkey brain. The original discovery was made in an area of the frontal lobe called area F5. Area F5 is a premotor area located ventrally in the lateral wall of the cerebral hemispheres. Area F5 is anatomically connected with the rostral sector of the inferior parietal lobule. In this region of the monkey brain there are two areas, called area PF and area PFG, that also contain mirror neurons (Rizzolatti and Craighero, 2004). Thus, there exists in the primate brain a fronto-parietal mirror neuron system that codes the actions performed by the individual and the actions of other people that the individual simply observes. This fronto-parietal mirror neuron system seems an ideal neural system for facilitating social understanding. By coding the actions of the self and of other people in a similar way, the mirror neuron system may provide a simple mechanism for the recognition of the actions of other people and of the intentions associated with those actions.

The neurophysiological studies in monkeys on mirror neurons led to the investigation of similar neural mechanisms in humans. In evolutionary terms, however, there are several intermediate steps from monkeys to humans. It makes sense to hypothesize an evolution of the mirror neuron system from monkeys to humans. The physiological properties of mirror neurons seem tailored for imitation, a process that requires the copying of the actions of other individuals. Imitation is highly developed in humans, while limited in monkeys. Indeed, the human mirror neuron system seems a critical neural system for imitation, as we will see in the next section of this chapter.

Mirror Neurons and Imitation

Imitation seems a cornerstone of social cognition during development. It has been associated with the development of understanding the mental states of other people and with empathy. Imitation is also obviously an excellent form of learning skills, as it allows time-consuming trial-and-error forms of learning to be bypassed. The interest of scientists in imitation dates back at least to Darwin, who left detailed descriptions of mimicry in honeybees.

The debate on the definition of imitation has occupied social scientists for decades. One of its crucial aspects was whether the imitated action already belonged to the motor repertoire of the imitator or not. According to the most stringent definition of imitation, true imitation occurs only when the imitated action is novel and the imitator had never performed it in the past (Hurley and Chater, 2005). However, when we investigated for the first time the neural basis of imitation in humans with the goal of understanding whether or not human brain areas with mirroring properties were involved in imitation, the operational definition of imitation that we adopted was much simpler: the act of replicating actions made by other people.

The study of the role of the human mirror neuron system in imitation was obviously not performed with the same technique of single-cell recordings obtained with intracranial electrodes that was used with monkeys. This technique is too invasive to be used in healthy volunteers. The techniques adopted with humans were functional brain imaging and non-invasive brain-stimulation techniques such as transcranial magnetic stimulation (TMS). The very first brain-imaging study on imitation in human subjects used functional magnetic resonance imaging (fMRI). This fMRI study made the following assumptions. In monkeys, mirror neurons fire during both action execution and action observation. However, the firing rate of mirror neurons is quite different during action execution and action observation. Since the very first recordings on mirror neurons, neurophysiologists had observed a higher firing rate during action execution than during action observation. Indeed, during action observation mirror neurons tend to discharge at approximately half the firing rate at which they discharge during action execution. The brain imagers that used fMRI to study imitation in humans assumed a similar pattern of signal change in human mirror neuron areas. Human mirror neuron areas were assumed to activate during both action observation and action execution, but the signal increase during action observation was assumed to be approximately half of the signal increase during action execution. Given that imitation involves both action observation and action execution, the predicted signal increase in human mirror neuron areas during imitation was assumed to be approximately the sum of the signal increases measured during action observation and action execution, as shown in Figure 3.1.

The fMRI study of imitation of finger movements revealed two human brain areas with this predicted pattern of activity. The anatomical location of these brain areas corresponded well with the anatomical location of the monkey brain areas in which mirror neurons were recorded (Iacoboni et al. 1999). Indeed, as in the monkey, the mirror neuron areas were located in the posterior part of the inferior frontal gyrus and in the anterior part of the posterior parietal cortex.

Subsequent studies have also investigated the causal links between neural activity in these areas and imitative behavior, and the functional role of human fronto-parietal mirror neuron areas in imitation. Indeed, even though functional brain imaging provides wonderful opportunities to study brain activity *in vivo*, the limitation of this technique is that it provides only correlational information between brain activity and sensory, motor, or cognitive tasks. Brain imaging cannot tell us whether the activation of a given brain area during a task is essential to the task.

Marco Iacoboni

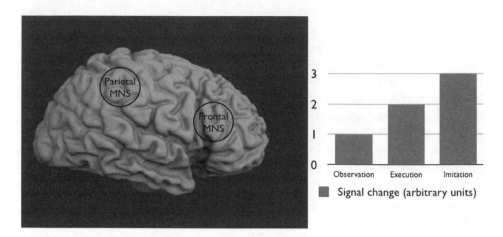

Figure 3.1.   Human mirror neuron areas identified with a finger imitation paradigm
Source: Iacoboni et al. (1999).

This interpretational limitation is especially important when the activated brain area is known to be relevant to other tasks. Indeed, the human inferior frontal mirror neuron area overlaps, at least in the left hemisphere, with Broca's area, a major language area of the human brain. On the one hand, such overlap supports evolutionary theories that posit a critical role of mirror neurons in language evolution. On the other hand, such overlap generates concerns that the activation observed during imitative tasks in Broca's area may simply be due to covert speech (Heyes, 2001). Although it is difficult to see how covert speech can generate in Broca's area the pattern of activity predicted on the basis of the firing rate of mirror neurons in monkeys, there is a way of testing directly the causal links between Broca's area and imitation. TMS can induce *transient lesions* in stimulated areas. By stimulating Broca's area during imitation, it is possible to test whether such stimulation interferes with imitation. A recent study adopting this approach has indeed demonstrated a causal role of the activity of Broca's area – and of its homologue in the right hemisphere – during imitation, thus rejecting the hypothesis that the activation of these areas during imitation is due to epiphenomenal covert speech (Heiser, Iacoboni, Maeda, Marcus, & Mazziotta, 2003).

Brain-imaging studies have also demonstrated that the inferior frontal mirror neuron area is mostly concerned with the goal of the action to be imitated (Koski et al. 2002) and is highly active during *mirror* imitation (Koski, Iacoboni, Dubeau, Woods, & Mazziotta, 2003). Mirror imitation is a form of face-to-face imitation. When the model and the imitator are face to face, the imitator tends to imitate the model as if in front of a mirror. This form of imitation is strongly predominant early in life (Wapner and Cirillo, 1968) and seems associated with intimacy and rapport. A study on imitation of postures during regular class periods found that, the higher the rapport in the classroom, the higher the mirroring. In another study, perceived mirroring in face-to-face interactions was also judged to convey more solidarity, involvement, and "togetherness" (Hatfield, Cacioppo, & Rapson, 1994).

Obviously, it is practically impossible to obtain brain-imaging data in such naturalistic contexts. However, it makes sense to hypothesize the involvement of mirror neurons in the spontaneous mirroring behavior of people, especially in the light of the brain-imaging data on mirror imitation. The intimacy of self and other that imitation and mirror neurons facilitate may be the first step toward empathy, a building block of social cognition, as I discuss in the next section of the chapter.

Mirror Neurons and Empathy

About a century ago, Theodore Lipps equated empathy to some form of *inner imitation*. He pointed out that, when we see the acrobat on the wire at the circus, we feel we are inside him (Gallese, 2001). Through the inner imitation of the actions and facial expressions of other people, we are able to feel what they feel, and to understand their emotional states. Mirror neurons seem the ideal brain cells for this kind of inner imitation, which, in modern cognitive jargon, is often called *simulation*. They fire, in our own premotor cortex, when we see others' actions.

Given the critical role of mirror neurons in imitation, the hypothesis that mirror neurons are also important neural elements for empathy predicts some links between imitation and empathy. Indeed, a well-controlled social psychology experiment has demonstrated these links. It is well known that humans tend automatically to imitate each other during social interactions. This phenomenon is called the "Chameleon Effect." There are, however, individual differences in the tendency to imitate others. Some people seem to be chameleons more than other people. It turns out that the tendency to imitate others correlates with the tendency to empathize with other people. The more empathic one individual is, the more that individual tends to imitate the posture, mannerisms, and facial expressions of other people (Chartrand and Bargh, 1999).

From the standpoint of neural systems, however, the link between mirror neurons and empathy begs the question: how are mirror neuron areas connected with more classical emotional brain centers, such as limbic structures? From what we know about connectivity patterns in the primate brain, there is one structure that connects the fronto–parietal mirror neuron areas with the limbic system. This structure is the insula (Augustine, 1996). Thus, the anatomical connections between mirror neuron areas and the limbic system through the insula provide a plausible neural substrate for the functional mechanisms of empathy first hypothesized by Lipps. When we see others' actions and facial expression, our mirror neurons provide an inner imitation of those actions and facial expressions. By sending signals to the limbic system through the insula, mirror neurons help us feel what we would feel if we were the ones making those actions and facial expressions. The large-scale network composed by mirror neuron areas, the insula, and the limbic system would then represent the cortical circuitry for empathy in the human brain.

To test this hypothesis, my group performed a brain-imaging experiment. We presented emotional facial expressions to our subjects and asked them to imitate those facial expressions or simply to watch them. Our predictions were as follows: if we understand the emotions of other people with an inner imitation of their facial expressions provided by mirror neurons that send signals to the limbic system through the insula, the whole network composed by mirror neuron areas, the insula, and limbic system should be active during both observation of facial emotional expression and imitation of those expressions. However, mirror neuron areas have higher activity during imitation than during observation of facial emotional expressions. Thus, if mirror neuron areas are the ones sending signals to the limbic system, there should be increased activity during imitation – compared to observation of facial emotional expressions – not only in mirror neuron areas, but also in the insula and in limbic areas, since the increased mirror neuron activity should spread throughout the network. Our imaging data supported both predictions (Carr, Iacoboni, Dubeau, Mazziotta, & Lenzi, 2003), thus suggesting that we understand the emotions of other people with a sort of simulation process, by which we pretend we are making those actions and facial expressions ourselves, and by so doing we feel what other people feel.

Our brain-imaging study provided evidence in support of a plausible neural mechanism for empathy based on the inner imitation of the actions of other people implemented by mirror neurons. However, our study did not provide direct links between this neural circuit and the capacity of empathizing with other people. A series of recent experiments that followed up our study investigated this issue directly. In another brain-imaging study performed by my group, activity in mirror neuron areas while subjects observed everyday actions – for instance, grasping a cup – correlated with subjects' ability to empathize (Kaplan and Iacoboni, 2006). In another study from a different group, activity in mirror neuron areas while subjects listened to sounds associated with actions also correlated with the tendency to empathize with other people (Gazzola, Aziz-Zadeh, & Keysers, 2006). Thus, it seems that, the more active is one's own mirror neuron system, the more empathic that individual is. This suggests that the mirror neuron system is a critical neural system for social cognition and interpersonal relations. Key questions that emerge from these considerations are about the development of the mirror neuron system and its possible dysfunctions. The next section of the chapter deals with these questions.

Development of the Mirror Neuron System

It is well known that very young infants are able to imitate some facial expressions and some simple hand movements (Meltzoff and Moore, 1977). Although there is no direct evidence of the existence of mirror neuron in newborns and young infants, it is likely that the imitative behavior of infants is made possible by some functioning mirror neurons. It is also very likely, however, that the reciprocal imitation between mother (or caregiver) and baby shapes the human mirror neuron system. For instance, if the baby smiles, the mother smiles back, and the baby's brain can associate the sight of somebody else's smile with the motor plan for smiling.

Several recent studies have investigated the human mirror neuron system at different ages and using different brain-imaging techniques. The youngest population investigated so far is composed of 6–7-month-old Japanese infants. The study was performed using near infrared spectroscopy (NIRS). This technique works by emitting light in the near infrared and by detecting the light that is reflected by the brain. The physiological brain processes that occur in response to neural activation influence the amount of light reflected. Thus, with NIRS it is possible to study the infant brain *in vivo* in a completely safe and non-invasive way. Indeed, NIRS allows the study of the infant brain in fairly natural settings. In the study on Japanese infants, the babies were shown either live actions from an adult or televised actions. Control conditions included the observation of moving toys that were moved by an unseen experimenter, or the observation of motion following physical laws. Periods of excessive movements of the babies were excluded from the analyses. The NIRS study found that motor areas were activated by the observation of actions, but not during the control conditions (Shimada and Hiraki, 2006). Evidently, this pattern of activity in motor areas probably reflects mirror neuron activity in the infant brain. Furthermore, the activity measured in motor areas while the infants were observing live actions was higher than the activity measured while the infants were watching televised actions, a pattern already observed in monkey's mirror neurons, which typically discharge robustly for live actions but weakly for actions shown on a monitor.

Another recent study has measured the suppression of the mu rhythm during action observation in children between 4 and 11 years of age. Mu suppression is typically considered an index of activation in central, motor areas. It has been argued that its presence during action observation is an index of mirror neuron activity (Hari et al. 1998). The children demonstrated mu suppression during action observation, thus suggesting again the presence of a functioning mirror neuron system in childhood (Lepage and Théoret, 2006).

We are studying typically developing children in a longitudinal experiment on social cognition in adolescents. The children are recruited when they reach 10 years of age and will be followed up for five years. The analyses of the data of the first visit demonstrate strong correlations between activity in mirror neuron areas and social competence. Mirror neuron activity during social mirroring was measured with fMRI while the children performed tasks of imitation and observation of facial emotional expressions. We found a robust correlation between mirror neuron activity during observation of facial emotional expressions and emotional empathy. We also found a robust correlation between mirror neuron activity during imitation and the social competence of the children (Pfeifer, Iacoboni, Mazziotta, & Dapretto, 2005).

Our results suggest that the mirror neuron system is some kind of bio-marker of human social competence. Indeed, the mirror neuron system seems to be a nuanced bio-marker of sociality. Emotional empathy is mostly a private experience – the ability to resonate emotionally with others. The correlation between emotional empathy and brain activity while children are simply *observing* other people's emotions reflects such private experience. On the other hand, the tendency to mimic the emotional expressions of others is a key aspect of smooth social interactions. If somebody displays intense happiness or deep sorrow while other people respond with a stone face, that person feels that he or she has not been understood. Thus, reciprocal mimicry is an important component of social interactions. The correlation between mirror neuron activity during overt imitation of emotional facial expressions and interpersonal competence that we found in our study reflects the key role of overt mirroring in social interactions.

If the mirror neuron system is such a critical neural system for social behavior, it makes sense to posit its dysfunction in diseases mainly characterized by social disorders. The hypothesis that the socially isolating condition of autism is due to a dysfunction in mirror neurons (Williams, Whiten, Suddendorf, & Perrett, 2001) has recently been tested by several labs. A variety of experimental approaches provided evidence in support of a mirror neuron dysfunction in patients diagnosed with Autism Spectrum Disorder (ASD). An MRI study has revealed structural changes in mirror neuron regions of ASD adolescents (Hadjikhani, Joseph, Snyder, & Tager-Flusberg, 2006), magnetoencephalography (MEG) has shown delayed activation in frontal mirror neuron areas in ASD subjects (Nishitani, Avikainen, & Hari, 2004), and electroencephalogram (EEG) has revealed reduced mu suppression during action observation in ASD patients (Oberman et al., 2005). Furthermore, TMS has shown reduced motor excitability during action observation in subjects with ASD (Lepage & Théoret 2006), and a recent fMRI study has demonstrated reduced mirror neuron activity in ASD patients during imitation of finger movements (Williams et al., 2006). However, none of these studies has tested the relationship between mirror neuron deficits and the severity of the clinical impairment.

We have recently investigated this relationship by using fMRI and activation tasks of imitation and observation of facial emotional expressions. Children with ASD demonstrated reduced mirror neuron activity while observing and imitating facial emotional expressions, compared to typically developing children. Critically, the impairment in mirror neuron areas correlated with the severity of the disease, as assessed by widely used clinical scales. The lower the mirror neuron activity, the more severe the autistic disorder (Dapretto et al., 2006). Our results strongly support the hypothesis that a deficit in mirror neurons is a core deficit in autism.

The deficit in mirror neuron activity in ASD fits well with the behavioral deficits in imitation observed in patients with autism (Rogers & Pennington, 1991). It also provides a rationale for using interventions based on imitation. Indeed, recent reports describing initial attempts to use imitation in ASD subjects as a form of treatment have provided very encouraging results (Escalona, Field, Nadel, & Lundy, 2002; Field, Sanders, & Nadel, 2001; Ingersoll & Gergans, 2006; Ingersoll, Lewis, & Kroman, 2006; Ingersoll & Schreibman, 2006).

Mirror Neurons and Self

There is a very intriguing developmental finding linking together imitation and self-recognition. In this study, two developmental psychologists investigated the amount of spontaneous imitation between pairs of children (Asendorpf & Baudonniere, 1993). They paired children on the basis of their ability to recognize their own face. Self-recognition typically develops toward the end of the second year of life. Even though younger children – say, 12 months old – seem to be endlessly fascinated by mirrors, when formally tested these younger infants typically fail the mirror self-recognition test. This test was developed by Gordon Gallup and allows an objective testing of self-face recognition (Gallup, 1970). The test works by placing an odorless mark on the forehead of the subject and by observing whether or not the subject looks at and touches the mark. In children, the mark is typically placed when the child is sleeping or by distracting the child while applying the mark (Keenan, Gallup, & Falk, 2003). Children who are able to recognize their own face immediately notice that something is different when they see the mark, and direct their behavior to the mark, touching it and using the mirror to look at the mark intently. Children who do not recognize themselves do not show mark-directed behavior at the mirror after the mark has been applied to their forehead.

Children who were able to self-recognize were paired with each other. These children imitated each other much more than the children who did not have mirror self-recognition. Thus, imitation and self-recognition seem to go together. Given that mirror neurons play a critical role in imitation, as we have seen in the previous sections of the chapter, is it possible that they also play a role in self-recognition?

My group has investigated the links between mirror neurons and self-recognition in two studies, using fMRI and TMS. In the first study, pictures of the subject were morphed with pictures of the subject's best friend. The morphs were made with different percentages of self and other, in 10 percent steps (100 percent self and 0 percent other, 90 percent self and 10 percent other, and so on). Subjects were supposed to recognize morphs that were made more of the *self* or more of the *other* by pressing one of two buttons. Brain activity when subjects were looking at morphs mostly made of self was compared to brain activity when subjects were looking at morphs mostly made of other. Mirror neuron areas in the right hemisphere were indeed much more active during self-recognition compared to other-recognition (Uddin, Kaplan, Molnar-Szakacs, Zaidel, E., Iacoboni, 2005).

Our explanation of these results is as follows. When one looks at one's own face reflected by the mirror, there are two selves facing each other. One is the *perceiving* self, the self as subject looking at his or her own picture. The other is the *perceived* self, the self as object, the face in the picture. What mirror neurons may be doing during self-recognition is to map the perceived self, the self as an object, onto the perceiving self, the self as subject, with a process akin to the one they implement when mirror neurons help to map the actions of other people onto the motor repertoire of the self. Indeed, there is evidence that even static pictures of other people can activate the human mirror neuron system (Urgesi, Moro, Candidi, & Aglioti, 2006).

In a subsequent study, we used TMS to test whether the activation in mirror neuron areas during self-recognition is essential for the self-recognition process (Uddin, Molnar-Szakacs, Zaidel, & Iacoboni, 2006). Indeed, the stimulation of the right parietal mirror neuron area induced a reliable impairment in self-recognition, whereas the stimulation of a control area did not. The TMS study shows a causal link between self-recognition and mirror neuron areas, those same areas that help us recognize and imitate the actions of other people. Thus, when one looks at mirror neurons, self and other appear as two sides of the same coin. I propose that mirror neurons may be the neural signature of a primary intersubjectivity. As we have seen earlier, a mechanism that probably shapes mirror neurons early in life is the reciprocal imitation between baby and mother. Thus, these cells may be formed at a time in which the baby has more a sense of *us* (mother and baby) than a sense of self. Mirror neuron activity, then, continues even later in life to be the neural signature of this sense of *us*, to which both self and other belong.

Concluding Remarks

Neural mirroring mechanisms in the primate brain reveal an aspect of intersubjectivity that has been emphasized by continental philosophers, especially the ones who can be grouped under the heading of existential phenomenologists. Rather than conceptualizing the self as a detached observer of the external world that includes others, as the classical Cartesian tradition suggested, phenomenologists have emphasized the notion that self and other are co-constituted. Dan Zahavi (2001) says of self and other that "they reciprocally illuminate one another, and can only be understood in their interconnection." The existential tradition, on the other hand, while pointing to our condition of being-in-the-world, alongside people and things, has also underlined the perspectival and limited view of the existential condition (Sartre, 1989). To analytic minds, the concept of the self as perspectival and limited and the concept that self and other are co-constituted cannot go together. These two concepts, however, have coexisted in existential phenomenology, drawing criticisms from the analytic tradition.

Mirror neurons show us neural mechanisms of simulation (or inner imitation) of the actions, intentions, and emotions of other people. These neural mechanisms provide a natural phenomenon that accounts for the seemingly incoherent claims of existential phenomenology. By simulating the actions, intentions, and emotions of others in our own brain, mirror neurons enable an intersubjective intimacy that allows us to overcome the perspectival and limited condition of our existence, grounding our sociality through mirroring.

References

Asendorpf, J. B., & Baudonniere, P. M. (1993). Self-awareness and other-awareness: Mirror self-recognition and synchronic imitation among unfamiliar peers. *Developmental Psychology*, 29, 88–95.

Augustine, J. R. (1996). Circuitry and functional aspects of the insular lobes in primates including humans. *Brain Research Reviews*, 2, 229–294.

Carr, L., Iacoboni, M., Dubeau, M. C., Mazziotta, J. C., & Lenzi, G. L. (2003). Neural mechanisms of empathy in humans: A relay from neural systems for imitation to limbic areas. *Proceedings of the National Academy of Sciences, USA*, 100, 5497–5502.

Chartrand, T. L., & Bargh, J.A. (1999). The chameleon effect: The perception-behavior link and social interaction. *Journal of Personality & Social Psychology*, 76, 893–910.

Dapretto, M., Davies, M. S., Pfeifer, J. H., Scott, A. A., Sigman, M., Bookheimer, S. Y., & Iacoboni, M. (2006). Understanding emotions in others: Mirror neuron dysfunction in children with autism spectrum disorders. *Nature Neuroscience*, 9, 28–30.

di Pellegrino, G., Fadiga, L., Fogassi, L., Gallese, V., & Rizzolatti, G. (1992). Understanding motor events: A neurophysiological study. *Experimental Brain Research*, 91, 176–180.

Escalona, A., Field, T., Nadel, J., & Lundy, B. (2002). Brief report: Imitation effects on children with autism. *Journal of Autism and Developmental Disorders*, 32, 141–144.

Ferrari, P. F., Gallese, V., Rizzolatti, G., & Fogassi, L. (2003). Mirror neurons responding to the observation of ingestive and communicative mouth actions in the monkey ventral premotor cortex. *European Journal of Neuroscience*, 17, 1703–1714.

Field, T., Sanders, C., & Nadel, J. (2001). Children with autism display more social behaviors after repeated imitation sessions. *Autism*, 5, 317–323.

Fogassi, L., Ferrari, P. F., Gesierich, B., Rozzi, S., Chersi, F., & Rizzolatti, G. (2005). Parietal lobe: From action organization to intention understanding. *Science*, 308, 662–667.

Gallese, V. (2001). The "shared manifold" hypothesis. *Journal of Consciousness Studies*, 8, 33–50.

Gallese, V., Fadiga, L., Fogassi, L., & Rizzolatti, G. (1996). Action recognition in the premotor cortex. *Brain*, 119(2), 593–609.

Gallup, G. G. (1970). Chimpanzees: Self-recognition. *Science*, 167, 86–87.

Gazzola, V., Aziz-Zadeh, L., & Keysers, C. (2006). Empathy and the somatotopic auditory mirror system in humans. *Current Biology*, 16, 1824–1829.

Hadjikhani, N., Joseph, R. M., Snyder, J., & Tager-Flusberg, H. (2006). Anatomical differences in the mirror neuron system and social cognition network in autism. *Cerebral Cortex*, 16, 1276–1282.

Hari, R., Forss, N., Avikainen, S., Kirveskari, E., Salenius, S., & Rizzolatti, G. (1998). Activation of human primary motor cortex during action observation: A neuromagnetic study. *Proceedings of the National Academy of Sciences, USA*, 95, 15061–15065.

Hatfield, E., Cacioppo, J. T., & Rapson, R. L. (1994). *Emotional contagion*. Cambridge: Cambridge University Press.

Heiser, M., Iacoboni, M., Maeda, F., Marcus, J., & Mazziotta, J. C. (2003). The essential role of Broca's area in imitation. *European Journal of Neuroscience*, 17, 1123–1128.

Heyes, C. (2001). Causes and consequences of imitation. *Trends in Cognitive Sciences*, 5, 253–261.

Hurley, S., & Chater, N. (2005). *Perspective on imitation: From neuroscience to social science*. Cambridge, MA: MIT Press.

Iacoboni, M., Woods, R. P., Brass, M., Bekkering, H., Mazziotta, J.C., & Rizzolatti, G. (1999). Cortical mechanisms of human imitation. *Science*, 286, 2526–2528.

Ingersoll, B., & Gergans, S. (2006). The effect of a parent-implemented imitation intervention on spontaneous imitation skills in young children with autism. *Research in Developmental Disabilities*, 28, 163–175.

Ingersoll, B., Lewis, E., & Kroman, E. (2006). Teaching the imitation and spontaneous use of descriptive gestures in young children with autism using a naturalistic behavioral intervention. *Journal of Autism and Developmental Disorders*.

Ingersoll, B., & Schreibman, L. (2006). Teaching reciprocal imitation skills to young children with autism using a naturalistic behavioral approach: Effects on language, pretend play, and joint attention. *Journal of Autism and Developmental Disorders*, 36, 487–505.

Kaplan, J. T., & Iacoboni, M. (2006). Getting a grip on other minds: Mirror neurons, intention understanding, and cognitive empathy. *Social Neuroscience*, 1, 175–183.

Keenan, J. P., Gallup, G. G., & Falk, D. (2003). *The Face in the Mirror: The Search for the Origins of Consciousness*. New York: Ecco.

Kohler, E., Keysers, C., Umiltà, M. A., Fogassi, L., Gallese, V., & Rizzolatti, G. (2002). Hearing sounds, understanding actions: Action representation in mirror neurons. *Science*, 297, 846–848.

Koski, L., Iacoboni, M., Dubeau, M. C., Woods, R. P., & Mazziotta, J. C. (2003). Modulation of cortical activity during different imitative behaviors. *Journal of Neurophysiology*, 89, 460–471.

Koski, L., Wohlschläger, A., Bekkering, H., Woods, R. P., Dubeau, M. C., Mazziotta, J. C., & Iacoboni, M. (2002). Modulation of motor and premotor activity during imitation of target-directed actions. *Cerebral Cortex*, 12, 847–855.

Lepage, J. F., & Théoret, H. (2006). EEG evidence for the presence of an action observation-execution matching system in children. *European Journal of Neuroscience*, 23, 2505–2510.

Meltzoff, A. N., & Moore, M. K. (1977). Imitation of facial and manual gestures by human neonates. *Science*, 198, 74–78.

Nishitani, N., Avikainen, S., & Hari, R. (2004). Abnormal imitation-related cortical activation sequences in Asperger's syndrome. *Annals of Neurology*, 55, 558–562.

Oberman, L. M., Hubbard, E. M., McCleery, J. P., Altschuler, E. L., Ramachandran, V. S., & Pineda, J. A. (2005). EEG evidence for mirror neuron dysfunction in autism spectrum disorders. *Brain Research: Cognitive Brain Research*, 24, 190–198.

Pfeifer, J. H., Iacoboni, M., Mazziotta, J. C., & Dapretto, M. (2008). Mirroring others' emotions relates to empathy and interpersonal competence in children. *NeuroImage*, 39, 2076–2085.

Rizzolatti, G., & Craighero, L. (2004). The mirror-neuron system. *Annual Review of Neuroscience*, 27, 169–192.

Rizzolatti, G., Fadiga, L., Gallese, V., & Fogassi, L. (1996). Premotor cortex and the recognition of motor actions. *Brain Research: Cognitive Brain Research*, 3, 131–141.

Rogers, S. J., & Pennington, B. F. (1991). A theoretical approach to the deficits in infantile autism. *Developmental Psychology*, 3, 137–162.

Sartre, J.-P. (1989). Existentialism is a humanism. In *Existentialism from Dostoyevsky to Sartre*, ed. W. Kaufman. New York: Meridian.

Shimada, S., & Hiraki, K. (2006). Infant's brain responses to live and televised action. *NeuroImage*, 32, 930–939.

Uddin, L., Molnar-Szakacs, I., Zaidel, E., & Iacoboni, M. (2006). rTMS to the right inferior parietal area disrupts self-other discrimination. *Social, Cognitive and Affective Neuroscience*, 1, 65–71.

Uddin, L. Q., Kaplan, J. T., Molnar-Szakacs, I., Zaidel, E., & Iacoboni, M. (2005). Self-face recognition activates a frontoparietal "mirror" network in the right hemisphere: An event-related fMRI study. *NeuroImage*, 25, 926–935.

Umiltà, M. A., Kohler, E., Gallese, V., Fogassi, L., Fadiga, L., Keysers, C., & Rizzolatti, G. (2001). I know what you are doing: A neurophysiological study. *Neuron*, 31, 155–165.

Urgesi, C., Moro, V., Candidi, M., & Aglioti, S. M. (2006). Mapping implied body actions in the human motor system. *Journal of Neuroscience*, 26, 7942–7949.

Wapner, S., & Cirillo, L. (1968). Imitation of a model's hand movement: Age changes in transposition of left–right relations. *Child Development*, 39, 887–894.

Williams, J. H., Waiter, G. D., Gilchrist, A., Perrett, D. I., Murray, A. D., & Whiten, A. (2006). Neural mechanisms of imitation and "mirror neuron" functioning in autistic spectrum disorder. *Neuropsychologia*, 44, 610–621.

Williams, J. H., Whiten, A., Suddendorf, T., & Perrett, D. I. (2001). Imitation, mirror neurons and autism. *Neuroscience and Biobehavioral Reviews*, 25, 287–295.

Zahavi, D. (2001). Beyond empathy: Phenomenological approaches to intersubjectivity. *Journal of Consciousness Studies*, 8, 151–167.

Chapter 4

The Inhibition of Imitative Behavior and Attribution of Mental States

Marcel Brass and Stephanie Spengler

Introduction

There is converging evidence from different fields of cognitive neuroscience suggesting that the observation of an action leads to a direct activation of an internal motor representation in the observer (Blakemore & Frith, 2005; Brass & Heyes, 2005; Iacoboni et al., 1999). It has been argued recently that these shared representations form a basis for imitation, action understanding, and social cognition (Gallese & Goldman, 1998; Rizzolatti & Craighero, 2004; Rizzolatti, Fogassi & Gallese, 2001). However, if there is a shared representational system of perception and action, the question arises how we are able to distinguish between internal motor representations and externally triggered motor representations (Jeannerod, 1999). In this chapter we first outline empirical evidence and theoretical accounts for the idea of shared representations. Furthermore, we report evidence suggesting that a crucial component of such a shared representation system is self–other distinction (Decety & Chaminade, 2003; Frith & Frith, 2006). In accordance with this assumption, recent data suggest that the inhibition of imitative behavior involves brain regions that are related to self–other distinction, perspective taking, and also the attribution of mental states (Brass, Derrfuss, & von Cramon, 2005; Brass, Zysset, & von Cramon, 2001; Spengler, von Cramon, & Brass, forthcoming). On the basis of these results and theoretical considerations, we argue that the inhibition of imitative behavior and mental state attribution share common functional mechanisms that are related to self–other distinction and perspective taking.

Shared Representations Are the Default State of the Motor System

In his seminal work, Piaget (1969) described the development of sensori-motor associations. The newborn starts to execute movements randomly. Such movements lead to specific sensory consequences in the environment, such as the visual impression of the moving limb and the proprioceptive feedback from the muscles. These perceived sensory consequences become associated with the motor command. Via bidirectional associations, the sensory consequences of the movement develop the potential to trigger the motor command. This leads to circular reactions: the movement triggers the sensory consequence, which triggers the movement again. This very simple mechanism of associating perceptual consequences of an action with the motor program is sufficient to constitute a shared representational system (Brass & Heyes, 2005; Greenwald, 1970). Because the motor program becomes associated with perceivable consequences of the action in the environment, observing such consequences in the environment can trigger the motor representation. In the beginning, the system does not differentiate between consequences in the environment that are produced by other agents or oneself. Seeing someone else's hand moving the hand automatically activates the associated motor representation within the observer. From this perspective, shared representations are the default state of the system. In the next step the system starts to develop a sense of agency. Specific sensory events in the environment are contingent upon one's own actions, while others are not. This experience, that other people are different from oneself, allows the system to develop a sense of self and agency. We will argue that self–other distinction is the precondition for attributing mental states to other people, for a theory of mind (TOM). Hence the basis for some social-cognitive skills is not the "like-me" experience (Meltzoff & Decety, 2003) but the "different-from-me" experience. Before we elaborate on this idea further, we outline theoretical accounts and empirical evidence for shared representations and the control of imitative response tendencies.

Demystifying Shared Representations as a Result of Motor Control

The basic idea that actions are controlled by their perceivable consequences is not a new one and actually goes back to the ideomotor principle formulated by William James (1890). Following up on this idea, Anthony Greenwald further developed this idea to a full-blown theory of motor control in the 1970s. The basic idea of the ideomotor theory can be directly derived from the concept of circular reactions. Perceivable consequences of an action become associated with the action and form the basis for motor representations. From the perspective of ideomotor theory, motor representations are anticipations of the sensory feedback from the action they represent. Because of this inherent property of motor representations, observing a movement automatically activates the corresponding motor plan via similarity. This basic idea led to the development of different theoretical accounts of motor control and imitation, which emphasize different aspects of the specific nature of motor representation and how associations are formed. The common coding approach by Wolfgang Prinz (1997), for example, proposes that shared representations are stored in an abstract format that is neither motor nor perceptual. This idea was further specified in the theory of event coding (Hommel, Musseler, Aschersleben, & Prinz, 2001), which provides a more specific account of how representations are shared by perception and action. The associative learning theory by Celia Heyes (2001) emphasizes the acquisition of shared representations by proposing general associative learning mechanisms as the basis for shared representations. Common to all these approaches, and derived from the basic idea that motor representations contain the sensory consequences of an action, is the set of empirical predictions that perceiving action should automatically activate the corresponding motor program. In the following paragraph we outline empirical evidence for this claim.

Behavioral Evidence for Shared Representations

The simplest way to test empirically whether observing an action leads to an activation of a corresponding motor program is to test whether action observation leads to a priming of the corresponding response. Since the year 2000 an increasing number of behavioral studies have addressed this issue (Blakemore & Frith, 2005; Brass & Heyes, 2005; Prinz, 2002). In a series of reaction time experiments Prinz and colleagues used interference paradigms to investigate the influence of movement observation on movement execution (Brass, Bekkering & Prinz, 2001; Brass, Bekkering, Wohlschläger, & Prinz, 2000; Stürmer, Aschersleben, & Prinz, 2000). This approach has been borrowed from stimulus response compatibility research and is based on a simple logical assumption. If the observation of an action leads to an activation of an internal motor representation, as assumed by ideomotor theory, observing an irrelevant action that does not match the instructed action should slow down reaction time, while observing an action that matches the instructed action should speed up reaction time. In accordance with this hypothesis, the experiments revealed that observing a congruent movement leads to faster reaction times than observing an incongruent movement (Brass et al., 2000; Brass, Zysset, & von Cramon, 2001; Heyes, Bird, Johnson, & Haggard 2005; Stürmer et al., 2000; Longo & Bertenthal, 2006). It was also demonstrated that motor priming by action observation cannot be reduced solely to spatial compatibility (Bertenthal, Longo, & Kosobud, 2006). Furthermore, the effect also occurs when the end position of the action is presented rather the whole movement being observed (Craighero, Bello, Fadiga, & Rizzolatti, 2002; Stürmer et al., 2000). A series of recent experiments revealed the influence of kinematic aspects of the observed action on the executed action (Edwards, Humphreys, & Castiello, 2003; Kilner, Paulignan, & Blakemore, 2003).

We have recently investigated whether this motor priming effect is driven simply by the movement itself or whether it matters whether the observer attributes an intention to the observed movement (Liepelt, von Cramon, & Brass, forthcoming).

The data suggest that intention attribution plays a crucial role in motor priming. When the observer assumes that an observed action was not intended, the motor priming effect becomes smaller.

Evidence from Neuroscience for Shared Representations

These behavioral studies provided strong evidence for the assumption that the mere observation of an action leads to an activation of an equivalent motor representation. Additionally, functional brain imaging studies make it possible to test more directly whether the motor system is involved in observing biological motion. An extensive literature on the observation of biological motion supports this assumption (for an overview, see Brass & Heyes, 2005; Decety & Grezes, 1999; Grezes & Decety, 2001). Observation of an action leads to the activation of a set of brain regions, some of which are also assumed to be partly involved in motor control. This network includes the lateral premotor cortex, the inferior frontal gyrus, areas along the intraparietal suclus, the inferior parietal lobe, as well as regions in the superior temporal sulcus. Furthermore, it was demonstrated that the activation in this network differs in the observation of biological agents and in that of non-biological agents such as robots (Perani et al., 2001). Moreover, the network is strongly modulated by motor experience with observed movement (Calvo-Merino, Glaser, Grezes, Passingham, & Haggard, 2005; Calvo-Merino, Glaser, Grèzes, Passingham, & Haggard, 2005). Observing movements that are highly practiced by the observer leads to a stronger activation of motor-related areas compared to observation of movements that are not well practiced.

The most persuasive empirical support for shared representations of perception and action was provided by Rizzolatti and colleagues from the University of Parma. Di Pelligrino, Fadiga, Fogassi, Gallese, and Rizzolatti (1992) found neurons in the premotor cortex (F5) of the macaque monkey that were active, both when the monkey observes an action and when it executes the same action. These neurons were dubbed mirror neurons. The activity of mirror neurons is restricted to the presentation of object-related actions. They do not respond to the mere sight of an object or a movement alone (Gallese, Fadiga, Fogassi, & Rizzolatti, 1996). Mirror neurons are not restricted to the visual domain but are also found in the auditory domain (Kohler et al., 2002). The discovery of mirror neurons impressively shows that common representations for observed and executed movements can be found even on a single cell level.

The Agency Problem of Shared Representations

The assumption of a shared representational system raises a fundamental issue that has so far not been addressed empirically. If the observation of an action leads to the activation of an internal motor representation, why does this externally triggered motor representation not automatically lead to imitative behavior in the observer? In order to avoid imitative behavior, the observer must be able to distinguish between his or her own motor intentions and the externally triggered motor representation (Jeannerod, 1999, 2004; Prinz, 2002). The confusion of self and other is already inherent in the concept of circular reactions. According to Piaget, newborns cannot distinguish between self-generated effects in the environment and effects that are produced by other individuals. It is only gradually that the baby develops a sense of agency.

However, if shared representations are the default state of the system, it should be possible to observe problems in distinguishing between self and other not only in newborns but also in adults. Since imitation is not adaptive in most everyday situations, the system must develop a standard solution for this problem. Nevertheless, it should be possible to provoke automatic imitative behavior by experimentally challenging this mechanism. As we outline below, there is some evidence that healthy adults display imitative response tendencies in specific communicative situations. Furthermore, we will report research on neurological and psychiatric patients with pathological imitative response tendencies.

Unintentional Imitation in Communicative Situations

A context where imitative response tendencies have been reported in adults is in social interactions. We all know the situation where we are involved in an interesting conversation and we suddenly find ourselves in the same posture as our conversation partner. This unconscious tendency to mimic the postures, mannerisms, and facial expressions of our social interaction partners has been called the "chameleon effect" and has been investigated systematically in social psychology (Chartrand & Bargh, 1999). Interestingly, imitative behavior seems to be relatively common in social situations and is displayed especially by empathic individuals. There also seems to be a preference to imitate others whom we like. We are usually unaware of such imitative behavior and as soon as we become aware of it we try to avoid imitation.

Moreover, recent research has suggested that imitation can be used to induce prosocial behavior toward the mimicker. In a series of experiments van Baaren, Holland, Kawakami, and van Knippenberg (2004) were able to show that participants felt more sympathy for the experimenter when he systematically imitated the movements and postures of the participant. This prosocial behavior was not restricted to the mimicker but extended to other people as well. Again it was crucial that the model was unaware of being imitated. But why do we feel more sympathy with someone who is imitating us? One possible answer to this question is related to the confusion of self and other. When we observe someone else doing what we do, the border between self and other becomes blurred. Therefore, the other becomes more like oneself, which leads to a positive evaluation. As soon as we become aware of the fact that the other person is imitating us, the effect disappears, because we become aware of the self–other distinction. The alternative interpretation would be that being imitated is rewarding in itself. If this interpretation holds, being imitated would induce a positive mood, which leads to prosocial behavior toward the environment.

At the moment, both interpretations are highly speculative, and further research is needed to evaluate these ideas. However, both interpretations lead to an interesting set of empirical predictions, which could be tested behaviorally and with functional MRI.

Imitative Response Tendencies in Neurological and Psychiatric Patients

In the previous paragraphs we have outlined how, under specific conditions, movement observation also exerts an influence on movement execution in adults. Furthermore, we have reported evidence from social psychology showing that people display unintended imitative behavior in social interactions. In some situations neurological patients with prefrontal lesions also show overt imitative response tendencies. Luria (1963) reported that these patients displayed what he called echopractic responses. He demonstrated that prefrontal patients tended to imitate observed behavior, rather than following a verbal instruction, when the verbal instruction and the observed behavior were incongruent. In a recent patient study we were able to replicate the finding of echopractic response tendencies in frontal patients under controlled experimental conditions (Brass, Derrfuss, Matthes-von Cramon, & von Cramon, 2003). Interestingly, in our study the patients were mostly aware of making errors.

This awareness of the inappropriateness of behavior contrasts with patients who suffer from so-called imitative behavior (Lhermitte, Pillon, & Serdaru, 1986; de Renzi, Cavalleri, & Facchini, 1996). Patients with this syndrome tend to imitate the experimenter overtly. When they were asked why they were imitating, they told the experimenter that they thought they were supposed to do so. These patients seemed to experience this externally triggered behavior as if they had intended it. Lhermitte (1986) assumed that imitation behavior is part of a broader syndrome, which he called the "social dependency syndrome." Patients with this syndrome have problems detaching their behavior from the social environment.

Another pathology where imitative response tendencies are observed is schizophrenia (DSM-IV). Schizophrenic patients sometimes obsessively imitate actions displayed by others (echopraxia). Furthermore, they imitate speech (echolalia). Interestingly, it has been proposed that one major problem of schizophrenic patients is distinguishing their own thoughts and actions from those of other people (Frith, 1992). Furthermore, it has been demonstrated that schizophrenics have problems determining agency of motor acts (Daprati et al., 1997).

These neuropsychological and psychiatric impairments provide some support for the idea that specific control mechanisms are needed to prevent unintended imitative response tendencies. Lhermitte's data also seem to suggest that some prefrontal patients confuse their intentions with externally triggered response tendencies.

Neural Correlates and Functional Mechanisms Involved in the Inhibition of Imitative Behavior

In order to gain deeper insights into the mechanisms that are needed to avoid imitative response tendencies, it is crucial to use methods that provide more detailed functional neuroanatomical information. We have carried out two functional MRI studies to investigate the neural circuits and functional mechanisms involved in the inhibition of imitative behavior (Brass, Bekkering, & Prinz, 2001; Brass, Derrfuss, & von Cramon, 2005). Two possible mechanisms might be crucial in this context. On the one hand, one can argue that imitative response tendencies do not differ from any other prepotent response tendency. If this holds true, one would expect brain areas to be activated that are involved in general cognitive control functions such as response inhibition and interference control. The cortical network involved in these processes is relatively well understood. It involves the lateral prefrontal cortex, the anterior cingulate cortex, the pre-supplementary motor area, and areas along the intraparietal sulcus (Duncan & Owen, 2000). The alternative possibility is based on the shared representation assumption and proposes that the inhibition of imitative behavior requires mechanisms that are involved in distinguishing between self and other, in determining self-agency, and in highlighting current motor intentions against externally activated response tendencies. Even though the brain areas involved in these processes are less well understood, there are some consistent findings suggesting that self–other distinction involves the temporo-parietal junction (TPJ) (Farrer & Frith, 2002; Farrer et al., 2003; Leube, Knoblich, Erb, & Kircher, 2003). Another line of research that systematically investigated self–other distinction is the study of perspective taking. Here participants have to distinguish a first-person perspective from a third-person perspective. A series of experiments by Perrine Ruby demonstrated that perspective taking in motor and non-motor tasks involves the TPJ and the anterior fronto-median cortex (Ruby & Decety, 2001, 2003). The median wall (including the precuneus) has also consistently been associated with tasks requiring self-referential processing (Northoff & Bermpohl, 2004).

In order to investigate the neural circuits involved in the inhibition of imitative behavior, we applied the so-called imitation-inhibition task in the fMRI scanner. In this task participants are required to carry out a lifting movement of the index or middle finger in response to a number (1 or 2) presented between the index and middle finger of a videotaped hand (Figure 4.1). In congruent trials

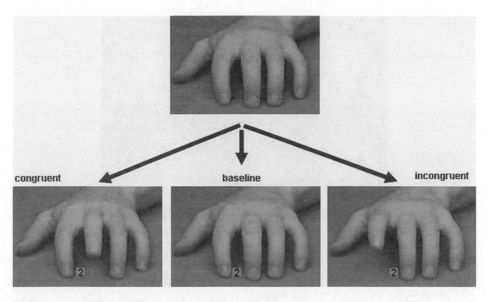

Figure 4.1. Schematic drawing of the imitation–inhibition task

Note: Participants were instructed to respond to a number displayed between the index and middle finger of a videotaped hand. When a "1" appeared, participants were instructed to lift their index finger, and when a "2" appeared, they were instructed to lift their middle finger. In congruent trials a movement that was identical to the instructed movement was displayed. In incongruent trials the alternative movement was display.

Source: Courtesy of Marcel Brass (previously unpublished, based on Brass et al., 2005).

participants observe a finger movement of the videotaped hand that is identical to the instructed movement. In incongruent trials the observed movement is different from the instructed movement. In neutral trials the hand on the computer screen remains still. Behaviorally, this paradigm very consistently yields an interference effect – that is, participants are slower in the incongruent than in the congruent condition. In order to address the question of which brain areas are involved in the inhibition of imitative behavior, we contrasted incongruent trials with congruent trials. Consistent with the hypothesis that the inhibition of imitative behavior involves brain regions that are related to self–other distinction and maintaining a self-perspective, we found activation in the TPJ and the anterior fronto-median cortex (aFMC) (Figure 4.2). Furthermore, we were able to show that the areas that were involved in the inhibition of imitative behavior did not overlap substantially with areas involved in the inhibition of other prepotent response tendencies. These data strongly suggest that the inhibition of imitative behavior is a special case of response inhibition. Because the observation of an action leads to a direct activation of an internal motor representation, participants have to distinguish their own motor intentions from the externally triggered motor representation.

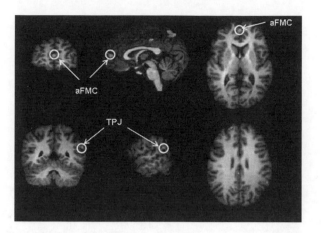

Figure 4.2.   Brain areas that are activated significantly more strongly in the incongruent than in the congruent condition of the imitation–inhibition task
Note: aFMC = anterior fronto-medial cortex; TPJ = temporo-parietal junction.
Source: Courtesy of Marcel Brass (previously unpublished, based on Brass et al., 2005).

The Inhibition of Imitative Behavior and Theory of Mind

If one takes a closer look at the areas that are activated for the inhibition of imitative behavior, it becomes clear that these areas are involved not only in self–other distinction and perspective taking, but also in more complex social-cognitive skills such as attributing mental states to others or to self, an ability that is related to having a "theory of mind" (TOM). Recently, there has been an extensive debate on the functional and neural mechanisms underlying TOM. One position is that the attribution of intentions is based on the mirror network (Gallese & Goldman, 1998). The basic idea behind this interpretation is that, because we experience that others are like our selves, we are able to understand the actions and mental states of others (Meltzoff & Decety, 2003). In other words, via a first-person simulation of other people's actions in one's own motor system, one experiences the similarity between self and other. However, this account has recently been criticized on the grounds of theoretical considerations (e.g. Jacob & Jeannerod, 2005; Saxe, 2005) and empirical findings (Saxe, 2006). One theoretical criticism is based on the argument that motor simulation is insufficient to deduce intentional states of others, because the same motor act can be based on different intentions. Moreover, motor simulation can be used only if the action is familiar and has been experienced by the person him or herself. Hence, if motor simulation is restricted to the motor act as such, it does not help in understanding other people's intentions (Jacob & Jeannerod, 2005), and other attribution mechanisms would have to come into play (Csibra & Gergely, 2006).

The empirical argument against a mirror account of mental state attribution stems from functional brain imaging studies using paradigms involving mentalizing. Studies that have investigated mental state attribution with functional MRI consistently report a network of brain activation that does not include brain areas with mirror properties (Frith & Frith, 1999, 2003). This network consists of the anterior fronto-median cortex, the TPJ, and the temporal poles.

But how does our finding of activations in classical TOM areas for the inhibition of imitative behavior relate to the discussion of the origins of mental state attribution? Here we propose that these findings provide further evidence for understanding the relation between the mirror system and TOM. We suggest an interpretation of mental state attribution that integrates different accounts. On the one hand, it assumes that shared representations are the first step for attributing mental states to other people. On the other hand, it assumes that the specific mechanisms that are involved in mental state attribution are related to the control of shared representations rather than to sharing representations (see also Decety & Grezes, 2006; Frith & Frith, 2006). Our interpretation is based on the ideomotor theory of action and assumes that shared representations are the default state of the sensorimotor system. As we have outlined above, because our motor representations contain the sensory consequences of our actions, perceiving an action automatically activates the equivalent motor representation in the observer. However, because our motor system is designed in such a way, the crucial requirement for attributing mental states to other people is not to share representations but rather to have mechanisms available that enable us to build different representations of self and other and to distinguish those. This thought is also reflected in Susan Hurley's shared representation model of mental state attribution (Hurley 2004). Here self–other distinction and inhibitory control play a crucial role: "The similarity of own and others" acts comes first, with mirroring. The job that remains is not to bridge a gap between oneself and other agents, but to track distinctions among them, especially when multiple other agents are in play." Along these lines we suggest that both the inhibition of imitative behavior and the understanding of other people's mental states require the ability to distinguish and enforce one's own mental representation from the other person's representation. We suggest that the system that has been developed to distinguish self and other in the motor domain can be generalized to more abstract representations such as mental states.

This interpretation of TOM allows us to integrate findings from different fields of cognitive neuroscience. First, it explains why the brain areas that are involved in mental state attribution are different from the brain areas that have mirror properties. When investigating the neural correlates of TOM, one sees not the shared representation system, which is underlying all conditions, but rather brain areas involved in separating self- and other-based representations. Secondly, this interpretation allows us to understand why the brain areas that are involved in TOM overlap with areas related to self–other distinction, perspective taking, and the inhibition of imitative behavior. All these tasks rely on the same computational processes implemented in overlapping brain regions. Thirdly, it explains why mental state attribution, which seems to be a specific human ability, involves brain regions (such as the TPJ) that are probably also existent in non-human primates.

The mechanism that underlies mental state attribution is phylogenetically relatively old. Only the abstraction from motor representations to mental states is specifically human.

Future Perspectives

The hypothesis that there is a tight relationship between the inhibition of imitative behavior, self–other distinction, and mental state attribution allows us to generate some interesting empirical predictions. First, this hypothesis would predict that neurological and psychiatric patients who have problems inhibiting imitative behavior should also be impaired in TOM tasks. We have recently investigated this prediction in neurological patients with prefrontal and posterior lesion (Spengler, von Cramon & Brass, forthcoming). Our preliminary results confirm our hypothesis and show that performance in a TOM task is highly correlated with the inhibition of imitative behavior in prefrontal patients.

Another patient group that might be of interest in this respect are individuals with Autism Spectrum Disorders (ASD). Recent research has focused on the integrity of the mirror system in autistic patients and has related this to poor social abilities and deficits in imitative performance in ASD (Williams, Whiten, Suddendorf, & Perrett, 2001). To date, this account is still being debated. In contrast to this hypothesis, we would predict that autistic patients likely to have problems in the control of imitative behavior rather then in imitation *per se*. Recent evidence has revealed no deficit in goal-directed imitation in autistic children, which speaks against a global failure in the mirror neuron system in ASD (Hamilton, Brindley, & Frith, forthcoming). It is, therefore, possible that the mirror system is not deficient in ASD, but that this system is not influenced by regions that distinguish between the self and other agents (Frith, 2003). Impairments of such a self–other system could, therefore, lead to egocentrism, abnormalities in self-awareness, and limitations in mentalizing, as they can be found in autism (Frith & de Vignemont, 2005). This would also predict that the control of imitation might be related to social abilities (for example, performance in TOM tasks) in individuals with ASD.

As a final point, our hypothesis about the relationship of imitation–inhibition and TOM leads to interesting predictions regarding normal development. It would predict that the inhibition of imitative behavior should be correlated with TOM abilities in infants, especially during time points in development where the system undergoes major phases of maturation.

Several developmental changes during childhood in egocentrism, perspective taking, and TOM have been described. With regard to mentalizing, two important developmental milestones have been highlighted (Frith & Frith, 2003), with the first one appearing at around 18 months of age, with unfolding abilities such as joint attention, pretend play, and an implicit understanding of mental states. By 4 years children begin to understand explicitly that people can hold different perspectives and distinguish between these different viewpoints – for example, they are able to construe a false belief in others (Wimmer & Perner, 1983). Linked to this development in representational and mentalizing abilities, different levels of self-awareness during childhood can be identified (Rochat, 2003), including early, precursory signs of self–other differentiation in specular images (at the age of 4 months) (Rochat & Striano, 2002), self–mirror recognition around 2 years, and a meta-cognitive self-awareness (4 years of age), allowing for the self to be seen from a third-person perspective. Self-awareness might be important in this context, as it includes the concept that one exists as an individual, separate from other people, with private thoughts, and may also include the understanding that other people are similarly self-aware with possibly different inner experiences.

Another time of further development for social-cognitive abilities may be adolescence, as the brain undergoes considerable structural development during this period, and changes in perspective-taking skills from adolescence to adulthood have been reported (Choudhury, Blakemore, & Charman, 2006).

These developmental landmarks might be interesting time points to explore the developmental changes in the control of imitative behavior and its relationship with different component abilities necessary for TOM. An important point might also be how the relationship and development of these functions are associated to executive functions (for example, inhibitory control) at different stages during development.

References

Bertenthal, B. I., Longo, M. R., & Kosobud, A. (2006). Imitative response tendencies following observation of intransitive actions. *Journal of Experimental Psychology: Human Perception and Performance*, 32(2), 210–225.

Blakemore, S. J., & Frith, C. (2005). The role of motor contagion in the prediction of action. *Neuropsychologia*, 43(2), 260–267.

Brass, M., Bekkering, H., & Prinz, W. (2001). Movement observation affects movement execution in a simple response task. *Acta Psychologica*, 106(1–2), 3–22.

Brass, M., Bekkering, H., Wohlschläger, A., & Prinz, W. (2000). Compatibility between observed and executed finger movements: Comparing symbolic, spatial, and imitative cues. *Brain & Cognition*, 44(2), 124–143.

Brass, M., Derrfuss, J., & von Cramon, D. Y. (2005). The inhibition of imitative and overlearned responses: A functional double dissociation. *Neuropsychologia*, 43(1), 89–98.

Brass, M., Derrfuss, J., Matthes-von Cramon, G. M., & von Cramon, D. Y. (2003). Imitative response tendencies in patients with frontal brain lesions. Neuropsychology, 17(2), 265–271.

Brass, M., & Heyes, C. (2005). Imitation: Is cognitive neuroscience solving the correspondence problem? *Trends in Cognitive Sciences*, 9(10), 489–495.

Brass, M., Zysset, S., & von Cramon, D. Y. (2001). The inhibition of imitative response tendencies. *NeuroImage*, 14(6), 1416–1423.

Calvo-Merino, B., Glaser, D. E., Grèzes, J., Passingham, R. E., & Haggard, P. (2005). Action observation and acquired motor skills: An FMRI study with expert dancers. *Cerebral Cortex*, 15(8), 1243–1249.

Calvo-Merino, B., Grèzes, J., Glaser, D. E., Passingham, R. E., & Haggard, P. (2006). Seeing or doing? Influence of visual and motor familiarity in action observation. *Current Biology*, 16(19), 1905–1910.

Chartrand, T. L., & Bargh, J. A. (1999). The chameleon effect: The perception–behavior link and social interaction. *Journal of Personality and Social Psychology*, 76(6), 893–910.

Choudhury, S., Blakemore, S. J., & Charman, T. (2006). Social cognitive development during adolescence. *Social Cognitive and Affective Neuroscience*, 1(3), 165–77.

Craighero, L., Bello, A., Fadiga, L., & Rizzolatti, G. (2002). Hand action preparation influences the responses to hand pictures. *Neuropsychologia*, 40(5), 492–502.

Csibra, G., & Gergely, G. (2006). "Obsessed with goals": Functions and mechanisms of teleological interpretation of actions in humans. *Acta Psychologica*, 124, 60–78.

Daprati, E., Franck, N., Georgieff, N., Proust, J., Pacherie, E., Dalery, J., et al. (1997). Looking for the agent: An investigation into consciousness of action and self-consciousness in schizophrenic patients. *Cognition*, 65(1), 71–86.

Decety, J., & Chaminade, T. (2003). When the self represents the other: A new cognitive neuroscience view on psychological identification. *Consciousness and Cognition*, 12(4), 577–596.

Decety, J., & Grezes, J. (1999). Neural mechanisms subserving the perception of human actions. *Trends in Cognitive Sciences*, 3(5), 172–178.

Decety, J., & Grezes, J. (2006). The power of simulation: Imagining one's own and other's behavior. *Brain Research*, 1079(1), 4–14.

de Renzi, E., Cavalleri, F., & Facchini, S. (1996). Imitation and utilisation behaviour. *Journal of Neurology, Neurosurgery and Psychiatry*, 61(4), 396–400.

di Pellegrino, G., Fadiga, L., Fogassi, L., Gallese, V., & Rizzolatti, G. (1992). Understanding motor events: A neurophysiological study. *Experimental Brain Research*, 91(1), 176–180.

Duncan, J., & Owen, A. M. (2000). Common regions of the human frontal lobe recruited by diverse cognitive demands. *Trends in Neurosciences*, 23(10), 475–483.

Edwards, M. G., Humphreys, G. W., & Castiello, U. (2003). Motor facilitation following action observation: A behavioural study in prehensile action. *Brain and Cognition*, 53(3), 495–502.

Farrer, C., Franck, N., Georgieff, N., Frith, C. D., Decety, J., & Jeannerod, M. (2003). Modulating the experience of agency: A positron emission tomography study. *NeuroImage*, 18(2), 324–333.

Farrer, C., & Frith, C. D. (2002). Experiencing oneself vs another person as being the cause of an action: The neural correlates of the experience of agency. *NeuroImage*, 15(3), 596–603.

Frith, C. (1992). *The Cognitive Neuropsychology of Schizophrenia*. Mahwah, N: Lawrence Erlbaum.

Frith, C. D., & Frith, U. (1999). Interacting minds: Biological basis. *Science*, 286: 1692–1695.

Frith, C. D., & Frith, U. (2006). The neural basis of mentalizing. *Neuron*, 50(4), 531–534.

Frith, U. (2003). *Autism: Explaining the Enigma*. Oxford: Blackwell.

Frith, U., & Frith, C. D. (2003). Development and neurophysiology of mentalizing. *Philosophical Transactions of the Royal Society London B: Biological Sciences*, 358(1431), 459–473.

Frith, U., & de Vignemont, F. (2005). Egocentrism, allocentrism and Asperger syndrome. *Consciousness and Cognition*, 14(4), 719–738.

Gallese, V., Fadiga, L., Fogassi, L., & Rizzolatti, G. (1996). Action recognition in the premotor cortex. *Brain*, 119(2), 593–609.

Gallese, V., & Goldman, A. (1998). Mirror neurons and the simulation theory of mind-reading. *Trends in Cognitive Sciences*, 2(12), 493–501.

Greenwald, A. G. (1970). Sensory feedback mechanisms in performance control: With special reference to the ideo-motor mechanism. *Psychological Review*, 77(2), 73–99.

Grezes, J., & Decety, J. (2001). Functional anatomy of execution, mental simulation, observation, and verb generation of actions: A meta-analysis. *Human Brain Mapping*, 12(1), 1–19.

Hamilton, Brindley, & Frith (forthcoming). Imitation and action understanding in Autistic Spectrum Disorders: How valid is the hypothesis of a deficit in the mirror neuron system? *Neuropsychologia*.

Heyes, C. (2001). Causes and consequences of imitation. *Trends in Cognitive Sciences*, 5(6), 253–261.

Heyes, C., Bird, G., Johnson, H., & Haggard, P. (2005). Experience modulates automatic imitation. *Brain Research: Cognitive Brain Research*, 22(2), 233–240.

Hommel, B., Musseler, J., Aschersleben, G., & Prinz, W. (2001). The Theory of Event Coding (TEC): A framework for perception and action planning. *Behavioral Brain Sciences*, 24(5), 849–878; discussion at 878–937.

Hurley, S. (2004). The shared circuits model. How control, mirroring, and simulation can enable imitation and mind reading. Paper presented at the ESF Conference: What do mirror neurons mean? [http://www.interdisciplines,org/mirror/papers/5]

Iacoboni, M., Woods, R. P., Brass, M., Bekkering, H., Mazziotta, J. C., & Rizzolatti, G. (1999). Cortical mechanisms of human imitation. *Science*, 286(5449), 2526–2528.

Jacob, P., & Jeannerod, M. (2005). The motor theory of social cognition: A critique. *Trends in Cognitive Sciences*, 9(1), 21–25.

James, W. (1890). *The Principles of Psychology*. New York: MacMillan.

Jeannerod, M. (1999). To act or not to act: Perspectives on the representation of actions. *Quarterly Journal of Experimental Psychology*, 52A, 1–29.

Jeannerod, M. (2004). Visual and action cues contribute to the self–other distinction. *Nature Neuroscience*, 7(5), 422–423.

Kilner, J. M., Paulignan, Y., & Blakemore S. J. (2003). An interference effect of observed biological movement on action. *Current Biology*, 13(6), 522–525.

Kohler, E., Keysers, C., Umilta, M. A., Fogassi, L., Gallese, V., & Rizzolatti, G. (2002). Hearing sounds, understanding actions: Action representation in mirror neurons. *Science*, 297(5582), 846–848.

Leube, D. T., Knoblich, G., Erb, M., & Kircher, T. T. (2003). Observing one's hand become anarchic: An fMRI study of action identification. *Consciousness and Cognition*, 12(4), 597–608.

Lhermitte, F. (1986). Human autonomy and the frontal lobes. Part II: Patient behavior in complex and social situations: the "environmental dependency syndrome". *Annals of Neurology*, 19(4), 335–343.

Lhermitte, F., Pillon, B., & Serdaru, M. (1986). Human autonomy and the frontal lobes. Part I: Imitation and utilization behavior: A neuropsychological study of 75 patients. *Annals of Neurology*, 19(4), 326–334.

Liepelt, R., von Cramon, D. Y., & Brass, M. (forthcoming). What is matched in direct matching? Motor priming effects are top-down modulated by intention attribution.

Longo, M. R., & Bertenthal, B. I. (2006). Common coding of observation and execution of action in 9-month-old infants. *Infancy*, 10, 43–59.

Luria, A. R. (1963). *Higher Cortical Function in Man*. New York, Basic Books.

Meltzoff, A. N., & Decety, J. (2003). What imitation tells us about social cognition: A rapprochement between developmental psychology and cognitive neuroscience.

Philosophical Transactions of the Royal Society London B: Biological Sciences, 358(1431), 491–500.

Northoff, G., & Bermpohl, F. (2004). Cortical midline structures and the self. *Trends in Cognitive Sciences*, 8(3), 102–107.

Perani, D., Fazio, F., Borghese, N. A., Tettamanti, M., Ferrari, S., Decety, J., et al. (2001). Different brain correlates for watching real and virtual hand actions. *NeuroImage*, 14(3), 749–758.

Piaget, J. (1969). *Nachahmung, Spiel und Traum*. Stuttgart: Klett.

Prinz, W. (1997). Perception and action planning. *European Journal of Cognitive Psychology*, 9, 129–154.

Prinz, W. (2002). Experimental approaches to imitation. In A. N. Meltzoff & W. Prinz (Eds.), *In the Imitative Mind: Development, Evolution, and Brain Bases* (pp. 143–163). Cambridge: Cambridge University Press.

Rizzolatti, G., & Craighero, L. (2004). The mirror-neuron system. *Annual Review of Neuroscience*, 27, 169–192.

Rizzolatti, G., Fogassi, L., & Gallese, V. (2001). Neurophysiological mechanisms underlying the understanding and imitation of action. *Nature Reviews Neuroscience*, 2(9), 661–670.

Rochat, P. (2003). Five levels of self-awareness as they unfold early in life. *Consciousness and Cognition*, 12(4), 717–731.

Rochat, P., & Striano, T. (2002). Who's that in the mirror? Self–other discrimination in specular images by four- and nine-months-old infants. *Child Development*, 73(1), 35–46.

Ruby, P., & Decety, J. (2001). Effect of subjective perspective taking during simulation of action: A PET investigation of agency. *Nature Neuroscience*, 4(5), 546–550.

Ruby, P., & Decety, J. (2003). What you believe versus what you think they believe: A neuroimaging study of conceptual perspective-taking. *European Journal of Neuroscience*, 17(11), 2475–2480.

Saxe, R. (2005). Against simulation: The argument from error. *Trends in Cognitive Sciences*, 9(4), 174–179.

Saxe, R. (2006). Uniquely human social cognition. *Current Opinion in Neurobiology*, 16(2), 235–239.

Spengler, S., von Cramon, D. Y., & Brass, M. (forthcoming). Linking control of imitation and social cognition: Neuropsychological: Evidence from frontal and temporo-parietal lesions.

Sturmer, B., Aschersleben, G., & Prinz, W. (2000). Correspondence effects with manual gestures and postures: A study of imitation. *Journal of Experimental Psychology: Human Perception and Performance*, 26(6), 1746–1759.

van Baaren, R. B., Holland, R. W., Kawakami, K., & van Knippenberg, A. (2004). Mimicry and pro-social behavior. *Psychological Science*, 15, 71–74.

Williams, J. H., Whiten, A., Suddendorf, T., & Perrett, D. I. (2001). Imitation, mirror neurons and autism. *Neuroscience and Biobehavioral Reviews*, 25(4), 287–295.

Wimmer, H., & Perner, J. (1983). Beliefs about beliefs: Representations and constraining function of wrong beliefs in young children's understanding of deception. *Cognition*, 13, 103–128.

Chapter 5

Social Perception: Understanding Other People's Intentions and Emotions through their Actions

Julie Grèzes and Beatrice de Gelder

Since most of the natural behavior of higher primates takes place within the context of social interactions, it is of interest to study the neural encoding of high-level social features, such as the emotional states or intention of another individuals. (Brothers, Ring, & Kling, 1990, p. 199)

Perceiving Other People's Actions and Motor Resonance

Humans are adapted to living in social groups with complex patterns of social interactions. Understanding the meaning of other people's behavior is an essential aspect of human communication, and a large amount of our daily life is spent watching and interpreting the actions of others (Barresi & Moore, 1996). The neural mechanism underlying our ability to represent others' goals by the mere observation of their motor actions has been the target of considerable research. Behavioral experiments had suggested that the system for generating and representing actions is also used in the perception of actions (Knoblich & Prinz, 2001). This approach was strengthened by the discovery of "mirror" neurons in the macaque monkey brain, a class of neurons found in the parietal and the premotor cortex. They were seen to discharge not only when the monkey performed an action but also when the monkey was observing an experimenter or another monkey performing the same action (di Pellegrino, Fadiga, Fogassi, Gallese, & Rizzolatti, 1992). Similarly, neuroimaging studies in humans have revealed parietal (PAR) and premotor (PM) activations both during execution and action observation, suggesting that action observation automatically triggers action representations (Grèzes, Armony, Rowe, & Passingham, 2003). The superior temporal sulcus (STS), involved in the perception of biological movements and in the observation of actions made by different body parts, was also active (Allison, Puce, & McCarthy, 2000). Finally, the correspondence between perception and action was shown to be somatotopically organized (Aziz-Zadeh, Wilson, Rizzolatti, & Iacoboni, 2006; Buccino et al., 2001; Gazzola, Aziz-Zadeh, & Keysers, 2006). Taken together these results provide support for the notion that, when one observes the action of another, the motor program of the observed action is activated in the observer's brain, thereby suggesting that the observer uses his or her own motor system to perceive the action of others.

Influence of the observer's motor abilities and of social relevance

Motor resonance seems to exist only for movements that respect the biomechanical constraints of our body, imposed by our skeleton and articulations, and that we are able to produce ourselves. Shiffrar and Freyd (1993) showed that it was possible to influence the subject's perception by varying the time of presentation between pictures of body positions. For instance, the first picture showed a person whose right forearm was over the left, while in the second picture the left was over the right. Under appropriate time conditions, observers reported seeing indirect trajectories that respected biomechanical constraints (for example, the left forearm turned around the right forearm), whereas, under shorter inter-stimulus intervals, subjects perceived direct and therefore biomechanically impossible trajectories (for example, the left forearm crossed the right forearm). Using positron emission tomography (PET), Stevens et al. (2000) investigated whether a change in brain activity accompanies this perceptual shift and demonstrated that premotor and parietal cortex were involved only during the perception of a biomechanically possible movement. Along similar lines, Buccino et al. (2001) observed less motor resonance when participants viewed images of actions by non-conspecifics. These findings suggest that the brain system for action representations is selectively tuned to process actions that conform to the biomechanical and the joint constraints of normal human movement.

A person's motor repertoire is constrained not only by human musculoskeletal anatomy but also by the skills that have been acquired and honed over time. For example, the motor simulation process is influenced by the individual motor abilities of each observer. During the first recordings in monkeys, mirror neurons discharged when the monkey observed a grasping action performed by the hand of an experimenter, but were silent if the same action was performed with a tool (Rizzolatti, Fogassi, & Gallese, 2001), an action that is not present in the motor repertoire of the monkey. This result suggests that action representations cannot strictly be based on observation alone, without concomitant motor action. To test this hypothesis, Grammont et al. (2006) trained their monkeys to grasp an object with a tool. They showed that the mirror neurons discharged to this type of action only after motor training, and that the responses were specific to the trained action and did not generalize to other tools. In humans, Reid, Belsky, & Johnson (2005) investigated individual differences in the development of the ability to perceive human action in 8-month-old infants. Their results clearly show that only young infants with relatively well-developed motor skills perceive the differences between possible versus impossible human movements. As for adults, functional magnetic resonance imaging (fMRI) was used to study differences in brain activity between watching an action that one has learned to do and an action that one has not (Calvo-Merino, Glaser, Grèzes, Passingham, & Haggard, 2005). Greater activations in STS, PAR, and PM where observed when expert dancers viewed movements that they had been trained to perform compared to movements that they had not. This effect could not be explained by visual familiarity (Calvo-Merino, Grèzes, Glaser, Passingham, & Haggard, 2006). To conclude, during action observation, there is activity in the parietal and premotor cortex as the subject internally simulates perceived movements, but the extent and level of activity within those regions will be constrained by the observer's motor abilities.

Finally, a recent paper by Kilner, Marchant, & Frith (2006) elegantly demonstrated that the activity during action observation is also modulated by social relevance – that is, by the degree of interaction between the actor and the observer. There is a modulation of activity only when the actor is facing the observer, and not when the actor is facing away.

Functions and possible limitations of motor resonance

This mechanism of shared motor representations was proposed as the basis of action understanding (Gallese, Keysers, & Rizzolatti, 2004; Grèzes & Decety, 2001; Iacoboni, 2005; Jeannerod, Decety, & Michel, 1994; Rizzolatti et al., 2001), and more recently it was suggested that it plays a role in action prediction (Csibra, 2007; Flanagan & Johansson, 2003; Kilner, Vargas, Duval, Blakemore, & Sirigu, 2004; Knoblich, Seigerschmidt, Flach, & Prinz, 2002). Fogassi et al. (2005), for example, demonstrated that the discharge of mirror neurons in monkeys during the observation of an act (grasping an object) is influenced by the type of act that follows it (for example, eating the food or putting it aside). Thus, these neurons not only code observed actions but also allow prediction of the next step of an action. In humans, the higher motor facilitation when subjects perceived the still picture of a hand caught in an ongoing but as yet incomplete grasping action pleads in favor of a role of motor simulation in anticipating the actions of others (Urgesi, Candidi, Ionta, & Aglioti, 2006). According to Gallese (2006), the mechanism of motor simulation could participate in interpreting the simple intentions of others.

Indeed, social interactions are less simple and less predictable than interactions between physical objects. Using transcranial magnetic stimulation, Gangitano, Mottaghy, & Pascual-Leone (2004) studied the observation of predictable and unpredictable grasping movements in human subjects. The profile of cortical excitability suggested that a motor representation of the perceived action was activated as soon as the action started. However, once it had been activated, it tended to proceed toward its completion, regardless of whether the end of the action was the same or not – that is, was predictable or unpredictable. Furthermore, using fMRI, we scanned subjects while they watched alternate videos of themselves and of others lifting a box, and judged whether the actors had a correct (predictable action) or false expectation (unpredictable and accidental action) about the weight of the box.

A parietal-premotor circuit, which reflects motor simulation, was activated during action perception. Still, the activity within this circuit did not dissociate unpredictable from predictable actions (Grèzes, Frith, & Passingham, 2004a. These results support the idea that the internal simulation of a perceived action plays a crucial role in predicting how the perceived movement will continue. But they also suggest that the motor simulation process does not dissociate intended from unintended actions or predictable from unpredictable ones and therefore may not be sufficient to understand the complex intentions of other people during social interactions. Still, it is suggested that the mirror neuron system, originally found in motor-related areas, could play an important role in social cognition (Gallese, 2006; but see Sommerville & Decety, 2006, for a discussion).

Understanding Other People's Intentions and Emotions from their Actions

The term "social cognition" proposed by Brothers (1990) is defined as "the processing of any information which culminates in the accurate perception of the disposition and intentions of other individuals." Premack (1978) coined the notion of "theory of mind," thereby referring to a hypothetical mental mechanism whereby social agents attribute mental states to each other. Since the mid-1990s, developmental psychology, social psychology, and neuroscience have investigated this ability (see reviews by Frith & Frith, 2003; Frith & Frith, 2006), using mostly verbal and static stimuli. Brain regions involved in the ability to infer mental states to others that have come to the foreground are the STS, the amygdala (AMG), the medial prefrontal cortex (MPFC), the anterior cingulate cortex (ACC), and the orbitofrontal cortex (OFC) (see review by Gallagher & Frith, 2003). These regions figure prominently as components of the social brain (Brothers 1990). The research on theory of mind has developed in parallel and independently from the research on action understanding. None of the experiments had explored the ability to understand mental states through the observation of dynamic human behavior, and therefore the question whether motor simulation sustains mental states attribution remains.

Violation of expectations

Subjects were scanned while watching videos of actors lifting a box. They were asked to judge whether the action reflected a correct or a false expectation of the weight of the box (Grèzes, Frith, & Passingham, 2004a or the intent to deceive about the weight of the box (Grèzes, Berthoz, & Passingham, 2006; Grèzes, Frith, & Passingham, 2004b). We found activations in the parietal and premotor cortex, suggesting that motor simulation was involved. However, when the subjects judged that the actors had a false expectation or an intent to deceive, there was also activity bilaterally in the STS, lateral orbitofrontal, and cingulate cortex. The inference that the actor was trying to deceive or had a false expectation was the difference between a prediction made by the observer and the action as perceived. People have a bias to judge other people's behavior as truthful (Levine, Park, & McCornack, 1999) and of attributing true beliefs to others' understanding of information (Bartsch & Wellman, 1995) that influence their predictions. The same biases were observed in our studies. Thus, the activations listed above may relate to the violation of the subject's prediction. In the STS, it was demonstrated that, when an observer's prediction was violated, the activity was higher compared with the situation in which the observer's predictions were met (Pelphrey, Singerman, Allison, & McCarthy, 2003; Saxe, Xiao, Kovacs, Perrett, & Kanwisher, 2004). The cerebellum may play a key role in signalling sensory discrepancy between predicted and actual consequences of movements (Blakemore, Frith, & Wolpert, 2001). Finally, activity in the orbital frontal cortex, as well as in the STS, has been reported when subjects perceived a mismatch between what they expected and what actually happened (Downar, Crawley, Mikulis, & Davis, 2001). We conclude that activations in the STS, cerebellum, and orbitofrontal cortex are best explained as reflecting the violation of the predictions made by the observer. When predictions are violated, the observer must update his or her representation of the mental state of the actor.

Communicative intent and personal involvement

Action observation can produce a strong emotional response, and can potentially induce or modify an observer's behavior, particularly when the content of the perceived action is directed at the observer him or herself. For example, it is particularly important to be able to distinguish whether a person is being honest or deceitful. Investigating this issue, we observed that communicative intent (deceit versus false expectation) and personal involvement influence the neural responses associated with the detection of deceit. Activations in the MPFC and AMG were found only for communicative intent as compared to non-communicative actions (Grèzes, Frith, & Passingham, 2004b. In the second study (Grèzes, Berthoz, & Passingham, 2006), subjects judged whether actors had been deceived about the real weight of a box. Personal involvement was manipulated by having the participants themselves among the actors. The STS and anterior cingulate cortex were activated irrespective of whether the participants detected that they themselves had been deceived by the experimenter or whether the other person had been misled. In contrast, the crucial factor determining AMG activation is subjective involvement, as there was activity in the AMG only in the condition in which participants observed themselves being deceived. The amygdala is said to play a key role in fast and automatic evaluation of the social significance of an event – for example, when the event constitutes a potential threat (Adolphs, 2003; Dolan, 2002). More importantly, Gloor (1972) reported that AMG stimulation induces subjective experiences of behavioral attitudes of others that the patients perceive as being directed at them (Gloor, 1972, cited by Brothers, 1990). However, Berthoz, Grèzes, Armony, Passingham, & Dolan (2006) contained judgments that were about social deception. We interpret the activation of the AMG in this situation as reflecting the greater emotional reaction elicited when the deceived one is oneself. In the same vein, we found more activity in the AMG when participants read stories narrating their own as opposed to others' intentional transgression of social norms (Berthoz et al., 2006).

These results suggest that, while simulation can be a predictive mechanism playing a role in the implicit understanding of other people's dispositions, mental states attribution also involves other brain areas that are part of a neural system underpinning the social brain. Prominent among these are the brain areas that process the type of action, its social context, and the observers' personal involvement.

Emotional contagion and motor simulation

If we grant that simulation may play a role in social cognition, it is also likely to be involved in perceiving actions that have a strong emotional component. It was demonstrated that a mechanism of shared representations, originally found in the motor-related areas, applies to emotions and sensations. The same brain areas (for example, the insula and anterior cingulate cortex) are involved when subjects experience disgust (Wicker et al., 2003) or pain (Jackson, Meltzoff, & Decety, 2005; Singer et al., 2004), and when they observe someone else experiencing the same emotion. Also, observing someone being touched elicits activity in the same area of the somatosensory cortex as being touched oneself (Blakemore, Bristow, Bird, Frith, & Ward, 2005; Keysers & Perrett, 2004). Thus, a direct and implicit form of understanding others is achieved by embodied simulation (Gallese, 2006). This ability to share other people's emotions facilitates social communication and social coherence, and may be at the origin of altruistic behavior and cooperation (see the review by de Vignemont & Singer, 2006).

But there is also support in the literature for a second mechanism involving both the action and the emotion circuits. Recent neuroimaging data show that perceiving emotional facial and body expressions presented as video films elicits activations both in the regions underlying motor representations (the premotor cortex) and also in the regions involved in emotional processing (the AMG) (Carr, Iacoboni, Dubeau, Mazziotta, & Lenzi, 2003; Decety & Chaminade, 2003; de Gelder, Snyder, Greve, Gerard, & Hadjikhani, 2004; Grèzes, Pichon, & de Gelder, 2007; Grosbras & Paus, 2006; Sato, Kochiyama, Yoshikawa, Naito, & Matsumura, 2004). It is, however, an open question whether the critical factor for understanding actions with an emotional component is the activity within motor-related areas as such (the mirror system) or the interaction between the emotion-processing areas and an action-related network. One explanation for enhanced activation in the premotor cortex for dynamic expression of emotion is that, when dynamic fear bodies are being viewed, an important priority for the brain is to represent the perceived emotional action. This would be in line with the findings of Adolphs, Tranel, and Damasio (2003) that patient B with extensive lesion of the ventral pathway, which includes the AMG, is able to recognize emotions from a dynamic facial expression but not from a static one. A second possible explanation takes into account that emotions are adaptive in the sense that they prepare the organism for a behavioral response to the current environment (Darwin, 1872; Lazarus, 1991; LeDoux, 2000; Panksepp, 1998). The enhanced activation in the premotor cortex could be due to the fact that the perception, for example, of a fear stimulus (whether this is a sound, face, or body) triggers a fear reaction in the observer that is based on activation of a fear motor program encoded in subcortical and cortical circuitry (Tomkins, 1963) and does not involve mirror neurons. Further investigations are needed to disentangle whether the activations detected in motor-related areas during the perception of emotional action reveal either the motor simulation of the action perceived or the preparation of the motor response that would be appropriate to the situation.

To conclude this section, starting from the postulate that the resonance phenomenon plays a role in social cognition, it is probably just a step in the chain of components necessary for adaptive behavior to the physical and social environment. Moreover, for this contagion mechanism to have explanatory value, its relationships with the other components must be clarified. This issue is *a fortiori* important to explain whether a dysfunction of the mirror system can influence the problems of communication and social interaction observed in autistic syndromes.

Implication for Autism and Conclusion

Autism is a complex disorder that is heterogeneous in its phenotypic expression and its etiology. Nonetheless, it is usually defined on the basis of common symptoms, and its core deficit is in poor social communication, a lack of imagination, the inability to understand others as intentional agents, a lack of empathy, imitation deficits, and stereotypical behaviors. These socio-cognitive deficits may be related to structural and functional abnormalities of many brain areas of the social brain: the STS, the AMG, the OFC, and the ACC (e.g. Abell et al., 1999; Baron-Cohen et al., 2000; Boddaert & Zilbovicius, 2002), and more recently with the mirror system (Hadjikhani, Joseph, Snyder, & Tager-Flusberg, 2007; Williams, Whiten, Suddendorf, & Perrett, 2001). There are currently many lines of research on the possible causes of impaired social communication and of deficits in processing emotional cues. Briefly, some authors think the social deficit could be a consequence of an AMG dysfunction, leading to functional abnormalities that impair the ability to detect socially relevant visual cues (Baron-Cohen et al., 2000). Another model speculates that this impairment may be the consequence of a malfunctioning mirror system (Williams et al., 2001), generating a deficit in the ability to represent the actions of others, and impairing higher-level cognitive functions involved in building intersubjectivity (Gallese, 2001).

Three recent studies have shown, however, that, in high-functioning individuals with autism, the system matching observed actions onto representations of one's own action is intact in the presence of persistent difficulties in higher-level processing of social information (Grèzes, Wicker, & de Gelder, forthcoming; Magnée, Stekelenburg, de Gelder, van Engeland, & Kemner, 2005; Sebanz, Knoblich, Stumpf, & Prinz, 2005). This raises doubts about the hypothesis that the motor contagion phenomenon – "mirror" system – plays a crucial role in the development of socio-cognitive abilities. One possibility is that this mirror mechanism, while functional, may be dissociated from socio-affective capabilities. In healthy subjects, a co-activation of those regions underlying motor resonance, on the one hand, and emotional processing (de Gelder, Snyder, Greve, Gerard, & Hadjikhani, 2004; Grèzes, Wicker, & de Geldre, forthcoming) or detection of intentions, on the other (Grèzes, Frith, & Passingham, 2004a, 2004b) is observed. A dissociation between these two mechanisms in autistic subjects seems plausible in the light of studies reporting problems in information processing at the level of the STS and the AMG (Boddaert et al., 2004; Castelli, Frith, Happé, & Frith, 2002) and problems in connectivity between these two regions. The superior temporal sulcus is, indeed, a brain region common to these three domains of motor and emotional contagion as well as intention detection. The data on the motor contagion for emotional expressions in autistic subjects do not address the issue of the feelings and emotional consciousness of these subjects, and the available results on the emotional contagion in autistic subjects are contradictory (Blair, 2003). Interactions between neural structures implied in intention and emotion recognition through action are an important topic for future research.

Finally, future studies also need to address the issue of variability between individuals, which is considerable (Frith, 2001) but is rarely taken into account in mind-reading tests or in neuroimaging studies using small samples. Correlation analyses between structure, function, and behavior will undoubtedly provide useful information for a better definition of neuro-cognitive phenotypes associated with inadequacy in everyday social relations that are the core deficit in autism, as well as for other psychiatric pathologies (for example, schizophrenia and personality disturbances) and degenerative neurological disorders (for example, fronto-temporal dementia). In the future a better characterization of these phenotypes will contribute significantly to more focused investigations into the genetic basis of these diseases (Leboyer Jamain, Betancur, Mouren-Siméoni, & Bourgeon, 2002) and for the development of therapeutic approaches (Baranek, 2002). More generally, an understanding of the cerebral mechanisms involved in the development of intersubjectivity in healthy subjects and of low-level mechanisms of social interactions is of great social relevance and promises new insights in these complex abilities.

References

Abell, F., Krams, M., Ashburner, J., Passingham, R. E., Friston, K. J., Frackowiak, R. S. J., Happé, F., Frith, C., & Frith, U. (1999). The neuroanatomy of autism: A voxel-based whole brain analysis of structural scans. *Neuroreport*, 10(8), 1647–1651.

Adolphs, R. (2003). Cognitive neuroscience of human social behaviour. *Nature Reviews Neuroscience*, 4(3), 165–178.

Adolphs, R., Tranel, D., & Damasio, A. R. (2003). Dissociable neural systems for recognizing emotions. *Brain & Cognition*, 52(1), 61–69.

Allison, T., Puce, A., & McCarthy, G. (2000). Social perception from visual cues: Role of the STS region. *Trends in Cognitive Sciences*, 4(7), 267–278.

Aziz Zadeh, L., Wilson, S. M., Rizzolatti, G., & Iacoboni, M. (2006). Congruent embodied representations for visually presented actions and linguistic phrases describing actions, *Current Biology*, 16(18), 1818–1823.

Baranek, G. T. (2002). Efficacy of sensory and motor interventions for children with autism, *Journal of Autism and Developmental Disorders*, 32, 397–422.

Baron-Cohen, S., Ring, H. A., Bullmore, E. T., Wheelwright, S., Ashwin, C., & Williams, S. C. (2000). The amygdala theory of autism. *Neuroscience & Biobehavioral Reviews*, 24(3), 355–364.

Barresi, J., & Moore, C. (1996). Intentional relations and social understanding. *Behavioral and Brain Sciences*, 19(1), 107–154.

Bartsch, K., & Wellman, H. (1995), *Children Talk about Mind*. New York: Oxford University Press.

Berthoz, S., Grèzes, J., Armony, J. L., Passingham, R. E., & Dolan, R. J. (2006). Affective response to one's own moral violations. *NeuroImage*, 31(2), 945–950.

Blair, J. R. (2003). Facial expressions, their communicatory functions and neuro-cognitive substrates. *Philosophical Transactions of the Royal Society B: Biological Sciences*, 358(1431), 561–572.

Blakemore, S. J., Bristow, D., Bird, G., Frith, C., & Ward, J. (2005). Somatosensory activations during the observation of touch and a case of vision–touch synaesthesia. *Brain*, 128 (7), 1571–1583.

Blakemore, S. J., Frith, C. D., & Wolpert, D. M. (2001). The cerebellum is involved in predicting the sensory consequences of action. *Neuroreport*, 12(9), 1879–1884.

Boddaert, N., Chabane, N., Gervais, H., Good, C. D., Bourgeois, M., Plumet, M. H., Barthelemy, C., Mouren, M. C., Artiges, E., & Samson, Y. (2004). Superior temporal sulcus anatomical abnormalities in childhood autism: A voxel-based morphometry MRI study. *NeuroImage*, 23(1), 364–369.

Boddaert, N., & Zilbovicius, M. (2002), Functional neuroimaging and childhood autism. *Pediatric Radiology*, 32(1), 1–7.

Brothers, L. (1990). The social brain: A project for integrating primate behavior and neurophysiology in a new domain. *Concepts in Neuroscience*, 1, 27–51.

Brothers, L., Ring, B., & Kling, A. (1990). Response of neurons in the macaque amygdala to complex social stimuli. *Behavioural Brain Research*, 41, 199–213.

Buccino, G., Binkofski, F., Fink, G. R., Fadiga, L., Fogassi, L., Gallese, V., Seitz, R. J., Zilles, K., Rizzolatti, G., & Freund, H. J. (2001). Action observation activates premotor and parietal areas in a somatotopic manner: An fMRI study. *European Journal of Neuroscience*, 13(2), 400–404.

Calvo-Merino, B., Glaser, D. E., Grèzes, J., Passingham, R. E., & Haggard, P. (2005). Action observation and acquired motor skills: An fMRI study with expert dancers. *Cerebral Cortex*, 15(8), 1243–1249.

Calvo-Merino, B., Grèzes, J., Glaser, D. E., Passingham, R. E., & Haggard, P. (2006). Seeing or doing? Influence of visual and motor familiarity in action observation. *Current Biology*, 16(19), 1905–1910.

Carr, L., Iacoboni, M., Dubeau, M. C., Mazziotta, J. C., & Lenzi, G. L. (2003). Neural mechanisms of empathy in humans: A relay from neural systems for imitation to limbic areas. *Proceedings of the National Academy of Sciences USA*, 100(9), 5497–5502.

Castelli, F., Frith, C., Happé, F., & Frith, U. (2002). Autism, Asperger syndrome and brain mechanisms for the attribution of mental states to animated shapes. *Brain*, 125(8), 1839–1849.

Csibra, G. (2007). Action mirroring and action understanding: An alternative account. In P. Haggard, I. Rosetti & M. Kawato (Eds.), *Sensorimotor Foundations of Higher Cognition. Attention and Performance XXII*. Oxford: Oxford University Press.

Darwin, C. (1872). *The Expression of the Emotions in Man and Animals*. London: John Murray.

Decety, J., & Chaminade, T. (2003). Neural correlates of feeling sympathy. *Neuropsychologia*, 41(2), 127–138.

de Gelder, B., Snyder, J., Greve, D., Gerard, G., & Hadjikhani, N. (2004). Fear fosters flight: A mechanism for fear contagion when perceiving emotion expressed by a whole body. *Proceedings of the National Academy Sciences USA*, 101(47), 16701–16706.

de Vignemont, F., & Singer, T. (2006). The empathic brain: How, when and why? *Trends in Cognitive Sciences*, 10(10), 435–441.

di Pellegrino, G., Fadiga, L., Fogassi, L., Gallese, V., & Rizzolatti, G. (1992). Understanding motor events: A neurophysiological study. *Experimental Brain Research*, 91(1), 176–180.

Dolan, R. J. (2002). Emotion, cognition, and behaviour. *Science*, 298(5596), 1191–1194.

Downar, J., Crawley, A. P., Mikulis, D. J., & Davis, K. D. (2001). The effect of task relevance on the cortical response to changes in visual and auditory stimuli: An event-related fMRI study. *NeuroImage*, 14(6), 1256–1267.

Flanagan, J. R., & Johansson, R. S. (2003). Action plans used in action observation. *Nature*, 424, 769–771.

Fogassi, L., Ferrari, P. F., Gesierich, B., Rozzi, S., Chersi, F., & Rizzolatti, G. (2005). Parietal lobe: From action organization to intention understanding. *Science*, 308, 662–667.

Frith, C. D., & Frith, U. (2006). The neural basis of mentalizing. *Neuron*, 50, 531–534.

Frith, U., & Frith, C. D. (2003). Development and neurophysiology of mentalizing. *Philosophical Transactions of the Royal Society B: Biological Sciences*, 358, 459–473.

Frith, U. (2001), Mind blindness and the brain in autism. *Neuron*, 32(6), 969–979.

Gallagher, H. L., & Frith, C. D. (2003). Functional imaging of "theory of mind". *Trends in Cognitive Sciences*, 7(2), 77–83.

Gallese, V. (2001). The "shared manifold" hypothesis. From mirror neurons to empathy, *Journal of Consciousness Studies*, 8, 33–50.

Gallese, V. (2006). Intentional attunement: A neurophysiological perspective on social cognition and its disruption in autism. *Brain Research*, 1079(1), 15–24.

Gallese, V., Keysers, C., & Rizzolatti, G. (2004). A unifying view of the basis of social cognition. *Trends in Cognitive Sciences*, 8(9), 396–403.

Gangitano, M., Mottaghy, F. M., & Pascual-Leone, A. (2004). Modulation of premotor mirror neuron activity during observation of unpredictable grasping movements. *European Journal of Neuroscience*, 20(8), 2193–2202.

Gazzola, V., Aziz-Zadeh, L., & Keysers, C. (2006). Empathy and the somatotopic auditory mirror system in humans. *Current Biology*, 16(18), 1824–1829.

Gloor, P. (1972). *The Neurobiology of Amygdala*. New York: Plenum.

Grammont, F., Instkirveli, U., Escaola, M. A., Rochat, P., & Rizzolatti, G. (2006). Personal communication.

Grèzes, J., Armony, J. L., Rowe, J., & Passingham, R. E. (2003). Activations related to mirror and canonical neurones in the human brain: An fMRI study. *NeuroImage*, 18(4), 928–937.

Grèzes, J., Berthoz, S., & Passingham, R. E. (2006). Amygdala activation when one is the target of deceit: Did he lie to you or to someone else? *NeuroImage*, 30(2), 601–608.

Grèzes, J., & Decety, J. (2001). Functional anatomy of execution, mental simulation, observation, and verb generation of actions: A meta-analysis. *Human Brain Mapping*, 12(1), 1–19.

Grèzes, J., Frith, C. D., & Passingham, R. E. (2004a). Inferring false beliefs from the actions of oneself and others: An fMRI study. *NeuroImage*, 21(2), 744–750.

Grèzes, J., Frith, C. D., & Passingham, R. E. (2004b), Brain mechanisms for inferring deceit in the actions of others. *Journal of Neuroscience*, 24, 5500–5505.

Grèzes, J., Pichon, S., & de Gelder, B. (2007). Perceiving fear in dynamic body expressions. *NeuroImage*, 35(2), 959–967.

Grèzes, J., Wicker, B., & de Gelder, B. (forthcoming). Perceiving whole body expressions of fear in high functioning autistic and Asperger subjects.

Grosbras, M. H., & Paus, T. (2006). Brain networks involved in viewing angry hands or faces. *Cerebral Cortex*, 16(8), 1087–1096.

Hadjikhani, N., Joseph, R. M., Snyder, J., & Tager-Flusberg, H. (2007). Abnormal activation of the social brain during face perception in autism. *Human Brain Mapping*, 28, 441–449.

Iacoboni, M. (2005). Neural mechanisms of imitation. *Current Opinion in Neurobiology*, 15(6), 632–637.

Jackson, P. L., Meltzoff, A. N., & Decety, J. (2005). How do we perceive the pain of others? A window into the neural processes involved in empathy. *NeuroImage*, 24(3), 771–779.

Jeannerod, M., Decety, J., & Michel, F. (1994). Impairment of grasping movements following a bilateral posterior parietal lesion. *Neuropsychologia*, 32(4), 369–380.

Keysers, C., & Perrett, D. I. (2004). Demystifying social cognition: A Hebbian perspective. *Trends in Cognitive Sciences*, 8(11), 501–507.

Kilner, J. M., Marchant, J. L., & Frith, C. D. (2006). Modulation of the mirror system by social relevance. *Social, Cognitive and Affective Neuroscience*, 1, 143–148.

Kilner, J. M., Vargas, C., Duval, S., Blakemore, S. J., & Sirigu, A. (2004). Motor activation prior to observation of a predicted movement. *Nature Neuroscience*, 7(12), 1299–1301.

Knoblich, G., & Prinz, W. (2001). Recognition of self-generated actions from kinematic displays of drawing. *Journal of Experimental Psychology: Human.Perception and.Performance*, 27(2), 456–465.

Knoblich, G., Seigerschmidt, E., Flach, R., & Prinz, W. (2002). Authorship effects in the prediction of handwriting strokes: Evidence for action simulation during action perception. *Quarterly Journal of Experimental Psychology*, 55A, 1027–1046.

Lazarus, R. S. (1991). *Emotion and Adaptation*. Oxford: Oxford University Press.

Leboyer, M., Jamain, S., Betancur, C., Mouren-Siméoni, M. C., & Bourgeon, T. (2002). Autisme: Le Point sur les études génétiques. *La Lettre des Neurosciences*, 12–14.

LeDoux, J. E. (2000). Emotion circuits in the brain. *Annual Reviews Neuroscience*, 23, 155–184.

Levine, T. R., Park, H. S., & McCornack, S. A. (1999). Accuracy in detecting truths and lies: documenting the veracity effect. *Communication Monographs*, 66, 125–144.

Magnée, M. J. C. M., Stekelenburg, J. J., de Gelder, B., van Engeland, H., & Kemner, C. (2005). Facial EMG and affect processing in autism, in 4th International Meeting for Autism Research (IMFAR), May 5–7, Boston, MA.

Panksepp, J. (1998). *Affective Neuroscience: The Foundation of Human and Animal Emotions*. New York: Oxford University Press.

Pelphrey, K. A., Singerman, J. D., Allison, T., & McCarthy, G. (2003). Brain activation evoked by perception of gaze shifts: the influence of context. *Neuropsychologia*, 41(2), 156–170.

Premack, D. (1978). Does the chimpanzee have a theory of mind? *The Behavioral and Brain Sciences*, 1, 515–526.

Reid, V. M., Belsky, J., & Johnson, M. H. (2005). Infant perception of human action: Toward a developmental cognitive neuroscience of individual differences. *Cognition, Brain, Behavior*, 9(2), 35–52.

Rizzolatti, G., Fogassi, L., & Gallese, V. (2001). Neurophysiological mechanisms underlying the understanding and imitation of action. *Nature Reviews Neuroscience*, 2(9), 661–670.

Sato, W., Kochiyama, T., Yoshikawa, S., Naito, E., & Matsumura, M. (2004). Enhanced neural activity in response to dynamic facial expressions of emotion: An fMRI study. *Brain Research: Cognitive Brain Research*, 20(1), 81–91.

Saxe, R., Xiao, D.-K., Kovacs, G., Perrett, D. I., & Kanwisher, N. (2004). A region of right posterior superior temporal sulcus responds to observed intentional actions. *Neuropsychologia*, 42(11), 1435–1446.

Sebanz, N., Knoblich, G., Stumpf, L., & Prinz, W. (2005). Far from action blind: Representation of others´ actions in individuals with autism. *Cognitive Neuropsychology*, 22, 433–454.

Shiffrar, M., & Freyd, J. (1993). Timing and apparent motion path choice with human body photographs. *Psychological Science*, 4, 379–380.

Singer, T., Seymour, B., O'Doherty, J., Kaube, H., Dolan, R. J., & Frith, C. D. (2004). Empathy for pain involves the affective but not sensory components of pain. *Science*, 303, 1157–1162.

Sommerville, J. A., & Decety, J. (2006). Weaving the fabric of social interaction: Articulating developmental psychology and cognitive neuroscience in the domain of motor cognition. *Psychological Bulletin Review*, 13(2), 179–200.

Stevens, J. A., Fonlupt, P., Shiffrar, M., & Decety, J. (2000). New aspects of motion perception: selective neural encoding of apparent human movements. *Neuroreport*, 11(1), 109–115.

Tomkins, S. S. (1963). *Affect, Imagery, Consciousness: 2. The Negative Effects*. New York: Springer Verlag.

Urgesi, C., Candidi, M., Ionta, S., & Aglioti, S. M. (2006). Representation of body identity and body actions in extrastriate body area and ventral premotor cortex. *Nature Neuroscience*, 10(1), 30–31.

Wicker, B., Keysers, C., Plailly, J., Royet, J. P., Gallese, V., & Rizzolatti, G. (2003). Both of us disgusted in My insula: The common neural basis of seeing and feeling disgust. *Neuron*, 40(3), 655–664.

Williams, J. H. G., Whiten, A., Suddendorf, T., & Perrett, D. I. (2001). Imitation, mirror neurons and autism. *Neuroscience & Biobehavioral Reviews*, 25(4), 287–295.

Chapter 6

Development of the Social Brain during Adolescence

Sarah-Jayne Blakemore

Introduction

Adolescence is the period of psychological and social transition between childhood and adulthood. The beginning of adolescence is characterized by large hormonal and physical changes (Coleman and Hendry, 1990; Feldman and Elliott, 1990). The transition from childhood to adulthood is also characterized by psychological changes in terms of identity, self-consciousness, and cognitive flexibility (Rutter, 1993). Recently, it has been demonstrated that various regions of the brain undergo dramatic development during adolescence and beyond. In the first half of this chapter I will describe the evidence for structural brain development during adolescence. In the second half I will discuss recent studies that have investigated social-cognitive development during adolescence.

Cellular development in the brain during adolescence

The notion that the brain continues to develop after childhood is relatively new. Experiments on animals, starting in the 1950s, showed that sensory regions of the brain go through sensitive periods soon after birth, during which time environmental stimulation appears to be crucial for normal brain development and for normal perceptual development to occur (Hubel & Wiesel, 1962). These experiments suggested that the human brain might be susceptible to the same sensitive periods in early development. Research on postmortem human brains carried out in the 1970s revealed that some brain areas, in particular the prefrontal cortex, continue to develop well beyond early childhood (Huttenlocher, 1979; Huttenlocher, De Courten, Garey, & Van Der Loos, 1983; Yakovlev & Lecours, 1967).

Two main changes were found in the brain before and after puberty. As neurons develop, a layer of myelin is formed around their axon. Myelin acts as an insulator and effectively increases the speed of transmission (up to one hundredfold) of electrical impulses from neuron to neuron. While sensory and motor brain regions become fully myelinated in the first few years of life, axons in the frontal cortex continue to be myelinated well into adolescence (Yakovlev & Lecours, 1967). The implication of this research is that the transmission speed of neural information in the frontal cortex should increase throughout childhood and adolescence.

The second difference in the brains of pre-pubescent children and adolescents pertains to changes in synaptic density in the prefrontal cortex (PFC). Early in postnatal development, the brain begins to form new synapses, so that the synaptic density (the number of synapses per unit volume of brain tissue) greatly exceeds adult levels. This process of synaptogenesis lasts up to several months, depending on the species of animal and the brain region. These early peaks in synaptic density are followed by a period of synaptic elimination (pruning), in which frequently used connections are strengthened and infrequently used connections are eliminated. This process, which occurs over a period of years, reduces the overall synaptic density to adult levels. In sensory regions of the monkey brain, synaptic densities gradually decline to adult levels at around 3 years, around the time monkeys reach sexual maturity (Rakic, 1995).

In contrast to sensory brain regions, histological studies of monkey and human PFC have shown that there is a proliferation of synapses in the subgranular layers of the prefrontal cortex during childhood and again at puberty, followed by a plateau phase and a subsequent elimination and reorganization of prefrontal synaptic connections after puberty (Bourgeois, Goldman-Rakic, & Rakic, 1994; Huttenlocher, 1979; Woo, Pucak, Kye, Matus, & Lewis 1997; Zecevic & Rakic, 2001). According to these data, synaptic pruning occurs throughout adolescence and results in a net decrease in synaptic density in the PFC during this time.

MRI studies of adolescent brain development

Until recently, the structure of the human brain could be studied only after death. The scarcity of postmortem brains in research meant that knowledge of human brain development was very scant. Since the advent of magnetic resonance imaging (MRI), a number of brain-imaging studies have provided further evidence of the ongoing maturation of the frontal cortex, and other regions, into adolescence and even into adulthood. A consistent finding from both cross-sectional and longitudinal MRI studies is that there is a steady increase in white matter (WM) in certain brain regions, particularly PFC and parietal cortex, during childhood and adolescence (e.g. Giedd et al., 1996; Giedd et al., 1999; Paus et al. 1999b; Pfefferbaum et al., 1994; Reiss, Abrams, Singer, Ross, & Denckla, 1996; Sowell et al., 1999; Sowell et al., 2003). While MRI studies diverge in terms of the precise brain regions in which WM density increases have been found, they generally agree on the pattern of WM change. Most studies point to a steady, more-or-less linear increase in WM with age (Barnea-Goraly et al., 2005; Giedd et al., 1999; Paus, Evans, & Rapoport, 1999a; Paus et al. 1999b; Pfefferbaum et al., 1994; Reiss et al., 1996; Sowell et al.,

1999). In the light of histological studies, this has been interpreted as reflecting continued axonal myelination during childhood and adolescence.

While the increase in WM in certain brain regions seems to be linear, changes in grey matter (GM) density appear to follow a region-specific, non-linear pattern. Several studies have shown that GM development in certain brain regions follows an inverted-U shape. In one of the first developmental MRI studies, Giedd et al. (1999) performed a longitudinal MRI study on 145 healthy boys and girls ranging in age from about 4 to 22 years. The volume of GM in the frontal lobe increased during pre-adolescence, with a peak occurring at around 12 years for males and 11 years for females. This was followed by a decline during post-adolescence. Similarly, parietal lobe GM volume increased during the pre-adolescent stage to a peak at around 12 years for males and 10 years for females, and this was followed by a decline during post-adolescence. GM development in the temporal lobes was also non-linear, and the peak was reached later, at about 17 years. In the occipital lobes, GM development had a linear course. A similar inverted-U shaped developmental trajectory of GM in various cortical regions has been found in several subsequent MRI studies (e.g. Gogtay et al., 2004; Thompson et al., 2000). Most studies show that sensory and motor regions mature first, while PFC, parietal, and superior temporal cortices continue to develop during adolescence and beyond.

In summary, several recent MRI studies have suggested that a perturbation in GM density more or less coincides with the onset of puberty. At puberty, GM volume in the frontal and parietal cortices reaches a peak, followed by a plateau after puberty and then a decline throughout adolescence continuing until early adulthood. The MRI results demonstrating a non-linear decrease in GM in various brain regions throughout adolescence have been interpreted in two ways. First, it is likely that axonal myelination results in an increase in WM and a simultaneous decrease in GM, as viewed by MRI. A second, additional explanation is that the GM changes reflect the synaptic reorganization that occurs at the onset of and after puberty (Bourgeois et al., 1994; Huttenlocher, 1979). Thus, the increase in GM apparent at the onset of puberty (Giedd et al., 1999) might reflect a wave of synapse proliferation at this time, while the gradual decrease in GM density that occurs after puberty in certain brain regions has been attributed to post-pubescent synaptic pruning.

The brain regions that undergo protracted development include PFC, parietal cortex, and superior temporal cortex (in some studies this has included superior temporal sulcus). These are regions that, in adults, have been activated in various functional neuroimaging studies of social cognition. This research will be described in the following section.

Social cognition in the brain

Mental state attribution, or "mentalizing," is defined as the ability to attribute mental states to other people in order to predict their behavior (e.g. Frith & Frith, 2003). Lesion studies have implicated the frontal cortex (Channon & Crawford,

2000; Gregory et al., 2002; Happé, Mahli, & Checkley, 2001; Rowe, Bullock, Polkey, & Morris, 2001; Stone, Baron-Cohen, & Knight, 1998; Stuss, Gallup, & Alexander, 2001; though see Bird, Castelli, Malik, Frith, & Husain, 2004) and superior temporal sulcus at the temporo-parietal junction (Apperly, Samson, & Humphreys, 2005; Samson, Apperly, Chiavarino, & Humphreys, 2004) in mentalizing. The neural basis of mentalizing has been investigated in many functional neuroimaging studies using a variety of tasks and stimuli, both verbal and non-verbal. There is remarkable agreement between these studies, demonstrating activation of the medial PFC (MPFC), the superior temporal sulcus (STS), the temporo-parietal junction (TPJ), and the temporal poles, when subjects infer mental states to story or cartoon characters (Frith & Frith, 2003).

So automatic and pervasive is this mind-reading mechanism that adults feel compelled to attribute intentions and other mental states and emotions to animated abstract shapes, simply on the basis of their movement patterns (Heider & Simmel, 1944). This has been exploited in neuroimaging studies in which participants view animations of moving shapes (e.g. Castelli, Happé, Frith, & Frith, 2000). The MPFC, STS, and temporal poles were activated by a comparison between animations that evoked mental state attributions (for example, one triangle mocking another) and animations in which triangles moved randomly. The same regions are activated when subjects look at cartoons or read stories that require mental state attribution (Gallagher et al., 2000), or think about their own intentions (den Ouden, Frith, Frith, & Blakemore, 2005).

The MPFC is activated when subjects think about psychological states, even if those states are applied to animals (Mitchell, Banaji, & Macrae, 2005). The MPFC is also activated by tasks that involve thinking about mental states in relation to the self (Johnson et al., 2002; Lou et al., 2004; Vogeley et al., 2001). The ability of humans to outwit each other and to use bluff and double bluff is an instance of advanced social skills that rely on an intuitive mentalizing ability. Since 2000, tasks have been devised in which subjects are instructed to withhold truthful responses and to answer with the opposite meaning to questions concerning recent autobiographical events (Spence et al., 2001), or to lie about a card's identity (Langleben et al., 2002; Langleben et al., 2005) or past events (Lee et al. 2002). These studies have found activations in components of the mentalizing system, including MPFC, when subjects are lying. In summary, a network of brain regions including MPFC and STS/TPJ seem to be involved in many aspects of social cognition.

There is a rich literature on the development of social cognition in infancy and childhood. Signs of social competence develop during early infancy, such that by around 12 months of age infants can ascribe agency to a system or entity (Johnson, 2003; Spelke, Phillips, & Woodward, 1995). The understanding of intention emerges at around 18 months, when infants acquire joint-attention skills – for example, they are able to follow an adult's gaze toward a goal (Carpenter, Nagell, & Tomasello, 1998). These early social abilities precede more explicit mentalizing, such as false-belief understanding, which usually emerges by about 4 or 5 years (Barresi & Moore, 1996). While normally developing children begin to pass theory-of-mind tasks by age 5, the brain structures that underlie mentalizing (MPFC and STS/TPJ) undergo substantial development beyond early childhood. Very little research has investigated the development of mentalizing, and its neural correlates, in late childhood or adolescence. In the next section I briefly describe recent empirical studies that have focused on social-cognitive development during adolescence.

Development of face processing during adolescence

Studies investigating the development of face processing have shown that there is an interruption at puberty in the developmental course of face recognition (Carey, Diamond, & Woods, 1980; Diamond, Carey, & Back, 1983). In one study the percentage of correct responses in a behavioral face-recognition task improved by over 20 percent between the ages of 6 and 10 (Carey et al. 1980). However, this improvement was followed by a decline around the age of puberty. Between age 10 and 12, participants showed a drop in accuracy of over 10 percent. Performance on the task recovered again during adolescence. In another study, face encoding was found to be worse in pubescent girls compared with pre- and post-pubescent girls matched for age (Diamond et al., 1983).

Recently, this result was replicated in a large sample (484 children and adolescents aged between 6 and 16 years – Wade, Lawrence, Mandy, & Skuse, 2006). In this study, subjects were instructed to match an emotional label (happy, sad, angry, fearful, disgusted, and surprised) to images of facial expressions. The recognition of fear and disgust showed the greatest linear improvements with age, while there was no improvement in the ability to recognize sad or angry expressions in this age range. In addition, pubertal status, independent of age, affected emotion recognition. Recognition of fear, disgust, and anger improved with pubertal development (Peterson, Crockett, Richards, & Boxer, 1988).The processing of facial expressions is associated with PFC activity (Sprengelmeyer, Rausch, Eysel, & Przuntek, 1998). Therefore, it was proposed that the structural development of the PFC and the concomitant change in the hormonal environment differentially affect neural circuits involved in particular aspects of emotion recognition.

Development of perspective taking during adolescence

Perspective taking is defined as the ability to take on the viewpoint of another person. The ability to take another's perspective is crucial for successful social communication. In order to reason about others, and understand what they think, feel, or believe, it is necessary to step into their "mental shoes" and take their perspective. Perspective taking is related to first-order theory of mind, in that it involves surmising what another person is thinking or feeling. Perspective taking includes awareness of one's own subjective mental states ("first-person perspective," or 1PP) and the ability to ascribe mental states to another person ("third-person perspective" or 3PP). Common brain areas are also activated when subjects perceive a visual scene or answer a conceptual question from their own, first-person, perspective and from another person's perspective. Functional neuroimaging studies have revealed that the inferior parietal cortex bordering with the TPJ and the PFC are associated with making the distinction between 1PP and 3PP at the motor (Ruby & Decety, 2001), visuo-spatial (Vogeley et al., 2004), conceptual (Ruby & Decety, 2003), and emotional (Ruby & Decety, 2004) level. In each of these contexts, superior frontal and right inferior parietal cortex are activated to a greater extent during 3PP than during 1PP.

In a recent study, the development of perspective taking during adolescence was investigated in a group of 115 participants between 8 and 36 years old (Blakemore, den Ouden, Choudhury, & Frith, 2007). The task involved answering questions that required the participant to imagine either how he or she would feel (1PP), or how a protagonist would feel (3PP), in various scenarios. The participant was asked to choose one of two possible emotional faces in answer to each question, as quickly as possible. The results demonstrated that the difference in reaction time to take the first- versus the third-person perspective decreased with increasing age. In other words, the difference in reaction time among adolescents was significantly larger than the difference among adults. The difference in reaction time in children and adolescents was spread almost equally in both directions. In contrast, adults showed no significant difference in reaction time to take the first- versus the third-person perspective. This finding suggests that the efficiency (or possibly the strategy) of perspective taking develops during adolescence, perhaps in parallel with the underlying neural circuitry. What underlies this change in perspective taking with age requires further investigation.

Development of the neural substrates for social cognition

In the past decade, functional magnetic resonance imaging (fMRI) has been used to investigate the development of the neural substrates for various social-cognitive abilities during adolescence. Several groups have investigated the neural processing of emotion in adolescents. Studies have demonstrated amygdala activation in normal adolescents in response to the perception of fearful faces (Baird et al., 1999) and of happy faces (Yang, Menon, Reid, Gotlib, & Reiss, 2003). Neither of these studies contained an adult or a younger child group, so comparisons before and after puberty of the neural processing of facial emotion could not be made. Furthermore, there was no exploration of how age affects emotion expression processing.

Thomas et al. (2001) addressed some of these issues by studying amygdala activation to fearful facial expressions in a group of children (mean age 11 years) and adults. Adults demonstrated greater amygdala activation to fearful facial expressions, whereas children showed greater amygdala activation to neutral faces. Slightly different results were obtained by Killgore, Oki, and Yurgelun-Todd (2001). Results indicated sex differences in amygdala development: although the left amygdala responded to fearful facial expressions in all children, left amygdala activity decreased over the adolescent period in females but not in males. Females also demonstrated greater activation of the dorsolateral PFC over this period, whereas males demonstrated the opposite pattern. In a recent study, bilateral PFC activity increased with age (from 8 to 15 years) for girls, whereas activity only in the right PEC was correlated with age in boys (Yurgelun-Todd & Killgore, 2006).

In a recent study (Monk et al. 2003) a group of adolescents (aged 7–17) and a group of adults (aged 25–36) viewed faces showing certain emotional expressions. While viewing faces with fearful emotional expressions, adolescents exhibited greater activation of the amygdala, orbitofrontal cortex, and anterior cingulated than adults When subjects were asked to switch their attention between a salient emotional property of the face (thinking about how afraid it made them feel) and a non-emotional property (how wide was the nose), adults, but not adolescents, selectively engaged and disengaged the orbitofrontal cortex. These fMRI results suggest that both emotion-processing and cognitive-appraisal systems develop during adolescence.

We have carried out a study to investigate the development during adolescence of the neural systems underlying mentalizing ability. We scanned a group of 19 adolescents (aged 11–17) and a group of eleven adults (aged 21–37) while they were thinking about intentional causality compared with physical causality. While the mentalizing network (cf. Frith & Frith, 2003) was active in both adults and adolescents when they were thinking about intentions, the relative roles of the various areas was significantly different between the age groups, with activity moving from anterior (MPFC) to posterior (STS) regions with age (Blakemore et al., 2007; for review see Blakemore, 2008).

Conclusion

The study of the development of social cognition beyond childhood is a new but rapidly evolving field. The finding that changes in brain structure continue into adolescence and early adulthood has challenged earlier views and since 2006 has given rise to a spate of investigations into the way cognition might change as a consequence. In this chapter I have briefly described research since 2000 that has investigated the development of social-cognitive processes during adolescence. Many questions remain unanswered. The role of hormones, culture, and the social environment in the development of the social brain are unknown. It is possible that changes in hormones and social environment (for example, changing school) interact with neural development at the onset of puberty. Future research is needed to disentangle the contributions of biological and environmental factors to the developing social brain.

Note

I am grateful to the Royal Society, UK, which funds my research.

References

Apperly, I. A., Samson, D., & Humphreys, G. W. (2005). Domain-specificity and theory of mind: Evaluating neuropsychological evidence. *Trends in Cognitive Sciences*, 9(12), 572–577.

Baird, A. A., Gruber, S. A., Fein, D. A., Maas, L. C., Steingard, R. J., Renshaw, P. F., Cohen, B. M., & Yurgelun-Todd, D. A. (1999). Functional magnetic resonance imaging of facial affect recognition in children and adolescents. *Journal of the American Academy of Child and Adolescent Psychiatry*, 38(2), 195–9.

Barnea-Goraly, N., Menon, V., Eckert, M., Tamm, L., Bammer, R., Karchemskiy, A., Dant, C. C., & Reiss, A. L. (2005). White matter development during childhood and adolescence: A cross-sectional diffusion tensor imaging study. *Cerebral Cortex*, 15(12), 1848–1954.

Barresi, J., & Moore, C. (1996). Intentional relations and social understanding. *Behavioral and Brain Sciences*, 19, 107–154.

Bird, C. M, Castelli, F., Malik, O., Frith, U., & Husain, M. (2004). The impact of extensive medial frontal lobe damage on "Theory of Mind" and cognition. *Brain*, 127(4), 914–928.

Blakemore, S.-J. (2008). The social brain in adolescence. *Nature Reviews Neuroscience*, 9(4), 267–277

Blakemore, S.-J., den Ouden, H. E. M., Choudhury, S., & Frith, C. (2007), Adolescent development of the neural circuitry for thinking about intentions. *Social Cognitive and Affective Neuroscience*, 2(2):130–139.

Bourgeois, J. P., Goldman-Rakic, P. S., & Rakic, P. (1994). Synaptogenesis in the prefrontal cortex of rhesus monkeys. *Cerebral Cortex*, 4, 78–96.

Carey, S., Diamond, R., & Woods, B. (1980). The development of face recognition: A maturational component. *Developmental Psychology*, 16(4), 257–269.

Carpenter, M., Nagell, K., & Tomasello, M. (1998). Social cognition, joint attention, and communicative competence from 9 to 15 months of age. *Monographs of the Society for Research in Child Development*, 63(4), i–vi, 1–143.

Castelli, F., Happé, F., Frith, U., & Frith, C. D. (2000). Movement and mind: A functional imaging study of perception and interpretation of complex intentional movement pattern. *NeuroImage*, 12, 314–325.

Channon, S., & Crawford, S. (2000). The effects of anterior lesions on performance on a story comprehension test: Left anterior impairment on a theory of mind-type task. *Neuropsychologia*, 38(7), 1006–1017.

Coleman, J. C., & Hendry, L. (1990). *The Nature of Adolescence* (2nd edn.) Florence, KY: Taylor & Frances/Routledge.

den Ouden, H. E., Frith, U., Frith, C., & Blakemore, S. J. (2005). Thinking about intentions. *NeuroImage*, 28(4), 787–796.

Diamond, R., Carey, S., & Back, K. (1983). Genetic influences on the development of spatial skills during early adolescence. *Cognition*, 13, 167–185.

Feldman, S. S., & Elliott, G. R. (Eds.) (1990). *At the Threshold: The Developing Adolescent*. Cambridge MA: Harvard University Press.

Frith, U., & Frith, C. D. (2003). Development and neurophysiology of mentalizing. *Philosophical Transactions of the Royal Society of London B Biological Sciences*, 358(1431), 459–473.

Gallagher, H. L, Happé, F., Brunswick, N., Fletcher, P. C, Frith, U., & Frith, C. D. (2000). Reading the mind in cartoons and stories: An fMRI study of "theory of mind" in verbal and nonverbal tasks. *Neuropsychologia*, 38(1), 11–21.

Giedd, J. N., Blumenthal, J., Jeffries, N. O., Castellanos, F. X., Liu, H., Zijdenbos, A., Paus, T., Evans, A. C., & Rapoport, J. L. (1999). Brain development during childhood and adolescence: A longitudinal MRI study. *Nature Neuroscience*, 2(10), 861–863.

Giedd, J. N., Snell, J. W., Lange, N., Rajapakse, J. C., Kaysen, D., Vaituzis, A. C., Vauss, Y. C., Hamburger, S. D., Kozuch, P. L., & Rapoport, J. L. (1996). Quantitative magnetic resonance imaging of human brain development: Ages 4–18. *Cerebral Cortex*, 6(4), 551–560.

Gogtay, N., Giedd, J. N., Lusk, L., Hayashi, K. M., Greenstein, D., Vaituzis, A. C., Nugent, T. F., 3rd, Herman, D. H., Clasen, L. S., Toga, A. W., Rapoport, J. L., & Thompson, P. M. (2004). Dynamic mapping of human cortical development during childhood through early adulthood. *Proceedings of the National Academy of Science, USA*, 101, 8174–8179.

Gregory, C., Lough, S., Stone, V., Erzinclioglu, S., Martin, L., Baron-Cohen, S., & Hodges, J. R. (2002). Theory of mind in patients with frontal variant frontotemporal dementia and alzheimer's disease: Theoretical and practical implications. *Brain*, 125(4), 752–764.

Happé, F., Malhi, G. S., & Checkley, S. (2001). Acquired mind-blindness following frontal lobe surgery? A single case study of impaired "theory of mind" in a patient treated with stereotactic anterior capsulotomy. *Neuropsychologia*, 39(1), 83–90.

Heider, F., & Simmel, M. (1944). An experimental study of apparent behavior. *American Journal of Psychology*, 57, 243–249.

Hubel, D. N., & Wiesel, T. N. (1962). Receptive fields, binocular interactions and functional architecture in the cat's visual cortex. *Journal of Physiology*, 160, 106–154.

Huttenlocher, P. R. (1979). Synaptic density in human frontal cortex – developmental changes and effects of aging. *Brain Research*, 163, 195–205.

Huttenlocher, P. R., De Courten, C., Garey, L. J., & Van Der Loos, H. (1983). Synaptic development in human cerebral cortex. *International Journal of Neurology*, 16–17, 144–154.

Johnson, S. C. (2003). Detecting agents. *Philosophical Transactions of the Royal Society of London: B Biological Sciences*, 358, 549–559.

Johnson, S. C., Baxter, L. C., Wilder, L. S., Pipe, J. G., Heiserman, J. E., & Prigatano, G. P. (2002). Neural correlates of self-reflection. *Brain*, 125(8), 1808–1814.

Killgore, W. D. S., Oki, M., & Yurgelun-Todd, D. A. (2001). Sex-specific developmental changes in amygdale responses to affective faces. *Neuroreport*, 12(2), 427–433.

Langleben, D. D., Loughead, J. W., Bilker, W. B., Ruparel, K., Childress, A. R., Busch, S. I., & Gur, R. C. (2005). Telling truth from lie in individual subjects with fast event-related fMRI. *Human Brain Mapping*, 26(4), 262–272.

Langleben, D. D., Schroeder, L., Maldjian, J. A., Gur, R. C., McDonald, S., Ragland, J. D., O'Brien, C. P., & Childress, A. R. (2002). Brain activity during simulated deception: An event-related functional magnetic resonance study. *NeuroImage*, 15(3), 727–32.

Lee, T. M., Liu, H. L., Tan, L. H., Chan, C. C., Mahankali, S., Feng, C. M., Hou, J., Fox, P. T., & Gao, J. H. (2002). Lie detection by functional magnetic resonance imaging. *Human Brain Mapping*, 15(3), 157–64.

Lou, H. C., Luber, B., Crupain, M., Keenan, J. P., Nowak, M., Kjaer, T. W., Sackeim, H. A., & Lisanby, S. H. (2004). Parietal cortex and representation of the mental self. *Proceedings of the National Academy of Sciences, USA*, 101(17), 6827–6832.

Mitchell, J. P., Banaji, M. R., & Macrae, C. N. (2005). General and specific contributions of the medial prefrontal cortex to knowledge about mental states. *NeuroImage*, 28(4), 757–762.

Monk, C. S, McClure, E. B., Nelson, E. E., Zarahn, E., Bilder, R. M., Leibenluft, E., Charney, D. S., Ernst, M., & Pine, D. S. (2003). Adolescent immaturity in attention-related brain engagement to emotional facial expressions. *NeuroImage*, 20(1), 420–428.

Paus, T., Evans, A. C., & Rapoport, J. L. (1999a). Brain development during childhood and adolescence: A longitudinal MRI study. *Nature Neuroscience*, 2, 861–863.

Paus, T., Zijdenbos, A., Worsley, K., Collins, D. L., Blumenthal, J., Giedd, J. N., Rapoport, J. L., & Evans, A. C. (1999b). Structural maturation of neural pathways in children and adolescents: In vivo study. *Science*, 283, 1908–1911.

Peterson, A. C., Crockett, L., Richards, M., & Boxer, A. (1988). A self-report measure of pubertal status: Reliability, validity and initial norms. *Journal of Youth and Adolescence*, 17, 117–133.

Pfefferbaum, A., Mathalon, D. H., Sullivan, E. V., Rawles, J. M., Zipursky, R. B., & Lim, K. O. (1994). A quantitative magnetic resonance imaging study of changes in brain morphology from infancy to late adulthood. *Archives of Neurology*, 51(9), 874–887.

Rakic, P. (1995). Corticogenesis in human and nonhuman primates. In M. S. Gazzaniga (Ed.), *The Cognitive Neurosciences* (pp. 127–145). Cambridge, MA: MIT Press.

Reiss, A. L., Abrams, M. T., Singer, H. S., Ross, J. L., & Denckla, M. B. (1996). Brain development, gender and IQ in children: A volumetric imaging study. *Brain*, 119(5), 1763–1774.

Rowe, A. D., Bullock, P. R., Polkey, C. E., & Morris, R. G. (2001). "Theory of mind" impairments and their relationship to executive functioning following frontal lobe excisions. *Brain*, 124, 600–16.

Ruby, P., & Decety, J. (2001). Effect of subjective perspective taking during simulation of action: A PET investigation of agency. *Nature Neuroscience*, 4, 546–550.

Ruby, P., & Decety, J. (2003). What you believe versus what you think they believe: A neuroimaging study of conceptual perspective-taking. *European Journal of Neuroscience*, 17, 2475–2480.

Ruby, P., & Decety, J. (2004). How would you feel versus how do you think she would feel? A neuroimaging study of perspective-taking with social emotions. *Journal of Cognitive Neuroscience*, 16, 988–999.

Rutter, M. (1993). *Developing Minds*. Harmondworth: Penguin.

Samson, D., Apperly, I. A., Chiavarino, C., & Humphreys, G. W. (2004). Left temporoparietal junction is necessary for representing someone else's belief. *Nature Neuroscience*, 7(5), 499–500.

Sowell, E. R., Peterson, B. S., Thompson, P. M., Welcome, S. F., Henkenius, A. L., & Toga, A. W. (2003). Mapping cortical change across the life span. *Nature Neuroscience*, 6(3), 309–15.

Sowell, E. R., Thompson, P. M., Holmes, C. J., Batth, R., Jernigan, T. L., & Toga, A. W. (1999). Localizing age-related changes in brain structure between childhood and adolescence using statistical parametric mapping. *NeuroImage*, 6(1), 587–97.

Spelke, E. S., Phillips, A. T., & Woodward, A. L. (1995). Infants' knowledge of object motion and human action. In D. Sperber, D. Premack, A. Premack (Eds.), *Causal Cognition: A Multidisciplinary Debate*. Oxford: Oxford University Press.

Spence, S. A., Farrow, T. F., Herford, A. E., Wilkinson, I. D., Zheng, Y., & Woodruff, P. W. (2001). Behavioural and functional anatomical correlates of deception in humans. *Neuroreport*, 12(13), 2849–53.

Sprengelmeyer, R., Rausch, M., Eysel, U. T., & Przuntek, H. (1998). Neural structures associated with recognition of facial expressions of basic emotions. *Biological Science*, 265(1409), 1927–1931.

Stone, V. E., Baron-Cohen, S., & Knight, R. T. (1998). Frontal lobe contributions to theory of mind. *Journal of Cognitive Neuroscience*, 10, 640–656.

Stuss, D. T., Gallup, G. G., Jr., & Alexander, M. P. (2001). The frontal lobes are necessary for "theory of mind". *Brain*, 124(2), 279–286.

Thomas, K. M., Drevets, W. C., Whalen, P. J., Eccard, C. H., Dahl, R. E., Ryan, N. D., & Casey, B. J. (2001). Amygdala response to facial expressions in children and adults. *Biological Psychiatry*, 49(4), 309–316.

Thompson, P. M., Giedd, J. N., Woods, R. P., MacDonald, D., Evans, A. C., & Toga, A. W. (2000). Growth patterns in the developing brain detected by using continuum mechanical tensor maps. *Nature*, 404, 190–193.

Vogeley, K., Bussfeld, P., Newen, A., Herrmann, S., Happé, F., Falkai, P., Maier, W., Shah, N. J., Fink, G. R., & Zilles, K. (2001). Mind reading: Neural mechanisms of theory of mind and self-perspective. *NeuroImage*, 14(1), 170–181.

Vogeley, K., May, M., Ritzl, A., Falkai, P., Zilles, K., & Fink, G. R. (2004). Neural correlates of first-person perspective as one constituent of human self-consciousness. *Journal of Cognitive Neuroscience*, 16, 817–827.

Wade, A. M., Lawrence, K., Mandy, W., & Skuse, D. (2006). Charting the development of emotion recognition from 6 years of age. *Journal of Applied Statistics*, 33(3), 297–315.

Woo, T. U., Pucak M. L., Kye, C. H., Matus C. V., & Lewis D. A. (1997). Peripubertal refinement of the intrinsic and associational circuitry in monkey prefrontal cortex. *Neuroscience*, 80, 1149–1158.

Yakovlev, P. A., & Lecours, I. R. (1967). The myelogenetic cycles of regional maturation of the brain. In A. Minkowski (Ed.), *Regional Development of the Brain in Early life* (pp. 3–70). Oxford: Blackwell.

Yang, T. T., Menon, V., Reid, A. J., Gotlib, I. H., & Reiss, A. L. (2003). Amygdalar activation associated with happy facial expressions in adolescents: A 3-T functional MRI study. *Journal of the American Academy of Child and Adolescent Psychiatry*, 48(2), 979–985.

Yurgelun-Todd, D. A., & Killgore, W. D. (2006). Fear-related activity in the prefrontal cortex increases with age during adolescence: A preliminary fMRI study. *Neuroscience Letters*, 406, 194–199.

Zecevic, N., & Rakic, P. (2001). Development of layer I neurons in the primate cerebral cortex. *Journal of Neuroscience*, 21, 5607–5619.

Chapter 7

How do we Understand Others' Intentions? An Attentional Investigation

Pines Nuku and Harold Bekkering

Introduction

Humans have a great desire for social interaction, anguish over the lack of communication with other conspecifics, and, thanks to their ability to understand the acts of others, reflexively shape their responses to the behavior of others (Blakemore & Decety, 2001; Blakemore & Frith, 2005). The present work aims to shed some more light on the mechanisms that allow for this behavioral "accommodation".

One of the most widely accepted views on the process of understanding others' action intentions suggests that the perception of another's acts activates in the perceiver a corresponding motor program. This proposal, which emerged originally in Lotze's "theory of local signs" (Lotze, 1852; for a historical overview, see Scheerer, 1984), suggests that space perception arises from the combination of a qualitative map of visual sensation and a quantitative map of metrics for focusing upon the object. The proposal, made available to the general scientific public by William James's "ideomotor theory" (James, 1870), holds that every action representation awakens to some degree the actual movement that is its object. Alterations to the ideomotor theory by Greenwald (1970), and especially by Prinz (1990), and the "common coding" framework, have confirmed this view, and have additionally proposed that perceived and planned actions might share or rely on common structural mechanisms.

Studies supporting this view typically measure the extent to which one's own motor behavior is affected when one observes another's motor acts. While this approach has provided numerous findings in visuo-motor processing, little space has been dedicated to measuring the extent to which one's own attentional behavior is affected by (observing) another's motor acts. The present work will treat this issue, investigating whether changes (that is, facilitations) in one's own attentional readiness may reflect the processing of another's (action) intentions, or, in other words, whether one's attention is affected by another performer's motor acts.

We start with a short overview of the action-understanding literature, and then, using illustrations from our own behavioral research, we provide some new insights into the mechanisms involved in this process. We show that not only observing, but also inferring and anticipating, others' acts facilitate the observer's attention.

Action understanding

Among several proposals explaining the action-understanding process, the direct-matching hypothesis system (Rizzolatti, Fogassi, & Gallese, 2001) seems the most favored.

According to it, visual representations of others' actions are automatically mapped onto our own motor representation, thanks to neural circuits that are active when one plans or executes a certain action as well as when one watches another person carrying out the same action (Blakemore & Decety, 2001; Iacoboni et al., 2005). This system is neurophysiologically grounded in the mirror neurons (di Pellegrino, Fadiga, Fogassi, Gallese, & Rizzolatti, 1992). These neurons, present in primate monkeys (Rizzolatti, Fadiga, Matelli, et al., 1996) and humans (Fadiga, Fogassi, Pavesi, & Rizzolatti, 1995; Iacoboni, Woods, Brass, Bekkering, Mazziotta, & Rizzolatti, 1999), are part of a fronto-parietal circuit connecting the superior temporal sulcus with the premotor cortex (Rizzolatti & Craighero, 2004) via the inferior parietal lobule (Fogassi et al., 2005). This circuit is active both when one performs and when one observes another person performing the same act intentionally (Gallese, Fadiga, Fogassi, & Rizzolatti, 1996; Gallese, Keysers, & Rizzolatti, 2004; Rizzolatti, Fadiga, Gallese, & Fogassi, 1996). Its processing was initially shown with transcranial magnetic stimulation (TMS) (for a review, see Rizzolatti & Craighero, 2004), but later on was also shown with studies using behavioral paradigms (see Brass, Bekkering & Prinz, 2001; Brass, Bekkering, Wohlschlager, & Prinz, 2000; Castiello, Lusher, Mari, Edwards, & Humphreys, 2002; Edwards, Humphreys, & Castiello, 2003; Heyes, Bird, Johnson, & Haggard, 2005; Vogt, Taylor, & Hopkins, 2003). Common to them is the assumption that "an action is understood [because] its observation causes the motor system of the observer to 'resonate'" (Rizzolatti et al., 2001, p. 661) and that one "understands the meaning of actions by internally simulating them" (Gallese et al., 2004, p. 396). In other words, the knowledge about another's action intentions is achieved by inferring and simulating them.

Action understanding and simulation
Following the direct-matching hypothesis, an action can be understood because observing it leads to a situation where both the movement planning (that is, the means) and the perceptual consequences of the action (that is, the goals) are activated in the motor cortex, even though the motor act is not executed. This view, derived from the "simulation theory" (see Goldman, 1989; Gordon, 1986), holds that an observer understands another's acts, not by relying on over-learned visual experiences or by logically calculating them, but by adopting the other's perspective (that is, by putting oneself in another's shoes). Humans develop their simulative

capabilities first by ascribing their own mental states to themselves, and consequentially by ascribing mental states to other individuals (Goldman 1989). This reflexive process is not only crucial to action understanding (see Chaminade, Meary, Orliaguet, & Decety, 2001; Knoblich & Flach, 2001) but is also determinant for joint attention.

Action understanding and joint attention

Most of the studies on "action understanding" rely on either a *non-mentalistic* or a *mentalistic* approach. Within the non-mentalistic approach, two theories seem to lead the discussion. The *interaction theory* (Gallagher, 2001) suggests that understanding others' behavior is socially "embodied" in humans and that humans are prone to interacting with others. The *associative learning theory* (Schultz & Dickinson, 2000), on the other hand, suggests that humans understand others' behavior because they understand the causal and predictive structure of our environment by associating actions with (action) outcomes, and especially by processing *unexpected* (action) outcomes that generate erroneous prediction (Schultz & Dickinson, 2000).

Within the mentalistic approach, the current debate centers on the *simulation theory* and the *theory theory*. Whereas the *simulation* theorists argue that understanding others' actions is rooted in the ability to simulate others' actions, the *theory* theorists suggest that action understanding involves the employment of theoretical stances: others' mental states, desires, and actions are represented as theoretical posits consisting of a set of causal laws relating external stimuli to inner states (Gallese & Goldman, 1998).

The simulative approach is crucial for *joint attention* – the ability to engage with another's attention deployed toward an external object. Joint-attention processes link the minds of two interacting partners, serving the initiation as well as the coordination of the partners (Sebanz, Bekkering, & Knoblich, 2006). In other words, joint attention links one's own perception with another's action, thus allowing one to predict the other's action intentions toward an object or event that is relevant to each of the interacting partners. Critical to this *triadic* (observer, agent, and object) process is the ability to *simulate* the agent's action intention (Deak, Flom, & Pick, 2000), with eyes and hands being the *mean* and the (gazed at/pointed at) object being the *goal* of the event (Woodward & Guarjardo, 2002). This way, by simulating the partner's eye or hand action, one understands the partner's goals, and interaction with the partner is facilitated (for a review, see Dijksterhuis & Bargh, 2001).

Joint Attention and Gaze (Priming)

Sensitivity to eye direction is intrinsic to human nature. Adults, for example, devote most of their face-processing time to exploring the eyes (Walker-Smith, Gale, & Findlay, 1977) or orienting reflexively to another's gaze (Driver et al., 1999; Emery, 2000; Friesen & Kingstone, 1998; Hietanen, 1999; Langton & Bruce, 1999). Eyes seem to convey several relevant bits of information about the bearers' identity (Bruce & Young, 1986), their emotional (Ekman, 1982) and mental (Kleinke, 1986) states, their intentions (Baron-Cohen, 1995; Baron-Cohen, Wheelwright, Hill, Raste, & Plumb, 2001), and their attention (Driver et al.,1999; Langton, 2000). Reflexive orienting to another's gaze direction relies on cortical areas, like the superior temporal sulcus (STS), an area that is part of the mirror neuron system, that are "specialized" in processing several aspects of the human face (Puce, Allison, Bentin, Gore, & McCarthy, 1998; Haxby, Hoffman, Gobbini, 2000) and eye motion (McCarthy, 1999). Interestingly, gaze orienting and covertly orienting attention activate the same brain areas (Dolan et al., 1997), confirming the importance of gaze (following) in visuo-spatial attention.

Sensitivity to eye direction emerges early in ontogeny (Hood, Willen, & Driver, 1998; Vecera & Johnson, 1995). Initially infants are sensitive to the "dyadic" (direct eye-to-eye) interaction (Farroni, Csibra, Simion & Johnson, 2002), and soon after they become sensitive to the "triadic" interaction, where they can shift their own (visual) attention toward external objects to which other people are also directing their (visual) attention (D'Entremont, Hains, & Muir, 1997). The triadic relation develops in two phases (Butterworth, 1998). Initially the observer starts changing his or her orientation and by so doing lets the other person know that an object of interest is or could appear at the gazed-at location. Subsequently, the relation evolves, involving a mental triangulation where the minds of two interacting agents "meet" when the object appears. The transition from a dyadic to a triadic interaction paves the way to joint attention, where one can monitor one's own attention (toward another person and the external object) as well as another's attention toward the external object (Tomasello, 1999).

Gaze "morphology"

Eye movement is crucial to the orienting of one's attention, because the morphology of the eye (that is, the sclera-to-iris ratio) seems to have evolved with the purpose of allowing easy discrimination of the location to which another individual is directing attention (Kobayashi & Kohshima, 1997), and because humans seem to have specialized areas in the anterior regions of the STS that mediate gaze processing (Allison, Puce, & McCarthy, 2000; Haxby, Hoffman, & Gobbini, 2000; Schuller & Rossion, 2001). Several behavioral studies show that the observation of real human faces (both frontal view – Driver et al., 1999 – and profile – Langton & Bruce, 1999) or of cartoon-like depictions of faces (Friesen & Kingstone 1998) facilitates the observer's attention.

Similarly, functional imaging (Haxby et al., 1999; Kanwisher, McDermott, & Chun, 1997; Puce et al., 1996), lesion (Campbell, Heywood, Cowey, Regard, & Landis, 1990), and neuropsychological (Vuilleumier, 2000) studies suggest that attentional alignment relies on specific areas within the temporal cortex that are also sensitive to gaze processing. Interestingly, however, there have not been many studies testing whether this "gazing phenomenon" relies on the eyes alone or on the eyes within the face context. Given that the observation of face features, like the human tongue, causes a reflexive alignment of the observer's attention with the tip of the other's tongue (Downing, Dodds, & Bray, 2004), and given that the face-processing area (FFA) responds more strongly to faces without eyes than to eyes alone (Kanwisher et al., 1997; Tong, Nakayama, Moscovitch, Weinrib, & Kanwisher, 2000), testing whether the "gazing" effect relies on eyes alone or on eyes within a face context is not trivial.

To this purpose, we ran a study (Nuku & Bekkering, forthcoming a) where we tested whether priming by virtue of eyes alone (that is, observing another's "iris-to-sclera-ratio" changes) yields comparable attentional effects to priming by virtue of eyes within a face (that is, observing another person's "iris-to-sclera-ratio" changes *within* a face context). As in all the studies described in this chapter, this study adopted a "simple detection task" paradigm (Posner, 1978), where a partici-pant's speed detection (that is, reaction times) to upcoming targets is measured via a manual response (that is, a button press). Typical to this paradigm is that responses to *primed* trials (that is, targets appearing on the side *cued* by the communicative signal) are compared with responses to *unprimed* trials (that is, targets appearing on the opposite side). This comparison gives an estimation of a priming effect.

The study consisted of two separate experiments. In the first experiment partici-pants saw two concentric geometric rings. These were presented either alone (in which case they were verbally coded as "circles, eyes alone"), or within a face context – a larger concentric circle representing the head, a horizontal line representing the mouth, and a small dot representing the nose (in which case they were verbally coded as "eyes within a face"). The circles, the eyes alone, and the eyes within a face were considered as *primes* and they were presented sequentially and blocked (that is, the "circle" block, the "eyes-alone" block, and the "eyes-within-a-face" block). In this experiment a typical trial started with the "circles" block, followed by the "eyes-alone" block, and finally by the "eyes-within-a-face" block. After the presen-tation of the circles on the screen, two black solid dots appeared within the circles, either on the left or on the right side. In the "eyes-alone" block as well as in the "eyes-within-a-face" block, the two black solid dots represented the two pupils *looking* to the left or to the right of the screen. Following one of three time intervals of 200, 350, or 500 ms from the presentation of the "pupils," the target, a red solid dot, appeared randomly either to the left or to the right of the screen. Since "circles" and "eyes alone" were perceptually identical, but conceptually different from each other, we argued that verbally coding the circles as "eyes" would trigger the observ-er's attention faster than the verbal coding of the circles as (socio-irrelevant) "circles." On the other hand, since "eyes alone" and "eyes within a face" were per-ceptually different, but conceptually similar to each other, we argued that the circles coded as "eyes within the face" would be more efficient in triggering the observer's attention than the circles coded as "eyes alone."

Surprisingly, we found that, despite being conceptually dissimilar, neither "circles" nor "eyes alone" did affect the observer's attention. As expected, however, we saw that the "eyes-within-a-face" prime did facilitate the target detection, with responses to targets appearing at the "gazed at" location being given faster than responses to targets appearing at the "non-gazed at" location, which suggests that observing a gazing face modulates the observer's orienting of visual attention. Alternatively, however, one can also argue that it was the *rich* context of the "eyes-within-a-face" prime, not the specific face context, that had affected the subjects' responses. To rule this alternative interpretation out, and to show that it was the direct observing of the "eyes-within-a-face" context that had facilitated the observer's attention, we ran a control experiment, with the circles embedded within a (stylized) house context and representing the windows of the house. As expected, the circles embedded within the context of a house, rather than a face, did not trigger the observer's attention.

Showing that not just any context, but rather a face context, is needed to highlight the functional properties (that is, the gazing) of the human eyes, we ran a third experiment, where we asked whether it was necessary for the observer *directly to see* the other's eyes (within the face) in order to benefit from their direction. In other words, can the mental representation of another's eye direction affect one's attention?

To test this hypothesis we ran the first experiment in the inverse order: the "eyes-within-a-face" block was presented first, the "eyes-alone" block second, and the "circles" block last. In compliance with our prediction, we saw that, once the observer had been presented with the "eyes-within-a-face" block, both the "eyes-alone" and the "circles" blocks facilitated the observer's alignment of attention with the target to be detected. This finding is in line with a study by Kingstone and colleagues (Kingstone, Tipper, Ristic, & Ngan, 2004) showing that the verbal coding of geometrical figures as "eyes" or "directional stimuli" activates different areas in the observer's brain, and only the "eyes" coding activates the sensitive face-processing STS area.

Taken together, these findings show that gaze morphology is crucial, though not fundamental, in triggering observers' attention. Additionally, it showed that *inferring* the gaze direction of another's eyes leads to attentional shifts by the observer.

Gaze "inference"

The above study indicated that inferring another's gaze direction facilitates the alignment of the observer's attention with the gazed-at target location. Nevertheless, one can also attribute such an effect to the stimuli that represent the eyes (within or outside the face context) being always visible on the screen. Being able to see the "pupils" within the eyes might have affected the observer's attention. To test this argument, we ran a second simple detection task study (Nuku & Bekkering, forthcoming a), where we tested whether *inferring* another's gazed-at region when it was not possible to see the other's eyes also triggered the observer's attention.

In the first experiment, we presented participants with a face with eyes that were closed (50 percent of the trials) or open (50 percent), with the eyes oriented to the left (50 percent) or to the right (50 percent) of the screen. The target, a red solid dot, appeared in random order to the left (50 percent) or to the right (50 percent) side of the face. In this way, the face direction and the type of eyes were unpredictive of the target location. The target detection was measured via a button press. Reaction times were submitted to a multivariate analysis of variance (MANOVA), with Prime Type (face with closed eyes, face with open eyes) and Validity (primed trials or trials in which the target appeared at the face-oriented location, unprimed trials or trials in which the target appeared opposite the face-oriented location) as within-subject factors. The analysis showed a Prime Type effect [($F(1,13) < 1, p > 0.05$)], suggesting that the detection of targets when the face appeared with open eyes (374 ms) was no different from the detection of targets when the face had the eyes closed (371 ms). Importantly, however, the analysis showed a reliable interaction between Prime Type and Validity [$F(1,13) = 8.7, p = 0.01$], indicating that the priming benefit (that is, responses to targets on primed trials being *faster* than responses to targets on unprimed trials) was significant only for the face with the open eyes. Specifically, when the face had the eyes open, the response difference between primed (367 ms) and unprimed (381 ms) trials was highly significant [$t(13) = -2.9, p = 0.01$)], whereas when the face had the eyes closed, the difference between primed (370 ms) and unprimed (372 ms) was not significant [$t(13) = 0.4, p = 0.7$]. Showing that the face with the eyes open did facilitate target detection while the face with the eyes closed did not argues in favor of the assumption that *seeing* another's eye direction facilitates the observer's alignment of attention. Alternatively, however, one could interpret the finding by arguing that one not only *sees*, but also *attends*, with open eyes. Seeing, thus, an agent with closed eyes is twice uninformative: neither can one know where the agent is looking nor can one infer where the agent is attending.

To test the alternative interpretation we ran a second experiment where the face had the eyes *obstructed* (made invisible) either by concealing sunglasses (through which one could see and attend) or by concealing occluders (through which one could neither see nor attend). We argued that, if *seeing* another's eye direction is crucial for aligning with his or her attended region of interest, neither the face with sunglasses nor the face with the occluders would facilitate the observer's attention. However, if one infers and subsequently aligns with the agent's *attended region of interest* (people look at another's eye direction because they want to know what has attracted the other's attention, not because they are interested in another's eyes direction *per se!*), only the agent wearing sunglasses could affect the observer's attention.

Except for this change in stimuli, the rest of the experiment was identical to the previous one. The measured reaction times to targets appearing at the side of the (occluded) face were submitted to a MANOVA with Prime Type (face with sunglasses, face with occluders) and Validity (primed trials, unprimed trials). The analysis showed that Prime Type did not reach the significance level ($p < 0.09$), indicating that target detecting in the "occluders" condition (381 ms) was not significantly different from responses in the "sunglasses" condition (389 ms). Importantly, however, the Prime Type x Validity interaction [$F(1,12) = 7.9, p < 0.016$]

indicates that the priming benefit was significant *only* for sunglasses. In the sunglasses condition, responses to primed trials (381 ms) were significantly (p < 0.05) faster than responses to unprimed trials (396 ms), whereas in the occluders condition responses to primed trials (384 ms) were no different (p > 0.35) from responses to unprimed trials (378 ms).

This finding suggests that participants' attention was affected only when seeing the agent with sunglasses. Considering that the agent's eye region was equally concealed in both the sunglasses condition and the occluders condition, this finding indicates that the participant's attentional facilitation could be attributed not to the *seeing* of the (open) eyes but rather to the *inferring* of the other's attended region of interest.

Gaze and (cross-modal) joint attention

The two previous studies showed how observing and inferring other's gaze direction facilitates the alignment of the observer's attention with the external gazed-at target. However, since most of our daily information is *received* in one modality and *released* in another (think of the condition when you *auditorily* hear someone's voice and *visually* search for his or her location), we furthered our investigation on the role of gaze priming, asking whether observing another's gaze direction might facilitate the detection of auditory targets. In other words, does the observing of another's gaze direction toward the location of an upcoming auditory target facilitate the observer's spatial attention?

To investigate this proposal, we ran a study (Nuku & Bekkering, forthcoming b) in a joint-attention 'paradigm'. Because joint attention is often regarded as the "tendency to spontaneously direct attention to where someone else is looking" (see Kingstone, Friesen, & Gazzaniga, 2000, p. 159), in this experiment we created a *triadic* scenario consisting of the observer (in front of a PC screen), the agent (on the PC screen), and the external auditory target. In other words, the sound represented the object of interest of both the agent and the observer.

The study, a simple cueing paradigm, consisted of three experiments, with identical design, measuring participants' reaction times. In the first experiment, participants saw a face turned to the left (50 percent of the trials) or to the right (50 percent) of the room with the eyes either open (50 percent) or closed (50 percent). In the room, 80 cm to the left and to the right of the observer (80 cm to the right and to the left of the agent respectively), we placed two tweeters, from which a (target) sound would be emitted. When the face direction was directed toward the tweeter from which the sound was emitted (50 percent chance), the auditory target was considered primed. In contrast, if the sounds were emitted from the tweeter opposite the face direction (50 percent chance), the auditory target was considered as unprimed. Subjects reported the target detection by pressing a button placed in front of them.

Correct reaction times contributed to means for each participant, and were submitted to a MANOVA, with Face Direction (congruent, incongruent) and Eye Type (eyes open, eyes closed) as within-subject factors. The analysis showed that neither Eye Type nor Face Direction reached significance (both $Fs < 1$, both $p > 0.05$), although they interacted significantly with each other [$F(1,15) = 6.4$, $p = 0.02$]. The response pattern for the face with eyes open [primed trials (209 ms) being detected faster than unprimed trials (214 ms) $t(15) = 2.0$, $p = 0.05$] was significantly different from the response pattern for the face with eyes closed [unprimed trials (219 ms) were faster than primed trials (209 ms), $t(15) = 2.3$, $p < 0.05$].

First, findings showed a cross-modal visuo-auditory orienting in a joint-attention setting: auditory targets appearing at the gazed-at sounds location were detected faster than auditory targets appearing at the non-gazed-at sounds location. Secondly, findings showed that the effect was inversed when the eyes were closed: auditory targets appearing at the non-gazed-at sounds location were detected faster than auditory targets appearing at the gazed-at sounds location. Although unexpected – considering that studies showing that primes other than the human gaze, namely the human tongue (Tipples, 2002), facilitate the observer's attention in a similar fashion to gaze cues – the second finding seems to suggest that the presence of the ear might have accounted, at least partially, for the facilitating in detecting sounds propagating from the ear's side.

In order to test the robustness of the "ear effect" we ran a second experiment, where we controlled the prominent position of the ear in the agent's face by taken the ear away. We argued that, if the ear prominence had indeed caused the "ear effect", with the ear taken away the effect would disappear.

Except for the stimuli (the face without the ear), the experiment was identical to the previous one. The measured reaction times contributed to means for each participant in each condition, and were submitted to a MANOVA, with Eye Type (eyes open, eyes closed) and Face Direction (congruent, incongruent) as within-subject factors. The analysis showed a significant effect for Face Direction [$F(1,13) = 12.5$, $p = 0.003$], but neither a main effect for Eye Type [$F < 1$, $p > 0.05$] nor an interaction between Eye Type and Face Direction [$F < 1$, $p > 0.05$]. This response pattern was quite different from that of the first experiment, with the response pattern between the eyes-open and eyes-closed conditions being similar here. More specifically, in the eyes-open condition responses to primed trials (272 ms) were faster than responses to unprimed trials (281 ms) [$t(13) = 3.20$, $p = 0.007$] and, similarly, primed trials (270 ms) were detected faster than unprimed trials (280 ms) [$t(13) = 2.75$, $p = 0.016$] in the eyes-closed condition too.

In addition to confirming a cross-modal visuo-auditory priming, these findings showed that sounds propagating from the eyes side were detected faster than the sound propagating from the ear side, even when the eyes were closed. This suggests that the prominence of the ear had indeed accounted for the "ear effect" in the first experiment.

Although the second experiment changed the findings of the first experiment, where we saw that sounds appearing at the ear side were detected faster than sounds appearing at the eyes side (if the eyes were closed), it was possible that taking the agent's ear away might have added unnaturalness to the agent's face. That is, since one cannot auditorily attend without the ear, with the ear being taken away we might have encouraged participants to align their attention with the face direction alone (that is, to ignore the gaze direction). To test for this possibility, we ran a third experiment, where the agent's ear could be considered as (visually) absent but (inferably) present at the same time. More specifically, we covered the agent's ear with either a "permeable" hat or an "impermeable" helmet, and argued that a (permeable) hat would allow one auditorily to attend to external sounds, whereas an (impermeable) helmet would not. Thus, if the "ear effect" in the first experiment was due to *inferring* the agent as "auditorily attending", participants' attention would be facilitated only when observing the agent wearing the hat. If the "ear effect" was due to the presence (that is, the prominence) of the ear in the agent's face, here the participants' attention would be facilitated only by the face direction, with the "hat" and "helmet" conditions yielding similar attentional effects.

Reaction times, submitted to a MANOVA with Eye Type (eyes open, eyes closed), Face Direction (congruent, incongruent), and Ear Cover (hat, helmet) as within-subject factors, showed no main effect for the Ear Cover [$F(1,15) = 1.3, p = 0.20$] factor, although it showed that Ear Cover interacted [$F(1,15) = 7.3, p = 0.01$] with Face Direction. This crucial interaction suggested that responses to auditory targets appearing at the location indicated by the agent's face were *faster* when the agent was wearing a hat (423 ms) than when the agent was wearing a helmet (430 ms). We explored this interaction in more detail by separating responses for "hat" and "helmet" conditions. In the hat condition, the MANOVA with Eye Type and Face Direction showed a highly significant interaction [$F(1,15) = 14.2, p = 0.002$], suggesting that, when the agent's eyes were open, responses to sounds appearing at the eyes side (420 ms) were *faster* than the responses to targets appearing at the ear side (426 ms) [$t(15) = 2.2, p = 0.058$]. In contrast, when the agent's eyes were closed, responses to targets appearing at the eyes side (432 ms) were *slower* than responses to targets at the ear side (422 ms) [$t(15) = 2.8, p = 0.014$]. The same analysis on the helmet data showed no interaction between Eye Type and Face Direction [$F < 1$, $p > 0.05$]. When the agent's eyes were open, responses to sounds appearing at the eyes side (423 ms) were similar to responses to targets appearing at the ear side (428 ms) [$t(15) = -1.2, p = 25$]. Similarly, when the agent's eyes were closed, responses to sounds appearing at the ear side (423 ms) were similar to responses (436 ms) to targets appearing at the ear side [$t(15) = 2.0, p = 0.064$].

In addition to confirming the cross-modal visuo-auditory orienting in a joint-attention setting, the present experiment dissociated between responses to targets primed by the agent wearing a hat and targets primed by the agent wearing a helmet, even though the agent's ear was in both cases invisible to the observer.

Taken together, these findings indicate that, if eye information is available (that is, the agent is attending with eyes open), observers cannot ignore the eyes and align to them reflexively. However, if the eye information is not available (that is, the agent's eyes are closed), observers focus on alternative face features if such features are considered informative with the regard to understanding the agent's attended region of interest. Thus, if the observer thinks that the agent cannot see but can still listen, the observer's attention can be facilitated by this inferring process.

Joint Attention and Hand Actions

Earlier we saw that, when humans communicate, they use *gazing* to support their communicative goals. This process, often referred to as "joint attention", does not rely exclusively on gaze acts, but benefits from changes in another's face direction (Langton, Watt, & Brue, 2000), grasping actions (Blakemore & Frith, 2005; Brass et al., 2001; Craighero, Bello, Fadiga, & Rizzolatti, 2002; Fadiga, Fogassi, Pavesi, & Rizzolatti, 1995; Vogt et al., 2003;), or pointing gestures (Brass et al., 2000; Stürmer, Aschersleben, & Prinz, 2000). However, most of the communication abilities have been studied within the visuo-motor reference frame. By focusing on how the observation of another's act affects the observer's motor behavior, we aim to investigate how the observation of a motor act affects an observer's attention behavior. Since hand gestures are highly informative with regard to another's action intention, in the following experiments we focused on these primes to test whether another's acts do indeed facilitate the observer's deployment of attention.

Hand actions in visual attention

One of the first studies to investigate how motor acts change an observer's attentional readiness showed that observing another's hand acts facilitates the observer's alignment of attention with a target appearing at the (hand) manipulated location (Fischer & Szymkowiak, 2004). In their study, Fischer and Szymkowiak presented participants with pictures of static pointing and grasping hands, seemingly priming (that is, either pointing at or grasping) one of the three tangerines arranged horizontally in front of the hand. Following a random delay of stimulus onset asynchrony (SOA) 300, 500, and 700 ms, a visual target appeared unpredictably over the left or right tangerine. This way, if the target appeared over the primed tangerine (that is, the one that was pointed at or grasped), the trial would be called primed; if it appeared over the tangerine opposite to the primed tangerine, it would be called unprimed; and if the hand primed the central tangerine, the trials would be considered neutral. Participants were required to report the target onset by pressing a button placed in front of them. The authors found that, in the pointing condition, participants were *faster* in detecting the target in the primed rather than the unprimed or neutral trials, whereas, in the grasping condition, participants were *slower* in detecting the target in the primed than in the neutral and unprimed trials. They interpreted this priming dissociation within the action-simulation processing (Gallese & Goldman, 1998), where an observer generates predictions on another person's actions by anticipating the occurrence of critical events and by coordinating his or her own actions with somebody else's (Knoblich & Jordan, 2003). Thus, the authors concluded that the encoding of spatially directed *ongoing* intentional postures (that is, the pointing hand) has attentional consequences for the observer, whereas postures depicting actions that have already been completed do not.

With this study as a starting point, we (see Nuku, Lindemann, Bekkering, & Fischer, forthcoming) investigated whether high cognitive processes such as *inferring* and *anticipating* the consequences of another's (hand) actions facilitate an observer's attention. In this study, we ran three experiments. The first one replicated Fischer and Szymkowiak's original study. Here we presented participants with a hand either pointing or grasping one of the three (coffee) cups presented on a table in front of the agent's hand. Subsequently, a target (that is, a black solid circle) would appear either on the pointed/grasped cup (50 percent of the trials) or on the opposite cup (50 percent). Participants signaled the target detection via a button press.

Reaction times were submitted to a MANOVA, with Posture Type (pointing, grasping), Validity (primed, unprimed, and neutral trials), and SOA (30, 500, 700 ms) as within-subject factors. The analysis showed a Posture Type x Validity interaction [$F(2,19) = 11.20$, $p < 0.001$]. Further investigations in this interaction showed that, in the pointing condition, primed targets were detected significantly *faster* (343 ms) than unprimed (352 ms) [$t(19) = -2.4$, $p < 0.05$] and neutral (355 ms) [$t(19) = -3.1$, $p < 0.05$]. In contrast, in the grasping conditions primed targets were detected significantly *more slowly* (355 ms) than unprimed (346 ms) [$t(19) = -2.1$, $p < 0.05$] and neutral (345 ms) [$t(19) = 2.0$, $p < 0.058$] targets. Thus, in agreement with Fischer and Szymkowiak, we confirmed the original (pointing–grasping) priming dissociation, showing that target detection was faster for targets preceded by the pointing hand (an ongoing action) than by the grasping hand (an already performed action).

Although this finding suggests that only the observation of pointing acts prompts the observer's attention, we argue that in Fischer and Szymkowiak's original paradigm the two primes – that is, the pointing and the grasping hands – were presented in two different locations. Pointing was presented far from the target location while grasping was presented near it (in the original study the grasping hand "approached" one of the three tangerines from a "resting" position). Since priming near the target location leads to inhibitory effects – inhibition of response (IOR), with inhibition occurring in trials where the prime-target (onset) delay exceeds 500 ms – while priming far from the upcoming target location does not (see Posner, 1987, 1980), we ran a control experiment to test whether this was the case with the pointing and grasping primes. Here, both primes were presented near the target location (that is, both "approached" the cup). This change in the experimental design had an immediate effect in the priming pattern. In contrast to the previous experiment, the reaction times submitted to a MANOVA with Posture Type (pointing, grasping), Validity (primed, unprimed, neutral trials), and SOA (300, 500, 700 ms) showed neither a Posture Type main effect not an interaction between Posture Type and Validity (both $Fs < 1$ and both $ps > 0.05$). Only the SOA main effect [$F(2,12) = 10.8$, $p < 0.01$] and the SOA x Validity interaction [$F(4,10) = 4.8$, $p < 0.05$] reached the significance level. A further investigation (paired samples t-tests) in this interaction showed that, in the pointing condition, the priming pattern (difference between the responses to unprimed and primed trials) in SOA 300 ms was facilitated [$t(13) = 3.36$, $p < 0.01$], while the priming pattern in SOA 700 ms was inhibited [$t(13) = -3.45$, $p < 0.01$]. Similarly, in the grasping condition, target detection at SOA 300 ms caused priming benefits [$t(13) = 3.10$, $p < 0.01$], while at SOA 700 ms it caused priming costs [$t(13) = -2.40$, $p < 0.05$]. In other words, this experiment showed that, if presented near the cup, both pointing and grasping yield a similar priming pattern: early response facilitation and late response inhibition. This finding argues in favor of our "spatial confound", suggesting that the (pointing–grasping) priming disparity in Fischer and Szymkowiak's original study (2004) was modulated by the prime location.

This finding, however, did not answer the main question of this study: does the (attentional) attuning to another's acts rely on (spatial) low (that is, seeing the hand action directly) or (cognitive) high (that is, anticipating the hand action) processes? In order to answer this question, we ran a third experiment, where the prime postures were related to objects in terms of a *causal* relationship. That is, participants observed the pointing or grasping hand approaching the object, and, when the hand retracted to its original position, the object moved with it. The object (that is, the coffee cup) displacement was perceived as caused by the hand and had to be reported by a simple button press.

The MANOVA with Posture Type (pointing, grasping), Validity (primed, unprimed, neutral), and SOA (300 ms, 500 ms, 700 ms) as within-subjects factors showed a SOA x Validity interaction [$F(4,10) = 4.8, p < 0.05$], suggesting a change in the priming pattern over time, as well as a Validity main effect [$F(2,15) = 9.4$, $p < 0.01$]. This latter finding shows that the detection of targets (that is, cups) that were "displaced" by the hand (that is, primed trials) was faster (330 ms) than the detection of targets that were not "displaced" by the hand (that is, unprimed trials) (341 ms) [$t(16) = -2.2, p < 0.05$] or that were neutral in this process (that is, neutral trials) (347 ms) [$t(16) = -3.3, p < 0.05$].

The experiment showed that the perceived *causal* relationship between the (manipulating) hand and the (subsequent) displacement of the cup did capture the observer's attention. This finding is in line with other studies showing how causal interaction of objects (for example, bottle–cork screw) affects the observer's attention (see Riddoch, Humphreys, Edwards, Baker, & Wilson, 2003).

Taken together, this study indicated that anticipating the outcome of another's actions affects the process of action understanding and facilitates the observer's attention.

Hand actions and "action simulation"

There is a variety of proposals regarding the purpose of mental simulation. For example, simulating, or mapping another person's body acts onto a mental representation of one's own body, seems to facilitate action imitation (Iacoboni et al., 1999; Rizzolatti et al., 2001) and interpersonal communication (Bavelas, Black, Lemery, & Mullett, 1986; Lakin & Chartrand, 2003), as well as enabling learning new and reproducing old acts (Blandin, Lhuisset, & Proteau, 1999). Watching a particular behavior primes the same behavior in the observer, facilitating the initiation and execution of the observed act (Dijksterhuis & Bargh, 2001; Jeannerod, 2001). Simulation is also the key to understanding other people's mental states (Arbib & Rizzolatti, 1996; Gallese & Goldman, 1998; Meltzoff & Decety, 2003;

Rizzolatti et al., 2001; Rizzolatti, Fogassi, & Gallese, 2002), although other studies (Jacob & Jeannerod, 2005; Saxe, 2005) suggest that it is not the "simulating" that facilitates the understanding of others' action intentions, but rather the understanding of others' actions that makes "simulation" possible (see Csibra, 2005).

Considering this dichotomy, we ran a study that could contribute to the debate, where we tested the observer's attention as a response to seeing simulatable and non-simulatable primes. Specifically, we compared priming effects from observing postures that were "mappable onto our body" (for example, hands) with postures that were "non-mappable onto our body" (for example, u-shapes), and argued that, if simulation is crucial to action understanding, then only simulable postures (that is, hands) would affect the observer's attention, with non-simulable postures (that is, u-shapes) having little effect in the observer's attention.

In a simple detection experiment (Nuku, Lindemann, & Bekkering, forthcoming), we presented participants with a picture depicting either two mirrored hands or two mirrored u-shapes. Although the design was identical for hands and for u-shapes, for simplicity we will illustrate the experimental design with the hand condition. In the hand condition, we started the trials by presenting the participants with a picture showing both an open hand (representing a reaching position) and a closed hand (depicting a precision grip or a pinching posture). In half the trials participants saw the open hand to the left and the closed hand to the right, while in the other half they saw open hand to the right and the closed hand to the left. Both hand apertures were presented centrally on the screen. After the two hands had been presented, participants saw two identical orbs on the screen (one orb near each hand aperture). In each case the two orbs were identical, and were either both large or both small. The pairs of large and small orbs were presented in a random order, with half of the trials receiving the large orbs and the other half receiving the small orbs. Since the two hands had different apertures (one large and one small), the two small orbs would "fit" only the precision-grip aperture, while the two large orbs would "fit" only "reaching" aperture. An upcoming target (that is, a solid red dot) appeared, in random order, either on the orb fitting the hand aperture (50 percent of the trials) or on the opposite orb (50 percent). Participants were required to press a button when they detected the target onset.

A two-way mixed-model analysis of variance (ANOVA), with Simulability (hands, u-shapes) as between-subject factor, and Validity (primed, unprimed) as within-subject factor, showed a Validity effect [$F(1,24) = 4.39, p < 0.05$], suggesting that overall responses to primed trials (340 ms) were faster than to unprimed trials (346 ms). Additionally it showed a Simulability x Validity interaction [$F(1,24) = 11.54, p < 0.01$], indicating that the priming effect depended on the prime type. That is, participants' responses were affected only when they observed the hands (346 ms for primed targets versus 356 ms for unprimed targets; $t(12) = -3.5, p < 0.01$), but not the u-shapes (338 ms vs 337 ms; $t(12) < 1.0$).

The present finding suggests that simulable primes (that is, hands) depicted as reaching or as pinching an object affected the observer's attention. Non-simulable primes, visually fitting the objects' size, did not.

In line with studies showing that observers not only reproduce others' actions but also *simulate* the sensory consequences of the motoric patterns (Blakemore & Decety, 2001; Rizzolatti et al., 2002; cf. Hommel, Müsseler, Aschersleben, & Prinz, 2001), we showed that observers access others' action intention, and, by so doing, facilitate their own visuo-spatial attention.

Conclusions

This chapter has aimed to show how people understand the actions and action intentions of other people. We have shown that humans can understand the behavior of others by observing and by inferring their eye or hand actions. Additionally we have shown that this pattern of action understanding is testable in both an unimodal (visual) as well as across-modal (visuo-auditory) orientation of attention. Our studies indicate that humans perceive the same scene differently in different situations: they perceive another person whose eyes are eyes open or occluded by (opaque) sunglasses as visually attending, while they perceive another person whose eyes are closed or occluded by a rectangle as non-visually attending but rather as auditorily attending. Similarly, humans consider a moving object in concomitance with a hand action as mere coincidence, although, depending on the context, they do interpret the same object motion as caused by the hand.

In addition to the existing visuo-motor literature, this chapter has shown that facilitations of one's own attentional readiness reflect the processing of the observed (other's) action intentions. We argue that humans represent the actions of others thanks to high cognitive processes such as adopting their perspective, inferring their intentions, simulating their actions, and attributing intentionality to their behavior. Such processes modulate both visuo-spatial and joint-attention mechanisms and facilitate the human ability to relate to external objects and to other people.

References

Allison, T., Puce, A., & McCarthy, G. (2000). Social perception from visual cues: Role of the STS region. *Trends in Cognitive Sciences*, 4, 267–278.

Arbib, M. A., & Rizzolatti, G. (1996). Neural expectations: A possible evolutionary path from manual skills to language. *Communication & Cognition*, 29, 393–424.

Baron-Cohen, S. (1995). *Mindblindness: An Essay on Autism and Theory of Mind*. Cambridge, MA: MIT Press.

Baron-Cohen, S., Wheelwright, S., Hill, J., Raste, Y., & Plumb, I. (2001). The reading the mind in the eyes test revised version: A study with normal adults, and adults with Asperger syndrome or high-functioning autism. *Journal of Child Psychology and Psychiatry*, 42, 241–251.

Bavelas, J. B., Black, A., Lemery, C. R., & Mullett, J. (1986). "I show how you feel": Motor mimicry as a communicative act. *Journal of Personality and Social Psychology*, 50, 322–329.

Blakemore, S. J., & Decety, J. (2001). From the perception of action to the understanding of intention. *Nature Reviews Neuroscience*, 2, 561–567.

Blakemore, S. J., & Frith, C. (2005). The role of motor contagion in the prediction of action. *Neuropsychologia*, 43, 260–267.

Blandin, Y., Lhuisset, L., & Proteau, L. (1999). Cognitive processes underlying observational learning of motor skills. *Quarterly Journal of Experimental Psychology: Human Experimental Psychology*, 52(A), 957–979.

Brass, M., Bekkering, H., & Prinz, W. (2001). Movement observation affects movement execution in a simple response task. *Acta Psychologica*, 106, 3–22.

Brass, M., Bekkering, H., Wohlschlager, A., & Prinz, W. (2000). Compatibility between observed and executed finger movements: Comparing symbolic, spatial, and imitative cues. *Brain and Cognition*, 44, 124–143.

Bruce, V., & Young, A. (1986). Understanding face recognition. *British Journal of Psychology*, 77, 305–327.

Butterworth, G. (1998). What is special about pointing? In F. Simion & G. Butterworth G. (Eds.), *The Development of Sensory, Motor, and Cognitive Capacities in Early Infancy: From Perception to Cognition* (pp. 171–190). Hove: Psychology Press/Lawrence Erlbaum.

Campbell, R., Heywood, C., Cowey, A., Regard, M., & Landis, T. (1990). Sensitivity to eye gaze in prospagnosics patients and monkeys with superior temporal sulcus ablation. *Neuropsychologia*, 28, 1123–1142.

Castiello, U., Lusher, D., Mari, M., Edwards, M., & Humphreys, G. W. (2002). Observing a human or a robotic hand grasping an object: Differential motor priming effects. In W. Prinz & B. Hommel (Eds.), *Common Mechanisms in Perception and Action: Attention and Performance XIX* (pp. 315–333). Oxford: Oxford, University Press.

Chaminade, T., Meary, D., Orliaguet, J. P., & Decety, J. (2001). Is visual anticipation a motor simulation? A PET study. *Neuroreport*, 12, 3669–3674.

Craighero, L., Bello, A., Fadiga, L., & Rizzolatti, G. (2002). Hand action preparation influences the responses to hand pictures. *Neuropsychologia*, 40, 492–502.

Csibra, G. (2005). Action mirroring and action interpretation: An alternative account. In P. Haggard, Y. Rosetti, & M. Kawato (Eds.), *Sensorimotor Foundations of Higher Cognition. Attention and Performance XXII*. Oxford: Oxford University Press.

Deak, G. O., Flom, R., & Pick, A. D. (2000). Perceptual and motivational factors affecting joint visual attention in 12- and 18-month-olds. *Developmental Psychology*, 36, 511–523.

D'Entremont, B., Hains, S. M. J., & Muir, D. W. (1997). A demonstration of gaze following in 3- to 6-month-olds. *Infant Behavior and Development*, 20, 569–572.

di Pellegrino, G., Fadiga, L., Fogassi, L., Gallese, V., and Rizzolatti, G. (1992). Understanding motor events: A neurophysiological study. *Experimental Brain Research*, 91, 176–180.

Dijksterhuis, A., & Bargh, J. A. (2001). The perception–behavior expressway: Automatic effects of social perception on social behavior. *Advances in Experimental Social Psychology*, 33, 1–39.

Dolan, R. J., Fink, G. R., Rolls, E., Booth, M., Holmes, A., Frackowiak, R. S. J., & Friston, K. J. (1997). How the brain learns to see objects and faces in an impoverished context. *Nature*, 389(9), 596–599.

Downing, P. E., Dodds, M. C., & Bray, D. (2004). Why does the gaze of others direct visual attention? *Visual Cognition*, 11(1), 71–79.

Driver, J., Davis, G., Ricciardelli, P., Kidd, P., Maxwell, E., & Baron-Cohen, S. (1999). Gaze perception triggers reflexive visuospatial orienting. *Visual Cognition*, 6(5), 509–540.

Edwards, M. G., Humphreys, G. W., & Castiello, U. (2003). Motor facilitation following action observation: A behavioural study in prehensile action. *Brain and Cognition*, 53, 495–502.

Ekman, P. (1982). *Emotion in the Human Face*. New York: Cambridge University Press.

Emery, N. J. (2000). The eyes have it: The neuroethology, function and evolution of social gaze. *Neuroscience and Biobehavioral Reviews*, 24, 581–604.

Fadiga, L., Fogassi, L., Pavesi, G., & Rizzolatti, G. (1995). Motor facilitation during action observation: A magnetic stimulation study. *Journal of Neurophysiology*, 73, 2608–2611.

Farroni, T., Csibra, G., Simion, F., & Johnson, M. (2002). Eye contact detection at birth. *Proceedings of the National Academy of Science*, 99, 9602–9605.

Fogassi, L., Ferrari, P. F., Gesierich, B., Rozzi S., Ch'ersi, F., & Rizzolatti G. (2005). Parietal lobe: From action organization to intention understanding. *Science*, 308, 662–667.

Fischer, M. H., & Szymkowiak, A. (2004). Joint attention for pointing but not grasping postures. *Cortex*, 40, 168–170.

Friesen, C. K., & Kingstone, A. (1998). The eyes have it! Reflexive orienting is triggered by non-predictive gaze. *Psychonomic Bulletin and Review*, 5(3), 490–495.

Gallagher, S. (2001). The practice of mind theory: Simulation or primary interaction? *Journal of Consciousness Studies*, 8(5–7), 83–108.

Gallese, V., Fadiga, L., Fogassi, L., & Rizzolatti, G. (1996). Action recognition in the premotor cortex. *Brain*, 119, 593–609.

Gallese, V., & Goldman, A. (1998). Mirror neurons and the simulation theory of mind-reading. *Trends in Cognitive Science*, 3, 493–501.

Gallese, V., Keysers, C., & Rizzolatti, G. (2004). A unifying view of the basis of social cognition. *Trends in Cognitive Science*, 8(9), 396–403.

Goldman, A. (1989). Interpretation psychologized. *Mind and Language*, 4, 161–185.

Gordon, R. (1986). Folk psychology as simulation. *Mind and Language*, 1, 158–171.

Greenwald, A. G. (1970). Sensory feedback mechanisms in performance control: With special reference to the ideomotor mechanism. *Psychological Review*, 77, 73–99.

Haxby, J. V., Hoffman, E. A., & Gobbini, M. I. (2000). The distributed human neural system for face perception. *Trends in Cognitive Science*, 4, 223–233.

Haxby, J., Ungerleider, L., Clark, V., Schouten, J., Hoffman, E., & Martin, A. (1999). The effect of face inversion on activity in human neural systems for face and object perception. *Neuron*, 22, 189–199.

Heyes, C. M., Bird, G., Johnson, H., & Haggard, P. (2005). Experience modulates automatic imitation. *Cognitive Brain Research*, 22, 233–240.

Hietanen, J. K. (1999). Does your gaze direction and head orientation shift my visual attention? *Neuroreport*, 10(16), 3443–3447.

Hommel, B., Müsseler, J., Aschersleben, G., & Prinz, W. (2001). The theory of event coding (TEC): A framework for perception and action planning. *Behavioral and Brain Sciences*, 24, 849–937.

Hood, B. M., Willen, J. D., & Driver, J. (1998). Adult's eyes trigger shifts of visual attention in human infants. *Psychological Science*, 9, 131–134.

Iacoboni, M., Molnar-Szakacs, I., Gallese, V., Buccino, G., Mazziotta, J. C., & Rizzolatti, G. (2005). Grasping the intentions of others with one's own mirror neuron system. *Public Library of Science*, 3, 529–535.

Iacoboni, M., Woods, R. P., Brass, M., Bekkering, H., Mazziotta, J. C., & Rizzolatti, G. (1999). Cortical mechanisms of human imitation. *Science*, 286, 2526–2528.

Jacob, P., & Jeannerod, M. (2005). The motor theory of social cognition: A critique. *Trends in Cognitive Science*, 9, 21–25.

James, W. (1870). *Principles of Psychology*. New York: Holt.

Jeannerod, M. (2001). Neural simulation of action: A unifying mechanism for motor cognition. *NeuroImage*, 14, 103–109.

Kanwisher, N. G., McDermott, J., & Chun, M. M. (1997).The fusiform face area: A module in human extrastriate cortex specialized for face perception. *Journal of Neuroscience*, 17, 4302–4311.

Kleinke, C. L. (1986). Gaze and eye contact: a research review. *Psychological Bulletin*, 100, 78–100.

Kobayashi, H., & Kohshima, S. (1997). Unique morphology of the human eye. *Nature*, 387, 767–768.

Kingstone, A., Friesen, C. K., & Gazzaniga, M. S. (2000). Reflexive joint attention depends on lateralized cortical connection, *Psychological Science*, 11, 159–166.

Kingstone, A., Tipper, C., Ristic, J., & Ngan, E. (2004). The eyes have it!: An fMRI investigation. *Brain and Cognition*, 55, 269–271.

Knoblich, G., & Flach, R. (2001). Predicting the effects of actions: Interactions of perception and action. *Psychological Science*, 12, 467–472.

Knoblich, G., & Jordan, J. S. (2003). Action coordination in groups and individuals: Learning anticipatory control. *Journal of Experimental Psychology: Learning, Memory, & Cognition*, 29, 1006–1016.

Lakin, J. L., & Chartrand, T. L. (2003). Using nonconscious behavioral mimicry to create affiliation and rapport. *Psychological Science*, 14, 334–339.

Langton, S. R. (2000). The mutual influence of gaze and head orientation in the analysis of social attention direction. *Quarterly Journal of Experimental Psychology: Human Experimental Psychology*, 53, 825–845.

Langton, S. R. H., & Bruce, V. (1999). Reflexive visual orienting in response to the social attention of others. *Visual Cognition*, 6, 541–567.

Langton, S. R. H., Watt, R. J., & Bruce, V. (2000). Do the eyes have it? Cues to the direction of social attention. *Trends in Cognitive Sciences*, 4(2), 50–59.

Lotze, R. H. (1852). *Medicinische Psychologie oder Physiologie der Seele*. Leipzig: Weidmann.

McCarthy, G. (1999). Physiological studies of face processing in humans. In M. S. Gazzaniga (Ed.), *The New Cognitive Neurosciences* (pp. 393–410). Cambridge, MA: MIT Press.

Meltzoff, A. N., & Decety, J. (2003). What imitation tells us about social cognition: A rapprochement between developmental psychology and cognitive neuroscience. *Philosophical Transactions of the Royal Society (Series B)*, 358, 491–500.

Nuku, P., & Bekkering, H. (forthcoming a). Joint attention: Inferring what others perceive (and don't perceive).

Nuku, P., & Bekkering, H. (forthcoming b). When one sees what the others hear: A crossmodal attentional modulation for gazed (and non-gazed) auditory targets.

Nuku, P., Lindemann, O., & Bekkering, H. (forthcoming). Grasping another's intention: Purposeful actions attract attention.

Nuku, P., Lindemann, O., Bekkering, H., & Fischer, M. (forthcoming). Joint attention in action observation: inferring another's action intentions modulates visual attention.

Posner, M. I. (1978). *Chronometric Explorations of Mind*. Hillsdale, NJ: Lawrence Erlbaum.

Posner, M. I. (1980). Orienting of attention. *Quarterly Journal of Experimental Psychology*, 32, 3–25.

Puce, A., Allison, T., Bentin, S., Gore, J. C., & McCarthy, G. (1998). Temporal cortex activation in humans viewing eye and mouth movements. *Journal of Neuroscience*, 18, 2188–2199.

Prinz, W. (1990). A common coding approach to perception and action. In O. Neumann & W. Prinz (Eds.), *Relationships between Perception and Action: Current Approaches* (pp. 167–203). New York, Berlin, & Heidelberg: Springer.

Riddoch, M. J., Humphreys, G. W., Edwards, S., Baker, T., & Wilson, K. (2003). Seeing the action: Neuropsychological evidence for action-based effects on object selection. *Nature Neuroscience*, 6, 82–89.

Rizzolatti, G., & Craighero, L. (2004). The Mirror-Neuron System. *Annual Review of Neuroscience*, 27, 169–192.

Rizzolatti, G., Fadiga, L., Gallese, V., & Fogassi, L. (1996). Premotor cortex and the recognition of motor actions. *Cognitive Brain Research*, 3, 131–141.

Rizzolatti, G., Fadiga, L., Matelli, M., Bettinardi, V., Paulesu, E., Perani, D., & Fazio, G. (1996). Localization of grasp representations in humans by PET: 1. Observation vs. execution. *Experimental Brain Research*, 111, 246–252.

Rizzolatti, G., Fogassi, L., & Gallese, V. (2001). Neurophysiological mechanisms underlying the understanding and imitation of action. *Nature Neuroscience Review*, 2(9), 661–70.

Rizzolatti, G., Fogassi, L., & Gallese, V. (2002). Motor and cognitive functions of the ventral premotor cortex. *Current Opinion in Neurobiology*, 12: 149–154.

Saxe, R. (2005). Against simulation: The argument from error. *Trends in Cognitive Science*, 9, 174–179.

Scheerer, E. (1984). Motor theories of cognitive structure: A historical review. In W. Prinz & A. F. Sanders (Eds.), *Cognition and Motor Processes* (pp. 77–97). Berlin: Springer.

Schuller, A.-M., & Rossion, B. (2001). Spatial attention triggered by eye gaze increases and speeds up early visual activity, *Neuroreport*, 12(11), 2381–2387.

Schultz, W., & Dickinson, A. (2000). Neural coding of prediction errors. *Annual Review of Neuroscience*, 23, 473–500.

Sebanz, N., Bekkering, H., & Knoblich, G. (2006). Joint action: Bodies and minds moving together. *Trends in Cognitive Science*, 10, 70–76.

Stürmer, B., Aschersleben, G., & Prinz, W. (2000). Correspondence effects with manual gestures and postures: A study of imitation. *Journal of Experimental Psychology: Human Perception and Performance*, 26(6), 1746–1759.

Tipples, J. (2002). Eye gaze is not unique: Automatic orienting in response to uninformative arrows. *Psychonomic Bulletin and Review*, 9(2), 314–318.

Tomasello, M. (1999). *The Cultural Origins of Human Cognition*. Cambridge, MA: Harvard University Press.

Tong, F., Nakayama, K., Moscovitch, M., Weinrib, O., & Kanwisher, N. (2000). Response properties of the human fusiform face area. *Cognitive Neuropsychology*, 17, 257–279.

Vecera, S. P., & Johnson, M. H. (1995). Gaze detection and the cortical processing of faces. *Visual Cognition*, 2, 59–87.

Vogt, S., Taylor, P., & Hopkins, B. (2003). Visuomotor priming by pictures of the hand: Perspective matters. *Neuropsychologica*, 41, 941–951.

Walker-Smith, G. J., Gale, A. G., & Findlay, J. M. (1977). Eye movement strategies involved in face perception. *Perception*, 6, 313–26.

Woodward, A. L., & Guarjardo, J. J. (2002). Infants' understanding of the point gesture as an object-directed action. *Cognitive Development*, 17, 1061–1084.

Vuilleumier, P. (2002). Facial expression and selective attention. *Current Opinion in Psychiatry*, 15(3), 291–300.

Part Three

Social Cognition
during Infancy

Editors' Introduction

The amazing increase in interest on social-cognitive issues since 2002 has produced a renaissance of thinking in the developmental sciences. Rapid change has occurred in terms of the construction of new paradigms and by the application of older experimental frameworks to fresh questions. At the same time, fundamental questions have been examined. What does it mean to be a social entity, and why have humans developed this capacity? What is the ontogeny of key social behaviors and how do these milestones come to pass? What are their precursors? Recently, electrophysiological evidence for social information-processing capacities has been investigated. This new strand of research stands to fill in many blanks, particularly in areas of development where the measurement of overt behavior fails to parse infant capabilities in complex social tasks, such as joint attention or emotion processing. The chapters in this section provide overviews of key issues in developmental psychology, together with new information on these topics. They show how this work can be of assistance to issues raised by related topics, such as autism research.

An area that has generated much debate (both heated and fruitful) derives from the infant's understanding of goal-directed action. Among key interpretations of infant abilities is the teleological stance. Ildikó Király presents new data from an imitation paradigm on how the teleological stance changes with the emergence of language skills. It is suggested that this ability is fundamental in the emergence of later memory abilities. Research into the understanding of goals and intentions in early infancy has produced some remarkable findings since 2000. Petra Hauf points out that work investigating action perception must be tied to action production. In her review of her recent work, she shows that these two abilities are indeed linked by 9 months of age. Birgit Elsner provides a comprehensive review of the effects of tool use on infant understanding of others and their goals. An issue that has fascinated us for some time is how humans early in development are capable of determining complex social information when other cognitive capacities, such as memory, are poor. Our attempt to explain these anomalies and how they can be reconciled has led to the construction of a model of infant information processing: the Directed Attention Hypothesis, which we outline in our chapter (Reid & Striano, Chapter 11), together with new evidence for its existence. Tobias Grossmann and Amrisha Vaish outline models of infant face-processing capacities. This work suggests that there are many areas that require exploration before definitive conclusions can be made on a host of key issues. This is despite face processing being perhaps the most well-investigated area of early social cognition. Finally, Stefanie Hoehl outlines new work on early emotion processing. This topic demonstrates the bridging of areas within developmental psychology. In the mid-1990s, eye gaze, facial expression, and intention were all being considered in isolation. Hoehl shows that this is no longer the case, with areas now merged together, thereby producing new testable theories on developmental processes that might otherwise have been left unnoticed.

The overall effect of this part is of a field that is in a state of remarkable change. Despite the accumulation of a wealth of knowledge over generations, it is clear that there is much more that is not known about social cognition in human development when that is contrasted with what is known. The problem for developmental psychology is how we advance the field from here and in which directions. The chapters in this section provide us with strong hints for both these questions.

Chapter 8

Memories for Events in Infants: Goal-Relevant Action Coding

Ildikó Király

Introduction: The Role of Goal Understanding in Memory Research

Research concerning adult event representation has revealed a remarkable body of evidence regarding the organizing role of goals. Investigations of different representational forms of events, such as narratives (Mandler & Johnson, 1977), observed action sequences (Lichtenstein & Brewer, 1980), and abstract knowledge of routine behaviours (Schank and Abelson, 1977), all share the basic assumption that adults appear to impose the interpretative framework of goal-directed action on the human behavior they encounter. The main knowledge structures that are based on goals support segmenting of the continuous flow of action sequences into actions with boundaries (like episodes in text reading – Black & Bower, 1979), identifying relevant knowledge (like scripts – Schank and Abelson, 1977), and establishing valuable hierarchical organization in memory (like plans – Lichtenstein & Brewer, 1980). Thus goal-based organization seems to play a primary role in adult event representations.

The problem of developmental continuity in the organization of event representations has initiated numerous studies investigating older children's event representations. As early as the age of 4, children display event representations that incorporate information about temporal order, causal relations, and goals: their verbal reports on earlier events are skeletal but include only such elements that adults would recount (Nelson & Gruendel, 1986). Thus, children's event memory resembles adult event memory with respect to goal-based organization, even if they use less complex forms of representations (Fivush, Kuebli, & Clubb, 1992; Nelson & Fivush, 2000). Nevertheless, much less evidence is available for younger children, such as non-verbal toddlers.

Support for early organized event representations comes from an experiment in which irrelevant elements were inserted into novel action sequences. The elicited imitation study of Bauer & Mandler (1989), revealed the assumption that causal-enabling relations between event components facilitate organization to entail better retrieval of action sequences. Infants (of 16 and 20 months) could retrieve novel events imitating their components while omitting or displacing their irrelevant components if there were causal relations between their event steps. Causal-enabling relations in an action determine the only meaningful temporal order of the event components that lead to the targeted outcome, and as such can support the memory organization of it. Events and actions in the world, however, do not always possess such inherent, enabling temporal organization; there are events with unbound temporal relations among their goal-relevant components. For instance, when someone would like to make a cup of cocoa, it is up to the actor's habit whether he or she puts milk or cocoa powder into the cup first, before mixing them to attain the very same tasty drink. According to Bauer and Mandler (1989), the improvement in retrieval of events containing enabling relations in comparison to events lacking such inherent structure was evidenced by superior ordered recall. This suggests that toddlers are sensitive to temporal irreversibility. Furthermore, causal structure as a source of information on temporal organization enhances memory tracing. An alternative explanation for the better "recall" of events containing enabling relations is that planning on the basis of goal-state configuration is enough for the reconstruction of these types of events, since goal information in itself can guide the threading of related event components.

In a further study, to test whether the improved recall performance of events containing enabling relations was due to problem solving rather then retrieval from memory, Bauer Schwade, Wewerka, and Delaney (1992) presented infants (of only 20 months) with the goal-state configuration both of enabling event sequences and of event sequences lacking such structure (the action sequences necessary to reach the goals were not demonstrated). The performance of infants after they had been encouraged to produce the entire event was poor; they rarely demonstrated the target sequences, and they were no more successful with enabling sequences than they were with arbitrary sequences. Somewhat in contradiction to this result, Bauer et al. (1999) showed that 20- and 27-month-old infants were able to use goal-state information to support their planning attempts in the case of novel enabling events, providing evidence on the assumption that goal-state configuration has a central organizational role, though in a problem-solving context.

A possible solution to the above puzzle is raised by a study by Carpenter, Call, and Tomasello (2002). The authors have shown that prior exposure to the end-state or outcome configuration of an action sequence, followed by full modelling of the target action sequence, results in superior performance in imitation of event components as compared to exposure just to the full modelling of the event. This result confirms that goal information plays a central role in the interpretation and encoding of events, and that it is a major factor in the organization of events for later retrieval, as prior information on the end-state of the event facilitates the monitoring of event components.

In a task that required infants to represent relations between temporally separated actions and their converging structure, in which multiple actions served to enable a single outcome, Travis (1997) was able to show that 24-month-olds were capable of representing and imitating elements of an event in relation to its goal-based hierarchical structure. In particular, in the case of an event with embedded goal-irrelevant steps (in which two otherwise independent actions enabled a third action), infants grouped actions related to a common goal temporally, and reproduced goal-relevant action more than goal-irrelevant actions. The results clearly prove that 2-year-olds are able to represent converging causal structure, which is a characteristic of goal-directed action organization.

The importance of the early availability of goal-based organization can be apprehended in the fast parsing and identification of event types, and probably in forming general event representations. Despite the fact that there is empirical evidence that goal information plays a central role in the organization of event representations in the first years too, in the domain of memory development the notion of teleological stance is not widely appreciated. Teleological stance – an early interpretative schema for action coding proposed by Gergely and Csibra (1998) – is a convenient frame for guiding the perception and encoding of relevant, adequate ("real") components of events, even after only one brief exposure to them. The significance of this model lies in its power to clarify the central role of goal information in action representations through describing the inference structure and basic mechanism of interpretation as mediated and triggered by the rationality principle.

The aim of the present chapter is to introduce the consequences and experimental implementation of the model of teleological stance in the domain of imitative learning and memory development.

Early Interpretative Scheme for Action Understanding: The Teleological Stance

The theory of the teleological stance is based on the results of a series of habituation studies (Csibra, Bíró, Koós, & Gergely, 2003; Csibra, Gergely, Bíró, Koós, & Brockbank 1999; Gergely, Nádasdy, Csibra, & Bíró, 1995) that demonstrated goal attribution in 9- and 12-month-olds. These studies pointed out that by at least 9 months of age infants can (a) attribute goals to observed actions; (b) do so even if the agents are unfamiliar abstract entities that lack human features; (c) evaluate the relative efficiency of the goal approach in relation to the situational constraints on actions; and (d), if the relevant environmental constraints change, expect the agent to modify or change its means action adaptively to achieve efficient goal attainment in the new situation (Csibra et al., 1999, Csibra et al., 2003; Gergely et al., 1995).

Findings since 2000 confirmed that even 6-month-olds are able to interpret an ongoing action within the frame of the teleological stance: at this age infants are willing to attribute goals to humans and human-like robots (Kamewari, Kato,

Kanda, Ishiguro, & Hiraki, 2005) and to any kind of inanimate object if it appears to be able to vary its goal approach (Csibra, forthcoming).

To account for these findings, Csibra and Gergely proposed that infants are equipped with an abstract and domain-specific action interpretation system, the teleological stance (Csibra & Gergely, 1998; Gergely & Csibra, 1998, 2003). Briefly, the teleological stance is a representational system that relates three kinds of elements in a specific type of (teleological) explanatory structure: (a) action: the observed behaviour, (b) goal: the consequent change of state in the world, and (c) situational constraints: the relevant aspects of the situation that constrain actions leading to the goal. An essential component of the teleological stance is the "principle of rational action". This principle is responsible for (a) driving inferences about goal-directed actions and, at the same time, for (b) providing criteria of well-formedness for teleological action interpretations. The importance of the rationality principle is rooted in the piece of evidence that it can guide the selection of goal-related (in contrast to unrelated), or goal-relevant (in contrast to goal-irrelevant) acts, as it can guide the online assessment of the ongoing action sequence. The mechanism of continuous evaluation by the rationality principle allows us to predict the outcome of an ongoing action just by assuming that it is a "direct way toward" an end-state or outcome or (in this case obviously) a goal.

Teleological Stance and Imitation: The Selective Interpretative Nature of Imitative Learning in Human Infants

In the domain of memory development, Meltzoff (1988) has demonstrated that infants are able to re-enact – that is, retrieve novel actions – after a one-week delay; in other words, infants are able very early on imitatively to learn novel means actions by way of observing others. In the most impressive task of the above mentioned study, 14-month-olds watched as a human model leaned forward from the waist and touched the top panel of a light box with her forehead, thereby illuminating it. A week later, 67 per cent of the infants re-enacted the novel "head action," while none performed it in a base-line control group for whom the action was not demonstrated. This result was an obvious indicator of long-term memory retention in infants for a specific event. Alternatively, this result seemed unexpected from the point of view of the 1-year-old's teleological stance (Csibra and Gergely, 1998), since, on the grounds of this model, one would have expected that in this task infants, as rational agents, should have performed the most efficient goal-directed action available to them (using their hand to contact the light box), instead of imitating the unique, but less efficient, "head action."

To clarify this situation, Gergely, Bekkering, and Király (2002) performed a modified version of Meltzoff's task (1988). They hypothesized that "if infants noticed that the demonstrator declined to use her hands despite the fact that they were free, they may have inferred that the head action must offer some advantage in turning on the light. They therefore used the same action themselves in the same situation" (Gergely et al., 2002, p. 755). To test this idea, Gergely and colleagues tested two groups of 14-month-olds varying the situational constraints of the model. In the "hands-occupied" condition, the model's hands were visibly occupied: she pretended to be chilly and wrapped a blanket around her shoulders, holding it with both hands while performing the "head action." In the "hands-free" condition, however, after wrapping the blanket around her shoulders, the model placed her hands onto the table, so that they were visibly free, before demonstrating the "head action."

When the model's hands were occupied, 14-month-olds were less likely to imitate the "head action" (21 percent). Instead, they illuminated the box by touching it with their hand, performing the simpler, and equally effective, emulative response available to them, but not to the model. In contrast, when the model's hands were free, but she still used her head to illuminate the box, 69 per cent of 14-month-olds imitated her "head action" (p < 0.02) (this result is a replication of Meltzoff's results of 1988). So, differential imitation in the two conditions suggests that imitative learning is not an automatic "copying" process invoked by identification with the human actor, nor is it due to automatic behavioral "copying" of the modeled action. Rather, imitative learning is a selective interpretative process that involves the evaluation of the rationality of the means in relation to the situational constraints of the actor. Thus, re-enactment of the novel means takes place only if (a) the action is judged as rational given the situational constraints of the model, and (b) the action is judged as more rational than other available alternatives given the situational constraints of the infant him or herself.

With their recent model of human pedagogy, Gergely and Csibra (2005) shed new light on the constraints of teleological action interpretation. Their theory's main argument is

> that Mother Nature's "trick" to make fast and efficient learning of complex – and, for the learner, cognitively "opaque" – cultural knowledge possible was to have humans evolve specialized cognitive resources that form a dedicated interpersonal system of mutual design in which one is predisposed to "teach" and to "learn" new and relevant cultural information to (and from) conspecifics. (pp. 471–472)

A fundamental statement of their argument is that expert humans who possess cultural knowledge are disposed not only to use, but also ostensively to manifest, their knowledge to inexpert conspecifics, and inexpert conspecifics are specially receptive to ostensive communicative manifestations of others.

Briefly, the model of Human pedagogy outlines three major constituents that serve pedagogical knowledge transfer. First, there is a design specification that an expert conspecific (a "teacher") *ostensively communicates* her cultural knowledge by *manifesting* it for the novice (the "learner") with the help of *referential cues* (such as eye contact, turn-taking contingency). Secondly, because of her *special kind of receptivity*, the learner is predisposed to interpret the teacher's ostensive-communicative cues that accompany her knowledge manifestation as evidence that the manifestation will convey *new* and *relevant* cultural information for her. As a consequence, this allows fast learning of the communicated content without any further need to test its relevance independently. Thirdly, the built-in *presumption of relevance* of pedagogically communicated knowledge manifestations also enables the acquisition of knowledge contents that are *arbitrary, conventional*, and causally/functionally *non-transparent*, which stand for many forms of cultural knowledge.

The selective imitational findings of the Gergely et al. (2002) study is a nice example of how pedagogy operates: how infants infer differentially in two conditions what is new and relevant information for them (see also the argument of Gergely & Csibra, 2005). In the "hands-occupied" condition of the head-on-box study, the novel outcome, including the presented property of the object (illuminability-upon-contact), is the *new* information, so it is going to be retained in memory and reproduced through action. Taking the teleological stance in this case, infants can infer that, given the physical constraints of the actor (hands occupied), touching the box with her forehead is justified as a sensible and efficient means to the goal, as the physical-causal efficiency of the "head action" is cognitively "transparent" here.

In the "hands-free" condition the situation is different. The goal state involving the newly experienced affordance of the box is *new* information here, too, so it will be reproduced. In contrast, when setting up a teleological interpretation as to what particular action would constitute the most rational/efficient means to the goal under these situational constraints, given the fact that the actor's hands were free, the infant must have identified the available "hand action" as the most efficient means to perform. Unexpectedly, however, the demonstrator chose not to use her free hands, but performed the unusual "head action" instead. This contrastive choice marked the "head-action" as *new* and *relevant* information that the ostensive-communicative manifestation conveyed. As a result, both the new goal *and the new means* were retained and imitated.

The head-on-box study (Gergely et al., 2002) from this perspective confirms that pedagogical cues are necessary factors for imitative learning in human infants, although (1) there is interpretative selectivity guiding what aspect of the modeled behavior will be imitatively learned, and (2) this is directed by the implicit assumptions of the infant's "pedagogical stance" – namely, that the observed individual is about to manifest "for" them some significant aspect of cultural knowledge that will be *new* and *relevant*.

Relevance-Guided Selective Imitation: Verbal Labels Serving Human Pedagogy

Regarding the domain of memory development, it is a normal and common feature of imitational paradigms that the target event is presented in a rich ostensive context, comprising *communicative-referential speech acts* and overt verbal instructions (for example, "Look, I'll show you something!") before the target action is demonstrated. Such speech acts or short verbal instructions (labels) could enrich any situation in a Gricean sense, letting the observer perceive the actor's/speaker's intent of presenting something new and relevant. These assumptions are directly analogous, if not identical, to the Gricean pragmatic assumptions of ostensive communication, as made obvious by Sperber and Wilson (1986). From a slightly different perspective, however, pedagogy is a primary adaptation for cultural learning that is not necessarily conscious but a cue-dependent fast-learning attitude, and not a specialized module dedicated to the recovery of the speaker's intent in linguistic communication, an assumption that has evolved later as a sub-module of human theory of mind (Sperber and Wilson, 2002). Mentalistic terms are not necessary for conceiving the understanding of relevance. Speech acts are ready to convey the intention of the speaker. At the same time, however, these verbal acts appear as part of the external situation: they convey intents or goals through setting up in advance a possible end-state and thus highlighting a possible goal as part of the external situation. This alternative goal can either correspond to or mismatch with the outcome/goal of the ongoing action sequence. Thus verbal labels can enhance the understanding of the ongoing action in terms of its goal: if the verbal act is in line with a specific end-state achieved in the following action (consistent with its "intention-in-action"), it helps the encoding of the relevant steps of the event sequence; if the uttered goal or intent and the goal of the action sequence do not overlap completely, it can alter the encoding of what is *relevant* in the situation by setting up a goal hierarchy.

Verbal instructions, as part of the communicative referential context (the external situation), can serve as overt articulation (*manifesto*) of what to learn (what is relevant) in the situation. For instance, a closer look at our example "Look, I'll show you something!" reveals that this verbal act can imply that manifestation of *new* and *relevant* information in general is a *goal* of the agent. The main purpose of a further study was to examine this supposition. To do this, we manipulated and controlled the verbal labels used in the experimental situation. Our aim was to investigate the role of verbal labels in highlighting the relevant features of the ongoing actions that are "to be encoded." Our hypothesis was that verbal labels pragmatically referring to the manifestation of new and relevant information bring about imitative learning of cognitively opaque subevents, while verbal labels that accord with the presented event sequence and end-state (that refer to a script) result in the omission of cognitively opaque subevents, even though they are part of a communicative context. To test this specific hypothesis and to reinforce the assumption that imitation is not "blind." we introduced a novel-enabling and a novel-arbitrary event, both with embedded irrelevant components, following the method of Bauer (1992; see also, Bauer & Mandler, 1989; Király, 2003;Travis, 1997). By introducing irrelevant components, the authors aimed to test the relevance-guided selective mechanism involved in imitation, since the omission or re-enactment of goal-irrelevant components of the modeled actions can inform us about the underlying mechanisms of coding and organizing processes. We would like to confirm the primary role of goal information in the encoding of actions, as well as the leading role of the teleological stance in the organization and recall of event memories in the form of imitation.

Method

Participants

The final sample consisted of seventy-seven 29-month-old infants (M = 28.9, SD = 2. 67 months, range = 24 months to 34 months), who were visited in local day-care centers and playing centers. Four additional infants were excluded from the sample, because of maternal help/interference (two) and shyness (two) during the test.

Test materials

Each infant in the experimental conditions was exposed to either a novel-enabling (Figure 8.1) or a novel-arbitrary event sequence. In the baseline-control groups infants could see only the props themselves.

Figure 8.1.   The event of "planting a flower"
Note: The presentation of the sequence was as follows: (1) taking a pot; (2) putting soil into it; (3) blowing on the flower (irrelevant step); (4) planting the flower.
Source: Courtesy of Ildikó Király (previously unpublished).

Both sequences were designed so that in each event sequence one of the event steps was irrelevant or unnecessary to the outcome of the event: one of their intermediary components was considered unimportant or irrelevant to the outcome of the event by adult raters.

Procedure

Infants were tested individually in the presence of their mothers in one of the kindergarten's playrooms. After a short warm-up period, they were seated on their mother's lap in front of a table, about 1 meter away, so that they could not reach the toy objects. The mothers were asked not to assist their children during the experimental sessions. The experimenter (an adult model) sat at the other side of the table. Elicited imitation procedure was used in which the experimenter modeled the target actions twice with the aid of the props, while commenting on these actions verbally in one of two ways, also making sure that the infant was paying attention. The sessions were video-recorded.

Two experimental conditions were introduced. In the "script or goal specification" condition, the presentation of the action sequence started with a reference to the event (by naming its purpose: "Look, I'm planting a flower" or "Look, I'm making a turtle"), while in the "pragmatically implied new information" condition the experimenter did not announce the aim of the event, instead referring to the pragmatic aim of the action itself as demonstrating new information ("Look, I'll show you something"). Her action sequence was the same in both conditions; thus she expressed the same "intention-in-action" too. In these experimental conditions the different types of events were presented to independent groups of infants. (There were 16 infants in the "pragmatic condition" with a novel-enabling event, 14 in the "script condition" with a novel-enabling event, 13 in the "pragmatic condition" with a novel-arbitrary event, and 10 in the "script condition" with a novel-arbitrary event.) During the test session the experimenter encouraged imitation with instructions such as "It is your turn now". Each of the infants was tested immediately after the modeling.

To assess the spontaneous production of target actions in the absence of adult demonstration, for each event a baseline-control group of 12 infants was exposed to the props.

Data analysis and scoring

The video-recordings of the test sessions were scored by two independent observers who were uninformed about which of the two conditions the children belonged to. The observers scored the presence or absence of each target action. Inter-observer reliability was calculated using kappa statistics ($\kappa = 0.912$).

An imitation score was calculated for each infant by summing the number of target actions produced during the test (the range for each event type was 0–4). The observers also registered the order. Using this source of data, a quantitative and also a qualitative variable were introduced to assess ordering errors. For the quantitative variable the correctly ordered pairs of actions were summed. Here, the acceptance criterion was the replication of the modeled step sequence with or without the omission of the irrelevant step. For the qualitative variable (borrowing the method from Bauer and Mandler, 1989), the subjects' performance was classified into one of three categories: (a) exact reproduction of the sequence (with the irrelevant step), (b) displacement or omission of the irrelevant component, but preserving the rest of the modeled order; (c) other ordering "errors" – for example, displacement or omission of any other target action(s).

Results

The mean imitation scores of infants in the experimental and control conditions were as follows:

novel-enabling event
    baseline control condition: Mean = 1.75 (SD = 0.62)
    script condition: Mean = 2.78, (SD = 0.57)
    pragmatic condition: Mean = 3.47, (SD = 0.5);

novel-arbitrary event
    baseline control condition: Mean = 0.53 (SD = 0.79)
    script condition: Mean = 3.1, (SD = 1.3)
    pragmatic condition: Mean = 3.5, (SD = 1.08).

An overall 2 (event type: novel enabling; novel arbitrary) × 3 (condition: pragmatic, script, baseline) analysis of variance was conducted to assess the possible quantitative differences in imitative performance in the different conditions for the novel-enabling compared to the novel-arbitrary sequence. First, there was no main effect for event type ($F(1,71) = 3.32$, n.s.); thus there was no significant difference between the performance on the novel-enabling compared to the novel-arbitrary sequence. However, there was a significant main effect for condition, $F(1,71) = 40.29$, $p < 0.001$, and there was also a significant event-type x condition interaction, $F(1, 71) = 8.07$, $p < 0.001$. Post-hoc analysis (Tukey test of significant differences at the 0.05 level) yielded that infants' performance was greater in each experimental (pragmatic and script) condition compared to the baseline-control condition. Thus, regarding both event types, infants in the experimental conditions produced more target actions than children in the baseline-control condition. The significant interaction described above can result from the variance in the difference between imitation scores in the experimental conditions, dependant on event type. To test this possibility, for each event type, imitation scores were subjected to a one-way analysis of variance.

    On the novel-enabling event sequence, there was a significant effect of condition: $F(2,39) = 17,19$, $p < 0.001$. Post-hoc analysis (Tukey test of significant differences at the 0.05 level) revealed that experimental conditions differ significantly from each other. In the pragmatic condition infants produced more target actions than in the script condition. This analysis confirmed that the performance in both experimental conditions differs significantly from baseline.

In the case of the novel-arbitrary event sequence there was a quantitative difference in infants' performance between conditions: $F(2,32) = 24.16$, $p < 0.001$. Post-hoc analysis (Tukey test of significant differences at the 0.05 level) yielded that, besides the significant difference between each experimental condition and baseline, there was no quantitative difference in the imitation scores in the two experimental conditions.

The difference between the mean of imitation scores in the experimental conditions do not clarify, however, whether this result is caused by a variation in the imitated pattern of components or not. It is likely that components are not equally produced or left out during imitation in the two experimental conditions. To test this possibility, we used non-parametric analysis to compare the number of imitators in the different experimental conditions (pragmatic versus script) for each event component, separately for event types.

In the case of the novel-enabling event, there was a significant difference only for the third component, the irrelevant step – Fisher's exact test: $p < 0.01$. In the case of the novel-arbitrary event, there was a significant difference only for the second component, again the irrelevant step – Fisher's exact test: $p < 0.05$. Table 8.1 shows the percentage of imitators for each event component in the experimental conditions.

Infants imitated the irrelevant component to a different extent in the two experimental conditions for both event types: in the pragmatic condition the imitation of the irrelevant component was more frequent than in the script condition, and this pattern of performance was the same for the novel-enabling and for the novel-arbitrary event.

In order to evaluate the performance in temporal ordering of event components, first a 2 (experimental condition: pragmatic versus script) × 2 (event type: novel arbitrary versus novel enabling) ANOVA was performed with the score for correctly ordered pairs. The descriptive statistics for the mean number of pair of actions produced in the modeled order are presented in Table 8.2. This analysis yielded a significant main effect for condition, $F(3,49) = 13.18$, $p < 0.001$, as well as for event type, $F(3, 49) = 19.0$, $p < 0.001$.

These results reflect that infants imitated more components in target order in the case of novel-enabling as compared to novel-arbitrary events. It also seems that the performance of retrieving event components in correct order was superior for the pragmatic condition; however, this effect can appear to be due to the higher imitation scores (which results in higher ordering scores). With the overall qualitative categories for ordering errors, this problem can be eliminated. Therefore, infants' performance was classified by whether they (a) reproduced the sequence exactly as modeled, (b) omitted (or displaced) the irrelevant component, but preserved the rest of the modeled order, (c) made other ordering errors. The percentage of infants in each category is shown in Table 8.2. To test whether there is a different pattern of ordering errors with respect to event type, a non-parametric test was conducted with combined data from the two experimental conditions. This analysis

Table 8.1. The percentage of imitators for each event component in the experimental conditions

	Condition	
Event sequence	*Pragmatic condition*	*Script condition*
Novel enabling: "Planting a Flower		
1 Taking a pot	100	86
2 Putting soil in it	100	100
3 *Blowing the flower*	**50**	**0**
4 Planting the flower	100	100
Novel arbitrary: "Making a Turtle"		
1 Fixing a leg to the "body"	80	85
2 *Throwing a little cube into it*	**100**	**61**
3 Fixing another leg to it	90	85
4 Putting the back on the turtle	80	85

Table 8.2. The mean number of pairs of actions produced in the modeled order and the percentage of infants in each category of ordering errors

	Condition	
Event sequence	*Pragmatic condition*	*Script condition*
Novel enabling: "Planting a Flower"		
Mean	2.45	1.71
SD	0.51	0.73
Correct ordering (%)	44	0
Omission (or displacement) of irrelevant component (%)	50	86
Other ordering errors (%)	6	14
Novel arbitrary: "Making a Turtle"		
Mean	1.54	0.61
SD	1.03	1.43
Correct ordering (%)	10	7.5
Omission (or displacement) of irrelevant component (%)	20	7.5
Other ordering errors (%)	70	85

yielded a significant difference between the pattern of ordering errors on the novel-enabling compared to the novel-arbitrary event, $\chi^2 = 25.58$ (df = 2), p < 0.001. A separate analysis for each event type revealed that ordering errors were more likely in the script conditions; however, in the case of the enabling sequence ($\chi^2 = 8,04$, df = 2, p < 0.05), as is clearly visible in Table 8.2, infants in the pragmatic condition were more likely to produce the components in the correct order with the irrelevant component, while, in the case of the novel-arbitrary sequence ($\chi^2 = 0,85$, df = 2, n.s.), there was no significant difference in the pattern of ordering errors between the two experimental conditions.

Discussion

Since one of the main purposes of the study was to emphasize the role of teleological stance in the encoding and organization of actions, two different event sequences were used, a novel-enabling and a novel-arbitrary one. Our studies reinforced that children of 28 months re-enacted the elements of novel-enabling and novel-arbitrary events equally well.

Children performed better in the recall of the novel-enabling event sequence as compared to the novel-arbitrary one in only one respect: the recollection of its original temporal order, which can be interpreted as a consequence of the difference in the teleological organization of the event. In the case of enabling events there is only one specific, optimal way of attaining the goal, and this coincides with the original order of presentation in the modeling situation. Meanwhile, in the case of arbitrary events, there are several possible arrangements that are equally efficient in arriving at the same outcome, one of which is presented in the modeling situation. With regard to "teleology," this means that in the case of novel-enabling events the presented order of the subevents is the most effective way for attaining the outcome, while in the case of novel-arbitrary events the presented order of the event steps is only one of several equally efficient possibilities. Thus, an ordering error in the case of an enabling event impairs its efficiency in goal attainment, while variations in temporal order in the case of an arbitrary event bring about the same end result. The differential degrees of re-enactment in the two conditions indicate that goal information is actively used by 28-month-olds to evaluate the causal relevance of event components and as a consequence confirmed our claim that imitation is not a "blind" process.

Our studies demonstrate the continued centrality of the teleological stance in encoding action sequences in terms of goals and suggest that goal information is a primary organizing factor in the formation of event representations. From the perspective of investigating the memory performance of infants, our study reinforced (1) that infants encode the components of novel enabling as well as novel arbitrary events, though (2) they do not recall (code) the ordering information in the case of arbitrary events.

An important claim of ours was that verbal labels (we systematically varied them in our conditions) guide what to encode as goal-relevant information in the situation. Even though the demonstrated events were identical, infants in the "pragmatically implied new information" condition produced more target actions than in the "script or goal specification" condition for both event types. Moreover, in the pragmatic condition the imitation of the irrelevant component was more frequent than in the script condition, and this pattern of performance was the same for the novel-enabling and the novel-arbitrary event. With the help of a speech act that referred to a forthcoming manifestation of something *new* and *relevant*, infants selectively imitated an irrelevant, thus new and cognitively opaque, subevent. Within the framework of human pedagogy, we can assume that the model's ostensive communicative cues led infants to attend to the modeling, ready to apply their explanatory schemes to infer which aspects of the manifested behavior convey *new* and *relevant* information. In the "script or goal specification condition" the verbal label underlines the goal of the ongoing action, by reinforcing its specific end-state. Applying the teleological stance towards actions, infants can infer that the utterance of the actor calls their attention to the most efficient, optimal attainment of the expressed goal. Accordingly, they encode (and recall in imitation) only the adequate event steps leading to the specific outcome – the most efficient way of achieving the goal – as new and relevant information. At the same time, they omit the irrelevant step that is incomprehensible for them in the given situation.

In the "pragmatically implied new information" condition the verbal label refers implicitly to the manifestation of something new and relevant *in general*. Our data reinforced that both the goal-relevant components and the unexpected, new-event component (that was irrelevant with respect to the outcome of the situation) were imitated. Accordingly, our results reinforce our claim that, though pedagogical context highlights what is new and relevant, and is thus worth learning in a situation, at the same time teleological action interpretation guides the selection of what is to be imitated. So we would argue that pragmatic verbal instruction alters the analysis and set-up of the goal hierarchy of the event. With the general aim being that of learning something new and relevant, the overall goal of the situation can be an "interesting" attainment of the same outcome. Therefore, infants carefully monitor the whole event sequence. They definitely apprehend the intention-in-action of the event; they encode the adequate event components leading to a specific outcome. Simultaneously, they focus on the cognitively opaque subevent highlighted by the pragmatic verbal label. In this case, the teleological interpretation is launched on a more sophisticated overall goal: to fulfill the requirements of effective attainment of this, infants encode and later imitate the interesting cognitively opaque subevent of it as well.

Both of the verbal labels we used appeared in an ostensive communicative context: the verbal labels served to point to what is relevant and new in the situation. It is a question of whether ostensive-communicative cues are in themselves sufficient to trigger imitation or not; however, we suppose that the behavior should receive an at least partially completed interpretation, an understanding highlighted by a "mode of construal" available to them. One of the prosperous candidates here is teleology, as it is able to account for selective imitation: teleological action interpretation can in itself be a scheme for what aspects of the observed behavior should be copied and what aspects should be omitted. Meanwhile, verbal labels as external sources of information take part in setting up the goal hierarchy of the situation. In the "pragmatically implied new information" condition the strong prediction of the pedagogical model in itself would be that only the new, irrelevant component emerges in the imitative performance of infants. Disputing with this claim, we would argue that, in the case of our action sequences, the relation of the means actions and the goal (thus their "intention-in-action") is quite transparent, so that the observer can conceive the means–end sequence with the help of teleological action interpretation. Our results confirmed that infants can encode and later retrieve not just the new and relevant event step but also the adequate means sequence in the pragmatic condition. Implicit, pragmatic reference to a forthcoming new and interesting information leaves a set of possible goals open, prevalent enough to help the encoding of the cognitively opaque subevent that is irrelevant with respect to the end-state achieved in the action. In the case of the script, verbal labeling of the goal expressed by the verbal act and the intention-in-action are in accordance, which deepens the encoding of the goal of the ongoing action as the most relevant information in the situation. Using the teleological interpretation, infants omit the cognitively opaque subevent, and selectively imitate the relevant event steps of the action.

In sum, we can conclude that two major interacting factors guiding action interpretation and encoding in infants are the teleological principle and the overall aim of the demonstration situation as expressed in the verbal label communicated in the pedagogical context by the demonstrator. While the former serves as a selective frame that determines the automatic selection of goal-relevant event components, the latter may reinforce this selection or extend it with novel, goal-irrelevant elements. Our study revealed the importance of the teleological stance in encoding action sequences in terms of goals and reinforced that goal information is a primary organizing factor influencing the mnemonic performance of infants through guiding the formation of general event representations.

Note

The research outlined in this paper was supported by a grant from OTKA (T 047071) and by a Bolyai Research Grant to Ildikó Király.

References

Bauer, P. J. (1992). Holding it all together: How enabling relations facilitate young children's event recall. *Cognitive Development*, 7, 1–28.

Bauer, P. J., & Mandler, J. M. (1989). One thing follows another: Effects of temporal structure on 1- to 2-year-olds' recall of events. *Developmental Psychology*, 25, 197–206.

Bauer, P. J., Schwade, J. A., Wewerka, S. S., & Delaney, K. (1999). Planning ahead: Goal directed problem solving by 2-year-olds. *Developmental Psychology*, 35(5), 1320–1337.

Black, J. B., & Bower, G. H. (1979). Episodes as chunks in narrative memory. *Journal of Verbal Learning and Verbal Behaviour*, 18, 309–318.

Carpenter, M., Call, J., & Tomasello, M. (2002). Understanding "prior intentions" enables 2-year-olds to imitatively learn a complex task. *Child Development*, 73, 1431–1441.

Csibra, G. (forthcoming). Goal attribution to inanimate agents by 6.5-month-old infants. *Cognition.*

Csibra, G., Bíró, S., Koós, O., & Gergely, G. (2003). One-year-old infants use teleological representations of actions productively. *Cognitive Science*, 27(1), 111–133.

Csibra, G., & Gergely, G. (1998). The teleological origins of mentalistic action explanations: A developmental hypothesis. *Developmental Science*, 1(2), 255–259.

Csibra, G., Gergely, G., Bíró, S., Koós, O., & Brockbank, M. (1999). Goal attribution without agency cues: The perception of "pure reason" in infancy. *Cognition*, 72, 237–267.

Fivush, R., Kuebli, J., & Clubb, P. (1992). The structure of events and event representations: A developmental analysis. *Child Development*, 63, 188–201.

Gergely, G., Bekkering, H., & Király, I. (2002). Rational imitation in preverbal infants. *Nature*, 415, 755.

Gergely, G., & Csibra, G. (2003). Teleological reasoning about actions: The naïve theory of rational action. *Trends in Cognitive Sciences*, 7, 287–292.

Gergely, G., & Csibra, G. (2005). The social construction of the cultural mind: Imitative learning as a mechanism of human pedagogy. *Interaction Studies*, 6, 463–481.

Gergely, G., Nádasdy, Z., Csibra, G., & Bíró, S. (1995). Taking the intentional stance at 12 months of age. *Cognition*, 56(2), 165–193.

Kamewari, K., Kato, M., Kanda, T., Ishiguro, H., & Hiraki, K. (2005). Six-and-a-half-month-old children positively attribute goals to human action and to humanoid-robot motion. *Cognitive Development*, 20, 303–320.

Király, I. (2003). Guidance by goals: The possible causes of irrelevant act omission in infants' imitative behaviour. Poster presented at Society for Research in Child Development. Tampa, USA.

Lichtenstein, E. H., & Brewer, W. F. (1980). Memory for goal-directed events. *Cognitive Psychology*, 12, 412–445.

Mandler, J., & Johnson, N. S. (1977). Remembrance of things parsed: Story structure and recall. *Cognitive Psychology*, 9, 111–151.

Meltzoff, A. N. (1988). Infant imitation after a one week delay: Long term memory for novel acts and multiple stimuli. *Developmental Psychology*, 24, 470–476.

Nelson, K., & Fivush, R. (2000). Socialization of memory. In E. Tulving & F. I. M Craik, (Eds.), *The Oxford Handbook of Memory* (pp. 283–295). Oxford: Oxford University Press.

Nelson, K., & Gruendel, J. (1986). Children's scripts. In K. Nelson (Ed.), *Event Knowledge: Structure and Function in Development* (pp. 47–69). Hillsdale, NJ: Lawrence Erlbaum.

Schank, R. C., & Abelson, R. (1977). *Scripts, Plans, Goals and Understanding.* Hillsdale, NJ: Lawrence Erlbaum.

Sperber, D., & Wilson, D. (1986). *Relevance: Communication and Cognition.* Oxford: Blackwell.

Sperber, D., & Wilson, D. (2002). Pragmatics, modularity and mind-reading. *Mind & Language*, 17(1), 3–23.

Travis, L. L. (1997). Gol-based organisation of event-memory in toddlers. In P. van den Broek, P. J. Bauer, & T. Bourg (Eds.), *Developmental Spans in Event Comprehension and Representation: Bridging Fictional and Actual Events* (pp. 111–138). Hillsdale, NJ: Lawrence Erlbaum.

Chapter 9

The Interchange of Self-Performed Actions and Perceived Actions in Infants

Petra Hauf

Action Production and Action Perception

Since the mid-1990s, there has been a resurgence of interest and research in the development of action understanding in infancy. Central to this research is the debate about whether infants need to understand other persons' actions before they are able to understand their own actions or whether infants first have to understand their own actions and only then are able to understand the actions of others. It is critical that research programs that address this issue include both aspects of action – namely, action perception and action production. Until now, however, studies have focused on either one or the other of these aspects. For that reason, the research reported in this chapter concentrates on the interplay of action production and action perception.

The value of actions for our everyday life is apparent. More than ever, actions and activity are keywords of the modern community. Actions define our way of life and, equally important, our way of thinking. Understanding the way other people's minds work is crucial to our interactions with other people and is tightly linked to our understanding of their actions. The understanding of other individuals' actions and their relatedness to one's own actions is significant for the development of social-communicative abilities. Human beings act and interact with their social environment from very early on in development. For that reason, it is essential to be capable of producing actions as well as understanding the actions of others. Alongside developmental research, there has been a resurgence of interest in action control in adults. Central to this research are the debates about how the two aspects of action control – namely, action production and action perception – are related to each other. For developmental research, the issue is how this relatedness develops during infancy. The common coding approach (Prinz, 1990, 1997) emphasizes the functional relationship between action production and action perception. Following this idea, to-be-produced actions and perceived actions share common representational resources and thus are linked to each other intimately. Research with adult populations has demonstrated a privileged connection between action production and action perception in cognitive psychology (for an overview, see Hommel, Müsseler, Aschersleben, & Prinz, 2001; Prinz, 2002) and in neuroscience (e.g. Gallese, 2003; Hamilton, Wolpert, & Frith, 2004; Iacoboni, 2005; Rizzolatti, Fadiga, Fogassi, & Gallese, 2002). Similarly, Meltzoff's "like-me" developmental framework (Meltzoff, 2005, 2007; Meltzoff & Gopnik, 1993) postulates that infants' fundamental interpersonal relations are based on their representation of action. Thereby, infants monitor their bodily acts and detect cross-modal equivalents between their own acts-as-felt and the acts-as-seen in others (Meltzoff, 2007). Nevertheless, studies investigating functional equivalence between performed and perceived actions are still rarely conducted in developmental research (see e.g. Hauf & Prinz, 2005). Central to this research is furthermore the question of how this connection develops and whether this connection is bidirectional from the begin-ning. There seems to be no doubt that perceived actions are influencing action production and performed actions are influencing action perception after infants have reached a functional equivalence between both aspects of action control (Hauf & Prinz, 2005; Meltzoff, 2002, 2007). Nevertheless, the question of how infants attain this functional equivalence remains an unsolved issue. It is still a matter of debate whether infants need to understand other persons' actions before they are able to understand self-generated actions or whether infants first have to under-stand their own actions and are only then able to understand the actions of others. As a result, typical developmental approaches deal with only one part of this question, focusing either on the influence of action perception on action produc-tion or vice versa.

The influence of action perception on action production

The question about the impact of perceived actions on produced actions is broadly spread throughout the field of infant imitation. In order to imitate, infants must watch actions performed by others, use this visually provided information as a source for an action plan, and then complete the corresponding motor output by themselves. Thus, imitation taps action perception, cross-modal coordination, action production, and memory. It requires not only learning actions by observa-tion, but also transferring this knowledge to their own actions. The range of inves-tigated imitative behavior covers facial and body movements as well as actions on objects, intended actions, and social goals (Meltzoff, 1995). Research on infant action imitation points out that imitative learning develops between 6 and 9 months of age (Barr, Dowden, & Hayne, 1996; Elsner, Hauf, & Aschersleben, 2007; Heimann & Nilheim, 2004; Meltzoff, 1988). In typical studies about action understanding, infants watch a model performing a new action with a new object and they observe the outcome of this action. Following the perception phase – immediately or with delay – infants are encouraged to perform the previously perceived action. Action understanding is defined as "correct" imitation. For a long time imitation studies have focused mainly on the memory aspect involved in imitative behavior. For example, Meltzoff (1988) has demonstrated long-term memory recall of novel actions in 14-month-old infants. Bauer and Mandler (1989) additionally showed that 1–2-year-olds' recall of complex actions is better with enabling action sequences (action steps that have to be performed in a specific order) than with arbitrary sequences (action steps that can be performed in any order). However, only recently research has started to focus on the relation between perception and production and the role of action goals and action effects (for an overview, see Hauf, 2007). For illustration, Meltzoff (1995) demonstrated in his influential study that 18-month-olds do not just copy the surface features of a failed attempt but that the infant infers the underlying intention of the perceived action (e.g., to pull apart a dumbbell). After watching an actor trying, but failing to achieve, the goal state of an action, infants performed this target action about as often as those infants who had observed a successful demonstration. By inferring the underlying goal of another person, they were able to complete the observed action correctly, thus achieving the actor's goal, which remained unfulfilled during demonstration. Furthermore, infants are able to differentiate between intentional and accidental actions (Carpenter, Akthar, & Tomasello, 1998). In this study infants imitated actions that were vocally marked as intentional ("There!") more often than actions that were marked as accidental ("Whoops!"). As demonstrated by Gergely, Bekkering, and Kiraly (2002), infants at this age also take into account the situational constraints that may have forced the model to choose a certain action. When the model used her forehead to cause a light to turn on, even though her hands were free, then infants imitated this seemingly irrational action (see also Meltzoff, 1988). But when the model's hands were occupied during the demonstration phase, then infants did not use their foreheads in order to switch on the light. In this context they used their hands, indicating that they considered this action to be the more rational way to switch on the light. Focusing on the goal can also trigger infants to produce different actions after watching the same demonstration. Carpenter, Call, and Tomasello (2005) showed 12- and 18-month-old infants an adult making a toy mouse hop across a mat. The mouse was then either placed into a house or ended up at the same location without a house. In the first case infants simply put the mouse into the house (without performing the hopping motion), whereas in the latter case infants copied the hopping motion (without ending at a special location). In both cases the infants were performing the final goal of the perceived action, which was either the end-state (mouse in the house) or the movement (hopping), depending on the context.

Further evidence for the impact of action perception on action production derives from research on the role of action effects for action understanding. In a study by Hauf, Elsner, and Aschersleben (2004), a three-step action sequence was demonstrated to 12- and 18-month-old infants introducing different action–effect contingencies. During the demonstration the experimenter took a cylinder off a barrier in front of a toy bear (1st step), shook it (2nd step), and returned it onto the barrier (3rd step). The experimental groups differed with respect to the presented action-effect contingency. Either the second action step ("shaking") or the third action step ("returning") was combined with an interesting sound effect, or none of the steps was combined with a sound effect. After watching this demonstration, infants produced action steps that differed with regard to the observed action–effect contingency. In general, infants produced the action step that was combined with an interesting acoustical effect first and faster, compared to an action step that did not bring out such an effect. To illustrate, infants who saw an actor producing a sound effect while shaking the cylinder showed the action step "shaking" first (before returning) and with shorter latency. Additionally, infants who saw an experimenter producing a sound effect while returning the cylinder to the toy bear produced "returning" first (before shaking) and with shorter latency. This difference did not occur in the condition without any additional sound effect. Thus, the observation of an action–effect relation led to the selective production of different actions steps, indicating a straight impact of action perception on action production (see also Klein, Hauf, & Aschersleben, 2006). This finding was replicated with even younger infants (9 but not 7 months of age) by using a less-demanding action step – a button press (Hauf & Aschersleben, 2008).

These examples impressively demonstrate that infants are not just blind imitators. In contrast, they are learning by observation efficiently and even flexibly. They learn about themselves and their capacities through observing others' actions. Thus perceiving the actions of another person influences the behavior of the infant.

The influence of action production on action perception

The question of the impact of agentive experience on the understanding of actions performed by others is of increasing relevance for ongoing developmental research. It is supposed that infants have first to acquire a specific level of reasoning about their own actions in order to be able to understand the actions of others (e.g. Barresi & Moore, 1996; Meltzoff, 1995; Tomasello, 1995, 1999). They do so by analogy to self-produced actions. The transfer of knowledge from self to others is a fundamental issue in the development of understanding other persons' goal-directed actions. As an illustration, with her habituation studies Woodward (1998, 1999) showed that infants as young as 6 months can understand perceived reaching and grasping movements as goal directed. She habituated infants to a human hand grasping one of two objects placed on separate locations on a stage. After habituation, the locations of the objects were switched and infants were presented with two different test events. In one test event the hand was grasping the same object as before but performing a new motion path, since the object's location had been changed. In the other test event the old motion path was preserved, but the hand grasped the new object. The infants dishabituated more to the event that maintained the physical properties of the reach – but changed the person's goal – than to the event that maintained the person's goal – but changed the physical properties. As these results were not found with mechanical devices (Woodward, 1998; but see Hofer, Hauf, & Aschersleben, 2005) nor with unfamiliar actions (Woodward, 1999; but see Hofer, Hauf, & Aschersleben, 2007), it was assumed that agentive experience plays a central role for the understanding of goal-directed actions performed by others. Notwithstanding that these studies do not control for the impact of self-performed actions, they rest upon the notion that infants must be able to grasp before they are able to understand the grasping action of others. It is assumed that the experience of grasping objects to achieve their own goals gives infants leverage for making sense of the grasping behavior of others (Meltzoff, 2007). During the first year of life infants contingently increase their action production and correspondingly their knowledge about actions. Nevertheless, only a few recent studies focus on the direct impact of action production on action perception.

Thus far the power of agentive experience has been mainly demonstrated in studies that have focused on aspects of cognition such as object representation, object exploration, or action memory. For example, like adults, $4^1/_2$-month-old infants recognize the boundaries of visually presented objects more clearly after they have felt the pattern of relative motion produced by themselves (that is, actively) rather than after they have felt the same motion pattern produced by others (that is, passively) (Streri, Spelke, & Rameix, 1993). Furthermore, recent studies have demonstrated the input of agentive object exploration on the development of explorative skills (Needham, 2001; Needham & Baillargeon, 1997, 1998). Early experience of object manipulation facilitates subsequent object-exploration behavior in infants as young as 3 months old (Needham, Barrett, & Peterman, 2002). In addition, 18-month-old infants who had practiced a perceived action sequence before the retention interval reactivated the target action more often and more accurately than those infants who had not (Hayne, Barr, & Herbert, 2003; for similar findings, see Meltzoff, 2007). To produce actions helps to remember actions.

Although, these studies impressively show the power of agentive experience, research about the importance of agentive experience for the development of action understanding has only recently become a topic in infant research. Hauf, Aschersleben, and Prinz (2007) demonstrated that 9- and 11-month-old infants who had previously played with a toy later on preferred to watch a video presenting an adult using the same toy instead of one showing someone using a different one. Sommerville, Woodward, and Needham (2005) enriched the object contact of 3-month-old infants by giving experience earlier than they would normally have done. Only after this enrichment session could the infants focus on the relation between the actor and her goal during a subsequent habituation task, which was not the case in infants who had not experienced an enrichment session.

These examples provide first evidence that infants' own motor experience influences subsequent action perception. Seemingly, they learn about actions by analogy to self-produced actions. Thus the infants' own action production influences their subsequent perception of other persons' actions.

Bidirectional Influence of Action Production and Action Perception

Background

As previously outlined, the impact of action perception on action production has been demonstrated, as has the impact of action production on action perception. But the reported findings do not provide evidence for a bidirectional influence of action perception and action production nor clarify how infants attain a functional equivalence of motor and perceptual systems. There are only a few recent studies that seem to support the notion of a direct link between both aspects of action control.

By using a means–end task (pulling a cloth to retrieve a toy), Sommerville and Woodward (2005) found that only 10-month-olds who were able to perform a cloth-pulling action in order to attain a toy were also able to understand a similar sequence presented in a visual task. Longo and Bertenthal (2006) tested whether action perception, like watching an overt reaching action, is sufficient to elicit the Piagetian A-not-B error. Infants either recovered a toy hidden at location A or observed an experimenter recover the toy. After the toy had been hidden at location B, infants in both conditions continued to reach to A, demonstrating that an active search by the infant is not necessary for the A-not-B error. Interestingly, 9-month-old infants continued only following observation of actions they themselves were able to perform, indicating a shared representation of perceived and to-be-produced actions at this age.

Research on imitation has indicated that young infants can represent the acts of others and their own acts in commensurate terms (Meltzoff, 2007). The ability of young infants to imitate perceived actions and to recognize that their own actions are imitated by another person suggests that produced and perceived actions share common representations. Meltzoff and Moore (1999) reported that, from 9 months of age, infants tend to look and smile more toward the imitating adult compared to the contingently acting, but not imitating, adult facing them. Moreover, infants systematically produced testing behaviors oriented preferentially toward the imitating adult. In this behavior, infants systematically modulated their own actions on the toy while looking at the adult, checking whether she is changing her imitative behavior accordingly. In line with this, Agnetta and Rochat (2004) demonstrated that 9-month-olds discriminated between an imitating and a contingent, but not imitating, adult. They preferentially looked at the imitating adult and tried to re-engage this person during a still-face period. The fact that infants recognize that they are being imitated (action perception) and change their own behavior (action production) in order to test the imitative capacities of the adult co-partner indicates that perceived and to-be-produced actions influence each other. These experiments were designed to investigate the detection of intentions in infant imitation. Nevertheless, they provide evidence for bidirectional influence of action production and action perception (Meltzoff, 2007).

Although these findings seem to indicate a close linkage between action production and action perception, it is critical that research programs on the functional equivalence of perceived and produced actions include both aspects of action. The assumed bidirectional interchange between these factors can be satisfactorily established only by research that uses the same experimental paradigms to investigate the influence of action production on action perception and vice versa. There have recently been a few studies that have addressed the issue of functional equivalence by applying the same paradigm. Sommerville, Woodward, and Needham (2005) used grasping actions to assess the potential reciprocal relation between action production and action perception. In this study, 3-month-old infants took part in an action task and a visual-habituation procedure. During the "action task" infants wore so-called sticky mittens – mittens with palms that stuck to the edges of toys. These allowed infants easily to pick up the toys. During the "habituation procedure," infants watched an actor reach for and grasp one of two toys sitting side by side on a stage. In subsequent test trials, the position of the two toys was reversed and the actor grasped either the same toy at a new location (path change) or the new toy at the same location (goal change). All infants participated in both tasks, but half of them started with the action task followed by the habituation procedure (reach-first infants), whereas the other half started with the habituation procedure followed by the action task (watch-first infants). The results demonstrate an influence of action production on subsequent action perception. The reach-first infants focused on the relation between actor and the goal during the habituation procedure, but the watch-first infants did not. Besides, watch-first infants did not produce more coordinate contacts with the toys during the action task in comparison to the reach-first infants. Thus, there was no evidence that action perception influenced subsequent action production. Although the same experimental paradigm was used for investigating the bidirectional influence of action production and action perception, the results were not equally profound in both directions. Whereas agentive experience enhanced infants' performance in a subsequent action-perception habituation procedure, this was not the case in reverse. Perceptive experience provided by the habituation procedure did not facilitate infants' subsequent action production (Sommerville, et al., 2005).

Taken together, these findings mostly indicate an impact of action production on action perception but do not provide strong evidence for a reciprocal influence of action perception on action production. On the surface, these results suggest that infants must be able to produce an action in order to understand this action when observing its production by others. Alternatively, and this is the view favored here, the direction of the relation between action production and action perception is bidirectional, but it is difficult to measure in young infants. For that reason, the research reported in the following section investigates this possible bidirectional relationship by means of less demanding tasks, such as combining a looking paradigm with an imitation paradigm.

Petra Hauf

Empirics

One series of experiments investigated how self-produced actions influence infants' perception of actions performed by others. For the first part of the experiment (production phase, see Figure 9.1), the parent and experimenter faced each other across a small table, with infants on their parents' laps. All infants (7, 9, and 11 months old; 12 infants in each age group) started to play with a toy (a car or ribbons) for a 90-second interval. During this time, infants had enough time to encode all features of the toys as well as to determine possible actions related to the toys. Immediately after this, the infants were given the chance to watch two short videos. For this second part of the experiment (perception phase, see Figure 9.1) infants were seated centered in front of two video screens. The two videos showed the same two adults sitting at a table face to face and alternately performing an action. Adult A acted upon the toy, whereas Adult B observed that action and repeated it once Adult A had finished the action. Subsequently, Adult A repeated the same action, and so on. The entire sequence lasted for 90 seconds. In one video, the two adults were alternately sliding the car whereas in the other video the two adults were taking turns to wave the ribbons. Depending on the toy the infants had played with during the production phase, either the car video or the ribbons video could be referred to as being the same-toy video or the different-toy video. The question was whether their experience during the production phase would influence infants' looking behavior during the subsequent perception phase.

(a) Action production → action perception

(b) Action perception → action production

Figure 9.1. Experimental set-up for action production followed by action perception (top) and action perception followed by action production (bottom)
Source: Petra Hauf, previously unpublished.

All infants were highly engaged during the look-at-toy and play-with-toy components of the production phase. Infants played for an equally long time with the car as those infants who played with the ribbons. Further, no age differences were evident in this component of the paradigm. A comparison of the mean looking time data during the perception phase demonstrated that 9- and 11-month-olds looked significantly longer at the same-toy video, whereas 7-month-olds did not. These findings indicate that self-performed actions influence the subsequent perception of the actions performed by others (Hauf, et al., 2007). These results suggest that infants are not only interested in acting on objects themselves, but that this experience increases their interest in the actions of other people with the same object.

However, what of the consequence of action perception on action production? In a second series of experiments, infants (7, 9, and 11 months old; 12 infants in each age group) first watched a video movie on a screen that depicted two adults acting upon a toy by taking turns (perception phase, see Figure 9.1). The presented videos were identical to those used in the first experiment. Thus half the infants watched the video where the two adults were alternately sliding the car. The other half of the infants watched the two adults taking turns with the ribbons. Following this, the infants were seated at a table and both toys (car and ribbons) were simultaneously presented within reach of the infant (production phase, see Figure 9.1). Thus, the infants had the chance to choose and to interact, either with the same toy that they had seen in the video, or with a different toy, for a 90-second interval. Of interest was whether infants' action perception during the perception phase would influence their acting behavior during the subsequent production phase.

All infants were highly interested in watching the presented videos. Infants watched the video with the car and the video with the ribbons for equal lengths of time, indicating that they were attracted by both actions and both objects. Nevertheless, the mean acting time of the infants during the production phase yielded no differences. In all age groups the infants played equally long with the toy that they had watched during the perception phase as with the new toy. Further, only a few infants produced the demonstrated target actions (sliding the car or waving the ribbons). These results suggest that the perception of actions performed by others does not influence the subsequent action production by the infants (Hauf, submitted).

Taken together, this series of experiments demonstrated that there is an impact of self-performed actions on action perception, but there is not an impact of action perception on self-performed actions. This is in line with recent findings emphasizing that the transfer of knowledge from self to others seems to be easier for infants than the transfer of knowledge from others to self. At first glance this conclusion supports the notion that infants must be capable of producing an action before they are able to understand similar actions performed by others. Nevertheless, it is surprising that the infants rarely imitated the demonstrated actions (sliding a car and waving ribbons), which were easy to perform. It is well known from imitation literature that infants at this age are able to imitate three-step action sequences – even after a delay (Barr et al., 1996; Elsner et al., 2007; Heimann & Meltzoff, 1996; Meltzoff, 1988). However, there is one large difference between typical imitation studies and the experiments reported here. Typical imitation paradigms demonstrate an action in front of the infant, and then hand the same object to the infant. This encourages the infant to produce the observed target action. But in the current study infants watched two adults performing the same action, thereby imitating each other without demonstrating the action directly to the watching infants. Afterwards infants were given the chance to play with two toys. Probably, infants did not interpret this production phase as a request to repeat what they have watched before. Therefore, follow-up studies investigated infants' imitation capacities with two distinct tasks.

The first task required 7-, 9-, and 11-month-old infants (12 infants in each age group) to watch a video with two adults acting upon the car or the ribbons alternately (same videos as used in the former study). But, following this, only the same toy was handed to the infant during the subsequent production phase. Note, the infants had no choice between toys and were thus prompted to act upon the same toy that they had seen in the video. The question was whether infants would repeat the perceived target actions under this condition. Again, all infants were highly attentive during the perception phase. During the subsequent production phase more infants produced the demonstrated target actions (sliding the car or waving the ribbons) than the number of infants who did not. Age-related analysis revealed significant differences in the amount of imitation at the age of 9 and 11 months, but not at the age of 7 months.

The second task required 7-, 9-, and 11-month-old infants (12 infants in each age group) to watch a video with two adults acting upon one toy in an alternate turn-taking fashion while ignoring the other toy. Accordingly this video not only demonstrated a target action, but, in addition, two adults were selecting the same toy in order to play. As the information presented in the video was much more demanding than in the previously reported studies – selection and imitation instead of imitation only – the question was whether infants would select the same toy as the adults and whether they would repeat the perceived target actions. All infants were highly attentive during the presentation of the videos. During the production phase, more infants selected the same toy than the different toy. Age-related analysis yielded that this was due to the selective behavior of the 9- and 11-month-olds rather than to that of the 7-month-olds. Interestingly, the 9- and 11-month-old infants did not only select the same toy, but additionally, they interacted reliably longer with the same toy than the different toy. This was not the case in 7-month-olds. It has to be stressed that, even though the 9- and 11-month-olds selected the same toy and interacted with it for a longer time, they only occasionally performed the corresponding target action (for more details, see Hauf, submitted).

Taken together, these studies suggest that there is indeed a bidirectional influence between action production and action perception. By applying the same experimental paradigm – a looking paradigm combined with an imitation paradigm – we were able to demonstrate an influence of action production on action perception (Hauf et al., 2007) as well as an influence of action perception on action production (Hauf, submitted) during the first postnatal year. Importantly, even the current studies failed to demonstrate this bidirectional influence, if they were just reversing the sequence of action production and action perception. For further research it is necessary to adjust the used tasks. Infants did not show any effect of perception on production, when the perception phase modeled a specific action with a specific object but the production phase required the infants to choose between objects. The influence of perceived actions was obvious only in tasks where the demands of perception and production phases happened to match. For example, demonstrating an action with one toy and requesting actions upon the same toy or modeling selection of one toy and requesting selection of the same toy. Infants as young as 9 months of age were capable of performing these tasks, indicating an influence of action perception on action production.

Conclusions

Studies on infant imitation demonstrate an impact of action perception on action production (e.g. Carpenter et al., 1998; Carpenter, Call, & Tomasello, 2005; Gergely et al., 2002; Hauf, submitted; Hauf et al., 2004; Hauf & Aschersleben, 2008; Klein et al., 2006; Meltzoff, 1995). Furthermore, recent studies on agentive experience of infants have revealed an explicit influence of action production on action perception (Hauf et al., 2007; Sommerville et al., 2005). But, most importantly, there is recent evidence that action perception and action production are tightly linked to each other (e.g. Longo & Bertenthal, 2006; Sommerville & Woodward, 2005) and that action perception and action producing influence each other in a bidirectional manner (Agnetta & Rochat, 2004; Hauf & Prinz, 2005; Meltzoff, 2007).

The results reported in this chapter in addition indicate that, by the age of 9 months, infants have reached a level of functional equivalence between self-produced actions and actions that they perceive performed by others. These are key findings for future research on the development of action understanding in infants. They support the notion of a bidirectional interchange of action production and action perception. Infants improve their perception of others' actions through agentive experience *and* they learn the possibilities of their own action production through observing others' actions.

Besides the substantial evidence on shared representations of perceived and to-be-produced actions in adults (Hommel et al., 2001; Prinz, 1990, 1997), recent research provides additional evidence that such a functional equivalence also holds true in infants. When infants have functional equivalence within the paradigm, their representation of knowledge about their own actions is similar to their representation of knowledge about others' actions. Certainly this knowledge can be used by the motor system in order to produce actions and also by the perceptual system in order to perceive and understand action performed by others. Nevertheless, the question of how infants attain functional equivalence between action perception and production remains an unsolved issue. The motor system and the perceptual system are important factors of the bidirectional relationship between action perception and production. Therefore, it seems reasonable that input from these systems plays an important role for establishing functional equivalence as well. Accordingly, further research must focus on the input of the motor system and the perceptual system on the development of action understanding (von Hofsten, 2004).

At least as important is the issue of whether the bidirectional influence of action production and action perception emerges at the same time and whether the development of these two directions is connected to each other. Based upon the common-coding perspective (Prinz, 1997), or the "supramodal representation" idea (Meltzoff, 2007), this question is not easy to answer. Both theoretical frameworks allow an influence in all directions at any time. Nevertheless, it has to be considered that the interchange of action production and action perception is tightly linked to the capacities of the perceptual system and the motor system. Surely, these capacities are not always at the same level or available in the same way for use in cognitive tasks. Further research has to specify the contribution of the perceptual system and the motor system during the first postnatal year.

From the literature on infant action understanding and action control, it appears reasonable that the impact of agentive experience on action perception is more distinct and emerges earlier than the impact of perceptual experience on action production. Indeed the presented results using the same experimental paradigm demonstrate a much clearer influence of action production on action perception (Hauf, 2007; Sommerville et al., 2005). However, both studies have their limitations. Regarding the study by Sommerville and colleagues (2005), it has to be assumed that the perceptual enrichment session provided by the habituation events was less rich than that provided by agentive experience. With the help of the "sticky mittens," the 3-month-olds were able to "grasp" objects – probably for the first time in their lives – providing them with a tremendously new experience. But 3-month-olds spend much time watching events in their environment. In contrast, therefore, watching habituation events was not challenging for them. Accordingly, they did not even establish an object–hand association that would have been useful for subsequent action production. In addition, the study by Hauf (submitted) found that applying the same experimental paradigm does not necessarily provide a sufficient starting point for reciprocal testing. These considerations, along with speculations regarding the central nature of action representation (Hauf, 2007; Meltzoff, 2007), suggest that the interchange of action production and action perception is indeed bidirectional, but it is ultimately difficult to measure in young infants.

Note

I appreciate the opportunity to collect my data on action production and action perception at the Max Planck Institute of Human Cognitive and Brain Sciences in Munich, Germany. I also wish to thank T. Striano and V. Reid for the motivation they provided in this project.

References

Agnetta, B., & Rochat, P. (2004). Imitative games by 9-, 14-, and 18-month-old infants. *Infancy*, 6(1), 1–36.

Barr, R., Dowden, A., & Hayne, H. (1996). Developmental changes in deferred imitation by 6- to 24-month-old infants. *Infant Behavior and Development*, 19, 159–170.

Barresi, J., & Moore, C. (1996). Intentional relations and social understanding. *Behavioural & Brain Sciences*, 19(1), 107–154.

Bauer, P. J., & Mandler, J. M. (1989). One thing follows another: Effects of temporal structure on 1- to 2-year-olds' recall of events. *Developmental Psychology*, 25(2), 197–206.

Carpenter, M., Akthar, N., & Tomasello, M. (1998). Fourteen- through 18-month-old infants differentially imitate intentional and accidental actions. *Infant Behavior and Development*, 21, 315–330.

Carpenter, M., Call, J., & Tomasello, M. (2005). Twelve- and 18-month-olds copy actions in terms of goals. *Developmental Science*, 8(1), F13–F20.

Elsner, B., Hauf, P., & Aschersleben, G. (2007). Imitating step by step: A detailed analysis of 9- to 15-month-old's reproduction of a three step action sequence. *Infant Behavior and Development*, 30(2), 325–335.

Gallese, V. (2003). The manifold nature of interpersonal relations: The quest for a common mechanism. *Philosophical Transactions of the Royal Society of London. Series B, Biological Sciences*, 358, 517–528.

Gergely, G., Bekkering, H., & Kiraly, I. (2002). Rational imitation in preverbal infants. *Nature*, 415, 755.

Hamilton, A., Wolpert, D., & Frith, U. (2004). Your own action influences how you perceive another person's action. *Current Biology*, 14, 493–498.

Hauf, P. (2007). Infants' perception and production of intentional actions. In C. von Hofsten & K. Rosander (Eds.), *Progress in Brain Research: From Action to Cognition*, 164, 285–301.

Hauf, P. (forthcoming). Baby see – Baby do! What infants learn from other persons' actions.

Hauf, P., & Aschersleben, G. (2008). Action-effect anticipation in infant action control. *Psychological Research*, 72, 203–210

Hauf, P., Aschersleben, G., & Prinz, W. (2007). Baby Do – Baby See! How action production influences action perception in infants. *Cognitive Development*, 22, 16–32.

Hauf, P., Elsner, B., & Aschersleben, G. (2004). The role of action effects in infants' action control. *Psychological Research*, 68, 115–125.

Hauf, P., & Prinz, W. (2005). The understanding of own and others' actions during infancy: "You-like-me" or "Me-like-you"? *Interaction Studies*, 6(3), 429–445.

Hayne, H., Barr, R., & Herbert, J. (2003). The effect of prior practice on memory reactivation and generalization. *Child Development*, 74(6), 1615–1627.

Heimann, M., & Meltzoff, A. N. (1996). Deferred imitation in 9- to 14-month-old infants: A longitudanal study of a Swedish sample. *British Journal of Developmental Psychology*, 14, 55–64.

Heimann, M., & Nilheim, K. (2004). 6-months olds and delayed actions: An early sign of an emerging explicit memory? *Cognitie Creier Comportament*, 8(3–4), 249–254.

Hofer, T., Hauf, P., & Aschersleben, G. (2005). Infant's perception of goal-directed actions performed by a mechanical device. *Infant Behavior and Development*, 28, 466–480.

Hofer, T., Hauf, P., & Aschersleben, G. (2007). Infants' perception of goal-directed actions on video. *British Journal of Developmental Psychology*, 25, 485–498.

Hommel, B., Müsseler, J., Aschersleben, G., & Prinz, W. (2001). The theory of event coding: A framework for perception and action planning. *Behavioral and Brain Sciences*, 24, 849–937.

Iacoboni, M. (2005). Neural mechanisms of imitation. *Current Opinion in Neurobiology*, 15, 632–637.

Klein, A., Hauf, P., & Aschersleben, G. (2006). A comparison of televised model and live model in infant action control: How crucial are action effects? *Infant Behavior and Development*, 29, 535–544.

Longo, M. R., & Bertenthal, B. I. (2006). Common Coding of observation and execution of action in 9-month-old infants. *Infancy*, 10(1), 43–59.

Meltzoff, A. N. (1988). Infant imitation and memory: Nine-month-olds in immediate and deferred tests. *Child Development*, 59, 217–225.

Meltzoff, A. N. (1995). Understanding the intentions of others: Re-enactment of intended acts by 18-month-old children. *Developmental Psychology*, 31, 838–850.

Meltzoff, A. N. (2002). Elements of a developmental theory of imitation. In A. N. Meltzoff & W. Prinz (Eds.), *The Imitative Mind: Development, Evolution and Brain Bases* (pp. 19–41). New York: Cambridge University Press.

Meltzoff, A. N. (2005). Imitation and other minds: The "Like Me" hypothesis. In S. Hurley & N. Chater (Eds.), *Perspectives on Imitation: From Neuroscience to Social Science* (vol. 2, pp. 55–77). Cambridge, MA: MIT Press.

Meltzoff, A. N. (2007). The "Like Me" framework for recognizing and becoming an intentional agent. *Acta Psychologica*, 124, 26–43.

Meltzoff, A. N., & Gopnik, A. (1993). The role of imitation in understanding persons and developing a theory of mind. In S. Baron-Cohen, H. Tager-Flusberg, & D. J. Cohen (Eds.), *Understanding Other Minds: Perspectives from Autism* (pp. 335–366). New York: Oxford University Press.

Meltzoff, A. N., & Moore, M. K. (1999). Persons and representation: Why infant imitation is important for theories of human development. In J. B. G. Nadel (Ed.), *Imitation in Infancy: Cambridge Studies in Cognitive Perceptual Development* (pp. 9–35). New York: Cambridge University Press.

Needham, A. (2001). Object recognition and object segregation in 4.5-month-old infants. *Journal of Experimental Child Psychology*, 78, 3–24.

Needham, A., & Baillargeon, R. (1997). Object segregation in 8-month-old infants. *Cognition*, 62, 121–149.

Needham, A., & Baillargeon, R. (1998). Effects of prior experience on 4.5-month-old infants' object segregation. *Infant Behavior & Development*, 21(1), 1–24.

Needham, A., Barrett, T., & Peterman, K. (2002). A pick-me-up for infants' exploratory skills: Early simulated experiences reaching for objects using "sticky mittens" enhances young infants' object exploration skills. *Infant Behavior and Development*, 25, 279–295.

Prinz, W. (1990). A common coding approach to perception and action. In O. Neumann & W. Prinz (Eds.), *Relationships between Perception and Action: Current Approaches* (pp. 167–201). Berlin, Heidelberg, New York: Springer.

Prinz, W. (1997). Perception and action planning. *European Journal of Cognitive Psychology*, 9(2), 129–154.

Prinz, W. (2002). Experimental approaches to imitation. In A. N. Meltzoff & W. Prinz (Eds.), *The Imitative Mind: Development, Evolution, and Brain Bases* (pp. 143–162). Cambridge: Cambridge University Press.

Rizzolatti, G., Fadiga, L., Fogassi, L., & Gallese, V. (2002). From mirror neurons to imitation, facts, and speculations. In A. N. Meltzoff & W. Prinz (Eds.), *The Imitative Mind: Development, Evolution, and Brain Bases* (pp. 143–162). Cambridge: Cambridge University Press.

Sommerville, J. A., & Woodward, A. L. (2005). Pulling out the intentional structure of action: The relation between action processing and action production in infancy. *Cognition*, 95, 1–30.

Sommerville, J. A., Woodward, A. L., & Needham, A. (2005). Action experience alters 3-month-old infants' perception of others' actions. *Cognition*, 96, B1–B11.

Steri, A., Spelke, E., & Rameix, E. (1993). Modality-specific and amodal aspects of object perception in infancy: The case of active touch. *Cognition*, 47, 251–279.

Tomasello, M. (1995). Joint attention as social cognition. In C. Moore & P. J. Dunham (Eds.), *Joint Attention: Its Origins and Role in Development* (pp. 103–130). Hillsdale, NJ: Lawrence Erlbaum.

Tomasello, M. (1999). Having intentions, understanding intentions, and understanding communicative intentions. In P. D. Zelazo, J. W. Astington, & D. R. Olson (Eds.), *Developing Theories of Intention: Social Understanding and Self-Control* (pp. 63–75). Mahwah, NJ: Lawrence Erlbaum.

von Hofsten, C. (2004). An action perspective on motor development. *Trends in Cognitive Sciences*, 8(6), 266–272.

Woodward, A. L. (1998). Infants selectively encode the goal of objects of an actor's reach. *Cognition*, 69, 1–34.

Woodward, A. L. (1999). Infants' ability to distinguish between purposeful and non-purposeful behaviors. *Infant Behavior and Development*, 22, 145–160.

Chapter 10

Tools and Goals: A Social-Cognition Perspective on Infant Learning of Object Function

Birgit Elsner

Introduction

The acquisition of tool use is a fundamental aspect of human culture (e.g. Tomasello, 1999). Humans developed tools to help them to fulfill their intentions and to attain their action goals. Tool use is intimately linked to the concept of object function. Tools are designed for a specific purpose, and they allow certain actions to be done with them (Bloom, 1996; German & Johnson, 2002; Nelson, 1973). Actions on tools lead to changes in the environment, and, thus, tool use usually involves intentional action in the sense that the user has a certain goal, and he or she performs a movement to produce the desired outcome (see Elsner & Hommel, 2001). Yet, intentions exist only in our minds and have to be induced from the observable components of our actions – that is, from the performed movements and the produced effects (e.g. Tomasello, Carpenter, Call, Behne, & Moll, 2005). Humans probably refer to their own action knowledge when interpreting others' intentions (Elsner, 2007). In situations that entail tool use, this requires some knowledge about the tool's function. For infants and children, learning about the function of artifacts enables them not only to reach their own action goals by using tools, but also to understand the goals that may underlie others' actions on objects.

One aspect of function is what can be done with a given object (e.g. Madole & Oakes, 1999; Nelson, 1973). Although infants may acquire functional knowledge by trial and error when exploring novel objects, this is not the most common way. Typically, infants first observe other persons before they start to handle a given object on their own (Tomasello, 1999). When watching others' tool use, infants may acquire different kinds of knowledge. First, they may acquire procedural knowledge about the use of the object: which movements have to be performed (for example, for cutting, a knife has to be moved back and forth), and which outcomes can be expected (for example, when cut with a knife, one object comes apart into two pieces). Secondly, infants may acquire semantic knowledge about the tool itself: how are its shape or parts related to its function – that is, which object features are functionally relevant (for example, the sharp edge of a knife's blade is used for cutting). When this information has been learned, infants may search for objects that feature the same parts and may transfer their functional knowledge to these entities (for example, objects with a blade may be used for cutting). By doing so, infants form categories of objects that serve the same function (e.g. Bloom, 1996; Nelson, 1973).

It is interesting to note that these aspects of infant learning about object function have been investigated in different lines of developmental research. Procedural learning of how to handle an object is mainly investigated in imitation studies, whereas the acquisition of knowledge about object function and the transfer of this knowledge to novel objects is examined in categorization studies. Yet, both lines of research are interested in what infants learn from observing other persons' actions on objects and hence involve some aspects of social learning. However, the research traditions stress the social aspect to different degrees. Moreover, they use different measures to assess what infants learn from watching the demonstration. Whereas imitation studies focus on the reproduction of the observed actions (e.g. Meltzoff, 1988a), categorization studies record measures of attention (e.g. Booth & Waxman, 2002; Madole, Oakes, & Cohen, 1993).

The goal of this chapter is to review categorization studies and imitation studies to give an integrative picture of what infants learn from observing other persons' actions on artifacts. Because learning about object function is closely related to the learning of tool use, the reviewed results may be informative for the questions of how the control and the understanding of goal-directed action develops during the first two years of life. In particular, this review addresses imitation and categorization studies from a social-learning perspective. For each line of research, the following questions will be discussed. How important is the presence of a human model for the acquisition of object function? What can the respective paradigms tell us about the mechanisms underlying functional learning in infancy? Which aspects of object function are acquired by infants in different ages – that is, do infants encode the observed movements, the effects, or both?

Categorization Studies on Infant Learning about Object Function

Categorization studies assess infant learning about object function by recording measures of attention. Several studies have tested whether, under which circumstances, and at which age infants categorize novel artifacts on the basis of functional information (for a review, see Madole & Oakes, 2005). These studies typically consist of two phases. In a familiarization phase, infants observe a human agent performing specific actions on several artifacts. The objects differ in their appearance, but resemble each other in terms of features that are functionally relevant (for example, their shape or certain object parts, such as wheels or loops). The actions performed on the familiarization objects usually lead to salient effects, like object motion or sounds. Infants are mostly not allowed to act on the familiarization objects, and looking time serves as a dependent measure. If infants are allowed to manipulate the objects, the measure of interest is the time spent examining the object – that is, with focused manual exploration (e.g. Träuble & Pauen, 2007). The critical question is whether infants would detect the commonalities in function, even though each familiarization object provides diverging perceptual information. If so, the looking or examining times should decrease across the familiarization trials, reflecting a habituation process.

In a subsequent test phase, infants are presented with one or several novel exemplars from the familiar category (that is, within-category test objects) and with one or several novel objects that do not serve the familiar function (that is, out-of-category test objects). The function of the test objects is not demonstrated. Again, looking or examining times are recorded to assess whether infants would notice the change, which would become apparent in an increase in the dependent measure from the within-category to the out-of-category test object (e.g. Madole et al., 1993; Perone & Oakes, 2006; Träuble & Pauen, 2007). An alternative procedure is to ask the infant to choose out of two test objects the one that is similar to the familiarization objects. Here, it is tested whether the within-category test object is chosen more often than what would be expected by chance (e.g. Booth & Waxman, 2002).

Learning the function of artifacts requires that the object is watched while it is used by another person. Function is a dynamic, transient property and is thereby distinct from static features such as color or shape (Perone & Oakes, 2006; Rakison, 2004). Therefore, it has been argued that, in infancy, learning about function may be more difficult than learning about appearance (e.g. Madole & Oakes, 1999). This assumption was supported by data showing that 10-month-olds mainly attended to the shape of familiarization objects, whereas 14-month-olds also attended to the demonstrated function. When infants were familiarized to two objects and two functions, the form–function relations were learned only by 18-month-olds (Madole et al., 1993). However, infants attend to human actions, their effects, and also to the goals that might be motivating them (e.g. Leslie, 1984; Meltzoff, 1995; Woodward, 1998). Therefore, other authors suggest that function may be more salient than static features (e.g. Bloom, 1996; Nelson, 1973) and should thus be easy for infants to learn. This assumption has recently been confirmed by Horst, Oakes, and Madole (2005), who showed that, for 10-month-olds, categories defined by appearance are more difficult to learn than categories defined by function. These studies reveal that, from 10 months of age, infants are able to learn about the function of objects when observing others' actions on these objects.

Additionally, this research may answer some questions that are relevant from a social-learning perspective. First, the familiarization phase comprises a social learning situation. Because other studies show that infants attend to the actions of other persons (e.g. Leslie, 1984; Woodward, 1998), it may be asked how important the presence of the model is for categorization tasks. Secondly, it may be asked which aspects of function are learned by the infants. In most studies, the demonstrated function consists of actions performed on the objects and of salient effects produced by these actions. If infants wanted to understand the goals of the model, they would have to encode both the actions and the effects, and ideally also the relations between these components.

Several studies imply that infants interpret hands acting on objects as goal-directed and causal agents (e.g. Leslie, 1984; Woodward, 1998) and may therefore be particularly attentive to actions on objects by agents (e.g. Booth, 2000; Horst et al., 2005; Träuble & Pauen, 2007). Research on joint attention shows that social cues may direct infants' interest to objects (e.g. Itakura, 2001; Striano, Chen, Cleveland, & Bradshaw, 2006). In these studies, infants were confronted with objects and with a person who directed her attention to one object and to the infant. Joint attention requires that infants consider the actions of others, and that they use this information to modify their own behavior. Nine-month-olds' learning about static object features was enhanced in these joint-attention situations. Thus, social cues may direct infants' attention, which in turn may facilitate the processing of the information provided by objects.

Booth (2000) investigated whether infants' attention to others' actions would enhance the formation of object categories. Fourteen-month-olds were familiarized with objects that could be grouped according to their color and/or shape. One group of infants watched a static presentation of the stimuli (baseline condition). In a second group (independent motion), the stimuli moved on their own in category-specific ways. In the third group (agent-produced motion), the experimenter produced the same stimulus motions, but with her hands fully visible to the infant. In a subsequent test phase, infants who had observed the agent-produced motions could better distinguish between the categories than infants in the independent-motion and the baseline conditions. Hence, only category-specific motion that was produced by a visible agent facilitated category differentiation. Other studies by Booth and colleagues (Booth, 2006; Booth & Waxman, 2002) suggested that not only the presence of a model, but also the behavior of that person, affected infant categorization. If the model just attracted the attention of 14–18-month-olds to the familiarization objects by saying "Look at this," infants did not form object categories. However, a demonstration of the objects' function enhanced categorization. Booth (2006) speculates that the causal relations between the agent's goals, her actions on objects, and the resulting dynamic outcomes might enable the infants to attend to similarities among objects that might not have been noticed otherwise.

Träuble and Pauen (2007) also found that the demonstration of function enhanced infants' processing of a static indicator of category membership (that is, part structure). In their study, 11–12-month-olds were presented with novel artifacts that could be grouped either according to their overall similarity or according to their similarity in one functionally relevant part. Without prior demonstration, infants classified these objects only by their overall similarity, but not by part similarity. However, after having seen the experimenter performing specific actions and producing effects with the functionally relevant parts, infants succeeded in classifying the stimuli according to part similarity. Thus, watching a short function demonstration affected later categorization of the artifacts.

Two studies (Booth & Waxman, 2002; Träuble & Pauen, 2007) suggest that the demonstration of salient action outcomes is relevant for enhancing infants' categorization of artifacts. These studies compared infants' performance in two conditions. One group of infants observed the actor demonstrating actions on objects that were followed by salient effects (for example, by a sound or by attachment to another object). In the other condition, the same actions were presented, but without producing any effects. In both studies, 11–18-month-olds learned function-related categories in the "movement-and-effect" conditions, but failed to do so in the "movement-only" conditions. The presentation of salient action effects may facilitate infants' understanding of function demonstrations.

If the understanding of intentional action contributes to the encoding of function demonstrations, infants should learn both the demonstrated movements and the effects, because both components may be informative about the model's action goals. Perone and Oakes (2006) found that 10-month-olds noticed when a novel action or a novel effect was shown that had not been present during familiarization (see also Horst et al., 2005). However, when infants were familiarized with one object, two actions, and two sounds, they did not dishabituate to novel combinations of the familiar actions and effects. Thus, it is questionable whether 10-month-olds actually learned function, because they did not encode action–effect relations. Perone and Oakes conclude that, at 10 months, causal perception appears still to be fragile, and thus task complexity may interact with the learning of causal relations.

The facilitative effects of function demonstrations on infant categorization reported so far may be due to different underlying mechanisms. Observed function may act as a general attention enhancer, leading infants to make global comparisons between the familiarization objects. Alternatively, function may act as a specific attention enhancer, highlighting a subset of object properties that are causally related to the demonstrated function. To test these possibilities, Booth (2006) familiarized 18-month-olds to four objects that looked similar and shared a functionally relevant part. At test, infants were presented with two novel objects, one of which resembled the familiarization objects but did not have the functionally relevant part, whereas the other had the relevant part but looked dissimilar. The results of several experiments provided support for both mechanisms. When the relations between function and the relevant part were difficult to detect, infants relied on global similarity to determine category membership. However, when the causal relations were tighter and more transparent, infants focused on the functional relevant object parts. Thus, task difficulty appears to determine which knowledge is extracted by the infant during the observation of other persons' actions and the resulting effects.

In sum, studies that assess infant learning of object function with attentional measures reveal aspects that may be important for infants' understanding and encoding of other persons' actions, and also reveal the mechanisms that underlie these abilities. First, the presence and the behavior of the model affect infants' behavior. Not only does the actor direct infants' attention to the objects, but the model's actions and their salient outcomes also enable the infants to construe the function demonstration as intentional behavior. This, in turn, may facilitate processing of the specific features of the objects. Secondly, the characteristics of the function demonstration affect infant learning about the functional properties of objects. Factors that facilitate learning of causal functional relations are transparent relations between the relevant parts and the function as well as the presentation of salient action outcomes.

Imitation Studies on Infants' Reproduction of Actions on Objects

Many imitation studies involve the demonstration of actions on objects, and, therefore, these studies also present infants with information about the function of artifacts. The typical procedure of imitation studies comprises a demonstration phase, in which infants observe a model repeatedly performing actions on objects. Typically, the target actions lead to salient action effects, such as sounds or lights. In a subsequent test phase, the infant is handed the test object(s), and it is recorded whether he or she reproduces the demonstrated target action(s). Typically, this measure is compared to the spontaneous production of target actions in control groups whose participants either have not seen any demonstration (baseline control) or have watched a model performing arbitrary control actions on the test objects (adult-manipulation control). If the number of target actions is higher in the demonstration condition than in the control conditions, infants are said to have learned the target actions by observing the model.

In imitation studies, infants first have to remember the function of a given test object in terms of which action was related to that object. Then, they have to coordinate their motor system in a way that the target action is performed. Since 2000, the focus of imitation studies has moved from the questions of whether and at which age infants are capable of reproducing observed actions (e.g. Meltzoff, 1988b) to the question of which aspects of the demonstration affect infants' reproduction of target actions (e.g. Elsner & Aschersleben, 2003; Huang, Heyes, & Charman, 2002). In this context, the issue of how infants understand the goals and intentions of the model has gained specific interest. It is now taken for granted that infants' interpretation of the observed actions and the resulting effects determines the reproduction of the behavior (e.g. Tomasello et al., 2005).

Until 2007, only a few imitation studies had addressed the issue of what infants learn about the objects involved. In studies that present infants with several objects and actions during demonstration (e.g. Huang et al., 2002; Meltzoff, 1988a), infants must be able to relate objects and actions in order to perform the "correct" target action on a given test object. Infants are able to succeed in those tasks at 9 months of age (Meltzoff, 1988b). However, generalization studies reveal that younger infants' ability to reproduce observed actions appears to be closely tied to the demonstration objects. For example, 12-month-olds generalized modeled target acts only to a novel test object that varied in color from the original demonstration object, but not to objects that varied in shape, or in both color and shape (Hayne, MacDonald, & Barr, 1997). In another study (Barnat, Klein, & Meltzoff, 1996) 14-month-olds generalized target acts to novel objects that varied in both color and size. However, infants' performance was best with the original objects. Thus, younger infants' ability to retrieve observed actions appears to rely on the presence of very specific objects.

However, if infants are allowed to practice actions on objects, this may facilitate generalization of actions to novel objects serving the same function. Hayne, Barr, and Herbert (2003) reported that only 18-month-olds who practiced the target actions on the demonstration objects generalized the actions to objects that differed in both color and shape. Similar results were found by Elsner and Pauen (2007) for 12- and 15-month-olds. Infants were given the opportunity to imitate actions with simple white objects that featured a functionally relevant side part that could be used to activate a button at an effect box, thereby producing a sound. After four imitation trials with the simple objects, infants were presented with colored objects that had four side parts, one of them being the functionally relevant part. Although the function of these objects was never demonstrated, infants brought the colored objects in contact with the box, and some of the 15-month-olds also performed the target actions with the colored objects. It is important to note that infants had not shown these behaviors in a baseline phase that was conducted prior to the first demonstration. Hence, infants are not only able to reproduce other persons' actions on objects, but they can also transfer these actions to perceptually dissimilar objects that share the same functional parts.

Imitation studies usually address the social-learning component more directly than studies on object categorization. Here again, it may be asked how important the presence of a human model is for infant imitation. If infants imitate because they attribute goals and intentions to the model, then imitation should be impaired when a non-human agent demonstrates the target actions, when no model is present, or when the model does not engage in social contact with the infant. Secondly, it may be asked which aspects of the demonstrated actions are learned by the infants. If infants wanted to understand the goals of the model, they should encode both the actions and the effects, and ideally also the relations between these components. Some studies on infant imitation have addressed these issues.

One of the earliest hints that the presence of a human model is necessary for infant imitation came from Meltzoff (1995). In his study, one group of 18-month-olds observed a human model trying, but failing, to pull apart a dumbbell-shaped toy into two pieces. Another group watched a mechanical set of pincers performing the same movement. Infants never saw a successful action or the respective end result. The question was whether infants would copy the observed movement, or if they would "re-enact" the successful action (thereby producing the effect that was probably intended by the actor). Meltzoff found that infants re-enacted the failed attempts of the actor, but not of the machine. This was taken as evidence that infants attribute goals exclusively to humans. Further support for this assumption came from studies that recorded infants' looking times to goal-directed actions of human versus mechanical agents (e.g. Leslie, 1984; Woodward, 1998).

However, Johnson, Booth, and O'Hearn (2001) found that 15-month-olds re-enacted the failed attempts of a non-human agent. In their study, the failed attempt was modeled by a toy monkey that embodied some characteristics thought to imply the presence of a mind, like self-generated behavior, the presence of a face and hands, and the ability to engage in contingent interactions. Johnson et al. speculate that infants produced the target actions in their failed-attempt condition because they viewed the monkey as an agent with unfulfilled goals. In contrast, in Meltzoff's study (1995), the pincers embodied none of the features that characterize mentalistic agents. Thus, characteristics of the model and the model's behavior affect infants' reproduction of observed actions.

This assumption has recently been supported by Nielsen (2006), who confronted 18- and 24-month-olds either with an actor who engaged in social interactions (for example, smiling, eye contact) with the child while demonstrating the target actions (Social condition) or with an actor who avoided engaging with the child (Aloof condition). The target actions consisted in touching a switch with an object to open a box. The actor's behavior had a different impact in the two age samples. The 18-month-olds opened an equal number of boxes in both conditions, but they used the object more often in the Social condition. Thus, infants were more likely to copy the target actions when the actor acted socially toward them. The 24-month-olds opened more boxes in the Social than in the Aloof condition, but they used the object equally often in both conditions. Thus, these infants copied the model's actions in both conditions, but they needed social reinforcement (which was not present in the Aloof condition) to go on trying in trials where they failed to open the box at the first attempt. These results suggest that the interaction style of the model influences how infants copy observed actions.

Given these findings, it seems surprising that infants sometimes produce target actions in the absence of a human model. In a study by Thompson and Russell (2004), one group of 14–26-month-olds watched a human model demonstrating a counterintuitive action to obtain an out-of-reach toy that rested on a cloth. In a second group ("ghost condition"), the cloth and the toy were moved in the same fashion by a small invisible motor. Infants' behavior depended on the complexity of the task. When infants had to pull one cloth to obtain the toy that rested on another cloth, they produced fewer target actions in the ghost condition than in the modeling condition. Yet, when infants had to push a single cloth away to obtain a toy resting on that cloth, they performed more actions in the ghost condition than in the modeling condition. Hence, infants can learn an action from observing the spatiotemporal contingencies between the motion of an object and the resulting effects. Yet, infants need to observe easily understandable movement-outcome contingencies to be able to infer the necessary actions. In Thompson and Russell's study, the ghost condition of the single-cloth task provided this kind of information.

In a recent study, Huang and Charman (2005) also found evidence that 17-month-olds learn target actions from observing object movements. Infants were exposed to video films displaying the end-state of an action, either together with an actor demonstrating the target actions, or with only the movements of the objects without the actor being visible, or with only the movements of the actor without the objects being visible. The number of target actions was comparable in the object-movement and the full-demonstration group, but was significantly lower in the hand-movement group. Huang and Charman propose that the displayed object movements were easily understandable, and perhaps more interesting than the apparently non-goal-directed hand movements. However, infants in the full-demonstration condition adopted a more efficient strategy, in that they less often touched a demonstration-inconsistent object part and generated fewer non-target actions before succeeding. Hence, although infants inferred the target actions from seeing merely the end result and the object movements, their performance was more efficient after observing the model's action.

Infants' behavior in object-movement conditions can be described as emulation learning, which involves learning about the properties of, or causal relations between, the objects involved in observed actions (Tomasello, 1999; Want & Harris, 2002). The discussion about imitation or emulation is closely related to the question of what infants learn from observing others' actions. In emulation learning, the observer focuses on the displacements and the function-related properties of the involved objects, instead of attending to the model's actions and their effects. The studies reviewed so far indicate that the presence of a human model enhances infant imitation, but that, in some conditions, infants can also learn target actions from observing the spatiotemporal contingencies between object movements and the resulting effects. This implies that, at the end of the second year, infants have both imitation and emulation available to them. However, for emulation to occur, the observed object movements must display easily understandable movement–outcome relations. Additionally, infants must be able to infer the action that allows the transfer of a given state of the test object into the demonstrated end-state. There is evidence that infants rely on their own knowledge about actions and effects when emulating unseen target actions (see Elsner, 2007). Hence, as long as movement–outcome contingencies are too complex, infants may need to see a human model demonstrating both the target actions and the effects.

Several studies suggest that the presentation of salient action effects enhances infants' imitation of observed actions. Infants tend to copy "effect-less" movements less reliably than full demonstrations of target actions and effects (e.g. Bellagamba & Tomasello, 1999; Huang et al., 2002). Hauf, Elsner, and Aschersleben (2004) presented 12- and 18-month-olds with two actions, only one of which was followed by a salient action effect. Most infants reproduced both actions, which rules out that the action effect just enhanced infants' attention for one action. Nevertheless, the majority of infants performed the "effective" action as their first action. A probable explanation for this preference is that, during full demonstrations, infants relate the observed movement to the observed effect, thus forming a movement–effect association. In the test phase, they re-activate the representation of the action goal, leading to an activation, and a preferred reproduction, of the modeled movement (Elsner, 2007; Tomasello et al., 2005). Infants' preference for "effective" actions would thus depend on their ability to learn movement–effect associations by observation.

Infants' ability to relate observed actions and effects appears to undergo developmental changes during the first two years of life. Infants seem to begin to learn relations between actions and effects between 10 and 13 months of age (Carpenter, Nagell, & Tomasello, 1998). At this age, infants not only reproduced a modeled action but also checked whether the observed effect would occur. On the contrary, 9-month-olds copied the actions of the model but seemed to be oblivious to the produced effects. A similar developmental trend was revealed by Elsner and Aschersleben (2003). In their study, 9-month-olds did not learn the relations between two demonstrated movements and two effects. Twelve-month-olds, however, learned that performing the target actions produced interesting effects, but they did not encode which of the actions led to which effect. Only 15- and 18-month-olds encoded the specific relations between movements and effects, which enabled them to detect novel combinations of the familiar components. Hence, infants' ability to encode relations between actions and effects appears to improve substantially during the first two years of life. One reason for this may be older infants' growing attentive and memory capacities, which enable them to process more of the information that is provided by the demonstration.

During the second year of life, infants also appear to learn increasingly specific relations between objects and actions. In the study by Elsner and Pauen (2007), 12- and 15-month-olds were presented with an effect box and two simple white objects. One object featured a pin-like side part that could be inserted into a hole in the box, thereby producing a sound. The other object featured an anchor-like side part that did not fit into the hole. The model demonstrated the same target action with each object, producing the sound with the effective object and merely touching the hole with the ineffective object. Infants in the two age groups differed according to the specificity of the acquired functional knowledge. Fifteen-month-olds preferred the effective object when performing the target act or touching the box – that is, they chose the object that had produced a salient action effect during demonstration. Contrary to this, 12-month-olds showed no preference for the effective object, neither when performing the target act nor when touching the box. This indicates that the older infants had encoded the specific function of the side part when observing the model's actions, and that they applied this information in their own actions. Hence, imitation studies suggest important progress with respect to infants' learning about artifact function in social situations in the second year of life.

Conclusion

Imitation studies and categorization studies provide evidence that social cues affect infants' learning of object function. One aspect of object function is defined as actions that can be produced on a given object. When learning this aspect of object function, infants benefit from seeing how a human agent performs actions on objects. The social cues provided by human agents may be helpful in directing infants' attention to functionally relevant object parts. Full demonstrations of actions and effects seem to be especially captivating for the child, as compared to conditions in which the actions are presented without salient effects or to conditions in which the model just attracts infants' attention to the objects.

The social cues and goal-directed actions provided by the model appear to be especially relevant in categorization studies, where infants have to relate the demonstrated actions to functionally relevant object parts and to use the acquired functional knowledge to identify novel objects that may serve the same function. In imitation studies, where infants have to perform the "correct" target action on a given test object, infants can sometimes infer the necessary action by watching the spatiotemporal contingencies between the motion of the objects and the resulting effects, in the absence of a model. However, whether or not infants are able to emulate the actions in such conditions depends on the action knowledge acquired so far. If the demonstrated contingencies are too complex, infants need to see full demonstrations of actions and effects to be able to produce the target actions.

It may be speculated that full demonstrations of actions and effects by a human model are especially facilitating for infant learning of object function, because these demonstrations may be interpreted as intentional action. Infants are very attentive to human goal-directed actions, and this may lead to an enhanced encoding of the demonstrated object function – that is, of the actions performed on the objects and the effects that result from these actions. However, infants' ability to relate observed actions and effects, and thus to learn function, seems to undergo developmental changes during the first two years of life. Imitation and categorization studies reveal that 9–10-month-olds do not detect novel combinations of familiar actions and effects. However, infants of this age are able to remember which action was performed on a given test object, and they detect when a novel action is performed on a familiar object. By 14 months, infants can learn specific relations between observed actions and effects. Infants of this age detect perturbations in familiar action–effect relations, and this also influences their imitation behavior.

Although the acquisition of tool use is an important component of human culture, this review reveals that learning about artifact function is quite a vdemanding task. It typically requires the infant closely to monitor others' actions, to understand the relations between an object's shape or parts and its function, and also to encode the relations between the observed actions and the resulting effects. Furthermore, infants need to organize their own imitative behavior, and they need to transfer knowledge from one situation or one object to another to build up function-based artifact categories. Keeping the complexity of these demands in mind, it does not come as a surprise that social learning of artifact function shows considerable progress throughout the first two years of life.

References

Barnat, S. B., Klein, P. J., & Meltzoff, A. N. (1996). Deferred imitation across changes in context and object: Memory and generalization in 14-month-old infants. *Infant Behavior & Development*, 19, 241–251.

Bellagamba, F., & Tomasello, M. (1999). Re-enacting intended acts: Comparing 12- and 18-month olds. *Infant Behavior & Development*, 22, 277–282.

Bloom, P. (1996). Intention, history, and artifact concepts. *Cognition*, 60, 1–29.

Booth, A. E. (2000). The facilitative effect of agent-produced motions on categorization in infancy. *Infant Behavior & Development*, 23, 153–174.

Booth, A. E. (2006). Object function and categorization in infancy: Two mechanisms of facilitation. *Infancy*, 10, 145–169.

Booth, A. E., & Waxman, S. (2002). Object names and object functions serve as cues to categorization for infants. *Developmental Psychology*, 38, 948–957.

Carpenter, M., Nagell, K., & Tomasello, M. (1998). Social cognition, joint attention, and communicative competence from 9 to 15 months of age. *Monographs of the Society for Research in Child Development*, 63, 1–176.

Elsner, B. (2007). Infants' imitation of goal-directed actions: The role of movements and action effects. *Acta Psychologica*, 124(1), 44–59.

Elsner, B., & Aschersleben, G. (2003). Do I get what you get? Learning about the effects of self-performed and observed actions in infancy. *Consciousness & Cognition*, 12, 732–751.

Elsner, B., & Hommel, B. (2001). Effect anticipation and action control. *Journal of Experimental Psychology: Human Perception and Performance*, 27, 229–240.

Elsner, B., & Pauen, S. (2007). Social learning of artefact function in 12- and 15-month-olds. *European Journal of Developmental Psychology*, 4(1), 80–99.

German, T., & Johnson, S. (2002). Function and the origins of the design stance. *Journal of Cognition and Development*, 3, 279–300.

Hauf, P., Elsner, B., & Aschersleben, G. (2004). The role of action effects in infants' action control. *Psychological Research*, 68, 115–125.

Hayne, H., Barr, R., & Herbert, J. (2003). The effect of prior practice on memory reactivation and generalization. *Child Development*, 74, 1615–1627.

Hayne, H., MacDonald, S., & Barr, R. (1997). Developmental changes in the specificity of memory over the second year of life. *Infant Behavior & Development*, 20, 233–245.

Horst, J. S., Oakes, L. M., & Madole, K. L. (2005). What does it look like and what can it do? Category structure influences how infants categorize. *Child Development*, 76, 614–631.

Huang, C.-T., & Charman, T. (2005). Gradations of emulation learning in infants' imitation of actions on objects. *Journal of Experimental Child Psychology*, 92, 276–302.

Huang, C.-T., Heyes, C., & Charman, T. (2002). Infants' behavioral reenactment of "failed attempts": Exploring the roles of emulation learning, stimulus enhancement, and understanding of intentions. *Developmental Psychology*, 38, 840–855.

Itakura, S. (2001). Attention to repeated events in human infants (Homo sapiens): Effects of joint visual attention versus stimulus change. *Animal Cognition*, 4, 281–284.

Johnson, S. C., Booth, A., & O'Hearn, K. (2001). Inferring the goals of a nonhuman agent. *Cognitive Development*, 16, 637–656.

Leslie, A. (1984). Infants' perception of a manual pick up event. *British Journal of Developmental Psychology*, 2, 19–32.

Madole, K. L., & Oakes, L. M. (1999). Making sense of infant categorization: Stable processes and changing representations. *Developmental Review*, 19, 263–296.

Madole, K. L., & Oakes, L. M. (2005). Infants' attention to and use of functional properties in categorization. In L. Carlson & E. van der Zee (Eds.), *Functional Features in Language and Space: Insights from Perception, Categorization, and Development* (pp. 275–292). New York: Oxford University Press.

Madole, K. L., Oakes, L. M., & Cohen, L. B. (1993). Developmental changes in infants' attention to function and form-function correlations. *Cognitive Development*, 8, 189–209.

Meltzoff, A. N. (1988a). Infant imitation after a 1-week delay: Long-term memory for novel acts and multiple stimuli. *Developmental Psychology*, 24, 470–476.

Meltzoff, A. N. (1988b). Infant imitation and memory: Nine-month-olds in immediate and deferred tests. *Child Development*, 59, 217–225.

Meltzoff, A. N. (1995). Understanding the intentions of others: Re-enactment of intended acts by 18-month-old children. *Developmental Psychology*, 31, 838–850.

Nelson, K. (1973). Some evidence for the cognitive primacy of categorization and its functional basis. *Merrill-Palmer Quarterly*, 19, 21–39.

Nielsen, M. (2006). Copying actions and copying outcomes: Social learning through the second year. *Developmental Psychology*, 42, 555–565.

Perone, S., & Oakes, L. M. (2006). It clicks when it is rolled and it squeaks when it is squeezed: What 10-month-old infants learn about object function. *Child Development*, 77, 1608–1622.

Rakison, D. H. (2004). Infants' sensitivity to correlations between static and dynamic features in a category context. *Journal of Experimental Child Psychology*, 89, 1–30.

Striano, T., Chen, X., Cleveland, A., & Bradshaw, S. (2006). Joint attention social cues influence infant learning. *European Journal of Developmental Psychology*, 3, 289–299.

Thompson, D. E., & Russell, J. (2004). The ghost condition: Imitation versus emulation in young children's observational learning. *Developmental Psychology*, 40, 882–889.

Tomasello, M. (1999). *The Cultural Origins of Human Cognition*. Cambridge, MA: Harvard University Press.

Tomasello, M., Carpenter, M., Call, J., Behne, T., & Moll, H. (2005). Understanding and sharing intentions: The origins of cultural cognition. *Behavioral and Brain Sciences*, 28, 675–735.

Träuble, B., & Pauen, S. (2007). The role of functional information for infant categorization. *Cognition*, 105(2), 362–379.

Want, S. C., & Harris, P. L. (2002). How do children ape? Applying concepts from the study of non-human primates to the developmental study of "imitation" in children. *Developmental Science*, 5, 1–13.

Woodward, A. L. (1998). Infants selectively encode the goal object of an actor's reach. *Cognition*, 69, 1–34.

Chapter 11

The Directed Attention Model of Infant Social Cognition: Further Evidence

Vincent Reid and Tricia Striano

Introduction

Since the mid-1980s, research into infant social-cognitive capacities has shown that infants have some remarkable social abilities. These are surprising, given the complex, continuous, and dynamic nature of other humans and their actions. Indeed, it has even been suggested that there are no environmental sources as complex as another person (Gallagher et al., 2000). How can this be reconciled with the human infant's limited attention span, limited working memory, and initial lack of social experience? The aim of this chapter is to explain these skills via added support for the Directed Attention Model of infant social cognition (Reid & Striano, 2007). We conclude that the human infant uses social information to determine what is relevant in the environment. In doing so, the infant uses each successive aspect of the social world to reduce the overall amount of available information, such that the infant can successfully process the information, despite a limited processing capacity.

When compared with the highly skilled social abilities of the human infant, working memory capacity of infants is remarkably poor. For example, Ross-Sheehy, Oakes, and Luck (2003) found that visual short-term memory changed rapidly over infancy, but that skills by 13 months of age were still highly limited. In their preferential-looking paradigm, infants viewed changing and non-changing stimulus streams. Infants looked longer when they could recall the colors of the squares from the first presentation and if they changed in a subsequent presentation. Infants who were 4 and 6 months old looked longer only when a one-object stimulus stream changed color. However, by 10–13 months, infants could detect changes in displays with 2–3 items. In terms of perceptual development, when infants at $4^{1}/_{2}$ months of age see an object alone and then see it next to a novel object, this prior experience allows them to determine the location of a boundary between the two objects (Needham, 2001). This ability is not evident before 4.5 months of age, despite the very basic nature of the perceptual mechanisms involved.

When these memory and perceptual capacities are compared with the number of components present during social communication, such as in a triadic interaction between the infant, another person, and an external referent such as an object or a location, then there is clearly some form of differential processing occurring between the components of visual processing and working memory and the cognitive processes involved in social situations. For instance, 3-month-old infants can process relations between themselves, an object, and another person (Striano & Stahl, 2005). From an information-processing viewpoint, the social situation is clearly *more* complex than the demands of the task in the visual working memory study. For example, the changing color within the object stimulus streams is present in one location – the computer presentation monitor. In actual social situations, the surrounding environment must be monitored to determine locations and relations of central aspects of interest, such as the face of the social partner or the external referent.

In order to explain how infants exhibit complex social responses despite limited attentional resources and working memory capacities, we proposed an information-processing account of how an infant may reduce the environment to key factors that are relevant for the social situation (Reid & Striano, 2007). This framework was termed the Directed Attention Model, and was based on known social-cognitive abilities of infants. For example, when posed with the question "What needs to be processed in a social situation for socially appropriate responses to occur," we can proceed to dissect the perceptual stages needed before the infants discern enough of the environment for them to produce a socially correct response. In some respects, this is reverse engineering infant behavior. However, when the infant is provided with specific social information from an environment, we believe that this model, with its defined hierarchy of processes, may lead to predictions for infant behavior within any given scenario. Infant data strongly suggest that, through removing elements of the environment that are not socially relevant, infants effectively filter extraneous information away, thereby allowing their limited attentional resources to focus on more complex components of the social situation.

We have proposed that key cognitive tasks must occur in a semi-rigid sequence in order for an infant to react successfully during a social situation: the detection of socially relevant organisms (Stage One); the identification of socially relevant organisms (Stage Two); assessment of the locus of attention of the observed individual in relation to the infant (Stage Three); detection of the location of directed attention or object engagement by the observed individual (Stage Four). If these four components of the social situation are assessed, then the infant can: infer the observed goal, and/or, prepare an appropriate response (for example, establish contact, disengage, vocalize, and so on) (Stage Five). Each component will be discussed briefly, together with illustrations backing placement of each process within the listed hierarchy of tasks.

Stage One. The Detection of Socially Relevant Organisms

The first task that an infant needs to complete successfully in order to produce socially appropriate responses is to detect those components of the environment that are socially relevant. Many studies have indicated that infants are sensitive to distinctions between animate and inanimate objects (e.g. Mandler & McDonough 1996; Poulin-Dubois, Lepage, & Ferland, 1996). These studies suggest very early capacities to discriminate animate and inanimate objects in terms of the classification of motion, such as its regularity and energy source. Movement alone does not confer animacy. Even though movement in peripheral regions of the visual field induces reflexive gaze orientation by humans, these cues can assist only tangentially in the detection of conspecifics. Many other aspects of the natural visual world move, such as most flora in wind. Infants must therefore be initially faced with the task of discerning movement that is biological from movement that is not biological.

The detection and interpretation of biological motion are critical for recognizing conspecifics (Bertenthal, Proffitt & Kramer, 1987). Behavioral research suggests that humans detect and interpret biological motion very early in development, as shown by a preference to attend to biological motion when compared with stimuli depicting other forms of motion, such as randomly drifting dots. Much behavioral research has been conducted on infants' perception of biological motion, depicted by points of light moving as if attached to the major joints and the head of a moving person. Such stimuli, known as point light displays (PLDs), convey little information regarding the schema of the underlying object or agent. They are thus a good method with which to assess the perception of biological motion, free from confounding factors such as body shape or color. Indeed, adult observers fail to report any relationship between static PLDs and the percept of a person. However, moving point lights are perceived by adults as depicting a human form in less than 0.5 seconds (Johansson, 1973). Infants of 3 and 5 months discriminate these same moving PLDs from ones in which the temporal patterning of the lights is perturbed.

It appears that stored knowledge of the human form contributes to the interpretation of PLDs throughout ontogeny (Bertenthal, 1993). In support, 5-month-old infants do not discriminate PLDs depicting unfamiliar agents, such as a four-legged spider, from a perturbed version, whereas they do discriminate when exposed to PLDs of familiar agents (Bertenthal & Pinto, 1993). These studies indicate that experience of observing biological motion is required in order for infants to discriminate it from other forms of motion. Nonetheless, given that 3-month-olds have some capacities to discriminate biological motion from other types of motion, this suggests some very early capabilities. Furthermore, one study investigating neural correlates to the perception of biological motion with eight infants found that 8-month-old infants process biological motion in parietal regions of the brain (as do adults) when contrasted with scrambled motion (Hirai & Hiraki, 2005).

These authors found that differences between biological and scrambled motion were evidenced from 100 ms after presentation of the stimuli in the right but not the left parietal regions. The effect over parietal channels found by Hirai and Hiraki (2005) was confirmed in a later study with a larger sample of infants, where upright and inverted biological motion PLDs were presented to infants (Reid, Hoehl, & Striano, 2006). The stimuli depicted were of a person walking and a person kicking. No difference was seen between the two forms of motion (kicking versus walking). However, the resulting event-related potentials (ERPs) indicated a right parietal increase in positive amplitude for the upright PLDs, when compared with the inverted PLDs, which exhibited relatively less amplitude. This difference was observed from 150 ms after presentation of the stimuli and continued for the entire epoch of presentation.

We suggested in Reid and Striano (2007) that the detection of biological motion is of high importance for detecting conspecifics and that this process is required in order for the identification of the specifics of the social interaction. Further evidence for this claim derives from the very early ERP latency in infants of 8 months, where disambiguation of biological from non-biological motion occurs rapidly after stimulus onset. This fundamental aspect of social cognition must occur before more complex social information can be processed.

Stage Two. The Identification of Socially Relevant Organisms

Once the detection of biological motion has taken place, it is beneficial to identify the specifics of the observed organism. This could occur as an identification of species or as an identification of an individual conspecific. Surprisingly, little work thus far has addressed the issue of infant sensitivity to human biological motion relative to biological motion produced by other species. However, much work has been conducted on how an infant discriminates between a familiar person, such as the mother, and an unfamiliar person. This research has focused exclusively on how infants process faces rather than on how they discriminate the person – body and face inclusive – relative to another person. It should be noted that work on the identification of individuals is different from work that demonstrates that early in postnatal development infants are able to perceive the differences between individual faces (Slater & Quinn, 2001) or voices (DeCasper & Fifer, 1980). It is work determining how infants detect distinct individuals via personal properties such as gait or clothing that has not yet been investigated.

Electrophysiological studies with older infants suggest some capacities to discriminate familiar and novel people. De Haan & Nelson (1999) presented 6-month-old infants with a photograph of their mother and a stranger. The infants showed evidence for a familiarity effect. The resultant ERP negative component (Nc) was larger in amplitude for familiar faces than that for unfamiliar faces. Subsequent research into the functional properties of the Nc suggests that it is a robust index of infant attention (Richards, 2003; see also Striano & Reid, Chapter 1, this volume).

The results of de Haan and Nelson (1999) suggest differential processing of familiar and unfamiliar female adults by infants at 6 months of age, as well as an increased allocation of attentional resources when viewing familiar faces. As the Nc is maximal in amplitude at around 400 ms, this suggests rapid encoding of key components of the human face in order to discriminate familiar from unfamiliar people. In terms of the stages of social processing required to complete this task, it is interesting to note that the Nc component indicates differences between familiar and novel faces at around 400 ms after the presentation of the stimulus. This latency is reasonably rapid. However, it is later than the time needed to determine biological from non-biological motion.

Stage Three. Assessment of the Locus of Attention

An early step in successful communication is determining when a social signal is directed at or intended for the self. Once the detection and identification of an organism have occurred, we speculate that the observing infant will attend toward characteristics that index the locus of attention of the observed organism. In the human face, this can be detected by observing the orientation of the eyes (Farroni, Csibra, Simion, & Johnson, 2002) and the orientation of the head coupled with the orientation of the eyes (see Farroni, Johnson & Csibra, 2004). How infants determine the orientation of attention when observing an entire human body rather than the direction of the face and head is currently unknown. This is most likely due to the need to reduce the number of variables involved for an effective experimental design. Interestingly, once interaction has been established, then brief breaks in mutual gaze do not appear to influence the infant's understanding of a mutually enabled interaction (Nadel, Carchon, Kervella, Marcelli, & Réserbat-Plantey, 1999). This underlines the point that infants are highly predisposed to communicate, reciprocate, and connect with other people (Striano, 2004; Trevarthen, 1979).

The human infant's discriminative abilities are highly robust with respect to elements of the human face that delineate the locus of attention. For example, Farroni, Csibra, Simion, and Johnson (2002) showed that newborn infants can discriminate between a face with eyes oriented toward the infant and eyes oriented away from the infant. These authors also demonstrated that 4-month-old infants differentially process faces with direct versus averted gaze and that this is processed rapidly (*c.*250 ms) after faces have been presented to the infants.

Newborns are sensitive to faces, voices, and eye contact (Rochat & Striano, 1999), but do not appear to have particular social expectations or to show reduced attention or affect toward a social partner who suddenly stops interacting. However, with only 6 weeks of interactive experience, infants show a strong effect when an adult suddenly ceases to interact with them (Bertin & Striano, 2006). The infants reduce their smiling and gazing and then attempt to re-engage the social partner with vocalizations and body movements. Also by 6 weeks, infants distinguish between an adult who interacts in a relevant way by providing contingent feedback such as smiles and vocalizations compared to someone who interacts in an irregular way, with delayed social feedback (Striano, Henning & Stahl, 2005). These studies suggest robust social capacities in very young infants in the domain of determining the locus of attention in another person.

We conjecture that this form of processing must occur before further socially relevant components of the environment can be determined. Certainly in terms of potential advances in our knowledge, this particular topic has not garnered the attention that it deserves.

Stage Four. Detection of the Location of Another's Attention

Infants use the direction of an adult's gaze to determine what is socially relevant in the surrounding environment. Determining the locus of attention of nearby conspecifics is crucial for predicting change in the environment. An infant's enhanced attention to relevant locations might allow the infant to predict what objects the adult will act upon, thereby providing time for the infant to react socially and emotionally to changes that occur in the setting following the adult's action.

Recent studies into eye gaze and object processing suggest an early capacity for discerning a relationship between a person and an object. In one study, 4-month-old infants watched a video presentation of an adult gazing toward one of two objects. When shown the objects via video a second time, infants gazed toward the uncued object significantly more – suggesting that it was more novel (Reid & Striano, 2005). This suggests that 4-month-old infants not only followed the gaze of the adult, but acquired information about the object that was the focus of the adult's attention. Further, they can use the direction of gaze of an adult to facilitate attention to a location. This in turn biases processing of information from that location relative to objects in other locations.

In one study investigating the neural correlates of observing eye gaze on object processing, infants viewed an adult's face on-screen, and the eyes of the adult gazed toward an object. In the test trials, infants viewed the objects a second time. Infants exhibited enhanced neural processing (indexed by an enhanced positive slow wave) of the uncued object during test trials (Reid, Striano, Kaufman, & Johnson, 2004). Thus, the cued object was more highly processed when the face and object were on the screen and was subsequently more familiar to the infant when presented a second time in comparison to the uncued object. Results investigating infant processing of an adult's object-directed gaze suggest that similar cognitive systems are involved (Hoehl, Reid, Mooney, & Striano, 2008).

The results of these experiments suggest that by 4 months of age infants use the gaze of an adult to facilitate attention to a location. This in turn biases processing of information from that location relative to objects in other locations. In recent research investigating the neural correlates of joint attention in 9-month-old infants, it has been shown that infants allocate significantly more attentional resources to objects that are the subject of joint-attention interactions relative to objects that are not involved in joint-attention situations (Striano, Reid & Hoehl, 2006; see also Striano & Reid, Chapter 1, this volume). This result suggests that infants increase attention to aspects of the environment that are more socially salient.

The results of these studies are perhaps the most compelling support for the Directed Attention Model of infant social cognition. These data demonstrate that infants use others as tools with which to reduce the amount of information available for them to process from the surrounding world. To this extent, they fit very well with the notion that infants direct their limited attentional resources and memory capacity to components of the world that are important for social relations.

Stage Five. Inference of Goals and/or Preparation of Response

Infants are capable of detecting and identifying others. They also have skills at a remarkably early age that allow them to determine the locus of another person's attention as well as their relationship to external components of the world, such as objects or locations. However, the ability to infer goals appears not to develop until the beginning of the second half of the first postnatal year. We suggest that infants are capable of processing intentions and goals only when earlier perceptual processes of the social environment have been resolved.

Much research suggests that markers of intentionality throughout human action may be critical to understanding goal direction. At least by 9 months infants are capable of discerning intentional from accidental action (Woodward, 1999). Research also suggests that infants do not require the presentation of the end-state of an action in order to attribute a goal to an action, with infants at 8 months discriminating complete and incomplete actions and processing them differently at a neural level (Reid, Csibra, Belsky & Johnson, 2007). Other work suggests that infants of 9 months focus on the goals of an action over other components, such as the direction of the movement (Woodward, 2003).

One important issue is why younger infants fail to detect intentions embedded within human action. It may simply be that the number of variables that are required to be maintained in working memory produce the inability to detect goal-directed action in very young infants. Literally, there is too much information to maintain, and therefore the processing of additional information, in this case information pertaining to goal directions, will suffer. The Directed Attention Model can account for this in terms of overloaded working memory capacities. For example, the Directed Attention Model would predict that a young infant would be able to maintain information about one agent displaying a different emotional stance toward two objects, whereas two agents each displaying a separate emotional expression toward one object may be an observed social situation that is too complex for an infant to process. This is particularly the case if other components of the social situation take precedence in terms of infant attention. For example, if the infant first allocates attentional resources to determine the locus of an observed individual's attention in relation to the self, then tasks further downstream from that operation will suffer if the self–other information is required to be maintained over sustained periods of time. It is also possible that infants may produce a response at this stage in determining the parameters of the social situation. This may be due to the infant discerning enough information at this point in processing the situation to produce a socially correct response in the majority of settings, despite lacking awareness of the intentions or goals of others. Potentially, the detection of goals is not required in many social situations in order for an infant to produce a valid social response.

Conclusions

This information-processing model of social-cognitive skills is designed to provide a framework for conceptualizing infant abilities throughout development. In doing so, it may provide a basis for experimental predictions. For example, it predicts that the addition of biological motion to more complex aspects of the social environment, such as normal and disrupted human body schema, may help facilitate detection of aspects of body schema that would not otherwise be attended. This would be the case because biological motion is processed earlier and more rapidly than body schema, with components of body schema and biological motion overlapping. The discrimination of possible and impossible body schema may be a likely experimental outcome, which cannot be discriminated by infants at young ages when using static stimuli.

One caveat of this model is that it is a purely perceptual, information-processing account of how infants successfully resolve social information. The infant's role in this model is entirely passive. As any researcher interested in temperament and personality will inform you, in the real world, aspects of the infant determine outcomes from social events, as infants are highly interactive in their initiation of, and involvement in, social interactions. These factors will, of course, change the order of the sequence in the model. However, the individual components within each stage, such as detecting others and then determining their direction of attention, will probably not change.

This model is designed to describe social-cognitive processes. However, this inevitably has implications for general learning mechanisms throughout infancy. For example, word learning may be regarded as a purely cognitive task by those in developmental linguistics. However, learning to determine the referent of a novel word is an intrinsically social act, as is learning to speak (see Baldwin & Moses, 2001). Applying the Directed Attention Model to these social situations may predict the success of a given infant at these tasks because of the dynamics of the specific social situation.

The Directed Attention Model is the first attempt to produce a model that accounts for social capacities in infancy with limited cognitive skills. To the extent that use of this interpretative framework may generate new hypotheses, it is hoped that this simple model, and the further evidence for it provided in this chapter, will prove a useful platform for future research in the early development of social-cognitive information processing.

References

Baldwin, D. A., & Moses, L. J. (2001). Links between social understanding and early word learning: Challenges to current accounts. *Social Development*, 10(3), 309–329.

Bertenthal, B. I. (1993). Infants' perception of biomechanical motions: Intrinsic image and knowledge-based constraints. In C. Granrud (Ed.), *Visual Perception and Cognition in Infancy* (pp. 175–214). Hillsdale, NJ: Lawrence Erlbaum.

Bertenthal, B. I., & Pinto, J. (1993). Dynamical constraints in the perception and production of human movements. In M. Gunnar & E. Thelen (Eds.), *The Minnesota Symposia on Child Psychology: Systems in Development* (pp. 209–39). Hillsdale, NJ: Lawrence Erlbaum.

Bertenthal B. I., Proffitt, D. R., & Kramer, S. J. (1987). The perception of biomechanical motions by infants: Implementation of various processing constraints. *Journal of Experimental Psychology: Human Perception and Performance*, 13, 577–585.

Bertin, E., & Striano, T. (2006). The still-face response in newborn, 1.5-, and 3-month-old infants. *Infant Behavior & Development*, 29, 294–297.

DeCasper, A. J., & Fifer, W. P. (1980). Of human bonding: Newborns prefer their mothers' voices. *Science*, 208(4448), 1174–1176.

de Haan, M., & Nelson, C. A. (1999). Brain activity differentiates face and object processing in 6-month-old infants. *Developmental Psychology*, 35, 1113–1121.

Farroni, T., Csibra, G., Simion, F., & Johnson, M. H. (2002). Eye contact detection in humans from birth. *Proceedings of the National Academy of Sciences*, 99: 9602–9605.

Farroni, T., Johnson, M. H., & Csibra, G. (2004). Mechanisms of eye gaze perception during infancy. *Journal of Cognitive Neuroscience*, 16, 1320–1326.

Gallagher, H. L., Happé, F., Brunswick, N., Fletcher, P. C., Frith, U., & Frith, C. D. (2000). Reading the mind in cartoons and stories: An fMRI study of "theory of mind" in verbal and nonverbal tasks. *Neuropsychologia*, 38, 11–21.

Hirai, M., & Hiraki, K. (2005). An event-related potentials study of biological motion perception in human infants. *Cognitive Brain Research*, 22, 301–304.

Hoehl, S., Reid, V. M., Mooney, J., & Striano, T. (2008). What are you looking at? Infants' neural processing of an adult's object-directed eye gaze. *Developmental Science*, 11(1), 10–16.

Johansson, G. (1973). Visual perception of biological motion and a model for its analysis. *Perception & Psychophysics*, 14, 201–211.

Mandler, J. M., & McDonough, L. (1996). Drinking and driving don't mix: Inductive generalisation in infancy. *Cognition*, 59, 307–335.

Nadel, J., Carchon, I., Kervella, C., Marcelli, D., & Réserbat-Plantey, D. (1999). Expectancies for social contingency in 2-month-olds. *Developmental Science*, 2, 164–173.

Needham A. (2001). Object recognition and object segregation in 4.5-month-old infants. *Journal of Experimental Child Psychology*, 78(1), 3–22.

Poulin-Dubois, D., Lepage, A., & Ferland, D. (1996). Infants' concept of animacy. *Cognitive Development*, 11, 19–36.

Reid, V. M., Csibra, G., Belsky, J., & Johnson, M. H. (2007). Neural correlates of the perception of goal-directed action in infants. *Acta Psychologica*, 124, 129–138.

Reid, V. M., Hoehl, S., & Striano, T. (2006). The perception of biological motion by infants: An event-related potential study. *Neuroscience Letters*, 395, 211–214.

Reid, V. M., & Striano, T. (2005). Adult gaze influences infant attention and object processing implications for cognitive neuroscience. *European Journal of Neuroscience*, 21, 1763–1766.

Reid, V. M., & Striano, T. (2007). The directed attention model of infant social cognition. *European Journal of Developmental Psychology*, 4(1), 100–110.

Reid, V. M., Striano, T., Kaufman, J., & Johnson, M. (2004). Eye gaze cuing facilitates neural processing of objects in 4 month old infants. *Neuroreport*, 15, 2553–2556.

Richards, J. E. (2003). Attention affects the recognition of briefly presented visual stimuli in infants: An ERP study. *Developmental Science*, 6, 312–328.

Rochat, P., & Striano, T. (1999). Social cognitive development in the first year. In P. Rochat (Ed.), *Early Social Cognition* (pp. 3–34). Hillsdale, NJ: Lawrence Erlbaum.

Ross-Shirley, A., Oakes, L. M., & Luck, S. J. (2003). The development of visual short-term memory capacity in infants. *Child Development*, 74(6), 1807–1822.

Slater, A., & Quinn, P. C. (2001). Face recognition in the newborn infant. *Infant & Child Development*, 10(1–2), 21–24.

Striano, T. (2004). Direction of regard and the still-face effect in the first year: Does intention matter? *Child Development*, 75, 2, 468–479.

Striano, T., Henning, A., & Stahl, D. (2005). Sensitivity to social contingencies between 1 and 3 months of age. *Developmental Science*, 8(6), 509–519.

Striano, T., Reid, V. M., & Hoehl, S. (2006). Neural mechanisms of joint attention in infancy. *European Journal of Neuroscience*, 23, 2819–2823.

Striano, T., & Stahl, D. (2005) Sensitivity to triadic attention in early infancy. *Developmental Science*, 4, 333–343.

Trevarthen, C. (1979). Communication and co-operation in early infancy: A description of primary intersubjectivity. In M. Bullowa (Ed.), *Before Speech: The Beginning of Interpersonal Communication* (pp. 321–347). Cambridge: Cambridge University Press.

Woodward, A. (1999). Infants' ability to distinguish between purposeful and non-purposeful behaviors. *Infant Behaviour & Development*, 22(2), 145–160.

Woodward, A. L. (2003). Infants' developing understanding of the link between looker and object. *Developmental Science*, 6(3), 297–311.

Chapter 12

Reading Faces in Infancy: Developing a Multi-Level Analysis of a Social Stimulus

Tobias Grossmann and Amrisha Vaish

Introduction

The human face provides a wealth of socially relevant information. Healthy adults readily detect faces and decode all kinds of information from the face such as age, gender, familiarity, race, gaze direction, emotion, and so on. The importance of these face-reading capacities for social communication cannot be underestimated; this becomes especially clear when certain face-processing functions are impaired, as in certain neuropsychological conditions (for example, prosopagnosia). Although neuropsychological and neuroimaging work have helped identify a distributed network of specialized brain areas involved in adults' face-processing (Haxby, Hoffman, & Gobbini, 2000), the more basic question remains, how do these adult abilities develop and what are their precursors? It is thus crucial to look at the earliest stage of face processing: infancy. Therefore, the goal of this chapter is to review the accumulating work on the emergence of the face-processing system during infancy.

Before we turn to developmental work, let us consider a theoretical model of face processing, based on the neuroanatomical nature of the visual system in which visual information is processed via two routes, a subcortical and a cortical route. With respect to the face as a visual stimulus, it has been proposed that the subcortical route functions in face detection and relies on low spatial frequencies, whereas the cortical pathway is involved in face identification, eye-gaze perception, and emotional expression decoding, and relies on high spatial frequencies. Johnson (2005; Johnson & Morton, 1991) proposed that, in newborns, the subcortical face-processing route functions to detect and orient neonates toward faces, and to activate relevant cortical areas that later become specialized in processing specific aspects of faces. Following Johnson's logic, we first review work on newborns' face biases, and then review work on infants' developing abilities related to recognition, eye-gaze detection, and emotion decoding. Finally, we examine how infants apply these face-reading capacities in social situations. We will not discuss the neural bases and correlates of face processing in infancy, because these have been reviewed elsewhere (Nelson, 2001; Grossmann & Johnson, 2007).

The Newborn's Biases: Entering the World Prepared for Faces

One of the most debated questions in developmental psychology is whether newborns possess face-related preferences. In a series of experiments, Johnson, Dziurawiec, Ellis, and Morton (1991) showed that human newborns preferentially orient toward simple schematic face-like patterns as compared to control stimuli. Several studies have since been published supporting the notion that newborns are biased to attend to stimuli that possess certain characteristics of faces, a bias that is sufficient to elicit a preference for real faces in the natural environment (see Johnson, 2005). What stimulus characteristics are sufficient to elicit this bias? Based on earlier work, it was thought that a stimulus with three high-contrast blobs corresponding to the approximate location of the eyes and mouth might be enough to catch infants' attention. More recently, in a series of ingenious experiments by Farroni and colleagues (2005), this notion was refined and extended. In these experiments, newborns were found to show a preference for both schematic and naturalistic upright faces only under positive polarity (eye and mouth region dark, surrounding region lighter) and not under negative polarity (eye and mouth region light, surrounding region black) (see Figure 12.1). These findings are of particular

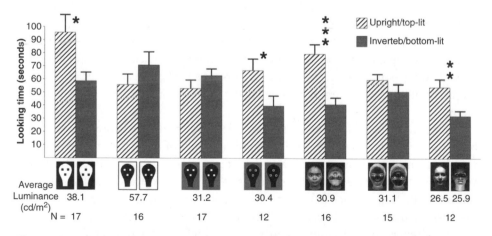

Figure 12.1. Stimuli and looking times in all experiments by Ferroni and colleagues
Note: Newborns' looking time to each of the pairs of stimuli was measured to reveal their preference. Significant differences are indicated by asterisks (* = P < 0.05; ** = P < 0.01; *** = P < 0.001). The numbers below the columns represent the number of newborns tested in the corresponding condition.
Source: Farroni et al. (2005).
Copyright © (2007) National Academy of Sciences, USA.

interest, because they rule out the recent proposal that newborns simply prefer up–down symmetrical patterns with more elements in the upper half (Turati, 2004), since this non-face-specific view would have predicted no effect of contrast polarity.

Another possible objection anticipated by Farroni and colleagues (2005) was that the absence of the effect in the reversed-contrast polarity condition might have been due to the low luminance of the negative polarity images, which prevented infants from exploring the details of the stimuli. Based on the hypothesis that one of the functions of newborns' orientation bias is to detect and establish eye contact (see Farroni, Csibra, Simion, & Johnson, 2002), the authors predicted that placing dark "irises" within the white squares in the negative polarity images would bring back the preference for upright faces. This prediction was supported. Furthermore, newborns were found to prefer human faces under natural lighting conditions (daylight or overhead illumination) as compared to bottom-lit faces. Note that a mechanism that is sensitive to overhead illumination could also explain the sensitivity to darker areas around the eyes and mouth.

There is thus compelling evidence for a face bias in newborns. What function might such a bias serve? Two accounts have been suggested (Farroni et al., 2005). One account stipulates that this bias in newborns allows detection of conspecifics in the environment, and that natural selection has thus sculpted a preference for invariant aspects of faces under natural lighting (top-lit). According to an alternative account, newborns' visual preferences have been selected for the function of detecting communicative partners. The latter is based on newborns' preferences for (1) upright faces and (2) eye contact and mutual gaze in an upright face. Simply to detect another human in the environment, a face in any orientation should be attended to, but only an upright face indicates a communicative partner, because human face-to-face communication takes only this form; moreover, mutual gaze in an upright face serves as a further communicative signal. Importantly, these two functional accounts are not mutually exclusive (Farroni et al., 2005). This is because a mechanism that relies on darker elements on a lighter background might help the infant find a top-lit face in the distance or the periphery but could also support eye-contact detection at close proximity; however, this idea remains to be tested. All in all, a face bias provides newborns with rich, socially relevant information, and might help detect conspecifics and/or communicative partners. In the following sections, we focus on infants' developing abilities to extract information about identity, eye gaze, and emotional expression.

Developing Face-Reading Capacities

Face recognition: Who are you?

Face recognition is the ability to discriminate among different exemplars of the face category and to recognize familiar faces. This ability capitalizes on recognition memory and thus differs from face detection – that is, the ability to discriminate faces from non-face visual objects. Evidence for early face recognition comes from work showing that, just hours after birth, infants exhibit a preference for their mother's face (Bushnell, 1991). Pascalis and de Schonen (1994) demonstrated that, after habituating to the photograph of an unfamiliar person and a retention interval of 2 minutes, newborn infants looked longer at a new face than at the face to which they had habituated. This suggests that newborns are capable of learning about individual faces. The question that arises is what information infants use in order to do so.

Pascalis, de Schonen, Morton, Deruelle, and Fabre-Grenet (1995) found that newborns' preference for their mother's face disappeared when the outer contour was masked and only the inner features of the face were visible. Infants thus seem to use outer contour features to identify their mother. This interpretation is consistent with findings on newborns' visual scanning of faces, which tends to be focused on high-contrast areas corresponding to the outer contour of the head or hairline (Maurer, 1983; Salapatek, 1968). Recent work shows that, although both inner and outer features are sufficient cues, outer features do have an advantage over inner features in eliciting newborns' face recognition (Turati, Macchi Cassia, Simion, & Leo, 2006). Another interesting finding from this study was that inversion of the face stimuli disrupted recognition only when the inner part of the face was shown, indicating that newborns are sensitive not only to inner and outer features but also to the spatial relations of the local features (face-specific configuration). This finding might be related to the face detection biases for upright faces described in the previous section, and points to a possible interaction of face-detection and face-recognition processes.

An important next question concerns what role experience plays in the developing face-recognition system. Experience plays a critical role for the development of many perceptual and cognitive functions. For example, between 6 and 10 months, infants' ability to discriminate between native speech sounds improves, whereas the ability to discriminate among foreign speech sounds declines, owing to a lack of exposure (Kuhl, Williams, Lacerda, Stevens, & Lindblom, 1992). Nelson (2001) suggests that the system underlying face recognition might be similarly sculpted by experience, and predicts that, early in life, infants can discriminate among several different faces and have a broadly defined face prototype. With experience, infants' face processing becomes more attuned and restricted to faces they are most familiar with (that is, a more precise face prototype). Indeed, Pascalis, de Haan, & Nelson (2002) showed that, although adults and 6- and 9-month-old infants were equally good at discriminating human faces, only the youngest infants could also discriminate monkey faces.

Further evidence for a perceptual narrowing in face processing comes from the "other-race effect" – that is, the finding that adults find it easier to discriminate faces from their own ethnic group (Sangrioli & de Schonen, 2004). However, this narrowing can be countered with experience. Thus, 6-month-olds exposed regularly to monkey faces for 3 months and then tested at 9 months could discriminate monkey faces (Pascalis et al., 2005). Similarly, Korean adults who had been adopted by French families when they were 3–9 years old performed as well as French natives in a Caucasian faces discrimination task (Sangrioli, Pallier, Argenti, Ventureyra, & de Schonen, 2005), whereas Koreans who had moved to France as adults showed the other-race effect. Together, these findings highlight the importance of experience in the development of face expertise.

Eye-gaze perception: What are you looking at?

The detection and monitoring of eye-gaze direction is essential for effective social learning and communication among humans (Bloom, 2000; Csibra & Gergely, 2006). Eye gaze informs us about the target of others' attention and expression, and conveys information about communicative intentions and future behavior (Baron-Cohen, 1995). Sensitivity to eye contact is evident early in human ontogeny. From birth, infants prefer to look at faces with their eyes open (Batki, Baron-Cohen, Weelwright, Connellan, & Ahluwalia, 2000), and faces that engage them in mutual as compared to averted gaze (Farroni et al., 2002).

Averted gaze may trigger a reflexive shift of an observer's visual attention (e.g. Driver et al., 1999). Numerous studies have investigated the effects that perceived gaze direction has on adults' spatial attention (e.g. Friesen & Kingstone, 1998; Langton & Bruce, 1999). The robust finding is that observers are faster to detect a target stimulus occurring in the peripheral visual field if it is preceded by a face looking in the direction of the stimulus rather than in the opposite direction. Newborns are also faster in making saccades to peripheral targets cued by the direction of eye movements of a schematic face, suggesting a rudimentary form of gaze following (Farroni, Pividori, Simion, Massaccesi, & Johnson, 2004), and 3-month-olds are more likely to orient toward a target if it is preceded by a perceived gaze shift toward the target when photographic images of a face are used (Hood, Willen, & Driver, 1998). Although infants, in contrast to adults, need to see eye movements to show this effect, motion alone is insufficient to shift infants' attention, as gaze shifts in an inverted face do not elicit gaze following (Farroni, Mansfield, Lai, & Johnson, 2003). Moreover, to find this effect in infants, the face has to be removed before the target object is presented, a finding that may be linked to young infants' difficulty in disengaging from attractive stimuli (Johnson, 1990).

The youngest age at which infants follow the gaze of live partners is between 2 and 3 months (D'Entremont, Hains, & Muir, 1997). Again, the gaze-following response requires special triggering conditions, including constant infant-directed speech and target objects that are close to the presenter's face. By about 6 months, infants follow gaze to more distant targets (Butterworth & Itakura, 2000; Butterworth & Jarrett, 1991), and gaze following to a single target becomes reliable between 7 and 9 months (Flom & Pick, 2005). However, the precision of 9-month-olds' responses is still fragile when several potential targets are available (Flom, Deák, Phill, & Pick, 2004), because infants around this age usually gaze at the first object on the correct side (Morales, Mundy, & Rojas, 1998). Furthermore, 9-month-olds follow the head turn of someone whose eyes are closed, whereas only a month later they do not (Brooks & Meltzoff, 2005). Only by 12 months do infants encode the psychological relationship between a person and the target of her gaze (Woodward, 2003). However, until 14 months infants follow blindfolded people's head turns (Brooks & Meltzoff, 2002). At this age, infants start to take into account whether the other has visual access to the target object (Dunphy-Lelii & Wellman, 2004) and correctly integrate information from head and eye direction (Caron, Keil, Dayton, & Butler, 2002).

Gaze following is a critical social skill. It helps coordinate visual attention and thereby achieve joint attention with conspecifics (Tomasello, 1999). More specifically, it has been hypothesized to serve various functions, including (a) instrumental learning or obtaining rewards by directing sight to something interesting (Moore & Corkum, 1994), (b) identifying others' attentional or perceptual states (Baron-Cohen, 1991), and (c) finding out what the other person is communicating about (Csibra, forthcoming).

Emotion detection: How do you feel?

Discriminating and recognizing facial expressions permits detection of another's emotional state and provides cues about how to respond. *Discrimination* means the ability to perceive the difference between two or more stimuli (de Haan & Nelson, 1998). Expressions can be discriminated solely by detecting feature differences between them, such as the different shape and configuration of the mouth or eyes. *Recognition* implies more than discrimination; it involves understanding the "meaning" of the emotional expressions (Bornstein & Arterberry, 2003; Oster, 1981). Nonetheless, to assign meaning to expressions, infants need to discriminate them, making discrimination integral to recognition.

There is evidence that even newborns may discriminate between facial expressions (Field, Woodson, Greenberg, & Cohen, 1982). In this study, newborns were tested with happy, sad, or surprised facial expressions presented by a live female model. One expression was posed repeatedly until infants looked at it for less than 2 seconds, after which the other two expressions were presented. Field and colleagues found that infants' looking time increased when the expression changed, suggesting that newborns could discriminate among the expressions (but see Kaitz, Meschulach-Sarfaty, Auerbach, & Eidelman, 1988). More rigorous studies suggest that, certainly by 3 months, infants can discriminate happy from surprised and from angry faces (see Nelson, 2001), and can also discriminate different intensities of a happy expression (Kuckuck, Vibbert, & Bornstein, 1986). By 4 months, infants look longer at happy than angry or neutral expressions (LaBarbera, Izard, Vietze, & Parisi, 1976), and discriminate mild from intense examples of fearful faces (Nelson & Ludemann, 1986). Six-month-olds reliably discriminate varying intensities of happy and angry facial expressions (Striano, Brennan, & Vanman, 2002). Note, however, that order effects have been observed. For example, 7-month-olds in a habituation procedure can discriminate happy from fearful faces if they are habituated to happy but not if they are habituated to fearful faces (Nelson, Morse, & Leavitt, 1979). Overall, infants do discriminate among several facial expressions.

These studies do not indicate, however, whether infants' responses generalize beyond the model tested, nor whether infants discriminate based on local feature information (for example, raised versus lowered eyebrows) or respond to the invariant configuration of facial features that constitute an emotional expression. For a facial expression to be useful in communication, infants need to understand that the expression conveys the same "meaning" across individuals and remains the same despite changes in intensity. Researchers have thus assessed infants' abilities to categorize facial expressions. In one such study, Nelson et al. (1979) familiarized 7-month-old infants to happy expressions posed by two females. In the test phase, infants were shown a third model posing a happy and a fearful expression. Infants looked longer at the fearful expression, indicating that, despite the change in identity, they detected that the happy expression belonged to the same category, whereas the fearful did not. However, infants did not show categorization abilities when they were first familiarized to the fearful expression. These findings have since been replicated and extended (Kotsoni, de Haan, & Johnson, 2001; Ludemann & Nelson, 1988). Thus, perhaps infants can categorize a very familiar expression (for example, happy) and then discriminate it from a novel expression, whereas a novel expression (for example, fearful) is more difficult to categorize.

Kestenbaum and Nelson (1990) also found that 7-month-olds recognized the similarity of happy faces over changing identities and discriminated this expression from fear and anger when the facial stimuli were presented upright, but not when they were inverted. In a second experiment, Kestenbaum and Nelson showed that, regardless of orientation, 7-month-old infants were able to discriminate between happiness, fear, and anger posed by a single model. It was thus suggested that *categorization* of emotional expressions might depend upon infants' ability to attend to affectively relevant information, which relies on configurational processing of the face and is thus disrupted by inversion. *Discrimination*, however, can be performed on feature information irrespective of stimulus orientation.

The results of the reviewed studies suggest that (1) although even newborns might react differentially to facial expressions, it is by 3–4 months that infants can reliably discriminate among at least some expressions, and (2) infants can form categories of happy expressions by 5 months, although the ability to form categories of less familiar expressions might not develop until after 7 months.

We have identified three levels of information (identity, gaze, and emotion) that infants become sophisticated at gleaning from the face during the first year. In everyday interactions, these generally occur together and are thus best processed in an integrated fashion. We thus now consider when infants begin to integrate these levels of facial information. To do so, we examine infants' use of others' facial information to guide their own actions and to predict others' actions.

Using Others as Informants:
A Case for Multi-Level Integration

Social referencing is a communicative process whereby infants use others' interpretations of ambiguous situations to form their own interpretations of those situations and thereby to learn about their environment (Campos & Stenberg, 1981). Social referencing thus aids our basic survival and permits the successful transmission of culture (Tomasello, 1999). In a typical social referencing study, infants are presented with a novel stimulus about which an adult delivers emotional cues. If infants engage in social referencing, they should modify their behavior according to the cues provided. This phenomenon can occur via multiple modalities, but we focus here on the facial modality.

What minimum abilities are needed to social reference using facial cues? One obvious candidate is emotion reading: infants must discriminate and identify the emotion in order to use it appropriately. Additionally, infants must understand the referential nature of the cues, which, in the context of facial cues, means they must follow the adult's gaze to the stimulus. Critically, infants must integrate these pieces of information. Research suggests that infants display such integration by 12 months; younger infants respond only to the emotional information. Thus, Walden and Baxter (1989) found that, although 6–12-month-olds showed differential looking to their parents' positive versus fearful facial expressions, they did not appropriately regulate their behavior towards ambiguous toys, whereas infants older than 12 months did (see also Mumme, DiCorcia, & Wedig, forthcoming). In Sorce, Emde, Campos, and Klinnert's study (1985), most 12-month-olds on the shallow side of a visual cliff crossed the cliff if mothers expressed interest or joy, but few crossed if mothers expressed fear or anger (see also Camras & Sachs, 1991; Klinnert, 1984).

Emotional and referential cues can also be integrated to draw inferences and make predictions about the signaler – that is, about her stance and actions towards the stimulus. In one recent study (Phillips, Wellman, & Spelke, 2002), 12-month-olds were habituated and 14-month-olds familiarized to an experimenter (E) looking at and positively emoting about object A. Infants then saw two kinds of test events: *consistent* events entailed E looking at and positively emoting about object (B), and then holding B, whereas *inconsistent* events involved E looking at and positively emoting about A, but then holding B. Infants of 14 months, but not 12-month-olds, looked longer at the inconsistent than the consistent test events, which was interpreted as suggesting that by 14 months infants combine a person's gaze direction and emotional expression to predict his or her action (see also Sodian & Thoermer, 2004). However, it is unclear whether infants used both gaze and positive emotion cues, since using gaze cues alone would have led to the same prediction as using both cues.

Vaish and Woodward (forthcoming) addressed this problem by using negative emotions, which predict that the emoter will *not* reach for the object she has attended to. They familiarized 14-month-olds to an experimenter (E) looking into a cup and emoting happily or disgustedly while ignoring another cup. Test events involved E reaching into either the cup she had emoted about (Attended) or the other cup (Unattended). If infants understand emotions as action predictors, they should look longer at Unattended events in the happy condition but at Attended events in the disgusted condition. However, infants in both emotion conditions looked longer at Unattended events, suggesting that they used attention but not emotion cues to predict E's actions (although there was an order effect similar to that reported by Sodian and Thoermer, 2004). Thus, by 14 months, infants may not yet integrate gaze and emotional cues to predict others' actions, and might instead use only gaze cues to do so.

Can infants integrate identity with gaze and emotion cues? When social referencing, infants need to identify trustworthy and knowledgeable sources of information (Baldwin & Moses, 1996). Typically, since caregivers are familiar, trusted, and knowledgeable, infants need only identify caregivers (which we have seen they can do early in the first year), and use cues provided by them. What if familiarity and knowledge are found in different individuals? Extant work addressing this issue provides mixed results. Zarbatany and Lamb (1985) placed 12-month-olds in a room with either their mother or a stranger. Infants then saw a novel stimulus about which they received positive or fearful facial cues from the adult. Infants in the "mother" condition looked as much at mothers as infants in the "stranger" condition looked at the stranger, but only infants in the "mother" condition regulated their behavior toward the stimulus. This suggests that infants note the informant's identity and modify their behavior only in response to cues from the familiar and trusted informant. However, infants in the "stranger" condition might have been so stressed by the mother's absence that they were unable to use the stranger's signals (Klinnert, Emde, Butterfield, & Campos, 1986).

To counter this problem, Klinnert et al. (1986) had 12–13-month-olds play with an experimenter (E) while mothers sat some distance behind the infants. When a novel toy appeared, E displayed happy or fearful facial expressions. The results contrasted with those of Zarbatany and Lamb (1985): infants referenced E first and more than the mother, and, although most infants looked to their mothers (who were neutral) before acting, infant behavior was nevertheless influenced by E's cues. Thus, infants do not blindly use signals from a familiar person; rather, when an unfamiliar adult has more information than the familiar one (as in this case because mothers were farther away and thus less aware of the ambiguous situation than was E), infants do effectively use information from the more knowledgeable adult. Of course, in most situations, familiar persons are knowledgeable and are the only informants; only in situations in which familiarity and knowledge are found in two different people do infants need to pick knowledge over familiarity. Given the mixed findings, there is clearly need for more work assessing whether infants can do so.

Recent research (Gergely, Egyed, & Király, 2007) investigated whether infants can integrate identity, gaze, and emotional information to predict others' actions, but revealed that 14-month-olds cannot. This finding is not surprising given that 14-month-olds may not even predict others' actions by integrating gaze and emotion cues (Vaish & Woodward, forthcoming). Thus, although 12-month-olds can effectively combine a signaler's facial cues to modify their *own* behaviors towards target stimuli, even 14-month-olds may not yet integrate these cues to predict the *signaler*'s behavior appropriately.

Conclusions

This chapter was designed to review and integrate the accumulating work on early face-processing skills. We have shown that, despite major developments in face-processing abilities during the first year and beyond, there is also immense continuity. Infants come into the world prepared to attend to socially engaging faces and to possess rudimentary capacities for face identification, gaze following, and emotion processing. These skills quickly become sophisticated, and, by the end of the first year, are ready to be integrated. One capacity that emerges from such integration is social referencing, which, at a minimum, consists of the abilities to use emotional and referential information, but is in fact larger than the sum of these parts, as it allows infants to engage in an activity that is crucial for survival and enculturation (Tomasello, 1999). Twelve-month-olds use others' gaze, emotion, and, arguably, identity cues to modify their own behavior, but even 14-month-olds seem unable to construe others' behavior in terms of these cues. Thus, there is a significant difference in the way 12–14-month-olds use their face-processing skills for themselves rather than for understanding others, and the ability to construe others' actions in terms of these cues seems to be still developing in the second year.

Finally, it should be pointed out that infants live in a multimodal world in which most cues are provided not only by faces but also by voices, touch, and so on. Indeed, the face may not always be the most potent communicative modality. In particular, infants seem to respond to vocal cues from earlier on and more effectively than to the facial modality (e.g. Mastropieri & Turkewitz, 1999; Grossmann, Striano, & Friederici, 2005; 2007; Vaish & Striano, 2004). It is thus important to consider how voice processing develops in infancy, and, more generally, to examine not only how the dimensions of face processing are integrated but also how processing of the face is integrated with that of other modalities during development.

References

Baldwin, D. A., & Moses, L. M. (1996). The ontogeny of social information gathering. *Child Development*, 67, 1915–1939.

Baron-Cohen, S. (1991). Precursors to a theory of mind: Understanding attention in others. In A. Whiten (Ed.), *Natural Theories of Mind: Evolution, Development and Simulation of Everyday Mindreading*. Oxford: Blackwell.

Baron-Cohen, S. (1995). *Mindblindness: An Essay on Autism and Theory of Mind*. Cambridge, MA: MIT Press.

Batki, A., Baron-Cohen, S., Wheelwright, S., Connellan, J., & Ahluwalia, J. (2000). Is there an innate gaze module? Evidence from human neonates. *Infant Behavior & Development*, 23, 223–229.

Bloom, P. (2000). *How Children Learn the Meanings of Words*. Cambridge, MA: MIT Press.

Bornstein, M. H., & Arterberry, M. E. (2003). Recognition, discrimination and categorization of smiling by 5-month-old infants. *Developmental Science*, 6, 585–599.

Brooks, R., & Meltzoff, A. N. (2002). The importance of eyes: How infants interpret adult looking behavior. *Developmental Science*, 38, 958–966.

Brooks, R., & Meltzoff, A. N. (2005). The development of gaze following and its relation to language. *Developmental Science*, 8, 535–543.

Bushnell, I. W. R. (1991). Mother's face recognition in newborn infants: learning and memory. *Infant and Child Development*, 10, 67–74.

Butterworth, G., & Itakura, S. (2000). How the eyes, head and hand serve definite reference. *British Journal of Developmental Psychology*, 18, 25–50.

Butterworth, G., & Jarrett, N. (1991). What minds have in common is space: Spatial mechanisms serving joint visual attention in infancy. *British Journal of Developmental Psychology*, 9, 55–72.

Campos, J., & Stenberg, C. (1981). Perception, appraisal and emotion: The onset of social referencing. In M. E. Lamb & L. R. Sherrod (Eds.), *Infant Social Cognition* (pp. 273–314). Hillsdale, NJ: Lawrence Erlbaum.

Camras, L. A., & Sachs, V. B. (1991). Social referencing and caretaker expressive behavior in a day care setting. *Infant Behavior and Development*, 14, 27–36.

Caron, A. J., Keil, A. J., Dayton, M., & Butler, S. C. (2002). Comprehension of the referential intent of looking and pointing between 12 and 15 months. *Journal of Cognition and Development*, 3, 445–464.

Csibra, G. (forthcoming). Why human infants follow gaze: A communicative-referential account.

Csibra, G., & Gergely, G. (2006). Social learning and social cognition: The case for pedagogy. In Y. Munakata & M. H. Johnson (Eds.), *Processes of Change in Brain and Cognitive Development. Attention and Performance XXI* (pp. 249–274). Oxford: Oxford University Press.

D'Entremont, B., Hains, S. M. J., & Muir, D. W. (1997). A demonstration of gaze following in 3- to 6-month-olds. *Infant Behavior & Development*, 20, 569–572.

de Haan, M., & Nelson, C. A. (1998). Discrimination and categorization of facial expressions of emotion during infancy. In A. Slator (ed.), *Perceptual Development* (pp. 287–309). Hove: Psychology Press.

Driver, J., Davis, G., Ricciardelli, P., Kidd, P., Maxwell, E., & Baron-Cohen, S. (1999). Gaze perception triggers reflexive visuospatial orienting. *Visual Cognition*, 6, 509–540.

Dunphy-Lelii, S., & Wellman, H. M. (2004). Infants' understanding of occlusion of others' line of sight: Implications for an emerging theory of mind. *European Journal of Developmental Psychology*, 1, 49–66.

Farroni, T., Csibra, G., Simion, F., & Johnson, M. H. (2002). Eye contact detection in humans from birth. *Proceedings of National Academy of Science (USA)*, 99, 9602–9605.

Farroni, T., Johnson, M. H., Menon, E., Zulian, L., Faraguna, D., & Csibra, G. (2005). Newborn's preference for face-relevant stimuli: Effects of contrast polarity. *Proceedings of the National Academy of Sciences USA*, 102, 17245–17250.

Farroni, T., Mansfield, E.M., Lai, C., & Johnson, M.H. (2003). Infants perceiving and acting on the eyes: Tests of an evolutionary hypothesis. *Journal of Experimental Child Psychology*, 85, 199–212.

Farroni, T, Pividori D., Simion, F., Massaccesi, S., & Johnson M. H. (2004). Eye gaze cueing of attention in newborns. *Infancy*, 5, 39–60.

Field, T. M., Woodson, R. W., Greenberg, R., & Cohen, C. (1982) Discrimination and imitation of facial expressions by neonates. *Science*, 218, 179–181.

Flom, R., Deák, G. O., Phill, C. G., & Pick, A. D. (2004). Nine-month-olds' shared visual attention as a function of gesture and object location. *Infant Behavior & Development*, 27, 181–194.

Flom, R. & Pick, A.D. (2005). Experimenter affective expression and gaze following in 7-month-olds. *Infancy*, 7, 207–218.

Friesen, C. K., & Kingstone, A. (1998). The eyes have it! Reflexive orienting is triggered by non-predictive gaze. *Psychonomic Bulletin & Review*, 5, 490–495.

Gergely, G., Egyed, K., & Király, I. (2007). On pedagogy. *Developmental Science*, 10, 139–146.

Grossmann, T., Striano, T., & Friederici, A. D. (2005). Infants' electric brain responses to emotional prosody. *NeuroReport*, 16 1825–1828.

Grossmann, T., Striano, T., & Friederici, A. D. (2007). Developmental changes in infants' processing of happy and angry facial expressions: A neurobehavioral study. *Brain & Cogniton*, 64, 30–41.

Haxby, J. V., Hoffman, E., & Gobbini, M. I. (2000). The distributed human neural system for face perception. *Trends in Cognitive Sciences*, 4, 223–233.

Hood, B. M., Willen, J. D., & Driver, J. (1998). Adults eyes trigger shifts of visual attention in human infants. *Psychological Science*, 9, 131–134.

Johnson, M. H. (1990). Cortical maturation and the development of visual attention in early infancy. *Journal of Cognitive Neuroscience*, 2, 81–95.

Johnson, M. H. (2000). Cortical maturation and the development of visual attention in infancy. *Journal of Cognitive Neuroscience*, 2, 81–95.

Johnson, M. H. (2005). Subcortical face processing. *Nature Reviews Neuroscience*, 6, 766–774.

Johnson, M. H., Dziurawiec, S., Ellis, H. D., & Morton, J. (1991). Newborns' preferential tracking of face-like stimuli and its subsequent decline. *Cognition*, 40, 1–19.

Johnson, M. H., & Morton, J. (1991). *Biology and Cognitive Development: The Case for Face Recognition*. Oxford: Blackwell.

Langton, S. R. H., & Bruce, V. (1999). Reflexive social orienting. *Visual Cognition*, 6, 541–567.

Kaitz, M., Meschulach-Sarfaty, O., Auerbach, J., & Eidelman, A. (1988). A reexamination of newborns' ability to imitate facial expressions. *Developmental Psychology*, 24, 3–7.

Kestenbaum, R., & Nelson, C. A. (1990). The recognition and categorization of upright and inverted emotional expressions by 7-month-old infants. *Infant Behavior & Development*, 13, 497–511.

Klinnert, M. D. (1984). The regulation of infant behavior by maternal facial expression. *Infant Behavior & Development*, 7, 447–465.

Klinnert, M. D., Emde, R. N., Butterfield, P., & Campos, J. J. (1986). Social referencing: The infants' use of emotional signals from a friendly adult with mother present. *Developmental Psychology*, 22, 427–432.

Kotsoni, E., de Haan, M., & Johnson, M. H. (2001). Categorical perception of facial expressions by 7-month-old infants. *Perception*, 30, 1115–1125.

Kuckuck, A., Vibbert, M., & Bornstein, M. H. (1986). The perception of smiling and its experiential correlates in 3-month-olds. *Child Development*, 57, 1054–1061.

Kuhl, P. K., Williams, K. A., Lacerda, F., Stevens, K. N., & Lindblom, B. (1992). Linguistic experience alters phonetic perception in infants by 6 months of age. *Science*, 255, 606–608.

LaBarbera, J. D., Izard, C. E., Vietze, P., & Parisi, S. A. (1976). Four- and six-month-old infants' visual responses to joy, anger, and neutral expressions. *Child Development*, 47, 533–538.

Ludemann, P. M., & Nelson, C. A. (1988). The categorical representation of facial expressions by 7-month-old infants. *Developmental Psychology*, 24, 492–501.

Mastropieri, D., & Turkewitz, G. (1999). Prenatal experience and neonatal responsiveness to vocal expressions of emotion. *Developmental Psychobiology*, 35, 204–214.

Maurer, D. (1983). The scanning of compound figures by young infants. *Journal of Experimental Child Psychology*, 35, 437–448.

Moore, C., & Corkum, V. (1994). Social understanding at the end of the first year of life. *Developmental Review*, 14, 349–372.

Morales, M., Mundy, P., & Rojas, J. (1998). Following the direction of gaze and language development in 6-month-olds. *Infant Behavior & Development*, 21, 373–377.

Mumme, D. L., DiCorcia, J. A., & Wedig, M. M. (unpublished). Limitations in 10-month-old infants' emotional processing abilities.

Nelson, C. A. (2001). The development and neural bases of face recognition. *Infant and Child Development*, 10, 3–18.

Nelson, C. A., & Ludemann, P. M. (1986). The discrimination of intensity changes of emotion by 4- and 7-month-old infants. Paper presented at the Midwest Psychological Association, Chicago.

Nelson, C. A., Morse, P. A., & Leavitt, L. A. (1979). Recognition of facial expressions by 7-month-old infants. *Child Development*, 50, 1239–1242.

Oster, H. (1981). "Recognition" of emotional expression in infancy. In M. E. Lamb & L. R. Sherrod (Eds.), *Infant Social Cognition: Empirical and Theoretical Considerations* (pp. 85–125). Hillsdale, NJ: Lawrence Erlbaum.

Pascalis, O., de Haan, M., & Nelson, C. A. (2002). Is face processing species-specific during the first year of life? *Science*, 296, 1321–1323.

Pascalis, O., & de Schonen, S. (1994). Recognition memory in 3- to 4-day-old human neonates. *Neuroreport*, 8, 1721–1724.

Pascalis, O., de Schonen, S., Morton, J., Deruelle, C., Fabre-Grenet, M. (1995). Mother's face recognition by neonates: A replication and extension. *Infant Behavior and Development*, 18, 75–85.

Pascalis, O., Scott, L. S., Kelly, D. J., Shannon, R. W., Nicholson, E., Coleman, M., & Nelson, C. A. (2005). Plasticity of face processing in infancy. *Proceedings of the National Academy of Sciences USA*, 102, 5297–5300.

Phillips, A. T., Wellman, H. M., & Spelke, E. S. (2002). Infants' ability to connect gaze and emotional expression to intentional action. *Cognition*, 85, 53–78.

Salapatek, P. H. (1968). Visual scanning of geometric figures by the human newborn. *Journal of Comparative and Physiological Psychology*, 66, 247–248.

Sangrioli, S., & de Schonen, S. (2004). Recognition of own-race faces by three-month-old infants. *Journal of Child Psychology and Psychiatry*, 45, 1219–1227.

Sangrioli, S., Pallier, C., Argenti, A. M., Ventureyra, V. A. G., & de Schonen, S. (2005). Reversibility of the other-race effect in face recognition during childhood. *Psychological Science*, 16, 440–444.

Sodian, B., & Thoermer, C. (2004). Infants' understanding of looking, pointing, and reaching as cues to goal-directed action. *Journal of Cognition and Development*, 5, 289–316.

Sorce, J. F., Emde, R. N., Campos, J. J., & Klinnert, M. D. (1985). Maternal emotional signaling: Its effects on the visual cliff behavior of 1-year-olds. *Developmental Psychology*, 21, 195–200.

Striano, T., Brennan, P. A., & Vanman, E. (2002). Maternal depressive symptoms and 6-month-old infants' sensitivity to facial expressions. *Infancy*, 3, 115–126.

Tomasello, M. (1999). *The Cultural Origins of Human Cognition*. Cambridge, MA: Harvard University Press.

Turati, C. (2004) Why faces are not special to newborns: An alternative account of the face preference. *Current Directions in Psychological Science*, 13(1), 5–8.

Turati, C., Macchi Cassia, V., Simion, F., & Leo, I. (2006). Newborns' face recognition: Role of inner and outer facial features. *Child Development*, 77, 297–311.

Vaish, A., & Striano, T. (2004). Is visual reference necessary? Contributions of facial versus vocal cues in 12-month-olds' social referencing behaviour. *Developmental Science*, 7, 261–269.

Vaish, A., & Woodward, A. (unpublished). What will you do next? Infants' use of attention versus emotion cues as predictors of behavior.

Walden, T. A., & Baxter, A. (1989). The effect of context and age on social referencing. *Child Development*, 60, 1511–1518.

Woodward, A. (2003). Infants' developing understanding of the link between looker and object. *Developmental Science*, 6, 297–311.

Zarbatany, L., & Lamb, M. E. (1985). Social referencing as a function of information source: Mothers versus strangers. *Infant Behavior and Development*, 8, 25–33.

Chapter 13

The Perception of Emotional Expressions during Infancy

Stefanie Hoehl

Emotional expressions provide us with invaluable information about others' feelings toward objects, situations, and people as well as their emotional state and mood. They also give us clues in respect to others' future behavior. Emotional expressions help us guide our own behavior, especially in new or ambiguous situations. This holds especially true for infants, who continuously encounter new situations and meet people and objects that, for them, are ambiguous.

Developmental scientists have investigated the ontogenetic course of emotional expression processing from the first hours of life onwards until adulthood. Since groundbreaking behavioral studies were conducted in the 1970s (e.g. Young-Brown, Rosenfeld, & Horowitz, 1977), our knowledge about infants' skills in the detection, discrimination, and recognition of different emotional expressions has increased tremendously. Several important questions about developmental trajectories, underlying mechanisms, and related neural networks have been posed and explored. The development of emotion processing in infancy must be considered as a highly dynamic and interactional process. On the one hand, infants' emotion-processing skills are highly dependent on the personality and behavior of the caregiver. Even more strikingly, it is also affected by the infant's temperament (de Haan, Belsky, Reid, Volein, & Johnson, 2004). It is now widely acknowledged that infants must be seen not as passive perceivers in social interactions, but as agents whose perception of emotions depends on various factors localized in their environment as well as in their own temperament and behavior.

A basic question related to the development of emotional-expression processing concerns the sequence in which certain skills arise in the first postnatal years. Critical steps are the detection of emotional signals, the differentiation between distinct emotions, and finally the recognition of emotions. Detection involves the sensitivity of infants' perceptual systems to external stimuli, which prevail social information like faces or voices. A sensitivity to attend toward socially relevant stimuli is already evident in newborn infants. For instance, neonates preferentially follow schematic face-like stimuli with their heads and eyes compared to similarly complex non-face-like patterns (Goren, Sarty, & Wu, 1975; Johnson, Dziurawiec, Ellis, & Morton, 1991). The discrimination of emotional expressions, in contrast, relies more heavily on experience. The ability to discriminate between certain pairs of emotions becomes evident at different points in time during the first postnatal year (see, e.g., Nelson, 2001 for the visual domain). However, mere discrimination does not imply that adults and infants share a common understanding of the expressed emotion. Furthermore, it is hard to tell whether infants base their discrimination of emotional expressions on underlying representations of the respective emotions or on merely perceptual characteristics of the applied stimuli, such as the configuration of certain facial features. Finally, recognition of emotional expressions involves a cognitive interpretation process of others' expressive signals. It can be assumed that at least the recognition of the emotional valence of an expression is required for infants to be able to use emotional cues to regulate their behavior in response to novel situations or objects.

The aim of this chapter is to review the most important findings concerning infants' emotional-expression processing in experimental settings. I will describe studies addressing only one sensory modality, as well as studies concerned with dynamic interactions that involve multiple sensory channels at the same time. One focus will be the functional relevance of the described skills for infants in everyday situations. In addition to behavioral results, new findings regarding the neural correlates of emotional expression processing will be addressed. Our knowledge of infants' neural responses to different stimuli relies most heavily on electroencephalographic (EEG) measures. In developmental research the online assessment of electrophysiological brain responses has proved to be a valuable source of novel insights into infancy development (see de Haan, Johnson & Halit, 2003; also Webb, Long, & Nelson, 2005, for a review). One of the most frequently used methods of analyzing infant EEG data is exploring event-related potentials (ERPs). An ERP reflects transient changes in brain electrophysiology that are time-locked to the presentation of an event, such as a briefly presented image of a face or a spoken word (Allison, Wood, & McCarthy, 1986).

I will start with a review on findings from infant studies that applied both visual and auditory stimuli. In the next sections I will focus on findings from separable sensory domains – that is, visual, auditory, and tactile stimulation. Then I will discuss the impact of emotional expressions, especially from caregivers, on infants' behavior in ambiguous situations, and address the functional relevance of this kind of social information.

The Perception of Multimodal Emotional Information in Infancy

In her 1997 review Walker-Andrews proposes a non-modular approach to the development of emotion perception. She poses the question whether intermodal perception development implies integrating information from initially separated sensory channels, or whether, in contrast, the infant learns to differentiate receptive information, which at first has been perceived in a unified multimodal way. Walker-Andrews reviews empirical evidence that suggests that infants are first able to discriminate and recognize emotional expressions when multimodal information is available, and only later learn to discriminate emotions when information from only one sensory domain is available, such as isolated facial expressions. Some support for this notion comes from a study by Caron, Caron, & MacLean (1988). In a series of experiments, the ability of infants of 4–5 months to discriminate between happy, sad, and angry expressions was studied, when the amount of available information from visual and auditory channels was varied. The results indicate that infants are able to discriminate between emotion pairs first when dynamic visual and auditory stimuli are presented or when only vocal stimulation is given. These findings suggest that infants benefit more from emotional information provided by the voice compared to facial expressions in the early postnatal months. This makes sense, since the auditory system is more developed at birth than visual sensory channels.

The most commonly used paradigm to investigate intermodal matching in infancy is the intermodal preference method. Infants are presented with two visual and one auditory stimulus that corresponds to one of the visual stimuli but does not match the second one. For instance, infants are presented with a man's and a woman's face accompanied by a male voice (see Spelke & Owsley, 1979, for a more detailed description of this method). When presented with dynamic facial expression and corresponding or not matching voices, 2-month-olds did not show intermodal matching but preferred to look almost exclusively at the happy expression regardless of the accompanying voice. At 5 months, infants increased fixation to the corresponding facial expression when any emotional voice was presented, showing evidence for emotional intermodal matching (Walker-Andrews, 1997). Finally, at 7 months of age, infants even show preference for sound-matching pictures when no synchrony between lip movements and voice is perceivable because the lower part of the depicted face is occluded (Walker-Andrews, 1986).

The finding that 7-month-olds are sensitive to intermodal matching of emotional stimuli is further supported by a recent study investigating infants' electrophysiological brain responses to congruent and incongruent face–voice pairs expressing happy or angry emotions (Grossmann, Striano, & Friederici, 2006). ERPs from 7-month-old infants indicated increased attention when a face with an emotional expression (either happy or angry) was accompanied by a word that was spoken in an incongruent tone of voice compared to congruent face–voice pairs. These data also suggest that infants perceived congruent face–voice pairs as being more familiar.

Another intermodal matching approach has been introduced by Philips, Wagner, Fells, and Lynch (1990) and is termed "metaphorical matching". Infants in this study were presented with displays of emotional facial expressions accompanied by auditory events (for example, a descending tone) either matching the facial expression in emotional expressivity or not. Infants at the age of 7 months were sensitive to this manipulation and looked longer when the tone matched the depicted facial expression.

An important factor that influences intermodal matching and emotion discrimination is familiarity of infants with the presented actors. In a study by Montague & Walker-Andrews (2002), infants of $3\frac{1}{2}$ months preferred concordant happy or sad facial expressions with simultaneously presented happy or sad vocal expressions only when their mothers were expressing the emotions. In the same intermodal preference task, no differential looking was observed when a strange person or their father was expressing the emotion. Interestingly, measures of parent–child involvement – for example, time per week spent in direct interaction with the infant and involvement in caregiving activities – were positively correlated with infants' preference for matching stimuli in the intermodal matching task. This indicates that familiarity with certain individuals might facilitate infants' understanding of emotions. Family dynamics – that is, how much time family members are spending with the infant – seem to be an important factor in this developmental process.

The Discrimination and Recognition of Emotional Facial Expressions

Infants are especially attentive toward faces from the first hours after birth onward (e.g. Johnson et al., 1991). Field, Woodson, Greenberg, and Cohen (1982) presented empirical evidence that newborn infants already demonstrate emotion discrimination. A live female actor changed her emotional expression (either happy, sad, or angry) to another emotional expression after the newborn infant showed habituation to the first expression. Infants' looking times increased when the actor changed to a new expression. The interpretation of these data, however, must be somewhat cautious. No comparison group without change of emotion was tested. Thus, infants' change in looking behavior might also be due to constraints of the applied paradigm (de Haan & Nelson, 1998).

Several studies have investigated infants' discrimination of emotional expression pairs in the first postnatal year using habituation, familiarization, or visual-preference techniques (see de Haan & Nelson, 1998 for a review). Some of the results, however, are hard to interpret, because infants showed different discrimination abilities when different paradigms were applied. Sometimes discrimination of facial expressions was also dependent on the order of presentation – that is, which one of two emotions was used in familiarization or habituation trials and which one in subsequent test trials. Pre-existing preferences may also bias some of the results (de Haan & Nelson, 1998).

The finding that young infants can discriminate happy faces from surprised and angry faces from the age of 3 months onward is fairly consistent (e.g. Barrera & Maurer, 1981; Young-Brown et al., 1977). Four-month-olds prefer joyful faces over angry and neutral faces when moving stimuli are used (Wilcox & Clayton, 1968). A distinction between happy and sad faces seems to be harder for 3-month-olds (Young-Brown et al., 1977). Fewer studies have examined the discrimination of other emotion pairs in early infancy. It makes sense that infants are sensitive to happy facial expressions first, because positive interactions are probably most important to establish early attachment to the caregiver. As Lavelli and Fogel (2002) reported, infants' interactions with caregivers change within the first three postnatal months. Active and emotionally positive forms of attention toward the caregiver and complex sequences of interactive communication are increasingly elicited. Attention toward negative forms of emotional expressions such as fear and anger might become more relevant only later in life, when infants become increasingly independent from caregivers in terms of locomotion. Campos et al. (2000) reported that mothers' expression of anger toward their infants increases tremendously at the onset of their infants' locomotion. Experience and familiarity with the respective emotion seem to be an important factor that determines infants' discrimination and recognition abilities. As Ludemann and Nelson (1988) argue, experience with certain emotional expressions heavily influences categorization of the respective expressions in infants.

It is not yet clear what kind of information infants are using to discriminate facial expressions. There is converging evidence that young infants rely mostly on feature-based information rather than on holistic representations of the facial expression. For instance, when habituated to "non-toothy" angry or happy faces, infants of 4–7 months old infants dishabituate to "toothy" smiles, indicating that the presence of teeth in the picture is a more salient feature than the emotion itself (Caron, Caron, & Myers, 1985). Otherwise only infants who are habituated to "non-toothy" angry faces should show dishabituation to "toothy" smiling faces. Some researchers also used images of upright or inverted faces to investigate whether infants' processing of emotional facial expressions is feature-based or holistic. When faces are presented upside-down, their structure (or *gestalt*) is disturbed, leading to feature-based processing and impaired recognition in adults (Yin, 1969). Kestenbaum and Nelson (1990) demonstrated that inversion does not impair 7-month-old infants' ability to discriminate happy from angry or fearful faces. This finding also indicates feature-based processing of facial expressions in infancy.

Several investigators have raised the question whether the development of facial emotional-expression processing relies on an innately specialized neural "face-module" (see, e.g., de Haan & Nelson, 1998). This notion is questioned by evidence of simultaneously developing categorization skills for emotional and non-social stimuli. Furthermore, empirical evidence suggests that experience with caregivers in infancy and early childhood has a considerable influence on facial emotion processing. For instance, children reared by abusive parents show a response bias toward angry faces in emotion discrimination tasks (Pollak, Cicchetti, Hornung, & Reed, 2000). Studies with infants of depressed mothers or reared in institutionalized settings also suggest that atypical early experience with emotional expressions affects the processing of faces, both on a behavioral and on a neural level (Diego et al., 2004; Parker, Nelson & The Bucharest Early Intervention Project Core Group, 2005). From these findings, a strictly nativist position appears not to be appropriate. Most probably, systems and processes that are initially occupied with the processing of social as well as non-social information become more and more fine-tuned to the processing of faces, as this kind of information is encountered most frequently and provides specifically relevant information. Possibly, a "preparedness" for certain cortical structures involved in face processing – like parts of the fusiform gyrus – to specialize in the processing of faces is innate (Nelson, 2001). In this view, general perceptual mechanisms and neural structures become specialized with exposure to faces during development.

To explore the neural bases of emotional-expression processing, some researchers have also applied electrophysical measures of infants' brain activity. Nelson and de Haan (1996) investigated 7-month-olds' brain responses to different emotional expressions applying ERPs. The negative component (Nc) was affected by the presented emotional expression. This component is well known in infant ERP research and has consistently been related to attentional processes (de Haan et al., 2003). Seven-month-olds displayed an enhanced Nc for fearful compared to happy faces, indicating that infants at this age allocate more attention to fearful than happy faces. In contrast, there was no difference in amplitude of the Nc when fearful and angry faces were compared. In a more recent study applying different stimuli and a longer presentation period, the Nc was bigger in the angry-face condition compared to the fearful-face condition, indicating that infants at 7 months do process angry and fearful faces differently (Kobiella, Grossmann, Reid, & Striano, 2008).

ERPs have also been used to investigate the influence of maltreatment in the first year of life on facial-emotion processing at the age of 30 months (Ciccheti & Curtis, 2005). Comparisons between a non-maltreated control group and maltreated children revealed significant differences in Nc amplitude in response to happy and angry faces. While control children displayed a greater Nc in response to happy faces compared to angry faces, the opposite pattern was found in maltreated children. This finding indicates a specific attentional sensitivity toward angry faces for the maltreated group and is consistent with a bias toward negative emotions in an emotion-discrimination task found in maltreated children by Pollack et al. (2000). These results support the importance of early experience with emotional expressions for later processing of emotions. Infants seem to adjust to their social environment by developing sensitivity for emotional expressions of potential danger, like an angry face that is directed at them.

The Development of Auditory Emotion Processing

Only a few studies have explored infants' processing of emotions using auditory stimuli, even though it has been suggested that auditory expressions of emotion are recognized earlier than facial expressions in infancy (e.g. Fernald, 1993; Walker-Andrews, 1997). There is evidence that auditory emotional cues may even be more important or salient than visual ones, in terms of influencing infants' behavior in an ambiguous situation (Vaish & Striano, 2004).

Even newborn infants are sensitive to emotional contents in vocal expressions (Mastropieri & Turkewitz, 1999). Infants respond with differential eye opening behavior to happy compared to neutral vocal expressions when spoken in their maternal language, but not when spoken in another language. This indicates the relevance of prenatal exposure to emotional vocalizations for postnatal speech and prosody processing.

One study by Fernald (1993) investigated infants' looking behavior and changes in affect in response to approval and prohibition vocalizations that were spoken in a corresponding positive or negative emotional tone. The vocalizations were presented in different languages and were accompanied by static photographs of a neutral face. At 5 months of age infants reacted with more positive affect to approvals and negative affect to prohibitions, irrespective of the language in which these words were spoken, except Japanese. No differential looking behavior was observed. These results document infants' early sensitivity to vocal expressions of affect, even in the absence of emotional facial expressions. The authors conclude that auditory information may have an advantage in being processed in the first postnatal months compared to visual information.

The majority of studies that investigated infants' listening preferences were concerned with a comparison of infant-directed speech (ID, or "baby talk") and adult-directed speech (AD). A very consistent finding is that infants prefer ID to AD (e.g. Fernald, 1985). Recently Singh, Morgan, and Best (2002) presented evidence that this preference might actually be due to the fact that ID typically contains more positive affect than AD. Characteristics of ID are, for example, elevated pitch, increased pitch variation, reduced speech rate, elongated vowels, and long pauses between utterances. Singh et al. (2002) conducted a series of auditory preference experiments with 6-month-olds in which they controlled for differences in affect across AD and ID speech registers. When affect was held constant across AD and ID trials, infants showed no preference for either of them. Even more strikingly, infants preferred AD over ID when AD trials contained more positive affect, demonstrating that pitch characteristics as described in previous studies may not be the most crucial stimulus property. Infants, in fact, are sensitive to the affective content of speech and show an early preference to expressions of happiness. This is consistent with findings from the visual domain as cited above.

The only ERP experiment investigating processing of prosody in infants demonstrated that 7-month-olds display an Nc in response to words that are spoken in an angry tone, but not to happy or neutral prosody (Grossmann, Striano & Friederici, 2005). As with emotionally expressive faces, infants at this age allocate more attention toward angry vocal expressions, which supports the notion that infants are specifically sensitive to social cues indicating threat.

Infants' Sensitivity to Tactile Emotional Signals

Very few researchers have investigated the influence of tactile stimulation as an emotional signal, though it is reasonable to assume that touch is an appropriate sensory channel to communicate and elicit emotions (Hertenstein, 2002). Some studies have investigated the modulation of infants' arousal in response to tactile stimulation. For instance, the disturbing effect of a sudden still face is mitigated when mothers are allowed to touch their infants (Stack & Muir, 1990). However, the communication of specific emotions via the tactile sensory system remains largely unexplored. Hertenstein and Campos (2001) investigated how maternal touch affects 12-month-olds' exploration of unfamiliar objects. When mothers tensed their fingers around the infants' abdomen while inhaling abruptly, infants displayed more negative affect toward the object compared to a tension-decrease condition and a control condition without additional tactile stimulation. Infants in the tension-increase condition also waited longer to touch the object and touched the object less. Infants' exploratory behavior is influenced by maternal touch. It can be concluded that infants use tactile stimulation as emotional cues in ambiguous or new situations.

How do Infants use Emotional Expressions Provided by Caregivers and Strangers?

As reviewed above, much is known today about infants' skills in discriminating and recognizing emotional expressions. Another interesting issue is certainly the influence of emotional expressions on infants' behavior.

Very early in development, infants are active participants in mutually regulated social interactions. They are already sensitive in the first postnatal months to incontingencies in social interactions and react in a disturbed way when an adult suddenly stops an ongoing interaction and instead poses a still face (see Adamson & Frick, 2003, for a review). A consistent finding is that by 2 months of age infants react with reduced smiling and averted eye gaze to a sudden still face.

In dyadic interactions, infants are well aware of the effects of their own behavior on their counterpart's reactions (see also Murray & Trevarthen, 1985). The still-face paradigm is an ambiguous and disturbing situation for an infant. In this situation, emotional expressions provided by the caregiver modulate the infant's reaction. D'Entremont and Muir (1997) found that 5-month-old infants react with less smiling to a sad or neutral still face compared to a happy still face, even though in all still-face conditions smiling and gaze were reduced compared to a normal interaction. This indicates that a still-face effect is also elicited when the still face is smiling, but that its disturbing effect might be somewhat attenuated, as indicated by infants' smiling behavior. In a study by Striano and Liszkowski (2005) the still-face effect was modulated by emotional facial expression only in 9-month-old infants, not in younger infants. Nine-month-olds in this study showed a reduced still-face effect when they were first presented with a happy still face and then with a neutral still face. As mentioned above, tactile stimulation can also reduce infants' grimacing and increase smiles during the still-face paradigm (Stack & Muir, 1990). These findings show that very young infants are susceptible to others' emotional feedback in ambiguous or disturbing situations, especially when provided by the caregiver. The still-face effect represents a dyadic situation.

In other studies infants' behavior in ambiguous *triadic* situations – that is, situations that involve not only the interacting agents but also a third object that both agents refer to – was examined. Evidence for infants also using emotional signals to disambiguate novel or potentially dangerous triadic situations comes from studies applying a visual cliff. The visual cliff is a Plexiglas surface that covers an apparent drop. Infants are placed on one side of the cliff, while caregivers wait at the other side. Infants usually hesitate before crossing the cliff. This situation is highly ambiguous to the infant, and probably perceived as being dangerous. A common reaction is that infants turn toward the caregiver – that is, infants actively search for the caregiver's feedback in this ambiguous situation. This behavior is called social referencing. Sorce, Emde, Campos, and Klinnert (1985) investigated the effect of different facial expressions posed by the mother on infants' behavior when situated on the edge of a visual cliff. Subjects in this line of studies were 12 months of age and consistently displayed social referencing – that is, they turned to the mother, who was standing at the opposite side of the cliff. Mothers' emotional expressions had a tremendous influence on infants' behavior. When the mother posed a joyful or interested expression, more infants crossed the depth, compared to when mothers looked fearful or angry. Infants in this study actively used emotional expressions provided by the caregiver to disambiguate the situation. Recent studies on the visual cliff also investigated the influence of vocal emotional expressions on infants' behavior when faced with a visual cliff (Vaish & Striano, 2004). Infants were presented with positive facial or vocal or both facial and vocal cues expressed by the mothers. It was found that infants crossed the cliff faster when multimodal or only vocal cues were provided compared to only facial cues, indicating that multimodal or only vocal expressions might be more powerful in guiding infants' behavior than only facial expressions.

Emotional expressions provided by adults also influence infants' behavior toward novel objects. Hertenstein and Campos (2004) tested how infants' behavior toward a target object is affected by positive or disgusted emotional displays expressed by an adult. Eleven-month-olds reacted with less reaching and touching behavior when the delay between the adult's emotional expressions and the test period was short. In infants with 14 months of age these retention effects were also found if a one-hour delay was posed between first exposure and the test phase. Mumme and Fernald (2003) showed that 12-month-olds' behavior toward a target object is also influenced by televised positive, neutral, or negative emotional expressions directed at a novel object. Infants can also use emotional signals if those are not provided to them in the context of a real social interaction and the infant acts as a passive onlooker. Interestingly, infants' reactions toward target objects are specific and do not generalize to simultaneously presented distracter objects that are not the targets of emotional expressions by the adult. Moses, Baldwin, Rosicky, & Tidball (2001) investigated infants' sensitivity to referential cues in a social-referencing paradigm. Infants of 12 and 18 months were influenced by an adult's expression of emotions toward a novel object only when the adult was also expressing clear-cut signs that he or she was actually referring to that object – that is, when he or she was gazing toward the target object. No effect was found when the experimenter was equally noisy but outside the infant's field of view. In a second experiment, infants' reactions to an emotional outburst displayed by an adult were investigated. Infants actively checked the adult's face and followed his or her gaze to the target object. Their reaction to the adult's emotional expression was also stronger toward the target object, compared to a distracter, even though some generalization effects were found.

In sum, the findings reviewed in this section demonstrate that by the end of the first year infants actively search and use emotional cues from adults, especially when encountering an ambiguous situation or object. However, it is not yet clear at what age infants are able to use information conveyed by emotional expressions in combination with referential cues such as eye gaze. In a study by Flom and Pick (2005), 7-month-old infants displayed more gaze following and looked at the target object for a longer period of time when the adult posed a neutral facial expression, compared to a happy or sad expression. The authors argue that infants at this age may not understand the referential nature of affective expressions in combination with eye gaze. Another assumption is that infants' attention may be captured by the emotional expressions, while it can be more flexibly allocated in the neutral face condition. However, recent data suggest that at the age of 7 months infants use facial emotions in combination with eye gaze cues to detect threat in their environment (Hoehl & Striano, in press). We presented angry and fearful faces whose eyes were either directed at the infant or averted to the side. Amplitude of the Nc was enhanced for angry faces with direct eye gaze compared to fearful faces with direct or averted gaze and angry faces with averted gaze. An angry face that is directed at the infant is a proximate indicator of threat, which directly addresses the infant. A fearful face with eye gaze directed at the infant does not indicate threat for the infant and may be more ambiguous. Infants allocate more attention to faces when they display the more immediate threat. Indicators of immediate threat are more salient for infants, because in a potentially dangerous situation survival may depend on quick referencing to the caregiver. Adults, in contrast, seem to be more sensitive to facial displays of the more ambiguous threat. In a functional imaging study, it was recently shown that the amygdala, a brain structure that is especially relevant for the detection of threat, shows enhanced activity in response to fearful faces with direct eye gaze and angry faces with averted gaze (Adams, Heather, Baird, Ambady, & Kleck, 2003). The developmental trajectory of the detection of threat from facial expression in addition to eye-gaze direction, however, remains to be explored. Our findings indicate that infants do pay attention to the direction of an adult's eye gaze, even if he or she poses an emotional facial expression. At least they do so in the case of fearful and angry expressions, which were not investigated in the study by Flom and Pick (2005). It is reasonable that fearful and angry expressions, as indicators of threat, are processed differently compared to happy or sad expressions, because the latter do not convey as relevant information about the target of someone else's eye gaze as do fearful and angry expressions. It remains to be investigated how infants as young as 7 months of age actually process another person's eye gaze in relation to a target object while he poses a fearful or angry expression.

Striano and Vaish (2005) demonstrated that by 7 months of age infants actively seek information from an adult's face when she acts ambiguously – for example, when she teases the infant, instead of just giving him a toy. In a second study it was found that infants look reliably less at the adult's face during a teasing task if she is smiling at him compared to displaying a neutral expression. This shows that infants of this age group use information provided by the adult's facial expression to disambiguate the situation. The smiling reassures the infants that the adult is teasing them, while the neutral expression provides no such information to disambiguate the situation. It could thus be shown that infants use the emotional facial expressions of adults to interpret their behavior.

There is still a lack of studies of social referencing in triadic situations with younger infants. The developmental course or even onset of social referencing is currently unknown, since almost all studies in this field investigated infants from the age of 12 months onwards. Studies on younger populations might reveal social referencing behavior at a much earlier age.

Conclusion and Perspectives

In the current chapter I have reviewed empirical findings regarding the development of emotional-expression processing. It has been demonstrated that infants actively seek and use information provided by emotional expressions in face, voice, and touch to guide their own behavior, especially in novel or ambiguous situations. Instead of merely being perceivers, they actively take part in social interactions and are aware of the effects of their own behavior during social encounters.

In addition to behavioral results, recent findings from EEG studies have been presented. By looking at neurophysiological responses, an additional source of information about infant development can be obtained. Two components have consistently, but not exclusively, been associated with the processing of emotional and most of all facial expressions: the negative component, reflecting allocation of attentional resources, and the positive slow wave, reflecting memory updating. In infant ERP data, these components are the most evident on frontal and central channels and sometimes lateralized to the right hemisphere, most of all when facial stimuli are applied (de Haan et al., 2003).

Faces are highly salient cues for typically developing infants and provide them with important social information, specifically emotional expressions. A sensitivity to attend to faces is therefore important for infants, as it enables them to communicate with caregivers as well as representing a means for retrieving information about the environment from others, including potential threat. Some individuals are impaired in processing or using social information as given in facial expressions.

People suffering from Autism Spectrum Disorder (ASD), for instance, show deficiencies in obtaining information from other people's eyes (Baron-Cohen et al., 2000) and in face processing (Dawson, Webb, & McPartland, 2005). Early brain development is atypical in infants who go on to develop ASD (Courchesne & Pierce, 2005). One future direction might be longitudinal studies of emotion processing in infants at risk of developing ASD – for instance, siblings of children with autism. This might help to examine the onset and development of atypical processing of social and emotional information as well as its neural correlates.

To increase our understanding of the neural correlates of emotion perception another fruitful approach might be to investigate the development of the human mirror neuron system (MNS). Functional imaging studies have revealed that many brain structures that are involved in the experience of a certain emotion are also activated when we observe someone else experiencing the same emotion. For instance, the amygdala, an almond-shaped structure in the medial temporal lobes, has consistently been related to the perception of fear – both when fear was elicited in the tested subjects and when fearful facial expressions were presented (LeDoux, 2003). Another example is the insula, a section of the neocortex that is located within the fissura lateralis. This structure is activated when disgust is experienced – for instance, when subjects are exposed to an unpleasant smell (Murphy, Nimmo-Smith, & Lawrence, 2003). But insula activation is also recorded when disgust is perceived in someone else's facial expressions (Phillips et al., 1997). Structures involved in the affective components of a painful experience are also involved in seeing someone else being hurt (Singer et al., 2004).

Recently Iacoboni (2005) proposed a circuit of human imitation that comprises the superior temporal sulcus, which is involved in the perception of biological motion, and the human MNS – namely, the posterior inferior frontal gyrus and adjacent ventral premotor cortex as well as the rostral inferior parietal cortex. The latter regions are thought to code the goal of the action and a motor plan on how to achieve this goal. When emotions are concerned, this MNS interacts with the amygdala via the insula, which acts as a relay from action representation to emotion in this model. In this view the basis of understanding others' emotional states is a motor representation of their emotional facial expressions. Evidence for this model derives from studies on the imitation of emotional facial expressions and its relationship to empathic skills (Carr, Iacoboni, Dubeau, Mazziotta, & Lenzi, 2003; Dapretto et al., 2005).

A connection between motor representations of facial expressions and the respective emotions can also be assumed when considering facial feedback mechanisms. People are influenced in ratings on how funny a cartoon is just by contracting muscles that either mimic a smile or a frown, even if they do not consciously perform the emotional facial expression (Strack, Martin, & Stepper, 1988). The development of the human MNS, however, is largely unknown. New neuroimaging techniques that are suitable for infant studies, like near-infrared spectroscopy (Csibra et al., 2004), and theoretical developmental approaches, like Meltzoff's "like-me" approach (Meltzoff & Brooks, 2001), might prove very helpful for a better understanding of the developmental basis of human emotion perception and its relation to mirror mechanisms.

References

Adams, R. B., Heather, L. G., Baird, A. A., Ambady, N., & Kleck, R. E. (2003). Effects of gaze on amygdala sensivity to anger and fear faces. *Science*, 300, 1536.

Adamson, L. B., & Frick, J. E. (2003). The still face: A history of a shared experimental paradigm. *Infancy*, 4(4), 451–473.

Allison, T., Wood, C., & McCarthy, G. (1986). The central nervous system. In M. Coles, E. Donchin, & S. Porges (Eds.), *Psychophysiology: Systems, Processes, and Applications* (pp. 5–25). New York: Guilford.

Baron-Cohen, S., Ring, H. A., Bullmore, E. T., Wheelwright, S., Ashwin, C., & Williams, S. C. R. (2000). The amygdala theory of autism. *Neuroscience and Biobehavioral Reviews*, 24, 355–364.

Barrera, M. E., & Maurer, D. (1981). The perception of facial expressions by the three-month-old. *Child Development*, 52, 203–206.

Campos, J. J., Anderson, D. I., Barbu-Roth, M. A., Hubbard, E. M., Hertenstein, M. J., & Witherington, D. (2000). Travel broadens the mind. *Infancy*, 1, 149–219.

Caron, A. J., Caron, R. F., & MacLean, D. J. (1988). Infant discrimination of naturalistic emotional expressions: The role of face and voice. *Child Development*, 59, 604–616.

Caron, R. E., Caron, A. J., & Myers, R. S. (1985). Abstraction of invariant face expressions in infancy. *Child Development*, 53, 1009–1015.

Carr, L., Iacoboni, M., Dubeau, M.-Ch., Mazziotta, J. C., & Lenzi, G. L. (2003). Neural mechanisms of empathy in humans: A relay from neural systems for imitation to limbic areas. *Proceedings of the National Academy of Sciences*, 100, 5497–5502.

Cicchetti, D., & Curtis, W. J. (2005). An event-related potential study of the processing of affective facial expressions in young children who experienced maltreatment during the first year of life. *Development and Psychopathology*, 17, 641–677.

Courchesne, E., & Pierce, K. (2005). Why the frontal cortex in autism might be talking only to itself: Local over-connectivity but long-distance disconnection. *Current Opinion in Neurobiology*, 15, 225–230.

Csibra, G., Henty, J., Volein, A., Elwell, C., Tucker, L., Meek, J., & Johnson, M. H. (2004). Near infrared spectroscopy reveals neural activation during face perception in infants and adults. *Journal of Pediatric Neurology*, 2, 85–89.

Dapretto, M., Davies, M. S., Pfeifer, J. H., Scott, A. A., Sigman, M., Bookheimer, S. Y., & Iacoboni, M. (2005). Understanding emotions in others: Mirror neuron dysfunction in children with autism spectrum disorders. *Nature Neuroscience*, 9, 28–30.

Dawson, G., Webb, S. J., & McPartland, J. (2005). Understanding the nature of face processing impairment in autism: Insights from behavioral and electrophysiological studies. *Developmental Neuropsychology*, 27(3), 403–424.

de Haan, M., & Nelson, C. A. (1998). Discrimination and categorization of facial expressions of emotion during infancy. In A. M. Slater (Ed.), *Perceptual Development: Visual, Auditory, and Language Perception in Infancy* (pp. 287–309). London: University College London Press.

de Haan, M., Belsky, J., Reid, V., Volein, A., & Johnson, M. (2004). Maternal personality and infants' neural and visual responsivity to facial expressions of emotion. *Journal of Child Psychology and Psychiatry*, 45 (7), 1209–1218.

de Haan, M., Johnson, M. H., & Halit, H. (2003). Development of face-sensitive event-related potentials during infancy: A review. *International Journal of Psychophysiology*, 51, 45–58.

D'Entremont, B., & Muir, D. W. (1997). Five-month-olds' attention and affective responses to still-faced emotional expressions. *Infant Behavior and Development*, 20, 563–568.

Diego, M. A., Field, T., Jones, N. A., Hernandez-Reif, M., Cullen, C., Schanberg, S., & Kuhn, C. (2004). EEG responses to mock facial expressions by infants of depressed mothers. *Infant Behavior & Development*, 27, 150–162.

Fernald, A. (1985). Four-month-old infants prefer to listen to motherese. *Infant Behavior and Development*, 8, 181–195.

Fernald, A. (1993). Approval and disapproval: Infant responsiveness to vocal affect in familiar and unfamiliar languages. *Child Development*, 64, 657–674.

Field, T. M., Woodson, R., Greenberg, R., & Cohen, D. (1982). Discrimination imitation of facial expression by neonates. *Science*, 218, 179–181.

Flom, R., & Pick, A. D. (2005). Experimenter affective expression and gaze following in 7-month-olds. *Infancy*, 7(2), 207–218.

Goren, C. C., Sarty, M., & Wu, P. (1975). Visual following and pattern discrimination of face-like stimuli by newborn infants. *Pediatrics*, 56, 544–549.

Grossmann, T., Striano, T., & Friederici, A. D. (2005). Infants' electric brain responses to emotional prosody. *Neuroreport*, 16(7), 1825–1828.

Grossmann, T., Striano, T., & Friederici, A. D. (2006). Crossmodal integration of emotional information from face and voice in the infant brain. *Developmental Science*, 9, 309–315.

Hertenstein, M. J. (2002). Touch: Its communicative functions in infancy. *Human Development. Human Development*, 45(2), 70–94.

Hertenstein, M. J., & Campos, J. J. (2001). Emotion regulation via maternal touch. *Infancy*, 2(4), 549–566.

Hertenstein, M. J., & Campos, J. J. (2004). The retention effects of an adult's emotional displays on infant behavior. *Child Development*, 75(2), 595–613.

Hoehl, S., & Striano, T. (forthcoming). Neural Processing of Eye Gaze and Threat Related Emotional Facial Expressions in Infancy. *Child Development*.

Iacoboni, M. (2005). Neural mechanisms of imitation. *Current Opinion in Neurobiology*, 15, 632–637.

Johnson, M. H., Dziurawiec, S., Ellis, H. D., & Morton, J. (1991). Newborns' preferential tracking of face-like stimuli and its subsequent decline. *Cognition*, 40, 1–21.

Kestenbaum, R., & Nelson, C. A. (1990). The recognition and categorization of upright and inverted expressions by 7-month-old infants. *Infant Behavior and Development*, 13, 497–511.

Kobiella, A., Grossmann, T., Reid, V., & Striano, T. (2008). The discrimination of angry and fearful facial expressions in 7-month-old infants: An event-related potential study. *Cognition and Emotion*, 22(1), 134–146.

Lavelli, M., & Fogel, A. (2002). Developmental changes in mother–infant face-to-face communication: Birth to 3 months. *Developmental Psychology*, 38, 288–305.

LeDoux, J. (2003). The emotional brain, fear and the amygdala. *Cellular and Molecular Neurobiology*, 23, 727–738.

Ludemann, P., & Nelson, C. A. (1988). The categorical representation of facial expressions by 7-month-old infants. *Developmental Psychology*, 24, 492–501.

Mastropieri, D., & Turkewitz, G. (1999). Prenatal experience and neonatal responsiveness to vocal expressions of emotion. *Developmental Psychobiology*, 35, 204–214.

Meltzoff, A. N., & Brooks, R. (2001). "Like me" as a building block for understanding other minds: Bodily acts, attention, and intention. In B. F. Malle, L. J. Moses, & D. A. Baldwin (Eds.), *Intentions and Intentionality: Foundations of Social Cognition* (pp. 171–191). Cambridge, MA: MIT Press.

Montague, D. P. F., & Walker-Andrews, A. S. (2002). Mothers, fathers, and infants: The role of familiarity and parental involvement in infants' perception of emotion expressions. *Child Development*, 73, 1339–1352.

Moses, L. J., Baldwin, D. A., Rosicky, J. G., & Tidball, G. (2001). Evidence for referential understanding in the emotions domain at twelve and eighteen months, *Child Development*, 72, 718–735.

Mumme, D. L., & Fernald, A. (2003). The infant as onlooker: Learning from emotional reactions observed in a television scenario. *Child Development*, 74, 221–237.

Murphy, F. C., Nimmo-Smith, I., & Lawrence, A. D. (2003). Functional neuroanatomy of emotions: A meta-analysis. *Cognitive Affective and Behavioral Neuroscience*, 3, 207–233.

Murray, L., & Trevarthen, C. (1985). Emotional regulation of interactions between two-month-olds and their mothers. In T. M. Field & N. A. Fox (Eds.), *Social Perception in Infants* (pp. 177–197). Norwood, NJ: Ablex.

Nelson, C. (2001). The development and neural bases of face recognition. *Infant and Child Development*, 10, 3–18.

Nelson, C. A., & de Haan, M. (1996). Neural correlates of infants' visual responsiveness to facial expressions of emotion. *Developmental Psychobiology*, 29(7), 577–595.

Parker, S. W., Nelson, C. A., & The Bucharest Early Intervention Project Core Group (2005). An event-related potential study of the impact of institutional rearing on face recognition. *Development and Psychopathology*, 17, 621–63.

Philips, R. D., Wagner, S. H., Fells, C. A., & Lynch, M. (1990). Do infants recognize emotion in facial expressions?: Categorical and "metaphorical" evidence. *Infant Behavior and Development*, 13, 71–84.

Phillips, M. L., Young, A. W., Senior, C., Brammer, M., Andrew, C., Calder, A. J., Bullmore, E. T., Perrett, D. I., Rowland, D., Williams, S. C., Gray, J. A., & David, J. M. (1997). A specific neural substrate for perceiving facial expressions of disgust. *Nature*, 389, 495–498.

Pollak, S. D., Cicchetti, D., Hornung, K., & Reed, A. (2000). Recognizing emotion in faces: Developmental effects of child abuse and neglect. *Developmental Psychology*, 36, 679–688.

Singer, T., Seymour, B., O'Doherty, J., Kaube, H., Dolan, R. J., & Frith, C. D. (2004). Empathy for pain involves the affective but not sensory components of pain. *Science*, 303, 1157–1162.

Singh, L., Morgan, J. L., & Best, C. T. (2002). Infants' listening preferences: Baby talk or happy talk? *Infancy*, 3(3), 365–394.

Sorce, J. F., Emde, R. N., Campos, J., & Klinnert, M. D. (1985). Maternal emotional signalling: Its effect on the visual cliff behavior of 1-year-olds. *Developmental Psychology*, 21, 195–200.

Spelke, E., & Owsley, C. J. (1979). Intermodal exploration and knowledge in infancy. *Infant Behavior and Development*, 2, 13–27.

Stack, D. M., & Muir, D. W. (1990). Tactile stimulation as a component of social interchange: New interpretations for the still-face effect. *British Journal of Developmental Psychology*, 8, 131–145.

Strack, F., Martin, L. L., & Stepper, S. (1988). Inhibiting and facilitating conditions of the human smile: A nonobtrusive test of the facial feedback hypothesis. *Journal of Personality and Social Psychology*, 54, 768–777.

Striano, T., & Liszkowski, U. (2005). Sensitivity to the context of facial expression in the still face at 3-, 6-, and 9-months of age. *Infant Behavior and Development*, 28, 10–19.

Striano, T., & Vaish, A. (2005). Seven- to 9-month-old infants use facial expressions to interpret others' actions. *British Journal of Developmental Psychology*, 24, 753–760.

Vaish, A., & Striano, T. (2004). Is visual reference necessary? Contributions of facial versus vocal cues in 12-month-olds' social referencing behavior. *Developmental Science*, 7, 261–269.

Walker-Andrews, A. S. (1986). Intermodal perception of expressive behaviors: Relation of eye and voice? *Developmental Psychology*, 22, 373–377.

Walker-Andrews, A. S. (1997). Infants' perception of expressive behaviors: Differentiation of multimodal information. *Psychological Bulletin*, 121(3), 437–456.

Webb, S. J., Long, J. D., & Nelson, Ch. A. (2005). A longitudinal investigation of visual event-related potentials in the first year of life. *Developmental Science*, 8, 605–616.

Wilcox, B., & Clayton, F. (1968). Infant visual fixation on motion pictures of the human face. *Journal of Experimental Child Psychology*, 43, 230–246.

Yin, R. K. (1969). Looking at upside-down faces. *Journal of Experimental Psychology*, 81, 141–145.

Young-Brown, G., Rosenfeld, H. M., & Horowitz, F. D. (1977). Infant discrimination of facial expressions. *Child Development*, 48, 555–562.

Part Four

Social Cognition: The Challenge of Autism

Editors' Introduction

The great importance of social cognition can most clearly be observed when it is lacking or impaired for some reason. One of the most apparent areas in which social cognition is impaired is in the neurodevelopmental disorder autism. Autism now affects one in every 160 children. It is a disorder that becomes apparent in the early years of ontogeny and affects skills such as social perception and processing, imitation, language learning and intersubjectivity. In the prior sections of this volume we have seen how complex some of these skills can be even in the typically developing individual. Taking a closer look at autism, its ontogeny and underlying neural pathways is one way to understand social cognition in typical development. In turn, we think that the fields of development and neuroscience hold the key to understanding and tackling the range of social-cognitive impairments which make up the autism spectrum.

This section on autism opens with a chapter by Joseph and Tager-Flusberg. The authors focus on the problem of face and eye processing, two areas of social cognition which are generally impaired in those with autism. Joseph and Tager-Flusberg provide a range of evidence to suggest that many of the atypical processing strategies and deficits demonstrated among persons with autism derive from the way that eye gaze is processed. The authors highlight the complex interplay between attention, perception and affective processes as these relate to face and gaze processing and most importantly set forth new ideas on the interplay between early development and brain pathology.

In the next chapter, Hobson and Hobson turn to the critical question of how infants relate with others and how we may better understand interpersonal relatedness through the study of autism. Hobson and Hobson point out that understanding autism relies upon understanding interpersonal relatedness, that is, how others are perceived and recognized and the underlying mechanism that drives humans to be connected to and understand others. In contrast, von Hofsten shows that we can learn a great deal about social cognition as well as autism by assessing microanalytic behavior. In this instance, von Hofsten assesses infant anticipatory behavior by determining what they are looking at via use of an eye tracking system. Even when interpersonal relatedness or live interaction is left out of the picture, von Hofsten shows that we can glean essential information from studying subtle eye movements. Such findings will only be improved when these techniques are applied to interpersonal interactions (see Hobson and Hobson). Eventually these techniques may be informative in terms of identifying infants at risk for autism.

Griffin and Dennett take a more philosophical approach, and address issues with autism by discussing "commonsense psychology." This is how we figure out the thoughts and feelings of other people in order to engage in successful social interactions. The process is not as simple as determining when someone is looking at you, nor is the desire to relate to others enough, without the ability to use social information in an effective way. The authors show that impairment in these skills, as in the case of autism, is critical to understanding more mature forms of social cognition, representing the mind of the other. The final chapter in this section by Brock, Einav and Riby focuses on the social-cognitive impairments, or lack thereof, observed in populations with Williams syndrome. Just as it is the case that deficits observed in individuals with autism help us to understand the underlying mechanisms and development of social cognition, so too can comparing and contrasting the development and neural basis of Williams syndrome with autism help to shed new light on social cognition. In sum, the chapter demonstrates that Williams syndrome, like autism, is highly complex and consisting of a wide spectrum of impairments and skills that are subtle and highly intricate.

The chapters in this section are highly diverse in their thinking, their methodology and their approach. We think this reflects the state of the autism spectrum disorder and the state of research in this field. As demonstrated in these various chapters, the integration of the fields of development and neuroscience will be critical in future developmental disorder research as well as in discovering the basis and mechanisms of human social cognition.

Chapter 14

Face and Gaze Processing in Autism

Robert M. Joseph and Helen Tager-Flusberg

Introduction

Autism is a strongly heritable, polygenic disorder that is unusually heterogeneous in its clinical presentation and severity. Despite its biological underpinnings, autism is diagnosed solely on the basis of behavioral impairments and anomalies, specifically in the three core symptom domains of reciprocal social interaction, communication, and repetitive interests and activities, and its exact neurological causes remain unknown. Inattention to other people's faces is one of the most striking social-communicative symptoms of autism, apparent by 1 year of age (Osterling & Dawson, 1994; Osterling, Dawson, & Munson, 2002; Yirmiya & Ozonoff, 2007) and evident through early childhood (Kasari, Sigman, & Yirmiya, 1993). Children with autism are abnormally delayed in early face-related social milestones, such as looking at another person's face to share interest in objects and events (Joseph & Tager-Flusberg, 1997; Mundy, Sigman, Ungerer, & Sherman, 1986) and, by diagnostic definition, they fail to use eye-to-eye gaze and facial expression to regulate social interaction (APA, 1994).

Given the social importance of faces both as a means of personal identification and as a means of communication among human beings, the ability to process information from faces has been a longstanding topic of scientific inquiry into the cognitive and affective bases of autistic social-communicative impairments. Since 2000, research on face processing in autism has flourished, and efforts have turned to delineating better the precise nature and mechanisms that underlie the neurofunctional deficits and anomalies involved. Such efforts hold the promise of helping to elucidate the complex neurological and genetic underpinnings of autism and how these are expressed in the symptoms that define autism at the behavioral level.

This chapter summarizes some of the main empirical findings in two key domains of face processing in autism – namely, the processing of face identity and eye gaze.

First, we review the current literature on face-identity recognition and discrimination in autism, and we argue that deficits found in face-identification studies are not convincingly explained by a primary failure of holistic or configural face processing in autism. Then we consider research on gaze processing in autism and how anomalies in attention, perception, and affective responses in relation to gaze stimuli may contribute to suboptimal performance on laboratory tests of face recognition and, more importantly, may provide behavioral and neurofunctional markers for the core social-communicative impairments in autism. We begin by providing a brief outline of the distributed neural system face processing in humans.

A Distributed Neural System for Face Processing in Humans

Face perception is mediated by a distributed neural system (Bruce & Young, 1986; Haxby, Hoffman, & Gobbini, 2000) comprised of several brain regions that interactively process different attributes of faces. Face detection occurs via the lateral geniculate nucleus, superior colliculus, pulvinar, striate cortex, and amygdala, which provide a rapid analysis of a face's salient structural and emotive features (Palermo & Rhodes, 2006). As Haxby and colleagues (Haxby et al., 2000) have proposed, the core face-processing system can then be divided into two functionally and neuroanatomically distinct, but interactive, components: the lateral fusiform gyrus, which analyzes the invariant features of faces, involved in the perception of face identity, and the superior temporal sulcus, which analyzes changeable aspects of faces, including eye movements and expressions of emotion. An extended network of brain regions participates in face processing by, for example, retrieving "person knowledge" associated with a given face (anterior temporal cortex, anterior paracingulate, posterior cingulate) and by assessing the social-affective significance of faces and of transient facial movements (amygdala, insula, anterior cingulate, prefrontal cortex) (Gobbini & Haxby, 2006; Haxby et al, 2000; Philips, Drevets, Rauch et al., 2003). This model has guided research on autism, which has focused on whether there are impairments in specific components of face processing and particular nodes in the neural network, or whether faces processing impairments might reflect more widespread dysfunction, including deficits across several aspects of face processing and connectivity between components of the distributed neural system.

Face-Identity Processing in Autism

Not only are faces ubiquitous in the human social environment, but they also form an exceptionally homogenous class of stimuli, all of which consist of the same set of part features (that is, eyes, nose, and mouth) in the same basic configuration. Extensive evidence shows that faces engage specialized configural processing mechanisms that are particularly sensitive to the spatial relations among the parts (Diamond & Carey, 1986) and to the face as a non-decomposed whole (Farah, Tanaka, & Drain, 1995). (Note: for the purposes of this chapter, we do not distinguish between configural and holistic processing, but see Maurer, Le Grand, & Mondloch 2002 and Yovel & Duchaine, 2006).

The development of configural face processing, and the specialization of the region of fusiform cortex that supports it, require and are shaped by early experience with faces (LeGrand, Mondloch, Maurer, & Brent, 2003, 2004; Pascalis et al., 2005). Configural face-processing skills undergo a prolonged period of development from infancy through adolescence (Maurer et al., 2002), but by the age of 6 typically developing children already exhibit adult levels of core aspects of holistic processing (Freire & Lee, 2001; Tanaka, Kay, Grinnell, Stansfield, & Szechter, 1998).

Deficits and abnormalities in face learning and recognition have been well documented in experimental research on autism (e.g. Boucher & Lewis, 1992; Braverman, Fein, Lucci, & Waterhouse, 1989; Davies et al., 1994; Hauck, Fein, Maltby, Waterhouse, & Feinstein, 1998; Langdell, 1978; Klin et al., 1999; Ozonoff, Pennington, & Rogers, 1990; Tantam, Monaghan, Nicholson, & Stirling, 1989; see Sasson, 2006, for a comprehensive review), and researchers have often proposed that such deficits result from a failure of normative configural encoding processes in autism (Boucher & Lewis, 1992; Davies, Bishop, Manstead, & Tantam, 1994; Miyashita, 1988; Tantam, Monaghan, L., Nicholson, J., & Stirling 1989). In a seminal study, Yin (1969) first demonstrated the importance of configural information to face identification by showing that face recognition in normal adults was disproportionately impaired relative to recognition of non-face objects when stimuli were presented in inverted orientation. It has been argued that the inordinate effect of inversion on face recognition has been argued to be caused by a disruption of the expected spatial configuration to which configural or holistic face processes are specially tuned (Carey & Diamond, 1977).

Several early studies reported an absence of the face-inversion effect in autism (Hobson, Outson, & Lee, 1988; Langdell, 1978; Tantum et al., 1989), but these studies have been fairly criticized on methodological grounds (Lahaie et al., 2006) and more recent studies suggest that autistic face-processing deficits do not derive from a failure of configural or holistic processing *per se.* For example, Joseph and Tanaka (2003) used a whole – part method to assess recognition of face parts (eyes, mouths) alternately presented in isolation and presented in the context of the whole face in which the face part had been previously seen and encoded. Children with autism exhibited better recognition of face parts in the whole than in the part condition. In addition, when whole faces were presented in inverted rather than upright orientation, they exhibited a decrease in recognition accuracy (that is, a face-inversion effect). An important qualification, however, was that both of these effects pertained *only* to trials in which information from the mouth region of the face was necessary for recognition. These findings were consistent with those from a much earlier study by Langdell (1978), who reported that children with autism were better at recognizing photographs of their peers based on isolated information from the mouth region than from the eye region. Together, these studies suggest that autistic face-recognition deficits derive from eye-related attentional or perceptual abnormalities, rather than an absolute deficit in holistic processing.

More recent studies also indicate that configural face processing is intact in autism. Using reaction time as well as accuracy measures, Lahaie et al. (2006) reported a normal face-inversion effect in a sample of adolescents and adults with autism. Rouse, Donnelly, Hadwin, & Brown, (2004) examined configural face processing in school-age children with autism by testing their susceptibility to the Thatcher illusion (Thompson, 1980). In this test, the eyes and mouth are presented in inverted orientation within an upright face, giving the face a grotesque appearance. However, when the same face is presented in inverted orientation, the change in the spatial relations among the parts that gives the face a grotesque appearance is normally much more difficult to detect. Using both accuracy and reaction-time measures, Rouse and colleagues found that children with autism were as susceptible to the Thatcher illusion as the control group.

In a second study, Lahaie et al. (2006) used a priming method to assess configural face processing in individuals with autism. An advantage of a priming paradigm is that the rapid presentation of the priming stimulus lessens the possibility that the perceptual processes of interest will be confounded by atypical ways of attending to faces that may become operative with longer stimulus presentation times. Lahaie et al. primed recognition of recently learned faces with one, two, three, or four natural face parts (for example, eyes, nose, mouth, outer contour) or with arbitrary, puzzle-piece-like face parts that partially represented two or more face features and thus contained configural information. The logic of this approach was that increasing the number of primes in the natural-parts condition would produce accelerated gains in face-recognition time among configural face processors, mirroring the accelerated increase in configural information, whereas increasing the number of arbitrary primes, each of which already contained configural information, would result in a linear or at least a less accelerated gain in recognition time. Lahaie et al. found that individuals with autism exhibited the same pattern of an accelerating priming effect with an increasing number of natural parts and a relatively weaker acceleration of this function in the arbitrary parts conditions, as was observed in control participants. The one group difference they reported was that, in contrast to controls, individuals with autism were facilitated in face-recognition speed when primed by one natural face part alone, leading the authors to argue that local face-processing biases in autism may operate independently of any deficit in configural processing. These and other authors (Behrmann, Thomas, & Humphreys, 2006; Behrmann et al., 2007) have raised the question of how local bias and other atypicalities of attention and perception that are not specific to the social domain may contribute to face-processing deficits in autism.

Initial evidence from several neuroimaging studies that found hypoactivation of the lateral fusiform gyrus during face-viewing tasks in individuals with autism (Critchley et al., 2000; Hall, Szechtman, & Nahmias, 2003; Hubl et al., 2003; Pierce,

Muller, Ambrose, Allen, & Courchesne, 2001; Schultz et al., 2000) had also given credence to the idea of a fundamental impairment in the configural perceptual processes associated with this cortical area (Barton, Press, Keenan, & O'Connor, 2002; Rossion et al., 2000; Tarr & Gauthier, 2000). However, as with behavioral findings on configural processing in autism, more recent studies provide evidence that fusiform hypoactivation in autism is not an absolute deficit, but varies according to other factors, including familiarity, such that faces of known people evoke relatively normal fusiform activation in individuals with autism (Aylward et al., 2004; Pierce, Haist, Sedaghat, & Courchesne, 2004), and the extent to which individuals attend to inner features and particularly the eye region of the face (Dalton et al., 2005; Hadjikhani et al., 2004). In this regard, it is important to note that, although Schultz and colleagues (Schultz et al., 2000) originally proposed the possibility that primary pathology of the fusiform could be the cause of autistic face-processing impairments, more recently this group has pursued the hypothesis that fusiform hypoactivation is secondary to abnormalities at other nodes in the extended face-processing system, particularly the amygdala and its role in imbuing faces and the information they convey with affective value and social salience (Grelotti, Gauthier, & Schultz, 2002; Grelotti et al., 2005; Schultz, 2005). Similarly, Dawson and colleagues (Dawson, Webb, & McPartland, 2005) have hypothesized that abnormalities in the encoding and recognition of faces revealed by electrophysiological studies of children and adults with autism (Dawson, Carver, Meltzoff et al., 2002; Webb, Dawson, Bernier, & Panagiotides, 2006) derive primarily from disturbances in limbic or dopaminergic brain circuitry involved in social reward learning, leading to diminished social approach and attention to faces and, in turn, to deficient specialization of the fusiform cortex for face processing.

In sum, face-processing deficiencies in autism do not appear to be reducible to an etiologically primary dysfunction of the fusiform gyrus or its role in the configural perception of face identity. Instead, they are likely to involve more widely distributed abnormalities at other nodes in the face processing system or in their integrated functioning. We suggest that these would include brain regions involved in the perception and interpretation of information communicated through facial movements, such as shifts of gaze and emotional expressions. Unlike face identity perception, deficits in these functions would seem to be at the core of the social and affective impairments that are actually defining of autism. Here we focus specifically on one of these functions, gaze processing.

Gaze Processing in Autism

There is abundant research evidence that individuals with autism fail to use other people's eye gaze for social and communicative purposes, such as to establish shared attention (Mundy, Sigman, Ungerer, & Sherman, 1986), to learn the referents of novel words (Baron-Cohen, Baldwin, & Crowson, 1997), to regulate turn taking in conversation (Mirenda, Donnellan, & Yoder, 1983), or to decipher the goals and intentions (Baron-Cohen, Campbell, Karmiloff-Smith, Grant, & Walker, 1995; Phillips, Baron-Cohen, & Rutter, 1992) and the thoughts and feelings of other people (Baron-Cohen et al., 1995; Baron-Cohen, Wheelwright, Hill, Raste, & Plumb, 2001; Baron-Cohen, Wheelwright, & Jolliffe, 1997). Behavioral observation studies have found that children with autism are significantly delayed in spontaneous gaze following, that they tend to rely on other attention-orienting cues, such as head turns and verbal directives, and that the emergence of gaze following is strongly associated with verbal mental age, suggesting that the acquisition of gaze following is atypically dependent on verbal mediation (DiLavore & Lord, 1995; Leekam, Hunnisett, & Moore, 1998).

In studies using eye tracking and other novel methods to examine visual attention to faces, people with autism have repeatedly demonstrated decreased attention to the eyes, the region of the face that is normally most informative for face identification (Goldstein & Mackenberg, 1966; McKelvie, 1976; Sergent, 1984) and of critical value for discriminating between facial expressions of emotion (Baron-Cohen et al., 1997; Bassili, 1979; Calder Young, Keane, & Dean, 2000; Hanawalt, 1944). Pelphrey et al. (2002) reported reduced attention to all inner facial features, but particularly to the eyes, among adults with autism viewing static expressions of emotion (but see van der Geest, Kemner, Verbaten, & van Engeland, 2002). Klin, Jones, Schultz, Volkmar, & Cohen (2002) found reduced attention to eyes and increased attention to mouths among adolescents and young adults with autism viewing film clips of dramatized social interactions. Using the "Bubbles" method (Gosselin & Schyns, 2001), Spezio, Adolphs, Hurley, & Piven (2006) assessed the degree to which different regions of the face were used by adults with autism to identify facial expressions of fear and happiness. By revealing random portions of the same set of face stimuli over numerous trials, the bubbles method allows a calculation of the degree to which different face areas contribute to accurate judgments. Although Spezio and his colleagues found no difference in accuracy or speed of emotion recognition between their autism and control groups, the autism group demonstrated significantly less reliance on the eye region and significantly more reliance on the mouth region in their emotion judgments relative to controls. The authors also tracked participants' gaze behavior during the bubbles task and found that the frequency of fixations made by individuals with autism to the mouth region was consistent with their increased use of mouth information in judging emotions, but that their fixations to the eyes tended to exceed their actual use of information from the eye region to make emotion judgments. In other words, their pattern of visual attention to the face did not completely account for differences in the way they processed faces. In a follow-up study to Joseph and Tanaka (2003, see above), Joseph and Tager-Flusberg (2004) assessed whether cuing children with autism to look at the eyes might induce holistic processing of this region of the face in children with autism. They found that the cues led to increased fixations on the eyes and improved recognition in both whole and part conditions, but did not produce a relative whole advantage (but see Lopez, Hadwin, Donnelly, & Leekam, 2005). These findings, along with those of Spezio et al., suggest that eye-related face-processing abnormalities in autism are not simply of an attentional nature, but are likely to involve what are potentially more fundamental aberrations in the perception of or affective response to people's eyes and shifts of gaze.

One possibility is that individuals with autism are less attentive to other people's eyes because of *indifference* borne of social-perceptual impairments that make gaze cues uninformative. Supporting this possibility is experimental evidence of impaired perception of both mutual gaze and goal-directed gaze in autism. Mutual gaze serves to convey a person's interest or intentions, positive or negative, toward another person, and is reflected in our remarkable sensitivity in detecting when another person's gaze is directed toward us (Argyle & Cook, 1976; von Grunau & Anston, 1995). Both children and adults are normally more efficient at encoding faces with direct gaze than those with averted gaze (Hood, Macrae, Cole-Davies, & Dias, 2003), suggesting that direct gaze makes faces more socially salient. However, this does not appear to be the case for children with autism. For example, Senju and colleagues used visual oddball and visual-search paradigms to assess sensitivity to mutual gaze in children with autism and found that, in contrast to controls, they were no better at detecting faces with direct gaze than those with averted gaze (Senju, Yaguchi, Togo, & Hasegawa, 2003; Senju, Hasegawa, & Tojo, 2005). Although Senju and colleagues did not investigate the neural bases of the diminished perception of direct gaze in autism, neuroimaging studies of normal adults have found that faces with direct gaze, as compared to those with averted gaze, preferentially engage the amygdala in conjunction with the fusiform gyrus (George, Driver, & Dolan, 2001; Kawashima et al., 1999).

Using event-related functional neuroimaging, Pelphrey, Morris, and McCarthy (2005) investigated brain activation in response to goal-directed shifts of gaze in autism, of particular interest given the striking behavioral impairments in gaze following and joint attention in this disorder. In their study, participants viewed a virtual actor, who on alternate trials either gazed toward an object that appeared on the periphery or, instead, looked away from the object toward empty space. Pelphrey et al. found that individuals with autism, like controls, showed increased activation in the superior temporal sulcus (STS) in response to the actor's gaze shift. However, whereas control participants showed relatively increased STS activation when the actor's gaze direction was incongruent with the object location (see also Pelphrey, Singerman, Allison, & McCarthy, 2003), STS activation among participants with autism did not differ between the congruent and incongruent conditions. Thus, although individuals with autism were generally sensitive to shifts of gaze, they did not appear to perceive gaze as intentional and goal-directed (see also Castelli, Frith, Happé, & Frith, 2002).

A second explanation for reduced attention to the eye region of the face is that individuals with autism have an *aversion* to making eye contact, resulting from heightened emotional arousal in response to salient social stimuli. Abnormalities of emotional arousal have been broadly linked to dysfunction of the amygdala and other social-affective brain circuitry, including anterior cingulate, insular, and prefrontal cortex (Davidson & Irwin, 1999). Hirstein, Iversen, & Ramachandran (2001) examined electrodermal activity, a measure of amygdala-mediated autonomic response, in children with autism, finding that most children exhibited hyper-arousal in response to a social bid for eye contact (although a small subgroup exhibited hypoarousal in their electrodermal response). Two other research groups have reported that children with autism, unlike controls, exhibited heightened electrodermal response while looking at faces with direct (or mutual) gaze as com-pared to faces with averted gaze (Joseph et al., 2005; Kylliainen & Hietanen, 2006). In addition, Joseph et al. (2005) found that autonomic arousal in response to direct gaze in children with autism was strongly and inversely correlated with their per-formance in an independent test of face recognition. These findings seem to con-tradict those of Senju and colleagues described above, but may suggest that the normally faster detection time for faces with mutual gaze in, for example, an oddball paradigm is disrupted by a heightened, negatively valenced autonomic response in individuals with autism.

Combining eye tracking with functional magnetic resonance imaging (fMRI), Dalton et al. (2005) directly investigated the relationship between looking behavior toward faces and patterns of brain activation in two independent samples of chil-dren and adolescents with autism performing face-recognition tasks. Across studies, Dalton et al. found decreased fusiform gyrus activation and increased amygdala activation in children with autism as compared to controls. Moreover, across studies, fusiform and amygdala activation were strongly and positively correlated with the amount of time spent fixating the eyes in the autism group, but not in the control group. These findings led to the conclusion that fusiform hypoactivation in autism is more likely a function of how individuals scan faces rather than a dys-function of the fusiform *per se* (see also Hadjikhani et al., 2004) and that a height-ened emotive response to eye contact, mediated by the amygdala and possible other affective neural circuitry, leads to diminished eye fixation in autism. In a similar fMRI study of face processing in unaffected siblings of individuals with autism, Dalton et al. (2005) found that unaffected siblings exhibited decreases in eye fixa-tion and right fusiform activation comparable to those found in their autism group, and that eye fixation and fusiform activation were similarly correlated. However, eye fixations were only mildly correlated with amygdala activation in the unaffected siblings, in contrast to the strong correlations found in individuals with autism, but the study may have been insufficiently powered to establish this connection.

Thus, although Dalton et al.'s fMRI findings may be viewed as inconclusive regarding the possibility that amygdala hyperactivity might serve as a quantitative neural phenotype for autism susceptibility, the eye-tracking findings suggested that the amount of attention directed to the eyes may provide a behavioral index. Con-sistent with this view, a recent study on infant siblings at risk for autism found that about one-third of 6-month-old infant siblings showed reduced gaze toward their mothers' eyes, relative to her mouth, in contrast to only one of twenty-four control infants (Merin, Young, Ozonoff, & Rogers, 2007).

Complementing these fMRI studies, Nacewicz, Dalton, Johnstone, et al. (2006) investigated links between amygdala volume, parent-reported social symptom severity in early childhood, and concurrent eye fixation in an emotion judgment task in a sample of older children and young adults with autism. They found that decreased amygdala volume was associated with more severe social impairment in childhood and with decreased eye fixation concurrently. In addition, individuals who exhibited lower levels of eye fixation showed little increase in amygdala volume with age, whereas individuals with higher levels of eye fixation showed age-related increases in amygdala volume that were comparable to those found in the control group. Based on these findings, Nacewicz et al. propose an "allostatic load model" (McEwen, 2003) of amygdala development in autism, in which chronic social stress and hypersensitivity in more severely affected individuals contributes to an initial period of amygdala overgrowth in early childhood, consistent with previous findings (e.g. Schumann et al., 2004), followed by an excitotoxic process of atrophy through later childhood and adolescence (see also Schumann & Amaral, 2006). This model thus takes into consideration the effects of experience on neural development as well as the endogenous neuropathological processes that help to determine that experience.

In summary, individuals with autism exhibit abnormally decreased attention to the eye region of the face. There is evidence that this results from a perceptual or a higher cognitive impairment in reading intent in people's eyes and shifts of gaze, leading to a relative indifference to people's eyes and faces in general. There is also evidence that looking at other people's eyes is aversive to individuals with autism, possibly causing them to avoid eye contact so as to regulate affective arousal. Of course, these alternate possibilities are not mutually exclusive. In fact, impaired social perception and affective dysregulation would probably be mutually reinforcing. For example, heightened autonomic reactivity in response to looking at other people's eyes could conceivably be an acquired anxiety response in individuals who are regularly pressed to respond to gaze cues they do not understand.

Further Considerations and Future Research Directions

We have proposed, based on existing research evidence, that the atypical processing strategies and performance deficits demonstrated by individuals with autism on face-recognition tasks derive specifically from abnormalities in gaze processing. Although the research we have reviewed in support of this hypothesis has implicated dysfunction in mainly two brain regions, the amygdala and STS, their role in the etiology of face- and gaze-processing impairments needs to be investigated in two broader contexts.

The first context is of autism as a complex neurodevelopmental disorder, which involves significant impairments in, for example, language and social functioning, both of which depend on widely distributed neural systems. The distributed nature of the brain pathology in autism is perhaps best underscored by the most robust and replicated brain finding on autism thus far, that of early cerebral overgrowth that has not been reliably localized to any single brain region or tissue compartment (e.g. Hazlett et al., 2005; Hazlett, Poe, Gerig, Smith, & Piven, 2006; Redcay & Cour-chesne, 2005). In this context, structural pathology of the amygdala in autism resulting from primary regulatory defects in brain ontogenesis is likely to co-occur with more distributed pathology of other subcortical and cortical structures includ-ing those involved in social-emotional function. Likewise, abnormalities of STS activation related to a failure to ascribe intent based on gaze direction (Pelphrey et al., 2003) may extend to functionally overlapping cortical regions, such as those associated with mental-state attribution from social cues other than gaze, and recently described as part of the extended neural system for face perception (Gobbini & Haxby, 2006).

The second context is of autism as a disorder of development, which poses the challenge of disentangling primary from secondary impairments. The majority of studies discussed here have focused on older children and adults, but brain pathol-ogy and related functional deficits in autism can be completely understood only in developmental terms. To a large extent this is already reflected in many of the per-spectives presented in this chapter, including the hypotheses that face-processing deficits may be secondary to amygdala dysfunction (Nacewicz et al., 2006; Schultz, 2005) or to social- motivation deficits (Dawson et al., 2005), and our own perspec-tive that impaired social perception and affective dysregulation may be mutually reinforcing. However, these questions will be answered only when research on older individuals is complemented by longitudinal investigations of young children and infants at risk of developing an autism spectrum disorder. Prospective longitudinal studies beginning in the earliest months of infancy will help to delineate the earliest trajectories of face-processing impairments, providing an enriched perspective on the interplay between maturational and experience-dependent influences on the biological and cognitive mechanisms that underlie the social-affective impairments at the core of autism spectrum disorders.

References

APA (1994). American Psychiatric Association. *Diagnostic and statistical manual of mental disorders.* 4th edn. Washington: American Psychiatric Association.

Argyle, M., & Cook, M. (1976). *Gaze and Mutual Gaze.* Cambridge: Cambridge University Press.

Aylward, E., Bernier, R., Field, A., Grimme, A., & Dawson, G. (2004). Autism during the view of familiar faces. Poster presented at the International Meeting for Autism Research, Sacramento, CA.

Baron-Cohen, S., Baldwin, D. A., & Crowson, M. (1997). Do children with autism use the speaker's direction of gaze strategy to crack the code of language? *Child Development*, 68, 48–57.

Baron-Cohen, S., Campbell, R., Karmiloff-Smith, A., Grant, J., & Walker, J. (1995). Are children with autism blind to the mentalistic significance of the eyes? *British Journal of Developmental Psychology*, 13, 379–398.

Baron-Cohen, S., Wheelwright, S., & Jolliffe, T. (1997). Is there a "language of the eyes"? Evidence from normal adults and adults with autism or Asperger syndrome. *Visual Cognition*, 4, 311–331.

Baron-Cohen, S., Wheelwright, S., Hill, J., Raste, Y., & Plumb, I. (2001). The "reading the mind in the eyes" test revised version: A study with normal adults, and adults with Asperger's Syndrome or high-functioning autism. *Journal of Child Psychology and Psychiatry*, 42, 241–251.

Barton, J. J. S., Press, D. Z., Keenan, J. P., & O'Connor, M. (2002). Lesions of the fusiform face area impair perception of facial configuration in prosopagnosia. *Neurology*, 58, 71–78.

Bassili, J. N. (1979). Emotion recognition: The role of facial movement and the relative importance of upper and lower areas of the face. *Journal of Personality and Social Psychology*, 37, 2049–2058.

Behrmann, M., Avidan, G., Leonard, G. L., Kimchi, R., Luna, B., Humphreys, K., & Minshew, N. (2007). Configural processing in autism and its relationship to face processing. *Neuropsychologia*, 44, 110–129.

Behrmann, M., Thomas, C., and Humphreys, K. (2006). Autism: Seeing it differently. *Trends in Cognitive Science*, 10, 258–264.

Boucher, J., & Lewis, V. (1992). Unfamiliar face recognition in relatively able autistic children. *Journal of Child Psychology and Psychiatry*, 33, 843–859.

Braverman, M., Fein, D., Lucci, D., & Waterhouse, L. (1989). Affect comprehension in children with pervasive developmental disorders. *Journal of Autism and Developmental Disorders*. 19, 301–316.

Bruce, V., & Young, A. W. (1986). Understanding face recognition. *British Journal of Psychology*, 77, 305–327.

Calder, A. J., Young, A. W., Keane, J., & Dean, M. (2000). Configural information in facial perception. *Journal of Experimental Psychology: Human Perception and Performance*, 26(2), 527–551.

Carey, S., & Diamond, R. (1977). From piecemeal to configurational representation of faces. *Science*, 195, 312–314.

Castelli, F., Frith, C., Happé, F., & Frith, U. (2002). Autism, Asperger syndrome and brain mechanisms for the attribution of mental states to animated shapes. *Brain*, 125, 1839–1849.

Critchley, H. D., Daly, E. M., Bullmore, E. T., Williams, S. C. R., Van Amelsvoort, T. V., Robertson, D. M., et al. (2000). The functional neuroanatomy of social behavior: Changes in cerebral blood flow when people with autistic disorder process facial expressions. *Brain*, 123, 2203–2212.

Dalton, K. M., Nacewicz, B. M., Johnstone, T., Schaefer, H. S., Gernsbacher, M. A., Goldsmith, H. H., Alexander, A. L., & Davidson, R. J. (2005). Gaze fixation and the neural circuitry of face processing in autism. *Nature Neuroscience*, 8, 519–526.

Davidson, R. J., & Irwin, W. (1999). The functional neuroanatomy of emotion and affective style. *Trends in Cognitive Sciences*, 3, 11–21.

Davies, S., Bishop, D., Manstead, A. S. R., & Tantam, D. (1994). *Journal of Child Psychology and Psychiatry*, 35, 1033–1057.

Dawson, G. Carver, L., Meltzoff, A. N., Panagiotides, H., & McPartland, J. (2002). Neural correlates of face recognition in young children with autism spectrum disorder, developmental delay, and typical development. *Child Development*, 73, 700–717.

Dawson, G., Webb, S., & McPartland, J. (2005). Understanding the nature of face processing impairment in autism: Insights from behavioral and electrophysiological studies. *Developmental Neuropsychology*, 27, 403–424.

Diamond, R., & Carey, S. (1986). Why faces are and are not special: An effect of expertise. *Journal of Experimental Psychology: General*, 115, 107–117.

DiLavore, P., & Lord, C. (1995). Do you see what I see? Requesting and joint attention in young autistic children. Paper presented at biennial meeting of the Society for Research in Child Development, Indianapolis, IN.

Farah, M. J., Tanaka, J. W., & Drain, H. W. (1995). What causes the face inversion effect? *Journal of Experimental Psychology: Human Perception and Performance*, 21, 628–634.

Freire, A., & Lee, K. (2001). Face recognition in 4- to 7-year-olds: Processing of configural, featural, and paraphernalia information. *Journal of Experimental Child Psychology*, 80, 347–371.

George, N., Driver, J., & Dolan, R. J. (2001). Seen gaze-direction modulates fusiform activity and its coupling with other brain areas during face processing. *NeuroImage*, 13, 1102–1112.

Gobbini, M. I., & Haxby, J. V. (2006). Neural systems for recognition of familiar faces. *Neuropsychologia*.

Goldstein, A. G., & Mackenberg, E. (1966). Recognition of human faces from isolated facial features. *Psychonomic Science*, 6, 149–150.

Gosselin, F., & Schyns, P. G. (2001). Bubbles: A technique to reveal the use of information in recognition tasks. *Vision Research*, 41, 2261–2271.

Grelotti, D., Gauthier, I., & Schultz, R. T. (2002). Social Interest and the development of cortical face specialization: What autism teaches us about face processing. *Developmental Psychobiology*, 40, 213–225.

Grelotti, D. J., Klin, A. J., Gauthier, I., Skudlarski, P., Cohen, D. J., Gore, J. C., Volkmar, F. R., & Schultz, R. T. (2005). fMRI activation of the fusiform gyrus and amygdala to cartoon characters but not to faces in a boy with autism. *Neuropsychologia*, 43, 373–385.

Hadjikhani, H., Joseph, R. M., Snyder, J., Chabris, C. F., Clark, J., Steele, S., McGrath, L., Vangel, M., Aharon, I., Fekzco, A., Harris, G. J., & Tager-Flusberg, H. (2004). Activation of the fusiform gyrus when individuals with autism spectrum disorder view faces. *NeuoImage*, 22, 1141–1150.

Hall, G. B., Szechtman, H., & Nahmias, C. (2003). Enhanced salience and emotion recognition in autism: A PET study. *American Journal of Psychiatry*, 160, 1439–1441.

Hanawalt, N. G. (1944). The role of upper and lower parts of the face as the basis for judging facial expressions: II. In posed expressions and "candid camera" pictures. *Journal of General Psychology*, 31, 23–36.

Hauck, M., Fein, D., Maltby, N., Waterhouse, L., & Feinstein, C. (1998). Memory for faces in children with autism. *Child Neuropsychology*, 4, 187–198.

Haxby, J. V., Hoffman, E. A., & Gobbini, M. I. (2000). The distributed human neural system for face perception. *Trends in Cognitive Sciences*, 4, 223–233.

Hazlett, H., Poe, M., Gerig, G., Smith, R., & Piven, C. (2006). Cortical gray and white brain tissue volume in adolescents and adults with autism. *Biological Psychiatry*, 59(1), 1–6.

Hirstein, W., Iversen, P., & Ramachandran, V. S. (2001). Autonomic responses of autistic children to people and objects. *Proceedings of the Royal Society of London, B*, 268, 1883–1888.

Hobson, R. P., Outson, J., & Lee, A. (1988). What's in a face? The case of autism. *British Journal of Psychology*, 79, 441–453.

Hood, B. M., Macrae, C. N., Cole-Davies, V., & Dias, M. (2003). Eye remember you: The effects of gaze direction on face recognition in children and adults. *Developmental Science*, 6, 67–71.

Hubl, D., Bolte, S., Feineis-Matthews, S., Lanfermann, H., Federspiel, A., Strik, W., Poustka, F., & Dierks, T. (2003). Functional imbalance of visual pathways indicates alternative face processing strategies in autism. *Neurology*, 61, 1232–1237.

Joseph, R. M., Ehrman, K., McNally, R., & Tager-Flusberg, H. (2005). Affective response to eye contact in children with autism. Paper presented at biennial meeting of the Society for Research in Child Development, Atlanta, GA.

Joseph, R. M., & Tager-Flusberg, H. (1997). An investigation of attention and affect in children with autism and Down syndrome. *Journal of Autism and Developmental Disorders*, 4, 385–396.

Joseph, R. M., & Tager-Flusberg, H. (2004). The relationship of theory of mind and executive functions to symptom type and severity in children with autism. *Development and Psychopathology*, 16, 137–155.

Joseph, R. M., & Tanaka, J. (2003). Holistic and part-based face recognition in children with autism. *Journal of Child Psychology and Psychiatry*, 44, 529–542.

Kasari, C., Sigman, M., & Yirmiya, N. (1993). Focused and social attention of autistic children in interactions with familiar and unfamiliar adults: A comparison of autistic, mentally retarded, and normal children. *Development and Psychopathology*, 5, 403–414.

Kawashima, R., Sugiura, M. Kato, T., Nakamura, A., Hatano, K., Ito, K., et al. (1999). The human amygdala plays an important role in gaze monitoring: A PET study. *Brain*, 122, 779–783.

Klin, A., Jones, W., Schultz, R., Volkmar, F., & Cohen, D. J. (2002). Visual fixation patterns during viewing of naturalistic social situations as predictors of social competence in individuals with autism. *Archives of General Psychiatry*, 59, 809–816.

Klin, A., Sparrow, S. S., de Bildt, A., Cicchetti, D. V., Cohen, D. J., & Volkmar, F. R. (1999). A normed study of face recognition in autism and related disorders. *Journal of Autism and Developmental Disorders*, 29, 499–508.

Kylliainen, A., & Hietanen, J. K. (2006). Skin conductance responses to another person's gaze in children with autism. *Journal of Autism and Developmental Disorders*, 36, 517–25.

Lahaie, A., Mottron, L., Arguin, M., Berthiaume, C., Jemel, B., & Saumier, D. (2006). Face perception in high-functioning autistic adults: Evidence for superior processing of face parts, not for a configural face processing deficit. *Neuropsychology*, 20, 30–41.

Langdell, T. (1978). Recognition of faces: An approach to the study of autism. *Journal of Child Psychology and Psychiatry*, 19, 255–268.

Le Grand, R., Mondloch, C. J., Maurer, D., & Brent, H. P. (2003). Expert face processing requires visual input to the right hemisphere during infancy. *Nature Neuroscience*, 6, 1108–1112; erratum: 8, 1329.

Le Grand, R., Mondloch, C. J., Maurer, D., & Brent, H. P. (2004). Impairment in holistic face processing following early visual deprivation. *Psychological Science*, 15, 762–768.

Maurer, D., Le Grand, R., & Mondloch, C. J. (2002). The many face of configural processing. *Trends in Cognitive Sciences*, 6, 255–260.

McEwen, B. S. (2003). Mood disorders and allostatic load. *Biological Psychiatry*, 54, 200–207.

McKelvie, S. J. (1976). The role of eyes and mouth in the memory of a face. *American Journal of Psychology*, 89, 311–323.

Merin, N., Young, G. S., Ozonoff, S., & Rogers, S. J. (2007). Visual fixation patterns during reciprocal social interaction distinguish a subgroup of 6-month-old infants at-risk for autism from comparison infants. *Journal of Autism and Developmental Disorders*, 37, 108–121.

Mirenda, P., Donnellan, A., & Yoder, D. (1983). Gaze behavior: A new look at an old problem. *Journal of Autism and Developmental Disorders*, 13, 397–409.

Miyashita, T. (1988). Discrimination of facial components in autistic children. *Japanese Journal of Psychology*, 59, 206–212.

Mundy, P., Sigman, M., Ungerer, J., & Sherman, T. (1986). Defining the social deficits in autism: The contribution of nonverbal communication measures. *Journal of Child Psychology and Psychiatry*, 27, 657–669.

Nacewicz, B. M., Dalton, K. M., Johnstone, T., Long, M., McAuliff, E. M., Oakes, T. R., Alexander, A. L., & Davidson, R. J. (2006). Amygdala volume and nonverbal social impairment in adolescent and adult males with autism. Archives of General Psychiatry, 63, 1417–1428.

Osterling, J., & Dawson, G. (1994). Early recognition of children with autism: A study of first birthday home videotapes. *Journal of Autism and Developmental Disorders*, 24, 247–257.

Osterling, J. A., Dawson, G., & Munson, J. A. (2002). Early recognition of 1-year-old infants with autism spectrum disorder versus mental retardation. *Development and Psychopathology*, 14, 239–251.

Palermo, R., & Rhodes, G. (2006). Are you always on my mind? A review of how face perception and attention interact. *Neuropsychologia*.

Pascalis, O., Scott, L. S., Kelly, D. J., Shannon, R. W., Nicholson, E., Coleman, M., & Nelson, C. A. (2005). Plasticity of face processing in infancy. *Proceedings of the National Academy of Sciences*, 102, 5297–5300.

Pelphrey, K. A., Morris, J. P., & McCarthy, G. (2005). Neural basis of eye gaze processing deficits in autism. *Brain*, 128, 1038–1048.

Pelphrey, K. A., Singerman, J. D., Allison, T., & McCarthy, G. (2003). Brain activation evoked by perception of gaze shifts: the influence of context. *Neuropsychologia*, 41, 156–170.

Phillips, W., Baron-Cohen, S., & Rutter, M. (1992). The role of eye contact in the detection of goals: Evidence from normal toddlers and children with autism or mental handicap. *Development and Psychopathology*, 4, 375–383.

Phillips, M. L., Drevets, W. C., Rauch, S. L., et al. (2003). Neurobiology of emotion perception I: The neural basis of normal emotion perception. *Biological Psychiatry*, 54, 504–514.

Pierce, K., Haist, F., Sedaghat, F., & Courchesne, E. (2004). The brain response to personally familiar faces in autism: Findings of fusiform activity and beyond. *Brain*, 127, 2703–2716.

Pierce, K., Muller, R.-A., Ambrose, J., Allen, G., & Courchesne, E. (2001). Face processing occurs outside the fusiform "face area" in autism: Evidence from functional MRI. *Brain*, 124, 2059–2073.

Redcay, E., & Courchesne, E. (2005). When is the brain enlarged in autism? A meta-analysis of all brain size reports. *Biological Psychiatry*, 58, 1–9.

Rossion, B., Dricot, L., Devolder, et al. (2000). Hemispheric asymmetries for whole-based and part-based face processing in the human fusiform gyrus. *Journal of Cognitive Neuroscience*, 12, 793–802.

Rouse, H., Donnelly, N., Hadwin, J. A., & Brown, T. (2004). Do children with autism perceive second-order relational features? The case of the Thatcher illusion. *Journal of Child Psychology and Psychiatry and Allied Disciplines*, 45, 1246–1257.

Sasson, N. J. (2006). The development of face processing in autism. *Journal of Autism and Developmental Disorders*, 36, 381–394.

Schultz, R. T. (2005). Developmental deficits in social perception in autism: The role of the amygdala and fusiform face area. *International Journal of Developmental Neuroscience*, 23, 125–141.

Schultz, R. T., Gauthier, I., Klin, A., Fulbright, R. K., Anderson, A. W., Volkmar, F. et al. (2000). Abnormal ventral temporal cortical activity during face discrimination among individuals with autism and Asperger syndrome. *Archives of General Psychiatry*, 57, 331–340.

Schumann, C. M., & Amaral, D. G. (2006). Stereological analysis of amygdala neuron number in autism. *Journal of Neuroscience*, 26(29), 7674–7679.

Schumann, C. M., Hamstra, J., Goodlin-Jones, B. L., Lotspeich, L. J., Kwon, H., Buonocore, M. H., Lammers, C. R., Reiss, A. L., & Amaral, D. G. (2004). The amygdala is enlarged in children but not adolescents with autism; the hippocampus is enlarged at all ages. *Journal of Neuroscience*, 24, 6392–6401.

Senju, A., Hasegawa, T., & Tojo, Y. (2005). Does perceived direct gaze boost detection in adults and children with and without autism? The stare-in-the-crowd effect revisited. *Visual Cognition*, 12, 1474–1496.

Senju, A., Yaguchi, K., Tojo, Y., & Hasegawa, T. (2003). Eye contact does not facilitate detection in children with autism. Cognition, 89, B43–B51.

Sergent, J. (1984). An investigation into component and configural processes underlying face perception. *British Journal of Psychology*, 75, 221–242.

Spezio, M. L., Adolphs, R., Hurley, R. S. E., & Piven, J. (2006). Abnormal use of facial information in high-functioning autism. *Journal of Autism and Developmental Disorders*, 37(5), 929–939.

Tanaka, J. W., Kay, J. B., Grinnell, E., Stansfield, B., & Szechter, L. (1998). Face recognition in young children: When the whole is greater than the sum of its parts. *Visual Cognition*, 5, 479–496.

Tantam, D., Monaghan, L., Nicholson, J., & Stirling, J. (1989). Autistic children's ability to interpret faces: A research note. *Journal of Child Psychology and Psychiatry*, 30, 623–630.

Tarr, M. J., & Gauthier, I. (2000). FFA: A flexible fusiform area for subordinate- level visual processing automatized by expertise. *Nature Neuroscience*, 3, 764–769.

Thompson, P. (1980). Margaret Thatcher – a new illusion. *Perception*, 9, 483–484.

van der Geest, J. N., Kemner, C., Verbaten, M. N., & van Engeland, H. (2002). Gaze behavior of children with pervasive developmental disorder toward human faces: A fixation time study, *Journal of Child Psychology and Psychiatry*, 43(5), 669–678.

von Grunau, M., & Anston, C. (1995). The detection of gaze direction: A stare in the crowd effect. *Perception*, 24, 1297–1313.

Webb, S. J., Dawson, G., Bernier, R., & Panagiotides, H. (2006). ERP evidence of atypical face processing in young children with autism. *Journal of Autism and Developmental Disorders*, 36, 881–890.

Yin, R. K. (1969). Looking at upside-down faces. *Journal of Experimental Psychology*, 81, 141–145.

Yirmiya, N., & Ozonoff, S. (2007). The very early autism phenotype. *Journal of Autism and Developmental Disorders*, 37, 1–11.

Yovel, G., & Duchaine, B. (2006). Specialized face perception mechanisms extract both part and spacing information: Evidence from developmental prosopagnosia. *Journal of Cognitive Neuroscience*, 18(4), 580–593.

Chapter 15

Beyond Social Perception: The Case of Autism

Jessica A. Hobson and R. Peter Hobson

We are concerned with what happens "beyond social perception," in this sense: our experience of persons *as* persons is special in virtue of processes that are not encompassed by what most people think of as perception. If one wants to uncover how young children come to experience and then to understand persons as different from things, it is vital to consider the qualities of their relatedness toward others. To be sure, one *can* consider such relatedness as part and parcel of what social perception is, and, in this case, all to the good; but, with notable exceptions, this has not been the tradition in psychology. We shall argue that, from infancy onwards, there is structure to interpersonal perception and experience that provides the basis for so-called "theory of mind" understanding and for attendant *concepts* of mind that develop between the second and fourth years of life.

In addressing these issues, we shall adopt the approach of developmental psychopathology, with a specific focus on the syndrome of early childhood autism. Among persons with autism, we shall suggest, the capacity to perceive others as persons – or more accurately, to participate in those forms of relatedness that other people afford – may be weak or impaired. (In an ideal world, we would add some qualifications here, especially with regard to our view that autism is a systemic disorder of self-in-relation-to-other, but these points are sufficiently tangential to omit for the present purposes.) In order to understand this condition we need to concern ourselves with the ways in which affected children have difficulty in becoming engaged with and "moved by" other persons *as* persons with psychological orientations of their own. We follow the suggestions of Kanner (1943) that autism might best be viewed as a disturbance in interpersonal relations, where, in many cases at least, biologically based perceptual-affective abnormalities are critical in the development of the disorder. Through the case of autism, then, we may discern the nature and significance of otherwise elusive primary social-perceptual determinants of interpersonal relations, where such relations are foundational for psychological understanding. In following this investigative path, we trace the route through which infants travel in order to experience themselves as both connected to and distinct from other people as people with their own psychological orientations to the world. Such a journey may be necessary for children to acquire the capacity for flexible, creative, symbolic thinking itself.

What is Social Perception?

Social perception has been defined as the set of processes that involve the perception and understanding of other people. In a book entitled Social Perception, Zebrowitz (1990, p. 3) adopts a familiar position in suggesting how one needs to understand the covert psychological processes that underlie people's overt behavior. While there is obviously something captured by this approach, it is easy to overstate the degree to which the motives, intentions, and experiences of others are inner and hidden from the observer, who must infer or deduce their existence. As Cockburn (1990, p. 15) describes, according to this model one might think that the being that feels pain, gets angry, acts, and sees is not to be found in the world of extended, tangible entities.

Dijksterhuis and Bargh (2001, p. 9) appear to endorse such a view when they write:

> So what does a social perceiver perceive? First, social perceivers perceive what we may call observables. This class of behavior is easy to define. It involves behaviors that we can literally perceive. We perceive gestures and movements of others. We can see someone wave, scratch her head, or wiggle his foot. Furthermore, we can perceive various facial expressions. We see people smile or frown, for instance.

Although these authors qualify their position in acknowledging how we perceive more than is literally present, especially through imitation, still there appear to be tight boundaries to what social perception entails.

Heider (1944, 1958) offers us an alternative place from which we – and, in their own ways, infants – might begin to grasp what is foundational for human psychological engagement. Heider's abiding interest was in person perception (Weary, Rich, Harvey, & Ickes, 1980), in what he described (Heider 1958, p. 33) as "a process between the center of one person and the center of another person." He argued that:

> We must reject the prejudice which makes "inner realities" out of love, hate or anger, leaving them accessible to one single witness: the person who feels them. Anger, shame, hate and love are not psychic facts hidden at the bottom of another's consciousness: they are types of behavior or styles of conduct which are visible from the outside. Just as sorrow or shame or love can be expressively manifest through persons with bodies, so social perception is not something going on deep inside the person experiencing but also manifest, felt and seen.

Along very similar lines, Wittgenstein (1958) pointed out that we describe a face immediately as sad or bored, as a primary mode of perception. The upshot is that to perceive a person is at the same time to apprehend something of what it means to be a subject of experience, through affective responsiveness to what the person expresses through his or her body. Of course, this is *not* the same as conceptualizing what it means to be a person with a mind – an especially important consideration when it comes to considering the early months of life. Yet it *is* to be moved by the attitude of the other, in that a Mr Spock would not have the emotional wherewithal to engage in such feeling perception toward others. One might capture this dimension of social perception by stating that one individual orientates to, and is re-oriented *through*, the attitudes of others. This affectively coordinated experience-in-relation-to-others is what grounds our concept of persons as individuals with mental life. As Hamlyn (1974) has written, in order to perceive a person, one needs to stand in a personal relation to that which is perceived – so that understanding of persons is grounded in such relations. And, once again, Wittgenstein (1958) takes us one step further in pointing to our ability to apprehend meaning in others' actions and attitudes through our natural ability to transpose those actions and attitudes to one's own case.

Therefore we are led to consider how it is not merely emotional responsiveness to, but also alignment with, the perceptible stance of someone else that yields persons as objects of social perception. The ability to "mimic" reveals just how far the actions and attitudes we perceive in others are also actions and attitudes that we can come to assume. Such assimilation of another person's psychological orientation – or, more accurately, such identification with the other's orientation, given that the actions and attitudes are perceived *as* the other's – bestows uniquely important access to people who share our form of life.

The Beginnings of Person Perception

If it is in laughter that humans perceive joy, as Scheler (1954) expressed the matter, we need to analyze what goes into this form of perception. To achieve this, we need to consider how a person becomes a person for an infant. If we consider how it is not until around the middle of the second year of life that infants acquire concepts of self and other and come to understand what it means for a person to have a perspective (e.g. Hobson, 1993), then we need to specify how they arrive at these concepts.

For over a century, there have been theoretical writings on infancy that have explored how an infant's perceptual-affective propensities demarcate personal and non-personal spheres of existence. For example, Baldwin (1902) described how, through an instinctive capacity for sympathy with others, infants respond to suggestions of personality in other people. Darwin (1877) wrote: "An infant understands to a certain extent, and I believe at a very early period, the meaning or feelings of those who tend him, by the expression of their features" (pp. 293–294, cited in

Murray & Trevarthen, 1985). Even in the early months of life, there appears to be structure to infants' emotional connectedness with others: within and as a part of infants' experiences of social encounters, they register and feel as "other" something of the other's attitude, stance, and orientation. This is what human forms of sharing entail, even though the other-centeredness encompassed within such exchanges becomes unmistakable only with the advent of what Trevarthen and Hubley (1978) called secondary intersubjectivity toward the end of the first year of life.

Thus, around the time of a first birthday, one witnesses an infant's ability to register and be responsive to another person's attitudes toward a shared world, most obviously in social referencing and other "sharing" kinds of joint attention (Mundy, Kasari, & Sigman, 1992; Sorce, Emde, Campos, & Klinnert, 1985). We believe it is critical for subsequent developments in social understanding that, within such settings, the infant should be able to register his or her own movements in attitude *as* shifts across person-anchored perspectives. There is more to this than that the infant observes behavior from the outside; rather, the infant is moved to adopt a new orientation to a shared world through the other. It is on the basis of such non-inferential, non-intellectual role taking that, over the coming months, the infant will construct an understanding of selves as persons with their individual ways of experiencing and construing the world, and relate to the world as potentially meaningful in different ways to different people (including themselves).

Yet the conundrum remains: what gives differentiation to experience, such that certain of my experiences are of you as experiencing? A tradition of thinking about modes of sympathy, relatedness, and primary communication, which may be traced through writings in philosophy (e.g. Macmurray, 1961) and psychoanalysis (e.g. Winnicott, 1958) to contemporary psychology (e.g. Bråten, 1998; Decety & Chaminade, 2003; Meltzoff, 2002; Trevarthen, 1979), posits that a basic unit of study is self in relation to other persons. For example, Neisser (1988) describes an embodied direct perception that occurs when the self is engaged in immediate, unreflective social interaction with another person. If we can characterize the structure of infant perception that gives rise to experiences of self-in-relation-to others, then we may be in a position to account for the development of increasingly explicit forms of self/other differentiation and, in due course, conceptual understanding of what it means to be a self.

Early encounters

Consider the following vignette concerning Emma, the 5-month-old baby daughter of a colleague who joined us for a lunch meeting. As we adults were chattering away, Emma – positioned up against her mother's shoulder and directly across the table from me (JH) – turned to face me and began gazing intently into my eyes. As I looked into her eyes, my growing smile reflected the pleasure and enjoyment at making contact. Her look, reciprocated, now began to intensify, until her own face burst into smile. Simultaneously, she averted her gaze and turned away, still smiling. A moment later, in what seemed a flirtatious gesture, she looked back to catch my eye again. This pattern of mutual exchange was repeated more than once. Was Emma relating to a body? Was she engaging with a mind? It felt to me that she was both perceiving and engaging with me – a person – and sharing experiences. Already at the age of five months (which is not very old), Emma sought out and participated in this very special kind of contact. She also negotiated the rhythm and timing of the interaction as a successful partner in an interpersonal dance. To paraphrase Hamlyn, this child had entered into the kinds of personal relations that would serve as the basis for developing understanding of what persons are.

Evidence from Autism

When the system breaks down

One way of understanding social perception is to explore what happens when there are obstacles to perceiving what persons express. In the remainder of this chapter we consider how evidence from research in autism serves to illuminate the structure of interpersonal relatedness, and with this, we believe (although the evidence is circumstantial), the nature of social perception from early in typical development.

We begin by offering an illustrative case example. The following is a description of a brief series of events in a videotaped assessment with a 6-year-old girl we shall call Sarah with the diagnosis of early childhood autism. She was participating with me (JH) in the Autism Diagnostic Observation Schedule (ADOS-G: Lord et al., 2000), a semi-structured series of planned social presses in which children have opportunities to make requests, engage in joint attention vis-à-vis interesting activities and objects, and communicate with the tester in particular ways. The reason this instrument is so widely accepted is that it is powerful for eliciting certain kinds of exchange that are often limited in autism.

In this particular exchange, I (JH) was seated across and about 2 feet away from Sarah, and had surreptitiously placed a mechanical toy bunny on a table to her left and slightly behind her, but within my full view. I elicited Sarah's attention and exclaimed, "Sarah ... Look, look!" while nodding and gazing toward the rabbit. Sarah looked at my face quizzically. I repeated my attempt, pointing emphatically toward the bunny with my eyes as well as arm and hand gestures, and urging her to "Look!" With some confusion and hesitation, Sarah glanced down toward the floor in front of her, echoed my sound (an approximation of "look") and looked back at my face, seeming bewildered. When next I pointed directly at the rabbit with an outstretched arm and extended point, continuing to call her name and directing her to "look," Sarah looked at my outstretched arm and finger, tentatively extended her own finger, and oriented her hand and pointing finger to align spatially with mine. She did all this without looking at me. Then she looked at her own pointing finger and followed it to discover the mechanical bunny rabbit, which I then activated by depressing the switch near my feet. She watched the rabbit attentively as it hopped around and squeaked, but did not turn back to acknowledge me, the initiator and now sharer (or rather, onlooker) of the experience.

Sarah was attentive to the moving, squeaking object when I brought it over to the table. She smiled and examined it with interest. For what seemed like a long period of time she inspected the object (which did not seem to be a bunny for Sarah), but never once glanced at me. Although I sat with her, appreciating and enjoying the spectacle, it felt as though we were in two separate worlds. Sarah seemed and I felt very alone.

The quality of these exchanges is brought into relief when one compares what happened in a similar situation with a little 3-year-old girl we shall refer to as Emily, who does not have autism. When I glanced over at the rabbit, and before I had a chance to say, "Look!" Emily locked into my gaze and then seemed to bounce off my eyes as she located the object. When I brought it near, she held her hand out tentatively to the bunny's moving mouth, and, as it "nibbled" at her finger, gazed mischievously into my eyes and grinned. When I smiled, she jumped back in mock fear and pain as I queried (playfully): "Did he bite you?" This launched us into a repeat of the experience, as jointly we co-created and participated in a rich, symbolic world involving mutually coordinated exchanges expressed through bodily gestures and eye contact.

Social perception and autism

There is an extensive literature on deficits in social perception among individuals with autism. In one of the earliest experimental studies on emotion recognition, Hobson (1986) presented participants with videotaped facial and audiotaped vocal expressions four emotions. Children with and without autism who were similar in non-verbal ability were asked to select drawings and then photographs of emotionally expressive faces to correspond with these emotional displays and audio-taped vocal expressions of emotion. Although participants with autism did well on other indices of cross-modal matching – with reference to objects, for example – they performed less well in judging which faces corresponded with the portrayals of emotion. Subsequent studies building on this work (e.g. Hobson, Ouston, & Lee, 1989; Moore, Hobson, & Lee, 1997; Weeks & Hobson, 1987) demonstrated how emotional expressions do not seem to hold the same salience and/or meaning for individuals with autism as they do for matched participants without autism. There are now many studies (e.g., as reviewed by Hobson, 2005) illuminating the difficulties these individuals have with accurately perceiving facial and other gestural expressions (defined by Schultz, 2005, as recognition of the internal affective state of another individual) and also identity (defined by Schultz, 2005, as structural features of the face to define identity). In an overview of this issue, Schultz (2005) has stressed how the children's deficits in nonverbal communication encompass social perception, cognition, and motivation, with complex relations among those aspects of social functioning that have heavy reliance upon the amygdale–fusiform system.

One of the difficulties with many studies on social perception in autism is that they involve experimental materials that are quite different from what one might see in real life, or naturalistic social situations. To approximate online processing situations, Klin and colleagues (Klin, Jones, Schultz, Volkmar, & Cohen, 2002) have recently used eye-tracking methodology to capture where individuals with and without autism focus visually when viewing complex social situations on video. While most of us show preferential looking at the eyes of others, and this is seen in typical development even around the age of 3 months (Haith, Bergman, & Moore, 1979), individuals with autism show an unusual pattern of looking, in that they focus primarily either on mouth regions or on regions peripheral to the face. On the bases of these and similar findings, Klin and colleagues (Klin, Jones, Schultz, & Volkmar, 2005) argue that we need to move away from a focus on disembodied cognition and instead view autism through the approach of embodied cognition.

Klin and colleagues' enactive mind (EM) approach suggests that what might seem like social scenes to you or to me may not seem at all like social scenes to the viewer with autism who may be focusing on a light switch in the background rather than the actors kissing in the foreground. These authors (Klin et al., 2005, p. 698) argue that, "the overriding salience of social stimuli is not present. In its place is a range of physical stimuli, which attracts the child's selective attention . . . tools of thought are acquired outside the realm of active social engagement and the embodied experiences predicated by them." We agree with Klin and colleagues, but it remains to consider how and why social stimuli are not so salient for these children. In order to address this question, one must dig a little deeper into the nature of social experience itself.

Identification and Autism

Going beyond social perception: Background studies

Each of the following three studies of children with autism illustrates how individuals with this disorder have a limited propensity to identify with the subjective stance of another person. In our view, it is through this propensity that social perception becomes the kind of perception that it is. Just as others have stressed that perception has essential links with action toward the world-as-perceived, so we highlight how social perception is part and parcel of engagement with other-persons-as-perceived.

Perceiving subjectivity in emotional expressions
How are the actions and gestures of others perceived by individuals with autism? We (Moore, Hobson, & Lee, 1997) aimed to consider this question by studying how children and adolescents experience and describe a person presented through moving pinpoints of light, created by attaching reflective patches to the limbs and torso of a person. The point-light person enacted gestures of surprise, sadness,

anger, fear, and happiness, which were later displayed as brief video vignettes to the participants. In the anger sequence, for example, the point-light person gestured in an irritated manner with his arms while stamping his feet forcefully. Although participants with and without autism noticed and commented on the actions, the groups were markedly different in whether they referred to the subjective experiences of the person. Where a participant without autism would be likely to describe angry feelings, participants with autism would be likely to say "dancing to some music." The point-light person had meaning for the participants with autism, but it was meaning as viewed from the outside so to speak, without indication that these participants could get beneath the skin of the person they observed. These responses seem markedly similar to the outside-in definitions of social perception described above, where children with autism seem to have access only to the "observables."

Perceiving subjectivity in actions
In a paper entitled "Imitation and Identification in Autism," we (Hobson & Lee, 1999) tested groups of children with and without autism, matched according to verbal ability and chronological age, for their ability to imitate a person demonstrating four novel goal-directed actions on objects in two contrasting "styles," most often (but not exclusively) either harshly or gently. Despite almost all participants' ability to copy the goal-directed aspect of the actions, the children with autism were less likely to copy the styles with which the actions were demonstrated. We interpreted this finding in terms of the latter children's relative ability to copy simple goal-directed actions on objects, and their reduced propensity to *identify with* the person whose actions those were. Once again, the participants with autism seemed to view the actions from the outside rather than getting beneath the skin of the person they observed.

The findings yielded additional insight into the implications of social perception for subsequent behavior. The majority of participants without autism copied the "self-orientation" with which actions were demonstrated – for example, imitating how the experimenter positioned an object against his shoulder by positioning the object against *their own* shoulder. This pattern of responding was rare among the participants with autism, most of whom laid the object on the table in front of them. In our view, these results were not merely an index of imitative styles that *followed* perception; rather, they rendered explicit what the perception entailed in terms of registering and assimilating the stance of the person demonstrating the actions.

Self vis-à-vis *the other in communication*
The next study is best understood in the context of its origins, which were our own observations of a small typically developing girl we shall call Annie. Annie had very recently turned 4 and had met me (JH) on a few occasions to try out some of our tests for young children. On this particular occasion, as an incentive for playing with me, I brought along some stickers and offered a sheet to her so that she might

select one. She did so readily and she placed her chosen sticker onto her white jumper. In the spirit of playfulness, I asked Annie whether I might have a sticker for myself. She carefully selected another sticker from the sheet and handed the sticker to me. I smiled, held up my sticker in front of me, and asked her where I should place it. She thought about this for a moment, looked intently at me and pointed emphatically to her own shoulder (indicating that I should place the sticker onto my shoulder). Annie had anticipated that I would understand her communication by identifying with her identification with me. And each of us played our parts so naturally and unselfconsciously (I was not intending this as a test) that it was only when my co-author (PH), observing from across the room, pointed out the significance of this event, that we realised we might transform this into an experimental test.

As it turned out, our newly devised "sticker test" was effective in demonstrating how, in communication with someone else, participants with autism were less likely to point to *their own* bodies to indicate where the other person should place a sticker on *her own* body (Hobson & Meyer, 2005). It was not that children with autism did not communicate; rather, they pointed to what was "observable" to them – that is, to the literal location on my body where they wanted to see the sticker placed. This contrasted with what happened among children without autism, whose perception of and responsiveness to the communication of the tester was determined by their identification with the latter. Not only did they see the tester's actions as self-oriented (so they transposed the action to themselves); they also anticipated that the tester would identify with themselves (and place the sticker on herself) if they themselves communicated with a self-orientated action.

What's in a look?

The three studies described above each involve particular examples of the way in which children with autism perceive persons from the outside, rather than perceiving-and-engaging with others as subjective centers of experience. Another example of how the nature of children's social perception may be revealed is in their gaze.

The original descriptions of autism by Kanner (1943) highlight the children's limited participation in the subjective lives of others. One of the ways this was illustrated was by reference to markedly reduced or absent eye contact. For example, Kanner recorded that Elaine (case 11, aged 7, p. 241) "does not look into one's face." Of 5-year-old Paul (case 4, p. 228), Kanner wrote: "He never looked up at people's faces. When he had any dealings with persons at all, he treated them, or rather parts of them, as if they were objects." Donald (case 1, age 5, p. 218), "never looked at the person while talking and did not use communicative gestures."

Although Kanner primarily referred to the children as not making eye contact, there was also reference to the children's quality of gaze, as when he wrote of Virginia (case 6, age 11, p. 231) whose, "eyes had a blank expression."

A second "classic" set of clinical case descriptions are those recounted by Bosch (1970). Bosch, too, highlights disturbances in interpersonal gaze among individuals with autism, but in his descriptions we encounter children who showed gaze, but gaze that had unusual qualities. Of Hans R., Bosch wrote: "We never noticed that his gaze merged in mutual understanding with that of another . . . " (p. 8), and he described another person with autism as looking through others. Dieter E. was described in the following way (p. 24)

> If adults entered the playroom, he would look up briefly and glance fleetingly at them without letting his gaze rest on them. He only looked at people when he was asking them a question . . . but by the time the answer came his gaze had wandered somewhere else. If he was addressed, he would always look up but then look away again. His face remained motionless as if he was not at all involved.

The children's lesser tendency to look toward others, not only in frequency but also in intensity of eye contact, is characteristic and probably an early marker of the syndrome (e.g. Dawson, Osterling, Meltzoff, & Kuhl, 2000; DiLavore, Lord, & Rutter, 1995; Volkmar & Mayes, 1990; Wimpory, Hobson, Williams, & Nash, 2000). In the domain of joint attention, children with autism show a reduced tendency to use eye contact and deictic gestures (for example, pointing or showing) to coordinate attention and share experiences with social partners vis-à-vis objects or events in the world (McArthur & Adamson, 1996; Mundy, Sigman, Ungerer, & Sherman, 1986), even though they are able to disengage and shift attention (Leekam, López, & Moore, 2000), follow a head turn (Leekam, Hunnisett, & Moore, 1998), and detect what is at the focus of someone's gaze (Leekam, Baron-Cohen, Perrett, Milders, & Brown, 1997). There is evidence that they are less likely to share affect in episodes of joint attention (Kasari, Sigman, Mundy, & Yirmiya, 1990), they are more distinctive in their failure to point to and show rather than request things (Landry & Loveland, 1988; Mundy et al., 1986), and they are limited in their responsiveness to others in settings that would typically elicit social referencing (Charman et al., 1997; Sigman et al., 1992). These areas of impairment appear to involve not merely a lack of attentiveness or even affective responsiveness to other people (Sigman & Capps, 1997), but also a lack of sharing of the kind that entails a partial *movement into* or assimilation of the stance, the attitude, or the communicative intention of the other (Hobson, 1993, 2002/2004). Thus, we decided to embark on a new series of studies to test whether, indeed, the social perception of gaze involves more than meets the eye. One critical feature of social perception is that it differs from non-social perception in being a two-way street.

Sharing looks

The investigation we shall describe was built upon a previous study (Meyer & Hobson, 2004) in which we tested matched children with and without autism for their propensity to imitate self/other orientation in four different actions on objects. Although all the children copied the actions, those with autism were significantly less likely to imitate the self/other orientation of the actions. They tended, instead, to re-enact the actions as seen from their own point of view rather than from the point of view of the demonstrator transposed to the self. Our follow-up investigation (Hobson & Hobson, 2007) involved "blind" ratings of the videotapes from this recent study. We counted each look at the tester during the demonstration and imitation sequences over the eight trials – roughly 1–2 minutes per child. If the child looked at the tester because of an action or attention-gaining behavior on the part of the tester (such as calling the child's name, or providing praise or feedback), these looks were judged to be orienting looks. The other looks were distinguished on the basis of three features: depth, reciprocity, and affective contact. Those looks that involved depth into rather than at the tester's eyes, reciprocity (where the child was looking at the tester and was aware that the tester was looking back at him, rather than looking at the tester to see what she might say or do next), and affective contact were rated as being sharing looks. Those looks that involved checking out the situation with little or no personal contact were labeled checking looks. Inter-rater agreement was excellent.

The results were in keeping with three a priori predictions, as follows: (a) children with autism contrasted with control participants in spending more time looking at the objects acted upon and less time looking at the tester; (b) participants with autism showed fewer "sharing" looks toward the tester, and, although they also showed fewer "checking" and "orienting" looks, they were specifically less likely to show *any* sharing looks; and, critically, (c) within each group, individual differences in sharing looks (only) were associated with imitation of self/other orientation. Although only five of sixteen children with autism ever showed a sharing look, these same five were more likely (among the children with autism) to show role reversal in their imitation. And, despite the fact that the majority of children without autism showed sharing looks (eleven of sixteen), those who showed more sharing looks were relatively more likely to engage in role-reversal imitation compared with the other participants who did not have autism.

The results suggest that the mode of social perception that involves sharing looks is the very same mode of social perception that gives rise to self/other transpositions in imitation. Moreover, it is this mode of social perception – one that we believe implicates the process of identifying with someone else – that is especially impaired among many individuals with autism. Not only are such individuals less likely to look at another person when copying that person's actions on objects, but they are less prone to engage in sharing looks – and, when this is the case, they are also less likely to imitate the self/other-oriented aspects of the actions demonstrated.

"We-shared-that" looks

There are other aspects of looking that are revealing for social perception and engagement. For example, we devised a situation that would prompt self-conscious feelings of coyness and embarrassment among school-aged children (Hobson, Chidambi, Lee, & Meyer, 2006). There were twelve children with autism and twelve children without autism who each met with a familiar female tester (JH) in the context of another unrelated task. During the interaction, the tester introduced the children to a cuddly stuffed dog ("Doggie"). The tester began by nuzzling the dog against the face of a toy alien, saying: "Doggie likes . . ." with a rising intonation, until the child had made verbal or nonverbal reference to the alien. Next, the tester nuzzled the dog against the side of her own face and tilted her head affectionately, repeating "Doggie likes . . ." until the child made verbal or nonverbal reference to the tester. Finally, the tester playfully stated "And Doggie likes . . ." while inching Doggie toward the child, and then nuzzling it against the side of the child's face until the child made reference to himself or herself.

Although there were group differences in ratings of overall coyness, in that 12 of 19 participants without autism but only 7 of 20 with autism were rated as clearly showing coyness, the most striking finding was in the patterning of response to this situation. Children were very similar in showing self-conscious smiling and squirmy movements. Roughly half the children in each group showed both these manifestations of self-consciousness. However, almost two-thirds of the children without autism showed a re-engagement look following the experience – as if to say "we-shared-that" – and not a single child with autism showed such a look.

Guilty-looks
In another scenario (Hobson et al., 2006), we set up a situation (originally conceived by Barrett, Zahn-Waxler, & Cole, 1993) in which participants were faced with having inadvertently caused harm to the possession of another person. Here, after the tester expressed liking for a doll, which she explained to children she would be giving to her sister on the following day, the children were asked to make the dolly sit down. As the participants attempted to comply with these instructions, the tester looked away and rummaged through her bag. Unbeknownst to the children, the doll had been tampered with in advance to ensure that the attempt to make her sit down would result in her leg becoming detached while in the children's hands. Here, we aimed to look for evidence that the child might feel guilty toward the tester.

Amongst other ratings, there was one we added *post hoc* on the basis of what we had observed to be most striking about the clearest examples of guilty reactions on videotape. Although we did not select this item on the basis that it seemed to distinguish the groups, clearly the findings in this respect are in need of replication. The rating concerned the presence or absence of a "guilty look," defined as

> an active gaze pattern toward and/or away from the tester involving some combination of anxiety and reassurance-seeking, and then relief when the tester explained it was not the participant's fault. The quality of the exchange involves the rater emotionally, so that there is sympathy with the child's personal distress at harm done.

These "guilty looks" were judged to be present in 10 out of 12 participants without autism, and 2 out of 12 participants with autism. This was despite the lack of significant group differences in some other respects that might have been construed as expressions of guilt – and were indeed expressions of the participants' involvement in the unfolding events – such as attempts to repair the broken object.

Concerned looks

Finally, what about the way we react to the suffering of others? As Wittgenstein (1958, p. 286) observes: "If someone has a pain in his hand ... one does not comfort the hand, but the sufferer: one looks into his face." Cockburn (1990) reflects how this is not the same as watching the face of the other for signs of diminishing pain; instead, one looks into someone else's face in sympathy.

We respond to the suffering of others from very early in life. Studies of empathy in typical development reveal how newborn infants cry and show emotional arousal and distress in response to the sound of another crying infant. However, it is not until the beginning of the second year of life that infants begin to show unequivocal signs of directing empathic concern toward the other – for example, by showing concerned looks and attempting to give comfort. Around the age of 2 years, typically developing children are able to provide verbal articulation of empathy for another person (Zahn-Waxler & Radke-Yarrow, 1990).

There is evidence that young children with autism are relatively insensitive to the feelings of others in situations that might involve empathy. In a study conducted by Sigman and colleagues (1992), either an adult tester or the child's own caregiver pretended to injure herself while playing with a toy hammer. Children with autism showed far less concern and tended to look less at the adult than children without autism and those who were typically developing. These results were replicated with 20-month-old infants diagnosed with autism (Charman et al., 1997).

In a recent study of our own (Hobson, Harris, García-Pérez, & Hobson, 2008; Meyer, Hobson, García-Pérez, & Harris, 2006), we tested sixteen school-age children with autism and sixteen children without autism of similar age and verbal ability for showing concern toward another person whose drawing was torn by a second tester. The children were between the ages of 8 and 16 years, with a mean verbal mental age of about 7 years. In this study, the tester whose drawing was torn (JH) did not show any overt emotional reaction to the event, although she did witness its occurrence. Thus, it was not the case that her "observable emotional display" played a role in triggering participants' responses.

Two testers invited each child individually to play a game. The child was seated beside one tester and across from the other. Everyone drew an animal as part of an unrelated game. At the end of the game, the tester seated beside the child ascertained that the child knew who drew the turtle (the tester seated across) and then proceeded to tear the drawing in two. Both testers maintained a neutral facial expression. On another day, six months later, a similar scenario was repeated with the difference that the drawing torn was a blank note-card.

Video clips of the episodes were given to two raters who were blind to the experimental hypothesis. They were asked to find each look at the tester whose drawing was torn, and then evaluate which of those looks expressed concern. These were looks in which the child appeared to become involved with the tester whose drawing had been torn, apparently taking on her psychological stance (becoming upset on her behalf), experiencing concern for her feelings, or showing a sense of discomfort about her position (for example, through nervous laughter). Other looks were categorized as either (a) checking: when the child appeared to be assessing the situation to see what might happen next, or to be unsure what to do – here, the children seemed to be "looking around" but not making personal contact with the tester; (b) orienting looks: when the child looked at the tester whose drawing had been torn either in response to her speech or actions, or because the offending tester had made reference to her; or (c) sharing positive affect looks: when the participant showed interpersonal contact but without any concern, such as in finding the situation humorous.

The raters had excellent agreement on the occurrence and quality of the participants' looks. When the blank index card was torn, the children rarely looked at the tester seated across the table. When it was the tester's drawing that was torn, however, some of the children with autism but especially those without autism looked at her immediately after the event. More importantly, while on the "blank-drawing" condition only one child (a child without autism) ever showed a concerned look – and only once – on the "tear-drawing" condition ten out of sixteen children without autism showed between one and six concerned looks, while only three out of sixteen children with autism ever showed a concerned look.

Summary and Conclusions

Social perception implicates forms of relatedness toward (and paradigmatically with) other people. On the expressive side, what is going on "beneath the skin" is expressed through the body, but is more than bodily. The subjective dimension of personal life is not only observable for those who do not have autism, but also palpable (emotionally speaking).

We consider that, in order to understand the pathogenesis of autism, it is necessary to characterize affected individuals' limited intersubjective engagement with others, and, as a critical aspect of this, their abnormalities in social perception. We consider that, in many cases, a limited capacity to identify with others is the source of some of their most significant social-perceptual and social-cognitive impairments – and, beyond this, a critical factor in their difficulties in developing flexible, context-sensitive language and thought.

We have tried to illustrate how scientific methods that employ human raters to judge aspects of intersubjective engagement can yield insights into social perception, even when the focus of the ratings is constrained to different kinds of social looking. We take the view that, when scientists limit themselves to counts of what are now called "behaviors" such as numbers and lengths of look, then they are hard pressed to interpret the results in terms of meaningful human encounters. Yet, even to study observable phenomena such as "sharing looks" will take us only so far. We have suggested that, in order to reach the heart of the matter – that is, to apprehend the nature of social perception and the impairments in social perception that characterize autism – it is necessary to delve even deeper. If the syndrome of autism needs to be understood in the light of affected individuals' limited propensity to identify with others, then this reflects how such a propensity infuses social perception in typically developing human beings. Identification, like the sharing looks that are one expression of identification, is reciprocal, deep, and involves affective contact.

Imitation and embodiment

Partly in reaction to overly abstract and intellectual (or sometimes computational) accounts of social cognition, many social as well as developmental psychologists are stressing how embodiment is not only the key to understanding social perception, but also the grounding for social understanding. Yet what it means to perceive embodied mental states is still to be elaborated. Earlier in the chapter we voiced scepticism over the way that Dijksterhuis and Bargh (2001) write of the outward behavior of others as the "observables" of social perception. Yet these authors also write about an automatic social imitation (we often do what we see others doing) and cover a wide range of examples, from mothers imitating their babies' open mouths when feeding to partners who develop similar facial lines and grow to look more alike over time. They state: "These automatic forms of imitation are a consequence of the way we are wired. Perceptual representations automatically activate corresponding behavior representations. Like other species, such as fish, we automatically imitate others." Yet perhaps we are not so much like fish. The nature of our imitation – through identifying with others – is unique.

Niedenthal and colleagues (2005, p. 190) point out that, while it may feel intuitively accurate to consider that we "embody the behaviors of others online or when those others are physically present . . . it is perhaps more counterintuitive to imagine how embodiment enters into social perception offline, or when people are only present symbolically." These authors point out a historical background for the offline possibility, a background in psychoanalysis. For example, then report how Freud described sensory-motor symptoms as unconscious enactments of thoughts and memories involving other significant people (Breuer & Freud, 1893–1895/1955).

We would like to take up this notion of a historical link between psychoanalysis and current embodiment theories, and point out that Freud had much to say on related issues. Freud (1921/1955) explained how, through identification, one person's self is molded after the fashion of the someone else who has been taken as a model, a process that may be partial and apply to single characteristics of the person identified-with. He also wrote how such identifying-with is intrinsic to emotional ties between people. Laplanche and Pontalis (1973, p. 205) provide the following definition: "Psychological process whereby the subject assimilates an aspect, property or attribute of the other and is transformed, wholly or partially, after the model the other provides." Freud (1921/1955) not only linked this process with empathy and concern for others, but also considered it to be the means by which we take up any attitude at all toward another mental life. Yet, "identification is not simple imitation but *assimilation*" (Breuer & Freud, 1893–1895/1955, p. 150). In other words, identification may find expression in imitative acts, but it is more akin to what Merleau-Ponty (1964, p. 145) called mimesis (which he linked with the psychoanalytic term "introjection") – that is, "the ensnaring of me by the other ... that attitude whereby I assume the gestures, the conducts, the favourite words, the ways of doing things of those whom I confront." If the expression of attitudes is embodied (as Darwin, 1872/1904, believed), then identification is a further embodiment of the others' bodily expressed attitudes, albeit registered as "other" in experience.

Perhaps not surprisingly, this is an idea that is also increasingly popular among scientists who study the brain (see Gallese, 2003). Recent evidence from neuroscience, and more specifically functional MRI scanning that has had a focus upon the operation of "mirror neurons" and reflections of self/other psychological correspondence in interaction, have given us a picture of how something like identification may operate on a neurofunctional level (e.g. Decety & Sommerville, 2003; Gallese, 2001). For example, functional magnetic resonance imaging (fMRI) studies report similar changes in brain activity when painful electrical stimulation is applied to one's own or one's partner's hand (Singer et al., 2004). The same area of the brain becomes activated when smelling something disgusting and when watching a video of someone else expressing disgust (Wicker et al., 2003). Mirror neurons have been implicated in empathic responses, imitation, and the attribution of mental states, and, although there is a danger of overestimating how far a single, putative neurofunctional system underlies such processes, there is certain to be some kind of neurological bases for the phenomena of interpersonal linkage-cum-differentiation.

On autism: A final word

For some years, we have emphasized the significance of impairments in social perception for our understanding of autism. One reason is that, from very early in the life of a typically developing infant, such perception promotes intersubjective linkage and differentiation in relation to others. Such experience is critical if the very young child is to acquire increasingly explicit understandings of what it means to be a self with one's own mind, who exists in relation to other people with their minds. Hobson (1993, p. 45) described these emergent forms of "person-understanding" in the second year of life when he wrote about

> a concurrent set of developments manifest within social contexts: first, development in the awareness of other people not only as centres of consciousness with whom sharing is possible, but also as individuals who can feel distress or desire, who can be comforted or provoked, and for whom objects can have personal significance; second, development in the child's sense of herself as an individual; and third, development in the capacities to reflect on the characteristics and psychological states of individuals "selves," and to take action appropriately. It is most important to note the close interrelationships among these developing capacities.

This set of interrelated processes appears to be at the core of the difficulties faced by children with autism. When we consider the range and quality of the children's abnormalities in their self/other relations, including those implicated in empathy and social emotions, it is striking how children with autism have a relative dearth of engagement with other people's feelings *as* located in the other people *and* of importance for themselves in one way or another.

Since 1990 there have been a number of researchers conducting investigations that reveal how the children show disturbances in their ability to direct expressions of affect to another person, use facial expressions communicatively, and resonate to the emotions and bodily expressions of others (Bacon, Fein, Morris, Waterhouse, & Allen, 1998; Charman et al., 1997; Dawson, Hill, Spencer, Galpert, & Watson, 1990; Hobson & Lee, 1998; Mundy, Sigman, Ungerer, & Sherman, 1986; Sigman, Kasari, Kwon, & Yirmiya, 1992). Most notably, Mundy (1995, and Mundy & Burnette, 2005, p. 650) has emphasized how autism involves an "early onset of a dramatic reduction in the tendency of children with autism to initiate episodes of social sharing with other people." These authors have emphasized how far we have come since we understood the condition only in terms of a "pervasive lack of responsiveness to others" (American Psychiatric Association, 1980).

Mundy and Burnette (2005) describe how, in sharing an experience of something, one experiences both one's own attitude toward the object, as well as the social partner's awareness of and responses to the object and toward the self. This yields a kind of self/other comparison of experience that Mundy and Burnette judge to make a vital contribution to the development of the capacity of infants to simulate the mental states of others. In the same spirit, we invoke the process of identification to explain how sharing of experiences (Hobson, 1989), or adjustment of perspective through responsiveness to the attitudes of others, or the emergence of reflective self-awareness (Cooley, 1902; Hobson, 1990; Mead, 1934), or even the acquisition of context-sensitive language and creative symbolic thinking (Adamson, 1995; Hobson, 2000; Werner & Kaplan, 1963), emerge in the course of early development.

To conclude, this chapter has been less about the need to venture beyond social perception, and more about the need to transcend current conceptions of social perception. We have also indicated how there are profound developmental implications to the fact (if a fact it is) that human infants' social perception entails special kinds of engagement with others as persons.

Note

This work was supported by the Economic and Social Research Council, the National Institutes of Health, the Baily Thomas Charitable Foundation, and the Tavistock Clinic, London (with NHS R&D funding). We are grateful to the following schools for their participation in these projects: Edith Borthwick School, Helen Allison School, Springhallow School, and Swiss Cottage School. We also thank Dr David Williams, Valentina Levi, Ruth Harris, Susana Caló,

Dr Rosa García-Pérez, Dr Tony Lee, and Dr Gayathri Chidambi for their many contributions to the research.

References

Adamson, L. B. (1995). Joint attention, affect, and culture. In C. Moore & P. J. Dunham (Eds.), *Joint Attention: Its Origins and Role in Development* (pp. 205–221). Hillsdale, NJ: Lawrence Erlbaum.

American Psychiatric Association (1980). *DSM-III: Diagnostic and Statistical Manual of Mental Disorders.* 3rd edn. New York: American Psychiatric Association Press.

Bacon, A. L., Fein, D., Morris, R., Waterhouse, L., & Allen, D. (1998). Responses of autistic children to the distress of others. *Journal of Autism and Developmental Disorders, 28,* 129–142.

Baldwin, J. M. (1902), *Development and Evolution.* New York: Macmillan.

Barrett, K. C., Zahn-Waxler, C., & Cole, P. M. (1993). Avoiders vs. amenders: Implications for the investigation of guilt and shame during toddlerhood? *Cognition and Emotion, 7,* 481–505.

Bosch, G. (1970). *Infantile Autism,* trans. D. Jordan & I. Jordan. New York: Springer-Verlag.

Bråten, S. (1998). Infant learning by altercentric participation: The reverse of egocentric observation in autism. In S. Bråten (Ed.), *Intersubjective Communication and Emotion in Early Ontogeny* (pp. 105–126). Cambridge: Cambridge University Press.

Breuer, J., & Freud, S. (1893–95/1955). Studies on Hysteria. In J. Strachey (Ed.), *Standard Edition of the Complete Works of Sigmund Freud,* vol. 2. London: Hogarth.

Charman, T., Swettenham, J., Baron-Cohen, S., Cox, A., Baird, G., & Drew, A. (1997). Infants with autism: An investigation of empathy, pretend play, joint attention, and imitation. *Developmental Psychology, 33,* 781–789.

Cockburn, D. (1990). *Other Human Beings.* London: Macmillan.

Cooley, C. H. (1902). *Human Nature and the Social Order.* New York: Scribner.

Darwin, C. (1872/1904). *The Expression of Emotion in Man and Animals.* London: Murray.

Dawson, G., Hill, D., Spencer, A., Galpert, L., & Watson, L. (1990). Affective exchanges between young autistic children and their mothers. *Journal of Abnormal Child Psychology, 18,* 335–345.

Dawson, G., Osterling, J., Meltzoff, A., & Kuhl, P. (2000). Case study of the development of an infant with autism from birth to 2 years of age. *Journal of Applied Developmental Psychology, 21,* 299–313.

Decety, J., & Chaminade, T. (2003). When self represents the other: A new cognitive neuroscience view on psychological identification. *Consciousness and Cognition, 12,* 577–596.

Decety, J., & Sommerville, J. A. (2003). Shared representations between self and other: A social cognitive neuroscience view. *Trends in Cognitive Sciences, 7,* 527–533.

DiLavore, P. C., Lord, C., & Rutter, M. (1995). The pre-linguistic autism diagnostic observation schedule. *Journal of Autism and Developmental Disorders, 4,* 355–379.

Dijksterhuis, A., & Bargh, J. A. (2001). The perception-behavior expressway: Automatic effects of social perception on social behavior. In M. P. Zanna (Ed.), *Advances in Experimental Social Psychology* (vol. 33, pp. 1–40). San Diego, CA: Academic Press.

Freud, S. (1921/1955). Identification In J. Strachey (ed.), *The Standard Edition of the Complete Psychological Works of Sigmund Freud* (vol. xviii, pp. 105–110). London: Hogarth.

Gallese, V. (2001). The "shared manifold" hypothesis: From mirror neurons to empathy. *Journal of Consciousness Studies, 8,* 33–50.

Gallese, V. (2003). The manifold nature of interpersonal relations: The quest for a common mechanism. *Philosophical Transaction of the Royal Society of London*, 358, 517–528.

Haith, M. M., Bergman, T., & Moore, M. J. (1977). Eye contact and face scanning in early infancy. *Science*, 198, 853–855.

Hamlyn, D. W. (1974). Person-perception and our understanding of others. In T. Mischel (Ed.), *Understanding Other Persons* (pp. 1–36). Oxford: Blackwell.

Heider, F. (1944). Social perception and phenomenal causality. *Psychological Review*, 51, 358–374.

Heider, F. (1958). *The Psychology of Interpersonal Relations*. New York: John Wiley.

Hobson, J. A., & Hobson, R. P. (2007). Identification: The missing link between joint attention and imitation? *Development and Psychopathology*, 19, 411–431.

Hobson, J. A., Harris, R, Garcia-Perez, R., & Hobson, R. P. (2008). Anticipatory concern: A study in autism, *Developmental Science*, in press.

Hobson, R. P. (1986). The autistic child's appraisal of expressions of emotion. *Journal of Child Psychology and Psychiatry*, 27, 321–342.

Hobson, R. P. (1989). Beyond cognition: A theory of autism. In G. Dawson (Ed.), *Autism: Nature, Diagnosis and Treatment* (pp. 22–48). New York: Guilford Press.

Hobson, R. P. (1992). Social perception in high-level autism. In E. Schopler G. B. Mesibov (Eds.), *High-Functioning Individuals with Autism* (pp. 157–184). New York: Plenum Press.

Hobson, R. P. (1993). *Autism and the Development of Mind*. Hove: Lawrence Erlbaum.

Hobson, R. P. (2002/2004). *The Cradle of Thought*. Oxford: Oxford University Press.

Hobson, R. P. (2005). Autism and emotion. In F. R. Volkmar, R. Paul, A. Klin, & D. Cohen (Eds.), *Handbook of Autism and Pervasive Developmental Disorders* (pp. 406–424). Mahwah, NJ: Wiley.

Hobson, R. P., Chidambi, G., Lee, A., & Meyer, J. A. (2006). Foundations for self-awareness: An exploration through autism. *Monographs of the Society for Research in Child Development. Serial No. 284*, 71(2).

Hobson, R. P., & Lee, A. (1998). Hello and goodbye: A study of social engagement in autism. *Journal of Autism and Developmental Disorders*, 28, 117–126.

Hobson, R. P., & Lee, A. (1999). Imitation and identification in autism. *Journal of Child Psychology and Psychiatry*, 40, 649–659.

Hobson, R. P., & Meyer, J. A. (2005). Foundations for self and other: A study in autism. *Developmental Science*, 8, 481–491.

Hobson, R. P., Ouston, J., & Lee, A. (1988). What's in a face? The case of autism. *British Journal of Psychology*, 79, 441–453.

Hobson, R. P., Ouston, J., & Lee, A. (1989). Naming emotion in faces and voices: Abilities and disabilities in autism and mental retardation. *British Journal of Developmental Psychology*, 7, 237–250.

Kanner, L. (1943). Autistic disturbances of affective contact. *Nervous Child*, 2, 217–250.

Kasari, C., Sigman, M., Mundy, P., & Yirmiya, N. (1990). Affect sharing in the context of joint attention interactions of normal, autistic, and mentally retarded children. *Journal of Autism and Developmental Disorders*, 20, 87–100.

Klin, A., Jones, W., Schultz, R. T., & Volkmar, F. R. (2005). The enactive mind – from actions to cognition: Lessons from autism. In F. R. Volkmar, R. Paul, A. Klin, & D. Cohen (Eds.), *Handbook of Autism and Pervasive Developmental Disorders*. 3rd edn. (pp. 682–706). Mahwah, NJ: Wiley.

Klin, A., Jones, W., Schultz, R., Volkmar, F., & Cohen, D. (2002). Visual fixation patterns of naturalistic social situations as predictors of social competence in individuals with autism. *Archives of General Psychiatry*, 59, 809–816.

Laplanche, J., & Pontalis, J. B. (1973). *The Language of Psychoanalysis*. London: Hogarth.

Landry, S. H. & Loveland, K. A. (1988). Communication behaviors in autism and developmental language delay. *Journal of Child Psychology and Psychiatry*, 29, 621–634.

Leekam, S., Baron-Cohen, S., Perret, D., Milders, M., & Brown, S. (1997). Eye-direction detection: A dissociation between geometric and joint attention skills in autism. *British Journal of Developmental Psychology*, 15, 77–95.

Leekam, S. R., Hunnisett, E., & Moore, C. (1998). Targets and cues: Gaze-following in children with autism. *Journal of Child Psychology and Psychiatry*, 39, 951–962.

Leekam, S. R., López, B., & Moore, C. (2000). Attention and joint attention in preschool children with autism. *Developmental Psychology*, 36, 261–273.

Lord, C., Risi, S., Lambrecht, L., Cook, E. H., Jr, Leventhal, B. L., DiLavore, P. C., Pickles, A., & Rutter, M. (2000). The Autism Diagnostic Observation Schedule-Generic: A standardized observation of communicative and social behavior associated with the spectrum of autism. *Journal of Autism and Developmental Disorders*, 30, 205–223.

Macmurray, J. (1961) *Persons in Relation*. London: Faber & Faber.

McArthur, D., & Adamson, L. B. (1996). Joint attention in preverbal children: Autism and developmental language disorder. *Journal of Autism and Developmental Disorders*, 26, 481–496.

Mead, G. H. (1934). *Mind, Self, and Society from the Standpoint of a Social Behaviorist*. Chicago: University of Chicago Press.

Meltzoff, A. N. (2002). Elements of a developmental theory of imitation. In A. N. Meltzoff & W. Prinz (Eds.), *The Imitative Mind: Development, Evolution, and Brain Bases* (pp. 19–41). Cambridge: Cambridge University Press.

Merleau-Ponty, M. (1964). *Sense and Nonsense*, trans. C. Dreyfus & R. Dreyfus, Evanston, IL: Northwestern University Press.

Meyer, J. A., Hobson, R. P., García-Pérez, R., & Harris, R. (2006). Concern for others in children with and without autism. Poster presented at the International Meeting for Autism Research, June 1–3, Montreal, Canada.

Meyer, J. A., & Hobson, R. P. (2004). Orientation in relation to self and other: The case of autism. *Interaction Studies*, 5, 221–244.

Moore, D., Hobson, R. P., & Lee, A. (1997). Components of person perception: An investigation with autistic, nonautistic retarded and normal children and adolescents. *British Journal of Developmental Psychology*, 15, 401–423.

Mundy, P. (1995). Joint attention and social-emotional approach behavior in children with autism. *Development and Psychopathology*, 7, 63–82.

Mundy, P., & Burnette, C. (2005). Joint attention and neurodevelopmental models of autism. In F. R. Volkmar, R. Paul, A. Klin, & D. Cohen (Eds.) *Handbook of Autism and Pervasive Developmental Disorders* (pp. 650–681). Mahwah, NJ: Wiley.

Mundy, P., Kasari, C., & Sigman, M. (1992). Nonverbal communication, affective sharing, and intersubjectivity. *Infant Behavior and Development*, 15, 377–381.

Mundy, P., Sigman, M. D., Ungerer, J., & Sherman, T. (1986). Defining the social deficits of autism: The contribution of non-verbal communication measures. *Journal of Child Psychology and Psychiatry and Allied Disciplines*, 27, 657–669.

Murray, L., & Trevarthen, C. (1985). Emotional regulation of interactions between 2-month-olds and their mothers. In T. Field & N. Fox (Eds.), *Social Perception in Infants* (pp. 177–197). Norwood, NJ: Ablex.

Neisser, U. (1988). Five kinds of self-knowledge. *Philosophical Psychology*, 1, 35–59.

Niedenthal, P. M., Barsalou, L. W., Winkielman, P., Krauth-Gruber, S., & Ric, F. (2005). Embodiment in attitudes, social perception, and emotion. *Personality and Social Psychology Review*, 9, 184–211.

Scheler, M. (1954). *The Nature of Sympathy*, trans. P. Heath. Hamden, CT: Archon Books.

Schultz, R. T. (2005). Developmental deficits in social perception in autism: The role of the amygdala and fusiform face area. *International Journal of Developmental Neuroscience. Special Issue: Autism: Modeling Human Brain Abnormalities in Developing Animal Systems*, 23, 125–141.

Schultz, R. T., & Robins, D. (2005). Functional neuroimaging studies of autism spectrum disorders. In F. R. Volkmar, R. Paul, A. Klin, & D. Cohen (Eds.), *Handbook of Autism and Pervasive Developmental Disorders* (pp. 515–533). Mahwah, NJ: Wiley.

Sigman, M. D., & Capps, L. (1997). *Children with Autism: A Developmental Perspective*. Cambridge, MA: Harvard University Press.

Sigman, M. D., Kasari, C., Kwon, J. H., & Yirmiya, N. (1992). Responses to the negative emotions of others by autistic, mentally retarded, and normal children. *Child Development*, 63, 796–807.

Singer, T., Seymour, B., O'Doherty, J., Kaube, H., Dolan, J. D., & Frith, C. (2004). Empathy for pain involves the affective but not sensory component of pain. *Science*, 303, 1157–1162.

Sorce, J., Emde, R. N., Campos, J. J., & Klinnert, M. (1985). Maternal emotional signalling: Its effect on the visual cliff behavior of 1-year-olds. *Developmental Psychology*, 21, 195–200.

Trevarthen, C. (1979). Communication and cooperation in early infancy: A description of primary subjectivity. In M. Bullowa (Ed.), *Before Speech: The Beginning of Human Communication* (pp. 321–347). London: Cambridge University Press.

Trevarthen, C., & Hubley, P. (1978). Secondary intersubjectivity: Confidence, confiding and acts of meaning in the first year. In A. Lock (Ed.), *Action, Gesture, and Symbol: The Emergence of Language* (pp. 183–229). London: Academic Press.

Volkmar, F. R., & Mayes, L. C. (1990). Gaze behavior in autism. *Development and Psychopathology*, 2, 61–69.

Weary, G., Rich, M. C., Harvey, J. H., & Ickes, W. J. (1980). Heider's formulation of social perception and attributional processes: Toward further clarification. *Personality and Social Psychology Bulletin*, 6, 37–43.

Weeks, S. J., & Hobson, R. P. (1987). The salience of facial expression for autistic children. *Journal of Child Psychology and Psychiatry*, 28, 137–152.

Werner, H., & Kaplan, B. (1963). *Symbol Formation*. Oxford: Wiley.

Wicker, B., Keysers, C., Plailly, J., Royet, J. P., Gallese, V., & Rizzolatti, G. (2003). The common neural basis of seeing and feeling disgust. *Neuron*, 40, 655–664.

Wimpory, D. C., Hobson, R. P., Williams, J. M., & Nash, S. (2000). Are infants with autism socially engaged? A study of recent retrospective parental reports. *Journal of Autism and Developmental Disorders*, 30, 525–536.

Winnicott, D. W. (1958). *Collected Papers: Through Paediatrics to Psycho-analysis*. Oxord: Basic Books.

Wittgenstein, L. (1958). *Philosophical Investigations*. Oxford: Blackwell.

Zahn-Waxler, C., & Radke-Yarrow, M. (1990). The origins of emphatic concern. *Motivation and Emotion*, 14, 107–130.

Zebrowitz, L. A. (1990). *Social Perception*. Belmont, CA: Thomson Brooks/Cole Publishing.

Chapter 16

The Role of Looking in Social Cognition: Perspectives from Development and Autism

Claes von Hofsten and Gustaf Gredebäck

Looking plays a fundamental role during social interaction. In addition to exploring the surroundings and gathering visual information about objects, events, and people, it serves as an important communication device and an instrument for influencing other people. Looking is different from any other action in the sense that the transportation of body parts is minimal. When the eyes rotate in their sockets, the movements are only marginally affected by inertia and gravity. Therefore, saccadic eye movements can be extremely rapid. They usually last less than 200 ms and their maximum velocity can be almost 1,000°/s. Because there are no distal movements involved, looking is relatively independent of time. It does not take longer to shift a gaze from a close to a far position than to shift it between two close positions. Head movements are also involved in all larger gaze shifts. When this is the case, the head and the eyes start to move simultaneously, but, because of the greater inertia of the head, its movement ends later.

Facial expressions convey rich information about moods, emotions, and intentions, and our visual system is designed to extract that information. Faces provide information about the health of people and about their hormonal balance (Jones, Little, Burt, & Perrett, 2004; Little Jones, Penton-Voak, Burt, & Perrett, 2002). Men find women with a higher estrogen level more attractive, and women find men with higher testosterone more attractive. The importance of facial information is reflected in the fact that a special area in the temporal cortex, the fusiform area (FFA), is devoted to the processing of visual information about faces (Kanwisher, 2000).

Although visual information about the face and facial actions plays a privileged role in social interaction, it is also important to perceive and understand other actions. For instance, when a person throws a ball, grasps a glass of water, or positions a pen in the hand, it is useful to recognize what the person is doing and why, ahead of time. Hand gestures are an integrated part of all communication. For the deaf community, it is the primary mode of communication.

The understanding of other people's actions seems to be accomplished by the same neural system by which we understand our own actions. A specific distributed neural system, the mirror neuron system (MNS), is activated when perceiving as well as performing an action (Rizzolatti & Craighero, 2004). The MNS enables us to simulate other people's actions in our own motor system through a direct matching process in which observed actions are mapped onto our own motor representations of those actions. This enables us to understand the motives and goals of the observed actions and to repeat those actions ourselves. These neurons are intoned to the goal of the ongoing action.

When humans perform an action, like moving an object from one position to another, gaze moves to the goal before the hand arrives there with the object (Johansson, Westling, Bäckström, & Flanagan, 2001; Land, Mennie, & Rusted, 1999). When observing someone else performing the actions, adults (Flanagan & Johansson, 2003) move their gaze proactively to the goal in the same manner as they do when performing the actions themselves. Such predictive gaze behavior is observed only in the context of an agent (Flanagan & Johansson, 2003). It is important to note that the MNS does not create new motor competences. The motor representations of the observed actions correspond to what is spontaneously generated during everyday activities and whose outcome is known to the acting individual. Thus, imitation learning has to do with learning new instances of actions, including their purposes and goals, but not new modes of actions.

Looking itself provides important information about other people. We are very sensitive to where a person is looking, and this provides information about their direction of attention. This is an important social skill, because it facilitates referential communication. One can comment on objects and immediately be understood by other people, convey information about them, and communicate emotional attitudes toward them. The ability to perceive the gaze direction of others is thus a key component in social communication.

Adults' ability to discriminate gaze direction of a person is excellent (Cline, 1967; Gibson & Pick, 1963; Jenkins & Langton, 2003). Cline (1967), for instance, found that the standard deviation of the judgments of gaze direction when eyes and face moved together was 2° to 3.5° of visual angle or better. We are especially sensitive to determining whether we are being looked at. Cline (1967) found that the threshold for determining that one is being looked at is 0.75°, which translates to a gaze displacement of 1.27 cm in the horizontal dimension at a distance of 1 m. In other words, at this distance we can easily determine whether the person we are interacting with fixates our left or right eye.

It has been suggested that the contrast between the iris and its white surrounding (sclera) has evolved to facilitate the perception of gaze direction (Ricciardelli, Baylis, & Driver, 2000). The ability to discriminate eye direction is dependent on the contrast polarity between the iris and the sclera. If the sclera is dark and the iris is light (as in a negative photograph), the ability to determine gaze direction is dramatically impaired (Ricciardelli et al., 2000). Ricciardelli and colleagues proposed that the effect of contrast polarity on gaze processing arises because the visual system follows an inflexible contrast rule for gaze perception, invariably treating the dark part of the eye image as the part that does the looking. The perception of gaze direction is also affected by head direction but to a lesser extent. Judgement of gaze is more accurate when the head is in line with the eyes than when not (Gibson & Pick, 1963).

Last but not least, looking can be used as an executive device to influence other people. A "look" can be praise or a critique. We can catch the attention of other people simply by looking at them. We can get a person to look at an object, by repeatedly shifting our gaze between an object of interest and another person's face. We can show submission by looking down when someone looks at us or challenge the other person's authority by looking back. Two people who look into each other's eyes can perceive intense intimacy with each other. In summary, looking is not just a mode of perceiving but an instrument for social communication, maybe even the most important one. In kindergarten, blind children are easy to spot. They are very often isolated, sitting by themselves. Deaf children, however, do not have this problem. They are difficult to spot in a group of children because their ability to interact and play with the other children seems more or less unimpaired (Preisler, 1995). In the following we will discuss the role of looking in social development, how infants develop the ability to follow others' gaze direction, and how these abilities relate to Autism Spectrum Disorder (ASD).

Measuring Looking

Since the first measurements by Yarbus (1967), there have been relatively few attempts to study the behavior of looking directly. The reason is, of course, that, until the advent of eye-tracking technologies, measuring looking has been complicated and the analysis often very time consuming. Most studies have been made on infants and young children, where alternative methods for evaluating attention have not been available. Looking has been evaluated either online or from video by observers who have decided when subjects begin and stop looking at a scene and whether they look to the left or right. Based on such studies, researchers have been able to draw conclusions about what objects and events infants are interested in, how well they discriminate between them, and whether events that happen are expected or not. Literally thousands of studies have been performed using this method. Almost everything we know about infants' cognitive development originates from such studies.

However, drawing conclusions from such global aspects of looking to cognitive processes may be problematic (Aslin, 2007). When the looking duration to the left and right sides is unequal, there might be several different reasons for this. Even when the overall looking is equal, there might be differences in the patterns of looking that distinguishes the two sides.

More direct, precise, and reliable measurements of where gaze is directed at each point in time are needed to disambiguate some of these problems. Such methods are beginning to appear. They measure the reflection of infrared light sources on the cornea relative to the center of the pupil. In some of these methods no equipment is applied to the subject, who just sits in front of the apparatus. With appropriate calibration, the measurement of cornea reflection provides a good estimate of where a gaze is directed in the visual field. As these measures are being performed many times a second, they provide information about the microstructure of looking that might be needed to draw more firm conclusions about looking behavior.

The Role of Looking in Social Development

Looking is one of the earliest behaviors to develop. Newborn infants fixate and track face patterns (Goren, Sarty, & Wu, 1975; Morton & Johnson, 1991). They can distinguish between direct and averted gaze and they prefer to look at a face with direct gaze (Farroni, Csibra, Simion, & Johnson, 2002). In social situations, infants rapidly establish eye contact and engage in social interaction with their caretakers.

During the first months of life, the interaction is primarily focused on establishing a bond with the caretaker(s). Trevarthen (1979) called it the stage of primary intersubjectivity. Secondary intersubjectivity is established when the child and his or her caretakers begin to communicate with each other about objects in the surrounding. Looking plays a crucial role in this communication. The child looks at an object and the adult follows his or her gaze, and vice versa. The question is when infants begin to understand gaze direction and how well they understand it. Most researchers agree that infants reliably follow gaze from 10–12 months of age (Corkum & Moore, 1998; Deák, Flom, & Pick, 2000; Morales, Mundy, Delgado, Yale, Messinger, et al., 2000; Morales, Mundy, Delgado, Yale, Neal, et al., 2000; Morisette, Ricard, & D'ecarie, 1995; Scaife & Bruner, 1975; Woodward & Guajardo, 2002).

A common method has been to determine the side toward which the infants first turn their gaze (see, e.g., Corkum & Moore, 1998; Morales, Mundy, & Rojas, 1998). Moore, Angelopoulos, and Bennett (1997), for instance, found that some 9-month-olds, and presumably those with more advanced gaze-following skills, will turn in the direction indicated by a live but static face (left or right). Even 3–6-month-old infants have been found to be above chance in following a turning gaze to the correct side (D'Entremont, Hains, & Muir, 1997). A reasonable conclusion from these studies is that social directional cues can be utilized before 12 months as evidence of the probability that some interesting target will be seen to the left or right of the infant. However, to improve referential communication, the perception of gaze direction needs to convey information about what object the other person is looking at. Can infants discriminate eye and head poses in this more precise way to determine what object a person is looking at? In other words, will they tend to follow a gaze to the correct object on the correct side as opposed to a same-side distracter? The only evidence of this kind comes from studies of the paradigm originally created by Butterworth and Cochran (1980). An experimenter positioned in front of the infant looked at two different positions separated by 60° on the same side of the infant. One of these positions was in front of or to the side of the infant and the other was to the side or behind the infant. They found that 12-month-old infants did not follow a gaze to an object situated outside their own visual field, and they concluded that this is because at this age infants form only egocentric spatial representations. This is not necessarily the case. It is also possible that the infants could not discriminate the experimenter's fixation on a side position versus a position behind them. Thus, Deák et al. (2000) could not replicate the results by Butterworth and Cochran (1980). They found evidence that 12-month-old infants actually did follow a gaze in such a situation.

These discrepant findings raise several questions regarding the way gaze directions of the infants were evaluated. Butterworth and Cochran (1980) scored only the first gaze eye movement of the infant that occurred when the mother was fixating the target, whereas Deák et al. (2000) scored every fixation that was within 25° of the designated object. In Deák et al., gaze direction was evaluated by measuring the head angle on a video recording made from above the infant participant. All the head directions within 25° were considered to be on the target. Gaze following was then evaluated by subtracting the fixations on the distracter object from the fixations on the designated object. A problem with using head direction as indication of gaze direction is that, although head and eye movements tend to occur together, infants control them separately (von Hofsten & Rosander, 1997). Deák et al. (2000) found that the head direction, on average, deviated 13° from the target.

Thus it is possible that gaze movements other than those directed at the target were also scored as hits. A more precise way to measure gaze movements is needed to resolve these discrepant results. Von Hofsten, Dahlström, and Fredriksson (2005) used a gaze-movement camera that determined the gaze direction of the infant participants with a precision of less than a degree of visual angle. The infants were 12 months old, and static video images were used as stimuli. The experimenter performed one of three actions, looking towards one of four visible objects in front of him or her, looking and pointing at the objects, or just pointing at the objects while looking straight ahead. In the control condition the experimenter sat still and looked straight ahead. The angular deviation of the experimenter's gaze from straight ahead to the objects closest to the side was 28° and to the objects furthest out was 53°. If the infants used the static cues of attention direction, we expected them to follow the gaze action most consistently when the experimenter both looked and pointed and least consistently when the experimenter pointed while looking straight ahead. The objects were chosen because they were colorful and judged to be gender neutral (see Figure 16.1). If all the objects had been identical, the infant might have come to the conclusion that the adult's signal did not lead to an interesting sight.

The results show that 12-month-old infants correctly discriminated the gaze directions of the experimenter to the four object locations. Thus, social directional cues provided by eye and head direction of another person are utilized by 12-month-olds in a rather precise way. The spatial resolution of the infants' gaze perception was not a limitation in the present situation. The infants had no difficulties discriminating a 25° difference in gaze direction to two objects on the same side of

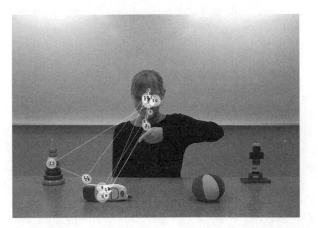

Figure 16.1. An example of the stimuli with the looking pattern of one of the subjects superimposed

Note: The hand is positioned in front of the woman's sweater. The grey spots and lines tell us what the subject looked at. The stimuli shown to the infants were, of course, without any lines or spots.

Source: von Hofsten, Dahlström, & Fredriksson, (2005). Reproduced by permission of the authors.

the experimenter. The times spent looking at the unattended object on the same side of the experimenter were the same as the times spent looking at the unattended objects on the other side of the experimenter. The results thus indicate that the finding of Butterworth and Cochran (1980) that infants fail to follow the gaze of a experimenter looking at an object position behind them is, at least, not due to an inability to discriminate gaze directions.

The infants did not require the attention-directing actions to be part of a live social interaction to be correctly perceived. They did not even require them to be dynamic. On the contrary, they could discriminate different directions of gaze from the static eye and head postures in still video images. Because discrimination of gaze direction is such an important social ability and attains such high precision in adults, it would be worthwhile determining the limits of infants' ability to perceive the gaze direction of another person and how it develops with age.

When the experimenter looked straight ahead and just used pointing to indicate the direction of attention, infants did not look significantly more at the indicated object. There may be at least five reasons for that. First, pointing may be more intimately associated with social interaction than just looking. According to Deák et al (2000), pointing follows the intention to redirect another's attention, whereas gaze shifts are seldom intended to redirect another's attention. Secondly, the ambiguous effect of pointing in the present study may partly stem from the gesture itself. In order to control for proximity between the pointing hand and the indicated object, the experimenter always put the pointing hand at the midline, close to the face. This is not the most natural way of using that gesture. In everyday life, pointing is used more as an extension of the body towards the object of interest. Thirdly, in the pointing condition the experimenter looked straight ahead. This produced a discrepancy between the indication of attention direction from eye and head, on one side, and the pointing, on the other side. The infants might therefore have scrutinized the face of the experimenter in an attempt to figure out what she "was up to." Finally, the face might also be more attractive when looking straight ahead. Farroni, Csibra, Simion, and Johnson (2002) found that newborn infants looked longer at a photograph of a face that was directed at them than at a face that looked to the side. When the experimenter looked straight at the subjects, it is also possible that they might have tried to establish eye contact and engage the experimenter in social interaction (Amano, Kezuka, & Yamamoto, 2004; Hains & Muir, 1996).

If infants are so sensitive to gaze direction in static images, it is expected that they should be even more sensitive in a dynamic situation. In a recent study, Gredebäck, Theuring, Hauf, and Kenward (forthcoming) measured infants' gaze following in response to movies of a experimenter who moved her eyes and head from a central location to fixate one of two toys. Infants of 12, 9, 6, and 5 months old were presented with these events (see Figure 16.2). Each infant always saw the same two toys and the experimenter always fixated the same toy (locations were counterbalanced across trials). This study was designed to evaluate how infants' gaze is related to the experimenter's gaze shifts and to evaluate how this ability develops during the first year of life.

As mentioned above, previous studies of gaze following have based their results either on the first response (often head turn) made by the infant or on the accumulated sum of all responses performed by an infant during each trial. The current study reported the accuracy of infants' gaze shifts from the experimenter's face to either toy (number of gaze shifts to the attended toy – number of gaze shifts to the unattended toy). This measure is referred to as a difference score (DS). A positive DS means that infants moved their gaze to the attended toy more often than to the unattended toy, and vice versa. In order to gain a sensitive measure of how infants' gaze following changed over time, infants' responses were first divided into a baseline segment (before the experimenter had initiated an object-directed gaze shift) and a gaze-direction segment (the experimenter's head movement and subsequent fixation to one of the two objects). The later (gaze-direction) segment, when the experimenter attended to a toy, was further divided into an early DS (measuring infants' first gaze shift from the experimenter's face to either toy) and a late DS (measuring infants' second gaze shift from the experimenter's face to either toy).

First of all, infants in each age group performed at random in the baseline segment of each trial. That is, infants equally often fixated both toys when the experimenter did not attend to any of the toys. In the gaze-direction segment, infants' initial response (early DS) was significantly more often directed at the attended toy at 12, 9, and 6 months of age. Infants of 5 months old performed at random. This finding suggests that infants develop the ability to follow others' gaze direction rapidly between 5 and 6 months of age. However, infants' second gaze shift from the experimenter's face to a toy (late DS) during each trial tell a somewhat

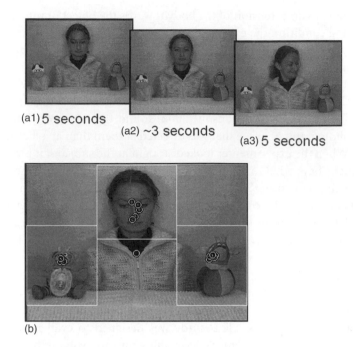

(a1) 5 seconds

(a2) ~3 seconds

(a3) 5 seconds

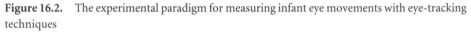

(b)

Figure 16.2. The experimental paradigm for measuring infant eye movements with eye-tracking techniques

Note: A: Successive events of each movie: a still picture of the model looking at the table (A1), the model looks up and turns (A2), and finally a still picture in which the model is fixating the attended toy (A3). B: The three areas of interest (AOIs) with example fixation data from a 9-month-old infant depicted as circles. Stimuli were presented in colour.

Source: von Hofsten, Dahlström, & Fredriksson, (2005). Reproduced by permission of the authors.

different story. Infants' second gaze shift from the experimenter's face was most often directed to the attended toy at 5, 6, and 9 months of age. Infants of 13 months old performed at random (see Figure 16.3).

Together these findings suggest that infants successively develop the ability to follow others' gaze direction. Direct gaze following occurs from 6 months of age, whereas younger infants can still follow others' gaze direction if they are provided with enough time to scan the scene. However, the development of gaze following is not complete at 6 months of age (as mentioned in the review above). Even the older infants change their scanning strategies. Infants of 12 months old followed the experimenter's gaze only on their first response (early DS). Perhaps infants at the end of their first year have become proficient enough, not only to follow gaze, but also to ignore this information (late DS) following their initial gaze shift. Please note that these temporal differences in infants' responses are dependent on having an experimental procedure (and dependent measures) that is sensitive to the temporal dynamics of infants' responses.

In a second study Theuring, Gredebäck, and Hauf (2007) presented 12-month-old infants with two sessions of similar movies. Each session included four of the

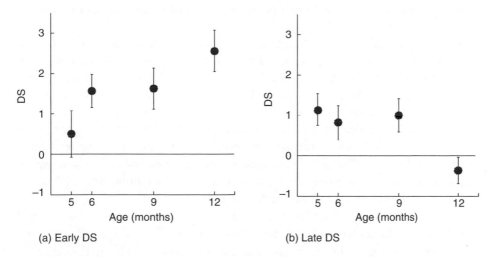

Figure 16.3.   Measuring early and late difference scores of infants' gaze shifts

Note: DS = difference score. Error bars show standard error. The tendencies of standard DS to increase and late DS to decrease with age are significant.

Source: von Hofsten, Dahlström, & Fredriksson, (2005). Reproduced by permission of the authors.

movies described in Figure 16.2, followed by two test phases at the end of each session. During the test phases the experimenter was absent and only the two objects remained (positions were counterbalanced). This study not only inquired about normal gaze following but also asked what relationship infants have to the goal object fixated by the adult experimenter. The toys were never manipulated nor did they ever move or make a sound. The only thing that differentiated the toys (other than their physical appearance) was the experimenter gaze.

The 12-month-old infants followed the experimenter's gaze (replicating the effect described above). However, in the test phase infants did not demonstrate any long-term difference between the two toys. The only measurable difference between the previously attended and the previously unattended toy was a brief novelty preference for the unattended toy. In summary, this study demonstrates that there is no close and obvious relationship between following the experimenter's gaze and attributing meaning to the goal of that action (the attended toy). It is also worth noting that infants in neither of the two studies (Gredebäck et al., forthcoming; Theuring, Gredebäck, & Hauf, 2007) learned to predict which object the experimenter would later look at. This is despite the fact that the experimenter always attended to the same toy throughout each session.

Action Understanding in Infancy

Social cognition is much more than just realizing where other people direct their attention. It has to do with understanding other people's actions, their motives and goals, and the emotions associated with them. In this portion of the chapter we ask, when do infants become able to understand and anticipate the action goals of others.

When we as adults perform simple manual actions we move our gaze to the goal of the ongoing action before our hand reaches the same area. This demonstrates that adults predict the outcome of their own actions (Johansson et al., 2001). In a similar manner, adults predict the goal of others' manual actions (Flanagan & Johansson, 2003). When presented with movies of a experimenter moving a series of blocks from one location to another, adult observers moved their gaze to the location where the block would later be placed before the experimenter's hand reached this location. The close fit between action execution and action observation suggests that there are strong similarities in how we (as adults) process manual actions, regardless of who actually performs the action.

According to Flanagan and Johansson (2003) these results support the so-called Matching Hypothesis and its claim that information on both others and one's own actions are analyzed in the same way, and that both types of information are processed by the same parts of the brain. In other words, we understand the actions of others by mapping them onto our motor representations of those actions.

The question of whether infants rely on a similar matching process to understand actions performed by others was addressed in a recent study by Falk-Ytter, Gredebäck, and von Hofsten (2006). In this study two groups of infants (of 6 and 12 months of age) and an adult control group were presented with different movies in which three balls were moved to a bucket. Participants' eye movements were measured in response to these events. Each movie included a female experimenter, three balls, and a bucket (see Figure 16.4).

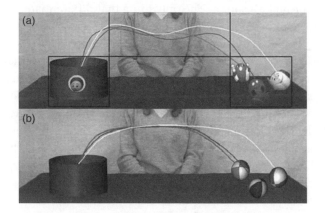

Figure 16.4. The stimuli presented to infants in the HA and SP condition (a) and MM condition (b)

Notes: The lines depict the trajectories of the balls as they were moved to the bucket in each respective condition. Boxes in (a) represent the location of areas of interest (AOIs).

HA: human-agent; SP = self-propelled; MM = mechanical-motion (conditions).

Source: von Hofsten, Dahlström, & Fredriksson, (2005). Reproduced by permission of the authors.

In one condition the experimenter moved the balls to the bucket in a normal fashion, reaching for each ball and transporting it to the bucket, one at the time – the human-agent condition (HA). The balls had some facial features, moved on curvilinear trajectories, and produced some distinct end effects as the balls were lowered into the bucket (a distinct sound and some small movement of a smiley attached to the bucket; see Figure 16.4a).

In the two other conditions the balls were not manipulated by the experimenter. Instead, each ball moved on its own from its starting position into the bucket. In one of these conditions – the self-propelled condition (SP) – the balls moved on identical trajectories to those created by the manual action in the HA condition. In this condition, all aspects of these movies (with the exception of the hand) were identical to the HA condition. The balls had some facial features, they moved on curvilinear trajectories, and the same end effects occurred as the balls entered the bucket (see Figure 16.4a).

In the third and final condition the balls were exchanged for simple colorful balls without facial features, and both the smiley and the end-effect sound were removed from the bucket. In addition, the balls moved on smooth curvilinear trajectories (again without any manual actions). This final condition is referred to as the mechanical-motion condition (MM) (see Figure 16.4b).

Two measures of performance were obtained. In each of these analyzes an area of interest (AOI) covered the bucket, another covered the initial location of the balls, and a third covered the trajectory of the balls (see Figure 16.4a). In the first analysis we measured when participants moved their gaze to the bucket (AOI) relative to when the experimenter's hand arrived there (see Figure 16.5a). In the HA condition both adults and 12-month-old infants predicted the arrival of the hand. Six-month-olds tracked the path of the hand in a reactive manner. Similar results were obtained from both 12-month-olds and adults in the two additional conditions (SP & MM).

The second analysis compared the time spent looking at the goal to the time spent lookingat the trajectory during the movement of each ball (see Figure 16.5b). This measure clearly demonstrated that both adults and 12-month-old infants fixated the goal for the majority of each movement but only in the HA condition. Six-month-olds appeared to track the ball, as did both adults and 12-month-olds in the other two conditions (SP & MM).

Together these findings suggest that 12-month-old infants and adults differentiate between these actions and that they fixate the goal (to a high degree and ahead of time) only when a hand moves the balls to the bucket. In all other conditions they track the ball without moving their gaze to the goal ahead of time. This result nicely fits the matching hypothesis and its assumption that we understand the actions of others by mapping them onto our motor representations of those actions. Thus, before infants have mastered a particular action, there will be no internal motor program to map it onto. Six-month-olds did not predict the goal of these actions, since they had not yet mastered the ability to move and drop objects into buckets. Because they lack a fluent motor repertoire for these actions, they are, in

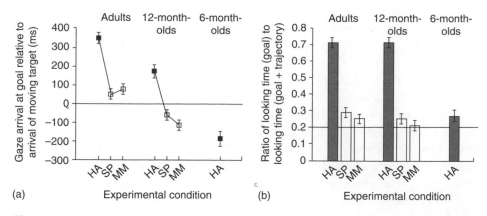

Figure 16.5.   Representations of predictive tracking in adults, 12-, and 6-month-old infants
Notes: (a) Gaze arrival at the bucket relative to the arrival of the ball in each of the three conditions (HA, SP, & MM) and three age groups (adults, 12-, & 6-month-olds). Positive numbers represent predictive tracking where the observer's gaze fixated the goal ahead of time. (b) Looking times at the bucket relative to the looking time at the trajectory of the ball. The line at 0.2 is the expected ratio if the observer tracked the ball.
    HA: human-agent; SP = self-propelled; MM = mechanical-motion (conditions).
Source: von Hofsten, Dahlström, & Fredriksson, (2005). Reproduced by permission of the authors.

essence, unable to comprehend the meaning of them, and as a consequence thereof they will track the balls instead of moving their gaze to the goal ahead of time.

   These findings harmonize well with resent suggestions that action understanding is mediated by specialized cells in the pre-motor cortex (called mirror neurons) that enhance our understanding of others' actions. Rizzolatti and colleagues (Rizolatti & Craighero, 2004; Rizzolatti, Fadiga, Gallese, & Fogassi, 1996) have demonstrated that mirror neurons are activated both when rhesus monkeys perform an action and when they observe others performing similar actions (for example, when the monkey eats nuts and when they observe a human eating ice cream). Similar effects have been observed in area 6–44 on humans using positron emission tomography (PET) (Iacoboni et al., 1999) and functional magnetic resonance imaging (fMRI) (Buccino et al., 2001).

How Looking is Impaired in ASD

It is well known that autism is associated with abnormal visual attention and that this abnormality primarily affects social functioning. Face perception has been found to be abnormal in autistic patients (Marcus & Nelson, 2001), and this effect is more pronounced in younger patients (Boucher & Lewis, 1992). The problem is that there are very few studies that have directly measured looking in autistic children when they are observing a social situation. Klin and associates (Klin, Jones,

(a) Normal 3-year-old   (b) Autistic child

Figure 16.6. Hotspots of looking at the conversation between two people for a 3–year-old normal child (a) and for an autistic child (b)

Note: The most intense looking is depicted red in the original pictures and comes out as invisible in the black-and-white copy. This corresponds to the area inside the rings in (a).

Source: von Hofsten, Dahlström, & Fredriksson, (2005). Reproduced by permission of the authors.

Schultz, Wolkmar, & Cohen, 2002a, 2002b; Klin, Jones, Schultz, & Wolkmar, 2003) recorded fixation patterns of highly performing autistic patients when they watched short videos taken from movies that displayed intense interaction between people engaged in rich socially expressive interactions. They found that the fixation patterns of the autistic patients were grossly different from those of normal controls. While the normal individuals fixated socially salient information in faces and body movements, the autistic patients tended to look at irrelevant inanimate details.

Von Hofsten, Adell, and Uhlig (2007) recorded the fixation patterns of ten preschool children with autism (3–6-year-olds) as they observed a conversation between two people. The conversation was 1.5 minutes long, and the speakers, who were turned toward each other, were filmed against a uniform background (see Figure 16.6). Half the children could not yet speak. These children were compared to two control groups with normal children. The first was made up of 3-year-old children (4 boys and 8 girls), this age being at the lower end of the autistic age interval. The second group was made up of considerably younger 1-year-old children (7 boys and 5 girls). This age was chosen because normal children clearly follow gaze at this age (see above) and show a number of other indications of social competence (Carpendale & Lewis, 2006). We found that the autistic children, on the average, looked at the faces of the speakers for 24 percent of the time, the normal 1-year-olds for 44 percent of the time, and the normal 3-year-olds for 70 percent of the time. In other words, the normal 3-year-olds looked at the faces of the speakers almost three times longer than the autistic children. These differences were more exaggerated when the time the children looked at the speaker was analyzed. The autistic children, the 1-year-olds, and the 3-year-olds looked at the face of the speaker for 14 percent, 26 percent, and 50 percent of the time, respectively. An illustration of the fixation pattern of a normal and an autistic 3-year-old child is shown in Figure 16.6.

As a control condition, the children were shown a video of two colorful egg-formed shapes positioned side by side, which moved up and down alternately and made sounds. The duration of each active period was approximately equal to the duration of the turn taking in the conversation. The visual extension of the "eggs" was also approximately equal to the speakers' faces. It was found that the normal 1-year-old and 3-year-old children looked about equally long at the "eggs" – that is, 54 percent and 59 percent of the time, respectively. The autistic children looked at the "eggs" for 44 percent of the time. These differences were not statistically significant.

In summary, the differences in fixation pattern between the normal and the autistic children were dramatic and they could not be explained in terms of differences in mental development. Even the performance of the 1-year-olds was more socially mature than the autistic children. These results demonstrate, in the same way as the results of Klin and associates (Klin et al. 2002a, 2002b; Klin et al., 2003), that the looking patterns of autistic children in dynamic social situations are fundamentally different from the looking patterns of normal children. It is not the fact that the two speakers alternate that makes the autistic children lose track, but the social interaction itself. They were perfectly able to fixate the two alternately moving objects. More studies like these ones are urgently needed, because they provide crucial information about the autistic syndrome. It is not that the autistic children totally lack a theory of mind. On the contrary, despite their pronounced social disability, they succeed in performing theory-of-mind tasks at different levels of complexity, and, in some situations, they are certainly capable of conversing with others about mental states (Klin et al., 2002b). Rather, the problem has to do with the complexity of the social world and how the very early emerging social adaptive mechanisms are tailored to deal with it. For instance, if the child's gaze is not attracted to another person's face, then there are far fewer opportunities to learn to perceive the social information conveyed by it. If the child does not develop a mechanism that makes him or her understand other people's actions like their own, the process of learning to understand and predict other people's actions becomes much more cumbersome. Autism seems to be a state where the contextualized social world becomes overwhelming and confusing and the child focuses on fragmented and isolated details instead.

Conclusions

Looking plays an extremely important role in social development. Most social interaction takes place at a distance, and vision is superb at extracting information about other people's emotions, intentions, and direction of attention. Looking is also crucially involved in communication. Vision can replace auditory communication in deaf children, while auditory perception cannot replace visually based communication in the same way. As a consequence, blind children are much more isolated in kindergartens than deaf children (Preisler, 1995). The understanding of social development requires us to study the visual behavior of the child, how infants look, what they look at, and how looking is geared to the social contexts encountered. The reported studies show that much insight can be gained into these social skills, even when the interactive component is eliminated. The children continued to apply socially relevant looking procedures and to extract information about attention direction and action goals from videos and photographs. Much more information will, of course, be available when similar measurements can be made in real-life situations. The availability of reliable methods for measuring looking with little or no constraints of movements is crucial for attaining these goals. They promise rapid accumulation of new data that will help us better understand the complex processes that constitute social development and what factors make a child fail to develop those skills.

Acknowledgement

The research reported here was funded by the Swedish Research Council (421-2004-1883, 421-2006-1794).

References

Amano, S., Kezuka, E., & Yamamoto, A. (2004). Infants shifting attention from an adult's face to an adult's hand: A precursor of joint attention. *Infant Behavior and Development*, 27, 64–80.

Aslin, R. N. (2007). What's in a look? *Developmental Science*, 10(1), 48–53.

Boucher, J., & Lewis, V. (1992). Unfamiliar face recognition in relatively able autistic children. *Journal of Child Psychology and Psychiatry*, 33, 843–859.

Buccino, G., Binkofski, F., Fink, G. R., Fadiga, L., Fogassi, L., Gallese, V., et al. (2001). Action observation activates premort and parietal areas in a somatotopic manner: An fMRI study. *European Journal of Neuroscience*, 13(2), 400–404.

Butterworth, G., & Cochran, E. (1980). Towards a mechanism of joint visual attention in human infancy. *International Journal of Behavioral Development*, 2, 253–272.

Carpendale, J., and Lewis, C. (2006). *How Children Develop Social Understanding*. Oxford: Blackwell.

Cline, M. G. (1967). The perception of where a person is looking. *American Journal of Psychology*, 80, 41–50.

Corkum, V., & Moore, C. (1998). The origins of joint visual attention in infants. *Developmental Psychology*, 34(1), 28–38.

Deák, G. O., Flom, R. A., & Pick, A. D. (2000). Effects of gesture and target on 12- and 18-month-olds' joint visual attention to objects in front of or behind them. *Developmental Psychology*, 36(4), 511–523.

D'Entremont, B., Hains, S. M. J., & Muir, D. W. (1997). A demonstration of gaze following in 3- to 6-month-olds. *Infant Behavior and Development*, 20(4), 569–672.

Falk-Ytter, T., Gredebäck, G., & von Hofsten, C. (2006). Infants predict other people's action goals. *Nature Neuroscience*, 9(7), 878–879.

Farroni, T., Csibra, G., Simion, F., & Johnson, M. H. (2002). Eye contact detection in humans from birth. *PNAS*, 99, 9602–9605.

Flanagan, J. R., & Johansson, R. S. (2003). Action plans used in action observation. *Nature*, 14(424), 769–771.

Gibson, J. J., & Pick, A. D. (1963). Perception of another person's looking behaviour. *American Journal of Psychology*, 76, 318–394.

Goren, C. C., Sarty, M., & Wu, P. Y. K. (1975). Visual following and pattern discrimination of face-like stimuli by newborn infants. *Pediatrics*, 56(4), 544–549.

Gredebäck, G., Theuring, C., Hauf, P., & Kenward, B. (forthcoming). The microstructure of infants' gaze as they view adult shifts in overt attention. *Infancy*.

Hains, S. M. J., & Muir, D. W. (1996). Infant sensitivity to adult eye direction. *Child Development*, 67(5), 1940–1951.

Iacoboni, M., Woods, R. P., Brass, M., Bekkering, H., Mazziotta, J. C., & Rizzolatti, G. (1999). Cortical mechanism of human imitation. *Science*, 286(5449), 2526–2528.

Jenkins, J., & Langton, S. R. H. (2003). Configural processing in the perception of eye-gaze direction. *Perception*, 32, 1181–1188.

Johansson, R. S., Westling, G., Bäckström, A., & Flanagan, J. R. (2001). Eye–hand coordination in object manipulation. *Journal of Neuroscience*, 21(17), 6917–6932.

Jones, B. C., Little, A. C., Burt, D. M., & Perrett, D. I. (2004) When facial attractiveness is only skin deep. *Perception*, 33, 569–576.

Kanwisher, N. (2000). Domain specificity in face perception. *Nature Neuroscience*, 3, 759–763.

Klin, A., Jones, W., Schultz, R., Wolkmar, F., & Cohen, D. (2002a). Visual fixation patterns during viewing of naturalistic social situations as predictors of social competence in individuals with autism. *Archives of General Psychiatry*, 59, 819–816.

Klin, A., Jones, W., Schultz, R., Wolkmar, F., & Cohen, D. (2002b). Defining and quantifying the social phenotype in autism. *American Journal of Psychiatry*, 159, 895–908.

Klin, A., Jones, W., Schultz, R., & Wolkmar, F. (2003). The enactive mind or from action to cognition: Lessons from autism. *Philosophical. Transactions of the Royal Society of London B*, 358, 345–360.

Land, M., Mennie, N., & Rusted, J. M. (1999). The roles of vision and eye movements in the control of activities of daily living. *Perception*, 28, 1311–1328.

Little, A. C., Jones, B. C., Penton-Voak, I. S., Burt, D. M., & Perrett, D. I. (2002). Partnership status and the temporal context of relationships influence human female preferences for sexual dimorphism in male face shape *Philosophical Transactions of the Royal Society of London B: Biological Sciences*, 269, 1095–1100.

Marcus, D. J., & Nelson, C. A. (2001). Neural bases and development of face recognition in autism. *CNS Spectrums*, 6, 36–59.

Moore, C., Angelopoulos, M., & Bennett, P. (1997). The role of movement in the development of joint visual attention. *Infant Behavior and Development*, 20(1), 83–92.

Morales, M., Mundy, P., Delgado, C., Yale, M., Messinger, D., Neal, R., et al. (2000). Responding to joint attention across the 6- to 24-month of age period and early language acquisition. *Journal of Applied Developmental Psychology*, 21, 283–298.

Morales, M., Mundy, P., Delgado, C. E. F., Yale, M., Neal, R., & Schwartz, H. K. (2000). Gaze following, temperament, and language development in 6-month-olds: A replication and extension. *Infant Behavior and Development*, 23, 231–236.

Morales, M., Mundy, P., & Rojas, J. (1998). Following the direction of gaze and language development in 6-month-olds. *Infant Behavior and Development*, 21(2), 373–377.

Morissette, P., Ricard, M., & D'ecarie, T. G. (1995). Joint visual attention and pointing in infancy: A longitudinal study of comprehension. *British Journal of Developmental Psychology*, 13, 163–175.

Morton, J., & Johnson, M. H. (1991). CONSPEC and CONLEARN: A two-process theory of infant face recognition. *Psychological Review*, 98(2), 164–181.

Preisler, G. M. (1995). The development of communication in blind and in deaf infants: Similarities and differences. *Child: Care, Health & Development*, 21, 79–110.

Ricciardelli, P., Baylis, G., & Driver, J. (2000). The positive and negative of human expertise in gaze perception. *Cognition*, 77, B1–B4.

Rizzolatti, G., & Craighero, L. (2004). The mirror-neuron system. *Annual Review of Neuroscience*, 27(16), 169–192.

Rizzolatti, G., Fadiga, L., Gallese, V., & Fogassi, L. (1996). Premotor cortex and the recognition of motor actions. *Cognitive Brain Research*, 3(2), 131–141.

Scaife, M., & Bruner, J. S. (1975). The capacity for joint visual attention in the infant. *Nature*, 253, 265–266.

Theuring, C., Gredebäck, G., & Hauf, P. (2007). Object processing during a joint gaze following task. *European Journal of Developmental Psychology*, 4(1), 65–79.

Trevarthen, C. (1979). The tasks of consciousness: how could the brain do them? *Ciba Foundation Symposium*, 69, 187–215.

von Hofsten, C., Adell, M., & Uhlig, H., Kochukhova, O. (2007). What eye movements reveal about autism. Unpublished typescript.

von Hofsten, C., Dahlström, E., & Fredriksson, Y. (2005). 12-month-old infants' perception of attention direction in static video images. *Infancy*, 8(3), 217–231.

von Hofsten, C., & Rosander, R. (1997). Development of smooth pursuit tracking in young infants. *Vision Research*, 37(13), 1799–1810.

Woodward, A. L., & Guajardo, J. J. (2002). Infants' understanding of the point gesture as an object-directed action. *Cognitive Development*, 17, 1061–1084.

Yarbus, D. L. (1967). *Eye Motion and Vision*. New York: Plenum Press.

Chapter 17

What Does the Study of Autism Tell us about the Craft of Folk Psychology?

Richard Griffin and Daniel C. Dennett

Introduction

Autism is a neurodevelopmental condition characterized by difficulties in social interaction (APA, 2000). Successful social interaction relies, in part, on determining the thoughts and feelings of others, an ability commonly attributed to our faculty of folk or common-sense psychology. Because the symptoms of autism should be present by around the second birthday, it follows that the study of autism should tell us something about the early emerging mechanisms necessary for the development of an intact faculty of folk psychology. Our aims in this chapter are threefold; (1) to examine the literature on "social-understanding" mechanisms in autism, particularly those assumed to develop in the first years of life; (2) to examine the related literature on typically developing infants and toddlers, and (3) to examine the theoretical approaches that attempt to characterize the early stages and development of this impressive skill. In doing so, we hope to help resolve some of the disagreements and sticking points that riddle the topic. In particular we will attempt to shift the focus from whether children have this or that specific mental-state concept (which they use to predict behavior of others) to a more developmentally friendly approach centered around the notion of reasons, recognizing that they may well exist *before they are represented*, and hence before they can be appreciated, or expressed.

The peer commentary in *Behavioral and Brain Sciences* following Premack and Woodruff (1978) – "Does the chimpanzee have a theory of mind?" – not only introduced the "false-belief" task (Dennett, 1978; Wimmer & Perner, 1983), but addressed a host of issues surrounding the characterization of second-order intentional systems, systems that may (or must) be interpreted as having *beliefs about beliefs* (or desires or intentions . . .), *desires about beliefs* (or fears or hopes. . . .), and so forth. Many of these issues remain unresolved thirty years later. While the commentators generally found the evidence of a "mindreading" chimpanzee less than convincing, Premack and Woodruff's claim that the attribution of "intentions" was at the basis of folk psychology has seen something of a resurgence. In the 1980s and 1990s, the child-development literature focused largely on what Bennett (1978) called the "rockbottom issue" of mental-state attribution – beliefs about beliefs – publishing hundreds of experiments on the topic (Wellman, Cross & Watson, 2001). Yet, with technical advances in probing the knowledge of infants and the ascendance of neuroimaging, the focus on belief has waned, and has shifted to the putatively "simpler" mental states of intentions, goals, and desires (Johnson, 2000).

According to a recent *New York Times* article entitled "Cells that read minds" (Blakeslee 2006), Premack and Woodruff's initial claim appears to have been vindicated. The article touts the properties, or at least certain claims about the properties, of "mirror" neurons, first discovered in the premotor cortex of macaque monkeys (Gallese, Fadiga, Fogassi, & Rizzolatti, 1996). The headline is not, as one might expect, a journalistic overstatement of the more cautious claims typically found in peer-reviewed journal articles. Iacoboni et al. (2005) state it baldly: "Thus, premotor mirror neurons . . . previously thought to be involved only in action recognition are actually also involved in understanding the *intentions* of others. To ascribe an intention is to infer a forthcoming new goal, and this is an operation that the motor system does automatically" (p. 529, italics added). In a similar vein, other "mirror-system" cells in the superior temporal sulcus, which respond to eye direction and object-directed reaching, are claimed to encode the "intentions behind" these acts, and even whether the agent under interpretation is "rational" (Mosconi, Mack, McCarthy, & Pelphrey, 2005).

The tug-of-war between "romantic" and "killjoy" interpretations described by Dennett (1983) continues to shape the experimental exploration of cognitive development in infants and the cognitive competence of animals, under various descriptions. Do preverbal infants infer the intentions of others (Bloom, 2000; Tomasello, Carpenter, Call, Behne, & Moll, 2005)? Do they also evaluate their rationality in some explicit fashion or are "the constraints embodied in the infant's naïve theories" (Csibra, Gergely, Bíró, Koós, & Brockbank, 1999, p. 2)? Are these constraints akin to the tacit assumption by visuo-motor systems that light travels in straight lines? There is a growing consensus that the false-belief task has set the mindreading bar too high (Johnson, 2000), and the game appears to have changed to limbo: how low can the bar go? There has been some nice work on the firing properties of "looming" neurons in locusts (Santer, Rind, Stafford, & Simmons, 2006). These neurons, in concert with descending contralateral motion-detector neurons, detect the forthcoming goals, or intentions, of approaching predators. How do we know this? We know this because the story does not end immediately after they fire; the locusts, if allowed, will then enter into elaborate evasive maneuvers. It seems to follow then that these are not simply *motion*-detection neurons, but rather *goal*-detection neurons. Since the most important goals (or intentions) to predict are those that have *you* as the target, with being eaten as the conditions of satisfaction, this role makes evolutionary sense. Indeed, there will be cases when these locusts' neurons, like mirror neurons, get it wrong about the agent's intentions, resulting in the locusts' frenzied flight for no good reason, or at least not the right reasons. Are we then obliged to say, in keeping with the principles of intentional-stance interpretation, that these neurons encode (or *have*?) both true and false beliefs about the intentions of others? Looking back in history (Lettvin, Maturana, McCulloch, & Pitts, 1965), should we say that the frog's eye *believed* what it told the frog's brain? And what *exactly* was the propositional message sent through the optic nerve? The fog of tug-of-war still obscures the path from intentional interpretation to inner mechanism.

To some, letting the lowly locust into the club of second-order intentional systems may seem to be a loose metaphor at best, or, worse, yet another instance of anthropomorphism gone wrong. Others might make this same charge against the claims of mindreading mirror neurons, which respond to relatively narrow classes of stimuli and cannot be said to have beliefs about anything. Some of the confusion here is probably due to confusing the *craft* of folk psychology – how we work the tools of the trade – with a few misleading elements of the *ideology* of folk psychology, the often benighted lore about how the craft works (Dennett, 1991). In particular, according to the ideology, there has to be some clear line between real believers/intenders and mere *as if* believers/intenders. A sea slug would seem to fit snugly into this latter category, and language-having humans are paradigmatic of the former. According to the ideology, as elaborated and elevated into constraints on *scientific* (non-folk) psychology by Fodor (1980) and others, there must be certain properties *internal* to the agent that serve as the definitive criterion for category membership. Lay folk psychologists don't have "brainoscopes" with which to peer inside heads (Baron-Cohen, 1995, p. 23), so we will have to leave it up to the experts to discover the essential properties of belief, whatever they might be. To most of us, gold and fool's gold are perceptually indistinguishable, but we can always rely on a trained chemist with a microscope to reliably distinguish the real from the fake (Putnam, 1981).

The ideology of folk psychology is realist and largely dualist (Bloom, 2004). But, when the ideology is combined with materialism, as it is with many educated adults, including scientists and philosophers, the realism remains but the dualism is replaced by one or another brand of reductionism, along with the mistaken assumption that looking inside heads will help us distinguish the real believers from the imposters. Now that we do have "brainoscopes" (for example, such techniques as neuroimaging, single-cell recording, and the like), this intuitive reduction has resulted in the discovery of neurons that represent an agent's intention to bring it about that *p*, a discovery eerily reminiscent of the imagined discovery of homunculi in sperm cells following the invention of the microscope.

The materialist reduction of the ideology is also reflected in (and infected by) opinions about how internal mental states cause behavior, via a system of presumably salient and distinct *attitudes* – belief, desire, intention, hope, fear, and so on – each with a slot for a propositional *content*, so that the mental state of belief that *it is raining* is distinct from the mental state of belief that *the cat is on the mat*, which is distinct from the *hope* that the cat is on the mat, and so forth. Thus, if behavior is caused by the *belief* that *p*, coupled with the *desire* to bring it about that *q*, a successful folk psychology is simply a matter of hooking up the correct attitudes with their proper *p*s and *q*s. But, of course, folk psychology can serve us quite well, whether or not propositional attitudes and their modulating contents are states discoverable – independently identifiable – somewhere in the neural architecture. The craft has been around far longer than functional neuroimaging. Fortunately, we should be able to determine how the craft does its work – in different species, and in human beings at different developmental stages – without having to wait until neuroscientists reach a consensus on the essential properties of adult belief.

Before we begin our review of "mindreading" mechanisms and of what might be going wrong in autism, we would like to point out another distinction that, if overlooked, has the potential to make mischief: the distinction between the mechanism (or the "performance" of the mechanism) and the competence. Roughly, competence-level descriptions characterize what a system can do (in a larger context) and mechanism-level descriptions characterize how the parts work or perform. (We assume that the characterization of mechanisms in this literature will be in functional rather than structural terms.) Competence models often specify far more than the actual work being done by the underlying functional mechanisms (Clark, 1990). For instance, the painstaking and detailed treatment of communication by Grice (1989) is compelling as an analysis of the competence that must exist *one way or another* for there to be genuine communication, but is well-nigh incredible as a description of internal machinery in the infant communicator. Thus, while an infant's impatient gestures will communicate to us that she wants us to hand over a certain toy, it is unlikely that she has *framed the intention* to bring it about that we hand over the toy by causing us, via those gestures, to believe that she wants us to do this, as Grice might put it. Her act already plays the functional role of communication, even though she has not yet grown into the role of a suitably circumspect communicator. Young children can be the beneficiaries of their own communicative acts without having to know that they are communicating, just as locusts can be the beneficiaries of their innate predator-detection modules without having to know what they are doing or how they are doing it. The reasons are implicit in the design of the mechanisms, and in the case of the child may eventually be represented in such a way that they can be both expressed and reflected upon, but the *representation* of the reasons is not, in simple cases, a design requirement on the mechanisms.

As a way of structuring our review of the literature, we will focus on "mindblindness," the model of autism introduced by Baron-Cohen (1995). While there are other accounts of autism, Baron-Cohen's model has not only delivered on a large number of its predictions (see Baron-Cohen, Tager-Flusberg & Cohen, 2000), but is the only cognitive model of autism that is explicit about the function and onset of mindreading mechanisms in the first few years of life, moreover, the model attempts to characterize the development of mental-state attribution in typically developing children as well, thereby allowing us to address some outstanding issues regarding the development of mental-state attribution in general.

Autism and Mindblindness: The Four Steps to Mindreading

Theory-of-mind mechanism (18–48 months)

While the false-belief task was the centerpiece of the work by Baron-Cohen, Leslie and Frith (1985) – "Does the autistic child have a 'theory of mind'?" – a large part of the motivation for the study surrounded the concept of pretense rather than the concept of belief. A lack of spontaneous pretend play, sometimes referred to as a failure in imagination (Wing & Gould, 1979), is one of the diagnostic criteria for autism (APA, 2000) and, for reasons that will become clearer below, the theory-of-mind mechanism (TOMM) (Baron-Cohen, 1995) is centered around the propositional attitude of pretense. This is despite the fact that children's pretense typically emerges around 18 months, whereas understanding false belief in others is not consistent until children are around 4 years old, a full $2^{1}/_{2}$ years later.

The function of TOMM is not only to represent the full range of mental states, but also to connect them into a coherent folk theory of mind. As mentioned above, the mechanism takes some years to develop, and its onset is heralded by children's engagement in pretense and shared pretense. The mechanism is borrowed from Leslie (1987), who argues that children's understanding of the propositional attitude of pretense is served by the maturation of a meta-representational "decoupler" mechanism, allowing children to hold online simultaneous representations of reality (for example, the banana is a banana) and of the content of the pretense (for example, the banana is a phone), without confusing the two. In accord with the ideology, Leslie sees this ability as indexing the distinction between propositional attitudes and propositional contents.

While the mental-state verb "to pretend" carries with it all the interesting properties of intentionality, such as aboutness and referential opacity (Dennett & Haugeland, 1987), simply engaging in pretense does not tell us much about how children understand acts of pretense. More important in this regard is how children interpret pretending in others. This is currently a topic of considerable debate (Friedman & Leslie, 2007; Lillard, 1998). A number of controlled experiments by Lillard and colleagues suggest that children may be interpreting pretense in behavioral rather than mentalistic terms, or as external actions rather than internal representations. For instance, most 4-year-olds will say that a hopping doll is *pretending* to be a kangaroo, even if they are told that the doll does not *know* that kangaroos hop, or was not *thinking* about kangaroos, or was not *trying* to hop like a kangaroo.

Despite these difficulties, their behavior during pretense tells us that they realize in some sense that pretend statements and actions need not be true of the world (for example, whoever is playing mommy is not really mommy), a property that is shared with belief. Yet belief states purport to represent reality correctly, whereas states of pretense do not. Perner (1995) claims that 2- and 3-year-olds have an amalgam concept of pretense and belief, which he calls "prelief." Only later in development is the child able to differentiate between pretense and belief, as indexed by understanding false belief. The concept of "prelief," Perner claims, does the work of "belief" in the young child's folk psychological reasoning schema (Perner, 1991, 1995), though the child cannot yet be considered to understand that minds are representational.

Fodor (1992) disagrees that "prelief" can do the work of belief. He writes: "Pretending involves acting as though one believes that P is true when, in fact, one believes that P is false. It would thus seem to be impossible for a creature that lacks the concept of a belief being false" (p. 290). For Fodor, the child's early theory of mind (his very simple theory of mind, or VSTM) consists of the standard two concepts – beliefs and desires – but not more complex concepts such as yens or suspicions, and so on. Because Perner's and others' data show that young children do not understand false beliefs, he avoids having the child's concept of pretense depend on the concept of false belief by construing it in behavioristic terms, as "acting *as if.*" Fodor claims that he cannot have this either, speculating as follows: "Presumably even young children know the difference between acting as if P because one is pretending that P and acting as if P because one believes that P" (p. 290, n. 9). Lillard's data, however, suggest that Fodor's seemingly innocuous assumption may not, strictly speaking, be the case. Her data appear to show that if you are not an x then acting as if you are an x = pretending – whether or not you believe you are an x or are x-ing. The "beliefs" that seem to be doing all the work are those of the interpreter, not the subject of the interpretation. Thus, while Fodor's second-order intentional description may be true of the child's competence, this description does not seem to reflect the reasoning by which children understand pretending in others. The evidence points to the fact that children can successfully engage in shared pretense without explicitly representing (namely, being capable of expressing the opinion) that their partner is pretending that P is true while at the same time believing that P is false. Certainly there are mechanisms that control the child's coherent behavior, but they do not appear to be doing so by explicitly representing the situation in these high-level terms – that is, in a language of thought with belief and desire concepts and slots for their contents.

Autism and pretense

As noted above, part of the diagnostic criteria for autism is reduced or absent pretend play. This is part of the DSM-IV largely as a result of the seminal work of Wing and Gould (1979) defining the triad of autistic features as abnormalities in *socialization*, *communication*, and *imagination*. Wing and Gould considered the paucity of pretend play to result from "problems in imagination," and clinicians currently take the existence of stereotyped and repetitive behaviors to reflect problems of this kind. Several empirical studies have confirmed Wing and Gould's contention that absent or reduced spontaneous pretend play is common in autism (for a review, see Jarrold, 2003). Pretend play is, however, sometimes seen in children with autism, though it is seen less frequently than in control groups, even those matched on receptive language ability (Jarrold, Boucher, & Smith, 1996).

More relevant to our question is whether these children will engage in *shared* pretense. Interestingly, several controlled studies have shown that children with autism will, in fact, engage in shared pretense if encouraged to do so (Lewis & Boucher, 1988). Indeed, in structured settings, children with autism will produce as many relevant pretend acts (for example, a doll wearing a silly hat or eating something biscuit-like) as matched control children (Charman & Baron-Cohen, 1997). Kavanaugh and Harris (1994) found that children with autism were even able to draw pretend consequences from pretend assumptions. For instance, they were able to say that a toy would be "wet" rather than dry after pretending to pour tea into it (the tea cup was empty). Importantly, they were not biased to the reality of the situation, as the target was, of course, still dry.

Thus, while the TOMMs of both Leslie (1987) and Baron-Cohen (1995) are based on the logical properties of the propositional attitude of pretense, as well as the diagnostic criterion of impaired pretend play, the ability of children with autism to engage in pretend scenarios with others argues against a straightforward connection. Moreover, the difficulty that typically developing children have with describing acts of pretense in terms of the mental states that underlie them suggests that the onset of pretense or even shared pretense may not index an understanding of propositional attitudes after all. Friedman and Leslie (2007) argue that toddlers have the innate concept PRETEND but not the concept MENTAL STATE. If this is the case, it would be a severely impoverished concept, in that PRETEND derives its meaning from the related concepts of BELIEF, IMAGINE, and ACTING AS IF. Baron-Cohen (1995) acknowledges the gap between engaging in pretense and attributing false beliefs, and the apparent need for additional mechanisms between the ages of 2 and 5 to fill this gap.

Shared-attention mechanism (9–14 months)

Baron-Cohen proposed two novel mechanisms in his model: A shared-attention mechanism (SAM) and an eye-direction detector (EDD). He suggested that autism is not merely the result of a faulty TOMM, but that a faulty TOMM is probably the result of a dysfunctional SAM, which emerges around the first birthday. The function of a SAM is to build triadic representations from pre-existing dyadic ones. Thus, while the infant might appreciate that she can see the toy (dyadic) and that mommy can see the toy (also dyadic), SAM combines these into a representation that is something like "I see that mommy sees the toy" or "mommy sees that I see the toy." This three-way relation typically includes the child, another individual, and an object/individual. The existence of a SAM may be indexed by gaze monitoring, where an infant follows the direction of another's gaze to an object, and looks back and forth between the object and the other's face. Pointing may also serve as an index, particularly if the child is pointing out an object to another to share interest. This is often referred to as protodeclarative pointing and is contrasted with its protoimperative counterpart, where children point out an object that they want, as a request or demand. While protoimperative pointing is also triadic (child–other–

object), Baron-Cohen (1995) argues that it need not require SAM. Indeed, pointing or gesturing to another for one's own wants and needs may be instrumental and does not require an understanding of attention, nor does it necessarily reflect a *"desire to share interest* with another person for its own sake" (p. 69, emphasis added). While there is little mention of issues of emotional connectedness (for example, a desire to share interest) in his (1995) model, it is reflected in later work on empathizing deficits (Baron-Cohen, 2003, 2005).

As of 2007 there is considerable debate whether gaze monitoring requires an understanding of attention or whether lower-level learning mechanisms are sufficient. Chimpanzees and monkeys will follow direction of gaze (or head direction), though they do not appear to need a concept of attention, or even seeing, in order to do so (Povinelli & Eddy, 1996; but see Tomasello, Call, & Hare, 2003). Even newborns will follow the direction of another's gaze, provided the target is within their own visual field (Farroni, Menon & Johnson, 2006). Could innate biases of this ilk, combined with correlational learning mechanisms, be enough to account for gaze-monitoring behaviors in infants and the other primates, or do these skills require more sophisticated conceptual tools? Even protodeclarative gestures are open to leaner, non-mentalistic, interpretations. "Showing" behaviors, for instance, may be a means to change the parents' overt emotional expression, or to induce positive feedback from them, rather than reflecting an understanding of attention or internal emotional states (Moore & Corkum, 1994; Perner, 1991).

Shared attention in autism

Children with autism show delays in both gaze monitoring and pointing (Leekam, Lopez, & Moore, 2000). Pointing does not typically appear until 20–30 months mental age (MA), and the ability to follow a point may arise earlier than the ability to follow a gaze (Mundy, Sigman, & Kasari, 1994). This is the reverse of typical development. Moreover, pointing in autism tends to be protoimperative in nature (for example, requesting or demanding) rather than protodeclarative (for example, showing or pointing out something of interest) (Baron-Cohen, 1989). This is also the reverse of typical development, where protodeclarative behaviors tend to precede protoimperative behaviors (Carpenter, Nagell, & Tomasello, 1998).

Spontaneous gaze following is present in children with autism, particularly if their verbal mental age is 4 years or older (Leekam, Hunnisett, & Moore, 1998). A verbal mental age of 4 is, however, quite sophisticated, and this finding jeopardizes claims of the necessary relation between gaze monitoring and language learning (Baldwin & Moses, 1994). The fact that the frequency of joint-attention behaviors, including gaze monitoring, predicts language ability in autism (Sigman & Ruskin, 1999) suggests that following gaze is an aid to comprehension and vocabulary, but that at least certain aspects of language learning can precede nonetheless without it.

While important social information can be obtained by following another's direction of gaze, even more social information can be obtained by noting another's emotional reaction toward an object/individual. This is called social or emotional referencing and, while not specifically addressed in Baron-Cohen's model (1995), it is an important subcategory of joint or shared-attention behaviors. Infants are particularly sensitive to the facial and vocal expressions of others and will modify their behavior toward various objects as a function of another's emotional expression. For instance, a parent's facial expression can influence whether a 12-month-old will cross a visual cliff or whether a 10-month-old will interact with a stranger (Feinman and Lewis, 1983; Sorce, Emde, Campos, & Klinnert, 1985). These particular examples may be explained by contagion, where the fear signals in a parent trigger fear in the infant, thus inhibiting their exploratory or interactive behavior. Other studies have found that older children can discern the particular object or referent of another's emotional expression, and will behave differentially toward that object as a function of the expression. Repacholi (1998), for instance, found that 14–18-month-old children would interact more with the target of another's happy display than a disgust display, even though the targets (toys) were hidden in boxes. These data show that these children were not, via a simple association mechanism, mapping the emotional displays to the box but likely understood that the expressions referred to hidden objects within the boxes.

Griffin and Baron-Cohen (2006) carried out Repacholi's study (1998) with 2- and 3-year-olds with Autism Spectrum Conditions (ASC). They found that, while all of the children would search for the contents of the boxes, apparently appreciating that the emotional displays signaled hidden contents, only the control groups were influenced by the emotional displays. The search behavior of the ASC group appeared to be random. Though the ASC group may have appreciated that the facial-vocal cues signaled something *inside* the box (apparently a triadic computation), they did not appear to use the emotional expressions as a source of information *about* those objects. A follow-up experiment using a preferential-looking technique found that the ASC children were capable of *distinguishing* between different emotional expressions (for example, happiness and fear), but simply distinguishing between expressions is not the same as understanding what they mean – that is, how they may relate to objects in the world or to internal states. It is not yet clear whether the difficulties with emotional referencing found in this study are due to problems understanding the referential nature of emotions or whether the deficit is more basic, reflecting an altered sensitivity to others' emotional states (Hobson, 2003).

Eye-direction detector (0–9 months)

The eye-direction detector (EDD) has three functions, two of which may be considered perceptual and a third of which is ostensibly conceptual. The perceptual functions include (1) detecting the presence of eyes, and (2) detecting the direction of gaze. The conceptual function is the inference that eyes are for "seeing." Thus during mutual contact, the EDD represents that "agent sees me" and "I see agent" (Baron-Cohen, 1995, 42–43).

Recent experiments by Farroni and colleagues suggest that the first two functions are present at birth (Farroni, Csibra, Simion & Johnson, 2002). Newborns can detect the difference between direct and averted gaze, and will look longer at the former. This effect, however, can be influenced by the location of the eyes within the face. The effect is not found when the face is inverted or when it is rotated 45 degrees (Farroni et al., 2006). Farroni and colleagues argue against the existence of a modular EDD, because of the fact that facial configuration can influence the effect, contending instead that their results reflect an innate face-processing template. However, Baron-Cohen (1994) argues that these modules need not be strictly informationally encapsulated in Fodor's sense (1983), so these findings are consistent with his characterization of EDD perceptual functions.

The perception of averted gaze will automatically trigger shifts of attention in infants only a few months old (Farroni, Johnson, Brockbank, & Simion 2000). In these studies, infants are faster at locating peripheral targets that are congruent with the direction of another's gaze than targets that are incongruent with the direction of gaze. To achieve this effect, however, a period of mutual gaze is necessary at the start of the procedure. Also, the centrally presented face must be extinguished before the targets appear (hence the procedure is typically done on a computer monitor). The continued presence of a face apparently demands more attentional resources than the peripheral targets for these young children (Johnson et al., 2005). The relation between the eyes and facial configuration makes a difference here as well, as the finding is not obtained when the face is inverted. It is important to note that this gaze-cueing effect is not properly a joint- or shared-attention behavior in that these children will not saccade to the location of the target *before* it appears (typically 1000 ms after the gaze cue), but simply show faster reaction times to the target after it has appeared (for a review, see Johnson et al., 2005). Even typically developing 3-year-olds, who will follow someone's gaze to almost any location, show this same pattern. Thus the mechanism that realizes this effect does not appear to be employing any notion of "seeing" or "attending" but is probably triggered by the direction of motion of facial features, particularly eyes or eye-like stimuli (Farroni et al., 2000).

Evidence for EDD's third function – the attribution of "seeing" – is not as straightforward, particularly in the first year of life. This is due to the fact that the concept of seeing derives its meaning from related concepts, such as attention or even knowledge, which are later emerging concepts according to the model. As Ryle (1949/2002) noted, "see" is what he called a success verb: you can look at something and fail to see it, so the attribution of seeing requires discerning – or hypothesizing – that success. ("She's looking right at us, but does she see us?" "Yes, now she's waving. At last she sees us.") But even 3-year-olds have trouble determining how knowledge is obtained through the various senses, and cannot accurately report whether they learned the identity of an object from seeing it, touching it, or inferring its presence from verbal clues (O'Neill & Gopnik, 1991). Such surprising gaps in their understanding are valuable reminders of how easy it is for adults to overestimate such competences. How tempting it is to think that anyone who can enjoy the game of hide and seek so much must have a solid appreciation of the perceptual sources of their own, and others', knowledge.

Eye-direction detection in autism

Baron-Cohen suggested that the EDD was intact in autism. Studies with school-age children with autism support this view in that they are able to determine whether someone is looking at them or at another object. They are also able to determine which object (among distractors) a person is looking at (Leekam, Baron-Cohen, Brown, Perrett, & Milders, 1997) and will use the word "see" in their everyday speech. While verbally able children with autism appear to have some notion of "seeing" or at least "looking at," they have difficulty in making the seemingly short leap to the axiom that "seeing leads to knowing." At least one study found these children could report that someone was "looking" in a box and that another person was "touching" the box, but were unable to determine which one "knew" what was in the box (Baron-Cohen & Goodhart, 1994). This is in keeping with Baron-Cohen's model in that "seeing" is computed by the EDD whereas "knowing" is computed by the TOMM.

But evidence with younger children with autism suggests that the EDD may not be spared after all. Johnson, Griffin and colleagues (Johnson et al., 2005) used the gaze-cueing paradigm described above with 2- and 3-year-olds with autism. They found that the children with autism were no faster at locating targets congruent with the direction of gaze than they were in the incongruent condition. That is, they did not show the gaze cueing effect. Nor did they show any problems shifting their own attention, a deficit which some have considered to be fundamental to the phenotype (Courchesne et al., 1994). In fact, the group with autism actually showed faster reaction times (RTs) than the controls in both the congruent and incongruent conditions, despite showing no evidence of cueing. These faster RTs have also been found by Chawaska, Klin, and Volkmar (2003) and may reflect a decreased attentional load to the centrally presented face (Johnson et al., 2005). If these children are not processing the face as fully or deeply as the control subjects, their attention may be more easily disengaged from the face, resulting in faster RTs to the peripheral targets (Lavie, Ro, & Russell, 2003).

Gaze cueing has also been studied with older children with autism. Senju, Tojo, Dairoku, and Hasegawa (2003) found that 10–12-year-olds with autism can be cued by gaze direction, and even by arrows. Yet, unlike an age-matched control group, the children with autism continued to be cued by the arrows even when they predicted the location of the targets on only 20 percent of the trials. This failure to show the differential sensitivity to the social nature of gaze cueing suggests that the group with autism may be using a different mechanism than typically developing children, treating the gaze direction as a symbolic cue. It is noteworthy that 2- and 3-year-olds do not show cueing to (non-social) arrows, which probably need to be understood as symbols that signify direction before this effect can occur (Charwaska, Klin & Volkmar, 2003).

Intentionality detector (0–9 months)

The intentionality detector (ID) is similar to the innate mechanism proposed by Premack (1990), who claimed that the mental state of "intention" is automatically attributed to anything that exhibits *self-propelled* or *self-initiated* motion. Baron-Cohen (1995) does not use the term "intention", owing to the fact that it is too closely linked to the concept of belief, instead claiming that the ID interprets motion stimuli in terms of "goals" and "desires" – for example, "Her goal is to go over there;" "It wants to get the cheese" (p. 33). The ID, like the EDD, can produce only dyadic mental representations. The output of each can be processed by the SAM so that their specific computations can be combined and the child can compute, for instance, that someone can desire (ID) the object he or she is looking at (EDD).

The studies that investigate intentionality detection in infants tend to focus on two main features of agency: motion properties (for example, self-initiated movement, action-at-a-distance, contingent interaction) and object-directed motion associated with agent-typical features such as eyes and hands. Our focus here will be on the former. The experiments investigating motion properties typically use simple geometric shapes, such as triangles and circles, which lack any agent-typical features. In adults, motion properties alone are enough to elicit elaborate folk psychological descriptions (Heider & Simmel, 1944), and infants may focus more on the motion properties of an object than the features that signal its kind of category (for example, color, shape) (Xu, Carey, & Quint, 2004).

At the time Baron-Cohen proposed his model, there was little evidence about the kinds of distinctions infants could make regarding motion properties. The ascendance of social-cognitive neuroscience and preferential-looking techniques with infants has begun to fill this gap. Perhaps the best evidence of goal attribution in infancy comes from a set of studies by Gergely, Csibra, and colleagues (Gergely & Csibra, 2003; Gergely, Nadasdy, Csibra & Bíró, 1995), who find that 9–12-month-old infants will disregard the perceptual similarity between two motion trajectories (for example, arcing or jumping), instead encoding its relation or directedness toward another object. An illustration will help to clarify.

Infants who are habituated to a ball jumping over a barrier (Figure 17.1, Habituation), will show "surprise" (will dishabituate) to a test condition with the same arcing motion, albeit with the barrier removed from its path (Figure 17.1, Old Action). Note that this is perceptually more similar to the habituation animation than the other test condition, where the ball moves in a direct path toward the other ball (Figure 17.1, New Action). While younger infants (6 months old) will dishabituate to the perceptually dissimilar condition (new action), most older infants (9–12 months old) will not, apparently because they expect the ball to move in a direct path toward the other ball. Gergely and Csibra argue that the older infants are representing the ball's "goal," which is to contact the other ball, and also that the goal will be satisfied by the optimal means available. They call this latter constraint the "principle of rationality." Importantly, they do not grant infants the means to attribute mental states as internal and *causal* to the action. The goals in

Habituation

Test

Old Action   *New Action*

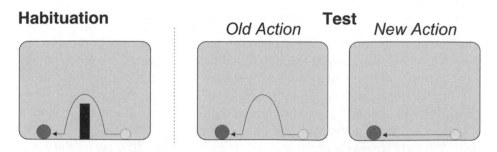

Figure 17.1. Stimuli from Gergely & Csibra that demonstrate infant sensitivity to rational action at 9 months of age

Note: For a full description of the paradigm, see p. 265.

Source: Gergely et al. (1995).

their model are the action outcomes – the act of getting to the other side, as it were. They call this the "teleological stance," whereby infants determine the future goal and then predict that agents will act in such-and-such a (rational) way *in order to* achieve that goal. "In order to" clauses signal teleological explanations. Gergely and Csibra's overall conceptual program is provocative, clearly articulated, and will be addressed in more detail below.

Intentionality detection in autism

Baron-Cohen speculated that the ID was intact in autism, based on the fact that reference to desires and goals sometimes occurs in their spontaneous speech and in experimental settings. Bowler and Thommen (2000) found that school-age children with autism were able to distinguish self-propelled from non-self-propelled motion in a Michotte-style launching event, and also that they described the Heider and Simmel (1944) stimuli using the same amount of mental-state language as controls. Abell, Happé, and Frith (2000) took the paradigm a step further, creating Heider and Simmel-style animations depicting three conditions: random movement, goal-directed movement, and "theory-of-mind" movement, of which the latter depicted the most sophisticated social scenarios (for example, tricking or mocking). They found that the autism group, when compared to typically developing 8-year-olds, produced less accurate mental-state language for the "theory-of-mind" condition, though the autism group did not differ from IQ-matched controls. Studies of this kind do not typically find impairments in the descriptions of goal-directed or simple purposive scenarios, such as chasing or fighting (see also Castelli, Frith, Happé, & Frith, 2002; Klin, 2000).

These studies test older, verbally able, individuals with autism. Because autism is not typically diagnosed before the age of 3, there are few data on toddlers and preschoolers with autism and almost no data on autism in early infancy. There are, however, a couple of studies that have investigated goal detection, broadly construed, in 2- and 4-year-old largely preverbal children with autism. Perhaps the best evidence of goal-detection capabilities in young children with autism comes from a study using Meltzoff's paradigm (1995) of "unfulfilled intentions" or "procedural imitation" (Aldridge, Stone, Sweeney, & Bower, 2000). In this paradigm, typically developing 14- and 18-month-old children who witness an actor unsuccessfully attempting to complete an act (for example, pulling apart miniature dumbbells), will complete that act if given the chance to do so (Carpenter et al., 1998). Because the children have not witnessed the completed act, some researchers claim that these infants have inferred the actor's *intention* to complete the act and are not merely copying an action. Aldridge et al. found that 2–4-year-old preverbal children with autism actually performed better than controls on these tasks, despite the fact that they showed no gestural imitation (for example, tongue protrusion, wiggling the ears with both hands) (see also Carpenter, Pennington, & Rogers, 2001). The authors were quite surprised by these results in that they expected, based largely on the work of Meltzoff and Gopnik (1993), that gestural imitation was a necessary precursor to the imitation of intentions. They assumed, moreover, that a "theory of mind" was necessary to complete these procedural tasks, echoing Premack & Woodruff (1978) (Aldridge et al., 2000, p. 300; but see Charman & Huang, 2002; Griffin, 2002; Griffin & Baron-Cohen, 2002). Interestingly, the "goals" of gestural imitation may not be as readily apparent as the outcomes of the procedural imitation conditions. To wiggle your ears in response to someone else's wiggling is likely to require, at the very least, an understanding that they "want" you to wiggle your ears as well. We could also construe this as an understanding of their intention for you to participate in the "ear-wiggling" game. Of course, even if this were understood, the child must be motivated to share emotions and activities with other individuals, an ability that may be lacking in children with autism.

Another study directly relevant to intentionality detection in preverbal children with autism was carried out by Griffin, Baron-Cohen, & Johnson (forthcoming), and used the stimuli from Gergely et al. (1995), depicted in Figure 17.1 above. While the studies reviewed above lead to the reasonable prediction that the ASC children would perform similarly to controls, the results are not kind to this prediction. After the groups had been familiarized to the ball surmounting a barrier (Figure 17.1, Habituation), the autism group, and only the autism group, looked longer at the perceptually dissimilar straight approach on the test trials (Figure 17.1, New Action). While these results do not fit with others that support the notion that young children with autism can predict goals (as event outcomes, at least), they fit well with another literature on autism that finds a pervasive bias to attend toward local rather than global features. This is sometimes referred to as weak central coherence (Happé, 1999). Because the ASC group in this study failed to incorporate the contextual constraints (for example, the barrier and/or the goal ball) and attended primarily to the salient perceptual feature of the stimuli (the arcing motion), the authors prefer an interpretation in perceptual rather than conceptual or "folk-theoretical" terms.

A bias toward local information can result in the omission of important contextual factors with which to constrain interpretation. Such integration failures have been found at a relatively low-level of visuospatial processing, and may account for why children with autism sometimes have difficulty seeing 2-D and 3-D visual illusions (Happé, 1996). A local processing bias can also result in enhanced performance when contextual factors typically interfere with performance, such as in the embedded-figures task, where individuals with autism outperform controls (for a review, see Happé, 1999). This processing bias is not by itself enough to account for theory-of-mind difficulties, as it is found across the spectrum, even with those who pass higher-order theory-of-mind tasks (Happé, 1995a).

The variation in age, IQ, number, and severity of traits, along with issues of comorbidity, virtually preclude any one cognitive or neurological model from characterizing the entire spectrum. Baron-Cohen's "mindblindness" model is most successful when applied to the subset in the medium-to-high functioning range, with enough language to participate in tasks that probe an understanding of mental-state concepts, and the research generating from the model shows us that it is not the power of language alone that gives rise to the idea of a representational mind. Typically developing children with a verbal mental age of 4 begin passing many theory-of-mind tasks, but children with autism require a verbal mental age of more than 9 years to achieve the same probability of success (Happé, 1995b). This suggests that they are using language as a crutch, as it were, to compensate for their impoverished inferential abilities in the social domain.

A possibility consistent with this is that individuals with autism, both children and adults, are the *only* people who really do have, and use, an articulated *theory* of mind (Dennett, 1990). That is, lacking the well-functioning mindreading *mechanisms* that permit typically developing children to adopt the intentional stance quite effortlessly (without even realizing they are doing it), individuals with autism must literally and explicitly consult the rules and generalizations of folk psychology in order to infer the likely mental states of those they encounter. While the generalizations of folk psychology could in principle be laid out in a (vast) list (for example, "People who are overtired are generally irritable"), the craft does not appear to require a "look-up" function of this imaginary list. Indeed, to be socially skillful, the *ceteris paribus* clauses endemic to these generalizations must be replaced with useful information. All things are not equal. A constructive criticism can be crushing to one individual and galvanizing to the next. People have different moods, interests, knowledge, opinions, status, and histories. A remark made to a sibling might not have the same social effects at school, at a dinner party, or at church.

Anecdotal evidence in support of this hypothesis comes from writers with autism such as Donna Williams (1998) and Temple Grandin (1995), who find themselves forced to ask some very difficult questions about the nature of folk psychology – questions about what it is to "like" something or "want" something, whether preferences and desires are caused by internal or external factors, and what the "self" has to do with all this (see Griffin, 2000). Articulate individuals with autism or Asperger sydrome may tell us more about the relationship between the ideology and the craft of folk psychology than those at the lower end of the spectrum. As many as 50 percent of people with autism will never speak, and the majority of children with autism have an IQ of 70 or less (APA, 2000; Volkmar & Klin, 2000). This "classic" autism is often accompanied by other medical or psychiatric problems as well as executive function deficits, the latter of which may be more diagnostic of the condition than theory-of-mind measures (Russell, 1997). Because a host of problems outside the domain of social cognition can and do accompany autism, Baron-Cohen considers "pure" autism to be reflected by those with Asperger sydrome, a condition where language deficits are not part of the diagnostic criteria and IQs range from normal to above average. When we look at this end of the spectrum, however, those with autism do not seem to have problems with the propositional attitudes, or even with embedding them into higher-order constructions (for example, Peter thinks that Jane thinks that . . .) (Bowler, 1992). Indeed, Ludwig Wittgenstein has been posthumously diagnosed with Asperger syndrome in a peer-review psychiatric journal (Fitzgerald, 2000), and, while he *certainly* had trouble with the propositional attitudes, it was not because he did not understand them as well as the typical layperson. His problems lay with the false premises of the ideology (Wittgenstein, 1953).

Indeed, finding "theory-of-mind" deficits in very high-functioning individuals on the spectrum requires far more sensitive measures, such as determining whether someone is contemplative, concerned, or dispirited, for example, from photographs of the eye regions of the face (Baron-Cohen, Wheelwright, Hill, Raste, & Plumb, 2001), or recognizing irony, sarcasm, or social faux pas (Baron-Cohen, O'Riordan, Stone, Jones, & Plaisted, 1999). While these problems clearly interfere with important "theory-of-mind" inferences, leading, for instance, to misunderstanding speakers' intentions, the reasons for these misreadings may be better understood as due not to a lack of "theory" but to impaired "evidence gathering" through misdirected attention (Klin, Jones, Schultz, Volkmar, & Cohen, 2002), failures to inhibit the more frequent associations, deficits in activating weaker, more distant, associations, or difficulties incorporating contextual constraints. These important quasi-perceptual talents need not be mutually exclusive. Each is necessary to note the difference between, say, content and content (or read, tear, bow, or row), and each is necessary to determine what someone means by "nice hat" (Brownell, Griffin, Winner, Friedman, & Happé, 2000). Individuals with right-hemisphere damage also show difficulties on these tasks, and, like that of high-functioning individuals on the autism spectrum, their performance may improve when time constraints are relaxed (Brownell et al., 2000; Griffin et al., 2006).

But real-world social interaction does not afford us the luxury of unlimited time to work through the possible meanings of an utterance, or of saying the right thing at just the right time. We all know the phenomenon of missing a double entendre or finding the perfect retort well after it was due. Most of us simply have the *knowhow* of the principles of relevance, clarity, quantity, or ambiguity, and so on, without reading Grice (1989), and without knowing *that* we were (typically) abiding by such principles. This is all part of the craft of folk psychology, and it is the part of the craft that is the least understood. We do not know *how* we know not to stand too close when speaking, read a "knowing" glance, or sense the proper rhythm of turntaking in conversation. These so-called undercurrents are where high-functioning individuals on the spectrum appear to have the most difficulty, and, because opinions about these mechanisms are not part of the ideology, they have remained largely outside the focus of empirical study.

Separating the Craft and the Ideology of Higher-Order Intentional Attributions

As we have seen, the theoretical accounts of early intentional interpretation tend to focus on children's beliefs about one or another of the propositional attitudes – more specifically, on the beliefs, goals, desires, or intentions of an agent. But when a child (or chimp) is shown to predict an agent's behavior, there is uncertainty whether he or she is representing, say, Big Bird's *intention* to p (or, better, bring it about that p), Big Bird's *desire* to (bring it about that) p, or Big Bird's *goal* to bring it about that p. (Philosophers insist that logic demands whole propositions, not mere verbs or verb phrases, as the permissible values of "p" and "q," but we will adopt a more casual and familiar usage here, counting on conscientious readers to supply the obligatory paraphrases, when needed.) It might seem to be more acceptable, less "mentalistic," to describe the child's competence in more "behavioristic" terms – for example, the child is representing that Big Bird is *attempting* to p, or *trying* to p, but these terms are not really less mind-involving, since only agents with minds (and goals, desires, intentions . . .) can *attempt* or *try*. Actions are a special class of events involving agent causation (Jackendoff, 2007). "Attempting," "trying," and the like refer to potential outcomes and provide reasons for an agent's actions, specifically those in the service of bringing p about. To see something as making an attempt is already to have adopted an intentional stance toward it.

Bare *event* descriptions, as contrasted with *action* descriptions, might then be closer to the mark. Perhaps the child is representing that Big Bird *will likely* p, or is *going to* p, or is *about to* p, and so forth. While p in each case may refer to a future (non-existent) state of affairs, predicting that someone or something is "about to" or "will likely" p, need not require a mechanism in the service of action explanation. Statistical or probabilistic learning could suffice. Just as we might predict that the falling bowl will hit the floor, or the cookie will get wet in the milk, a similar mechanism could predict that the doll (or mommy) will get wet in the bath. These predictions do not appeal to a purpose and describe events rather than actions. This difference is somewhat obscured by the fact that we speak casually about "reasons" in both kinds of cases: the "reason" the ice disappeared from the sidewalk is because it melted because the air got warmer, but the ice did not have this *purpose*, and neither did the air.

While philosophers have debated the fine points of these different descriptions (for example, attempting versus trying versus intending) and their implications for decades – are they descriptions of the same action (e.g. Anscombe, 1963; Davidson, 1980) or descriptions of different actions (e.g. Goldman, 1970)? – the task of developmental psychologists should be clear enough: to illuminate the mechanisms by which children encode and anticipate these behaviors. It is not clear that *any* of the action descriptions reflect the mechanisms that preverbal children use to predict actions or events. Language has a tendency to cut too fine in such cases. Differences in implication and assumption that can be discerned by adult philosophers may not engage any question that needs answering at the level of cognitive mechanisms in the child, and insisting on making such distinctions can tend to drive theorists toward a more *intellectualist* or "language-of-thought" perspective on these mechanisms than is warranted by any of the evidence.

In these simple scenarios, it may not appear to make much of a difference if the child characterizes an agent's reasons for acting as reflecting the agent's intention (and content) or desire (with the same content), but intentions and desires serve very different functional roles in the abstract calculus of folk psychology. The content of a desire (to bring it about that p) can be distinguished from the content of an intention (for example, to do such and such) in order to bring it about that p, in a variety of ways. Intentions and desires are different from beliefs in that they are neither true nor false, but are either fulfilled or unfulfilled (or pending). Studies that test whether children can distinguish between intentions and desires typically do so by creating scenarios with distinct satisfaction conditions for each. For instance, Phillips, Baron-Cohen and Rutter (1998) had children attempt to shoot targets in order to win a prize. The situation was manipulated such that children would (1) miss the target yet win the prize (satisfying the desire but not the intention), (2) hit the target and not win the prize (satisfying the intention but not the desire, (3) hit the target and win the prize (satisfying both), and (4) miss the target and not win the prize (satisfying neither). The test questions ask the children which target they "meant" to hit. Their answers belie their aim, tending to refer to the overall outcome – that is, whether (or not) they won the prize (desire content). Overall, these studies find that children are unable to distinguish accurately between intentions and desires until around the time they pass false-belief tasks (Feinfeld, Lee, Flavell, Green & Flavell, 1999; Shult, 2002). Because children with autism have difficulty with such tasks, Baron-Cohen relegates the concept of intention to the TOMM, along with epistemic states such as belief and knowledge.

In a recent, extended, defense of infant's understanding of intentions, Tomasello and colleagues (2005) write: "If we want to know how people understand intentional action, we must first have a model of exactly what intentional action is" (p. 676), and continue "the prototypical exemplar is, of course, the thermostat" (p. 676). Following Weiner (1948) and Ashby (1956), they go on to describe a model of intentions using the internal goal states, sensors, and feedback loops typical of cybernetic models. While the thermostat does provide a vivid minimalist example of an intentional system (Dennett, 1971), their citation of it may mislead people into thinking that all attribution of intentional action is *ipso facto* the attribution of some quite specific sort of internal mechanism – like the readily understood innards of a thermostat. It is important to bear in mind that, although thrifty engineering and conservative tradition restrict thermostat mechanisms to a handful of distinct types, there are in principle indefinitely many distinct mechanical ways of achieving the goal-directedness and feedback that constitutes a thermostat (you could even put a shivering or sweating midget inside, with a rule book to consult before acting – a literal homunculus).

More important than any specific prototypical mechanism is a folk conceptual analysis of these concepts (Jackendoff, 2007), and a breakdown of their function in folk psychological reasoning (Malle & Knobe, 2001). Such a breakdown provides a better yardstick against which to measure children's progress than an analysis of the feedback systems of heat-seeking missiles or thermostats. Intentions, unlike desires, involve action plans that signal a certain degree of commitment (Bratman, 1987). Moreover, one can desire to do something (one believes to be) impossible, but one cannot intend to do something (one believes to be) impossible. Malle and Knobe (2001) claim that social perceivers take desires (and beliefs and values) to be inputs to reasoning and intentions to be outputs, where they become the formation of the action plan. In this way, knowledge of an intention allows for greater predictive accuracy than knowledge of a desire. Intentions have action content of one's own actions, whereas the content of a desire can be much broader, and can include another's action or an unlikely outcome, and so on. For example, *I* can intend to spin the roulette wheel but I cannot intend *you* to spin it. I can *want* you to spin it, of course. Moreover, I cannot strictly speaking intend to win a million at the roulette table because it is out of my control. I can want, wish, or hope (desire verbs) to win, but I cannot intend, plan, or decide (intention verbs) to win. And, because intentions are closer to actions than desires, with more specific content, one cannot have conflicting intentions, even though one may have conflicting desires.

While there may be prototypical examples of intentions and desires, the degree of controllability and commitment can blur the lines between these attributions. Consider a more difficult shooting game than the one mentioned above. Someone with no shooting experience and poor eyesight might want to hit a bull's eye at 100 m but cannot intend to. If he purchased a scope, and set out practicing daily, we might shift from attributing to him a desire to hit the target to an intention to hit it (consisting of the action plan content, and because of his increasing skill and commitment).

Once someone has formed an intention, whether we consider the completed action *intentional* depends on whether it was executed as planned. Thus, even if he were an excellent shot, dropping the gun and hitting the bull's eye would not count as intentional, in most people's mind anyway (Knobe, 2003). He may have wanted to hit the target but he did not do so *intentionally*. We are not entirely consistent in these types of attributions, however. Say he wanted his neighbor dead and brought his gun to the hilltop to get a good angle. If he then tripped, dropped the gun, and killed the neighbor, a jury would probably find him guilty of *intentionally* killing the neighbor. Indeed, moral factors related to assessing blameworthiness will factor into whether we consider an action to be intentional. This blameworthy dimension of intentional attribution is seen in 4- but not 3-year-olds, again around the time they pass false-belief tasks (Leslie, Knobe, & Cohen, 2006).

In sum, there are many ways to distinguish between intentions and desires, but doing so will rely on other concepts such as belief, commitment, skill, the action's consequences, and so on (Jackendoff, 2007). An excellent case in point is a recent study of pointing and point following by infants (Tomasello, Carpenter, & Liszkowski, forthcoming), in which the authors first describe the surprisingly complex adult competence involved in pointing and point following, to wit: "she intends that I attend to X (and wants us to know this together) for some reason relevant to our common ground" (p. 10), and then go on to ask their central question: "the degree to which, and the ways in which, infant pointing shares all of the social-cognitive complexities of the adult version of this communicative gesture." Their conclusion about the competence they uncover in the year-old infants is remarkable for its mixture of insight and awkwardness: "they do this on a mental level involving the intentions, attention and knowledge of their partner" (p. 35). What is this "involving"? Is it explicit representing? Does it require, as Fodor would insist, *having the concepts* of intentions, attention and knowledge? Moses (2001) puts the problem clearly: "The difficulty, then, is to find a vocabulary that does justice to children's often impressive cognitive capacities without doing violence to the meaning of the full-blown adult concepts" (p. 69).

What Grice uncovered in his analysis of the (brilliant, sophisticated!) complexities of communication is parallel to the discoveries made by biologists of the (brilliant, sophisticated!) stratagems unwittingly pursued by animals. The low-nesting bird whose distraction display lures the predator away from the vulnerable fledglings in the nest is like the infant proto-communicator attracting his or her mother's attention. The bird is not just succumbing to paroxysms of fear and thrashing; she is monitoring the gaze direction of the predator, and making sure she wins the competition for attention, turning up the volume and allowing the predator to approach closer if the predator shows signs of giving up (Ristau, 1991). But the bird surely does not have to know she is doing all this! Neither does the pointing infant, who is "in some sense trying to influence her intentional/mental states" (Tomasello et al., forthcoming). An agent can X quite competently without having any explicit idea that he is Xing, or why Xing might be a good thing to do, or when to X and when not to X. All such an agent needs is a good Xing mechanism. Such an agent (and the agent's many other subsystems) is the beneficiary of all this timely Xing without anybody needing to be the wiser. In short (in philosophese), you can X without having the *concept* of Xing. You do need *something like* a concept; you need a designed mechanism that tracks, at least semi-reliably, the relevant phenomena. (A hand calculator almost perfectly tracks arithmetic, without having a (proper) concept of multiplication and division: after all, ten divided by three, times three, equals ten, not – as the calculator would have it – 9.99999999E.)

Do even articulate adults have *the* concept of communication, of intention, of belief? Probably only accomplished Griceans (and their critics), skilled novelists and playwrights, reflective con artists ... and a few other *virtuosi* would perform well on sophisticated tests of their knowledge of the conditions. We can imagine a challenging multiple-choice exam on the finer points of theory on which many adults would fall down rather badly. ("When X raised his eyebrows just then, what was he intending to do? A: acknowledge that he had understood Y's request but was refusing it. B: let Z know that Y's request betrayed Y's ignorance of the situation. C: cause Y to infer that X knew that Y wasn't serious in his request. D: none of the above.") A low grade on the test would hardly show that a person had not been communicating competently for years.

The mechanisms in the service of providing reasons need not be the same as those involved in predicting simple actions. All animals are in the business of behavioral prediction, but only humans are in the business of articulating reasons (Brandom, 2000). Only humans trade them. Being able to do so no doubt has more than a little to do with language and conceptual development. Young children are hit and miss with their reason ascriptions. In false-belief scenarios, children who fail the task are sometimes able to provide excellent (post-hoc) explanations that refer to mistaken beliefs, but even children who pass are not necessarily privy to their reasoning (for example, "He looked in the white box because that's his favorite color," to take one real-world case) (Bartsch, 1998). Coming up with reasons post hoc is probably easier than using them for prediction, for a couple of reasons; (1) the action to be explained has already transpired, so the outcome is a given, and (2) there is simply more time to come up with a reasonable story.

Children not only need to find reasons for other people's actions, but they need to do the same for themselves. Infants may have reasons for acting, but they are not yet their own reasons; they are the reasons that are presupposed by the design of the mechanisms that they are blessed with, "free floating rationales" (Dennett, 1995, 1996) that are not represented anywhere but are nevertheless discernible in the efficiency and effectiveness of their behavior. When we ascribe these reasons to them, this tends to create the illusion of more clear-cut content than actually exists. This overinterpretation can be useful as scaffolding, however, helping the child to come to be able to *distinguish* and then *adopt* such articulated mental states as his or her own (McGeer, 2004). It encourages a form of *approximating confabulation*, much like settling for the nearest miss in a poorly designed multiple-choice exam, when "none of the above" is not an option. We help children along in the dynamic process of composition ("Is *this* what you want?"), endorsement ("Thank you, that's exactly what I wanted!"), and revision ("No thank you. I'm not hungry right now") inherent in the refinement of reason-giving explanations. As their inferential abilities increase, so too will what follows from the reasons they give others and themselves, making them easier and easier to characterize as higher-order intentional systems, and making it easier for them to characterize us in the same way.

References

Abell, F., Happé, F., & Frith, U. (2000). Do triangles play tricks? Attribution of mental states to animated shapes in normal and abnormal development. *Cognitive Development*, 15, 1–16.

Aldridge, M. A., Stone, K. R., Sweeney, M. H., & Bower, T. G. R. (2000). Preverbal children with autism understand the intentions of others. *Developmental Science*, 3(3), 294–301.

Anscombe, G. E. M. (1963). *Intention*. Ithaca, NY: Cornell University Press.

APA (2000). American Psychiatric Association, *Diagnostic and Statistical Manual of Mental Disorders*. 4th edn., rev. text. Washington: American Psychiatric Association.

Ashby, W. R. (1956). *An Introduction to Cybernetics*: Boca Raton, FL, Chapman & Hall.

Baldwin, D., & Moses, L. J. (1994). Early understanding of referential intent and attentional focus: Evidence from language and emotion. In C. Lewis & P. Mitchell (Eds.), *Children's Early Understanding of Mind* (pp. 133–156). Hillsdale, NJ: Lawrence Erlbaum.

Baron-Cohen, S. (1989). Joint-attention deficits in autism: Towards a cognitive analysis. *Development & Psychopathology*, 1(3), 185–189.

Baron-Cohen, S. (1994). How to build a baby that reads minds: Cognitive mechanisms in mindreading. *Cahiers de psychologie cognitive*, 13, 513–552.

Baron-Cohen, S. (1995). *Mindblindness: An Essay on Autism and Theory of Mind*. Cambridge, MA: MIT Press.

Baron-Cohen, S. (2003). *The Essential Difference: Men, Women and the Extreme Male Brain*. London: Penguin.

Baron-Cohen, S. (2005). The empathizing system: A revision of the 1994 model of the mindreading system. In B. Ellis & D. Bjorklund (Eds.), *Origins of the Social Mind*. New York: Guilford.

Baron-Cohen, S., & Goodhart, F. (1994). The "seeing leads to knowing" deficit in autism: The Pratt and Bryant probe. *British Journal of Developmental Psychology*, 12, 397–402.

Baron-Cohen, S., Leslie, A. M., & Frith, U. (1985). Does the autistic child have a "theory of mind"? *Cognition*, 21(1), 37–46.

Baron-Cohen, S., O'Riordan, M., Stone, V., Jones, R., & Plaisted, K. (1999). Recognition of faux pas by normally developing children with asperger syndrome or high-functioning autism. *Journal of Autism & Developmental Disorders*, 29(5), 407–418.

Baron-Cohen, S., Tager-Flusberg, H., & Cohen, D. (Eds.) (2000). *Understanding Other Minds: Perspectives from Developmental Cognitive Neuroscience*. Oxford: Oxford University Press.

Baron-Cohen, S., Wheelwright, S., Hill, J., Raste, Y., & Plumb, I. (2001). The "reading the mind in the eyes" test revised version: A study with normal adults, and adults with Asperger syndrome or high-functioning autism. *Journal of Child Psychology & Psychiatry & Allied Disciplines*, 42(2), 241–251.

Bartsch, K. (1998). False belief prediction and explanation: Which develops first and why it matters. *International Journal of Behavioral Development*, 22(2).

Bennett, J. (1978). Some remarks about concepts. *Behavioral and Brain Sciences*, 1, 557–560.

Blakeslee, S. (2006). Cells that read minds. *New York Times*. Jan. 10.

Bloom, P. (2000). *How children learn the meaning of words*. Cambridge, MA: MIT Press.

Bloom, P. (2004). *Descartes' Baby: How the Science of Child Development Explains what Makes us Human*. New York: Basic Books.

Bowler, D. M. (1992). "Theory of mind" in Asperger syndrome. *Journal of Child Psychology and Psychiatry*, 33, 877–895.

Bowler, D. M., & Thommen, E. (2000). Attribution of mechanical and social causality to animated displays by children with autism. *Autism*, 4, 147–171.

Brandom, R. (2000). *Articulating Reasons: An Introduction to Inferentialism*. Cambridge, MA: Harvard University Press.

Bratman, M. E. (1987). *Intention, Plans & Practical Reason.* Cambridge, MA: Harvard University Press.

Brownell, H., Griffin, R., Winner, E., Friedman, O., & Happé, F. (2000). Cerebral lateralization and theory of mind. In S. Baron-Cohen, H. Tager-Flusberg, & D. Cohen (Eds.), *Understanding Other Minds: Perspectives from Developmental Cognitive Neuroscience* (pp. 306–333). Oxford: Oxford University Press.

Carpenter, M., Nagell, K., & Tomasello, M. (1998). Social cognition, joint attention, and communicative competence from 9 to 15 months of age. *Monographs of the Society for Research in Child Development, 63*(4).

Carpenter, M., Pennington, B. F., & Rogers, S. J. (2001). Understanding of others' intentions in children with autism and children with developmental delays. *Journal of Autism and Developmental Disorders, 31,* 589–599.

Castelli, F., Frith, C., Happé, F., & Frith, U. (2002). Autism, Asperger Syndrome and brain mechanisms for the attribution of mental states to animated shapes. *Brain, 125,* 1839–1849.

Charman, T., & Baron-Cohen, S. (1997). Brief report: Prompted pretend play in autism. *Journal of Autism and Developmental Disorders, 27,* 321–328.

Charman, T., & Huang, C. (2002). Delineating the role of stimulus enhancement and emulation learning in the behavioural re-enactment paradigm. *Developmental Science, 5,* 25.

Chawaska, K., Klin, A., & Volkmar, F. (2003). Automatic attention cueing through eye movement in 2-year-old children with autism. *Child Development, 74*(4), 1108–1122.

Clark, A. (1990). Connectionism, competence and explanation. *British Journal for the Philosophy of Science, 41,* 195–222.

Courchesne, E., Townsend, J., Akshoomof, N. A., Saitoh, O., Yeung-Courchesne, R., Lincoln, A. J., et al. (1994). Impairment in shifting attention in autistic and cerebellar patients. *Behavioural Neuroscience, 108,* 848–865.

Csibra, G., Gergely, G., Bíró, S., Koós, O., & Brockbank, M. (1999). Goal attribution without agency cues: The perception of "pure reason" in infancy. Cognition, 72, 237–267.

Davidson, D. (1980). *Essays on Actions and Events.* Oxford: Clarendon Press.

Dennett, D. C. (1971). Intentional systems. *Journal of Philosophy, 68,* 87–106.

Dennett, D. C. (1978). Beliefs about beliefs. *Behavioral and Brain Sciences, 4,* 568–570.

Dennett, D. C. (1983). Intentional systems in cognitive ethology: The "Panglossian Paradigm" defended (with commentaries). *Behavioral and Brain Sciences, 6,* 343–90.

Dennett, D. C. (1990) Abstracting from mechanism. *Behavioral and Brain Sciences, 13,* 583–4.

Dennett, D. C. (1991). Two contrasts: Folk craft versus folk science, and belief versus opinion. In J. D. Greenwood (Ed.), *The Future of Folk Psychology: Intentionality and Cognitive Science* (pp. 135–148). Cambridge: Cambridge University Press.

Dennett, D. C. (1995). *Darwin's Dangerous Idea: Evolution and the Meanings of Life.* New York: Simon & Schuster.

Dennett, D. C. (1996). *Kinds of Minds: Toward an Understanding of Consciousness.* New York: Basic Books.

Dennett, D. C., & Haugeland, J. (1987). Intentionality. In R. L. Gregory (Ed.), *The Oxford Companion to the Mind.* Oxford: Oxford University Press.

Farroni, T., Csibra, G., Simion, F., & Johnson, M. H. (2002). Eye contact detection in humans from birth. *Proceedings of the National Academy of Sciences, 99,* 9602–9605.

Farroni, T., Johnson, M. H., Brockbank, M., & Simion, F. (2000). Infants' use of gaze direction to cue attention: The importance of perceived motion. *Visual Cognition, 7*(6), 705–718.

Farroni, T., Menon, E., & Johnson, M. H. (2006). Factors influencing newborns' preference for faces with eye contact. *Journal of Experimental Child Psychology*, 95, 298–308.

Feinfeld, K. A., Lee, P. P., Flavell, E. R., Green, F. L., & Flavell, J. H. (1999). Young children's understanding of intention. *Cognitive Development*, 14, 463–486.

Feinman, S., & Lewis, M. (1983). Social referencing at 10-months: A second order effect on infants' response to strangers. *Child Development*, 54, 878–887.

Fitzgerald, M. (2000). Did Ludwig Wittgenstein have Asperger's syndrome? *European Journal of Child and Adolescent Psychiatry*, 9(1), 61–65.

Fodor, J. (1980). Methodological solipsism considered as a research strategy in cognitive psychology. *Behavioral and Brain Sciences*, 3, 63–73.

Fodor, J. (1983). *Modularity of Mind.* Cambridge, MA: MIT Press.

Fodor, J. A. (1992). A theory of the child's theory of mind. *Cognition*, 44(3), 283–296.

Friedman, O., & Leslie, A. (2007). The conceptual underpinnings of pretense: Pretending is not "behaving-as-if". *Cognition*, 105, 103–124.

Gallese, V., Fadiga, L., Fogassi, L., & Rizzolatti, G. (1996). Action recognition in the premotor cortex. *Brain*, 119, 593–609.

Gergely, G., & Csibra, G. (2003). Teleological reasoning in infancy: The naive theory of rational action. *Trends in Cognitive Sciences*, 7, 287–292.

Gergely, G., Nadasdy, Z., Csibra, G., & Bíró, S. (1995). Taking the intentional stance at 12 months of age. *Cognition*, 56(2), 165–193.

Goldman, A. (1970). *A Theory of Human Action.* Englewood Cliffs, NJ: Prentice-Hall.

Grandin, T. (1995). *Thinking in Pictures: And Other Reports from my Life with Autism.* New York: Doubleday.

Grice, H. P. (1989). *Studies in the Way of Words.* Cambridge, MA: Harvard University Press.

Griffin, R. (2000). Self, world, and order in Autism Spectrum Disorder. *Emotional & Behavioural Difficulties*, 5, 36–41.

Griffin, R. (2002). Social learning in the non-social: Imitation, intentions, and autism. *Developmental Science*, 5(1), 30–32.

Griffin, R., & Baron-Cohen, S. (2002). The intentional stance: Developmental and neurocognitive perspectives. In A. Brook & D. Ross (Eds.), *Daniel Dennett: Contemporary Philosophy in Focus* (pp. 83–116). New York: Cambridge University Press.

Griffin, R., & Baron-Cohen, S. (2006). Social referencing & categorical perception of emotions in toddlers with autism: A look at fear and disgust. Paper presented at International Conference on Infant Studies, Kyoto, Japan. June.

Griffin, R., Baron-Cohen, S., & Johnson, M. H. (forthcoming). Can preschoolers with autism take the teleological stance?

Griffin, R., Friedman, O., Ween, J., Winner, E., Happé, F., & Brownell, H. (2006). Theory of mind and the right cerebral hemisphere: Refining the scope of impairment. *Laterality*, 11(3), 195–225.

Happé, F. (1995a). *Autism: An Introduction to Psychological Theory.* Cambridge, MA: Harvard University Press.

Happé, F. (1995b). The role of age and verbal ability in the theory of mind task performance of subjects with autism. *Child Development*, 66, 843–855.

Happé, F. (1996). Studying weak central coherence at low levels: Children with autism do not succumb to visual illusions. A research note. *Journal of Child Psychology and Psychiatry*, 37, 873–877.

Happé, F. (1999). Autism: Cognitive deficit or cognitive style? *Trends in Cognitive Sciences*, 3, 216–222.

Heider, F., & Simmel, M. (1944). An experimental study of apparent behaviour. *American Journal of Psychology*, 57, 243–259.

Hobson, R. P. (2003). *The Cradle of Thought*. Oxford: Oxford University Press.

Iacoboni, M., Molnar-Szakacs, I., Gallese, V., Buccino, G., Mazziotta, J. C., & Rizzolatti, G. (2005). Grasping the intentions of others with one's own mirror neuron system. *Public Library of Science: Biology*, 3(3), e79.

Jackendoff, R. (2007). *Language, Consciousness, Culture: Essays on Mental Structure*. Cambridge, MA: MIT Press.

Jarrold, C. (2003). A review of research into pretend play in autism. *Autism*, 7(4), 379–390.

Jarrold, C., Boucher, J., & Smith, P. (1996). Generativity deficits in pretend play in autism. *British Journal of Developmental Psychology*, 14, 275–300.

Johnson, M. H., Griffin, R., Csibra, G., Halit, H., Farroni, T., de Haan, M., et al. (2005). The emergence of the social brain network: evidence from typical and atypical development. *Developmental Psychopathology*, 17(3), 599–619.

Johnson, S. (2000). The recognition of mentalistic agents in infancy. *Trends in Cognitive Sciences*, 4, 22–28.

Kavanaugh, R. D., & Harris, P. L. (1994). Imagining the outcome of pretend transformations: Assessing the competence of normal children and children with autism. *Developmental Psychology*, 30, 847–854.

Klin, A. (2000). Attributing social meaning to ambigious visual stimuli in higher-functioning autism and Asperger syndrome: The Social Attribution Task. *Journal of Child Psychology and Psychiatry*, 41, 831–846.

Klin, A., Jones, W., Schultz, R., Volkmar, F., & Cohen, D. (2002). Visual fixation patterns during viewing of naturalistic social situations as predictors of social competence in individuals with autism. *Archives of General Psychiatry*, 59, 809–816.

Knobe, J. (2003). Intentional action and side effects in ordinary language. *Analysis*, 63, 190–193.

Lavie, N., Ro, T., & Russell, C. (2003). The role of perceptual load in processing distractor faces. *Psychological Science*, 12, 510–515.

Leekam, S., Baron-Cohen, S., Brown, S., Perrett, D., & Milders, M. (1997). Eye-direction detection: A dissociation between geometric and joint-attention skills in autism. *British Journal of Developmental Psychology*, 15, 77–95.

Leekam, S. R., Hunnisett, E., & Moore, C. (1998). Targets and cues: Gaze-following in children with autism. *Journal of Child Psychology and Psychiatry and Allied Disciplines*, 39(7), 951–962.

Leekam, S. R., Lopez, B., & Moore, C. (2000). Attention and joint attention in preschool children with autism. *Developmental Psychology*, 36(2), 261–273.

Leslie, A. M. (1987). Pretense and representation: The origins of "theory of mind". *Psychological Review*, 94, 412–426.

Leslie, A., Knobe, J., & Cohen, A. (2006). Acting intentionally and the side-effect effect: "Theory of mind" and moral judgment. *Psychological Science*, 17, 421–427.

Lettvin, J. Y., Maturana, H. R., McCulloch, W. S., & Pitts, W. H. (1965). What the frog's eye tells the frog's brain. In W. S. McCulloch (Ed.). *Embodiments of Mind*, Cambridge, MA: MIT Press.

Lewis, V., & Boucher, J. (1988). Spontaneous, instructed and elicited play in relatively able autistic children. *British Journal of Developmental Psychology*, 6, 325–339.

Lillard, A. S. (1998). Playing with a theory of mind. *Child Development*, 69, 981–993.

Malle, B., & Knobe, J. (2001). The distinction between desire and intention: A folk-conceptual analysis. In B. F. Malle, L. J. Moses, & D. Baldwin (Eds.), *Intentions and Intentionality: Foundations of Social Cognition*. Cambridge, MA: MIT Press.

McGeer, V. (2004). Autistic self-awareness. *Philosophy, Psychiatry & Psychology*, 11, 235–251.

Meltzoff, A. (1995). Understanding the intentions of others: Re-enactment of intended acts by 18-month-old children. *Developmental Psychology*, 31, 838–850.

Meltzoff, A., & Gopnik, A. (1993). The role of imitation in understanding persons and developing a theory of mind. In S. Baron-Cohen, H. Tager-Flusberg, & D. J. Cohen (Eds.), *Understanding Other Minds: Perspectives from Autism*. Oxford: Oxford University Press.

Moore, C., & Corkum, V. (1994). Social understanding at the end of the first year of life. *Developmental Review*, 14(4), 349–372.

Mosconi, M. W., Mack, P. B., McCarthy, G., & Pelphrey, K. A. (2005). Taking an "intentional stance" on eye-gaze shifts: A functional neuroimaging study of social perception in children. *NeuroImage*, 27(1), 247–252.

Moses, L. J. (2001). Some thoughts on ascribing complex intentional concepts to young children. In B. F. Malle, L. J. Moses, & D. A. Baldwin (Eds.), *Intentions and Intentionality: Foundations of Social Cognition* (pp. 69–83). Cambridge, MA: MIT Press.

Mundy, P., Sigman, M., & Kasari, C. (1994). Joint attention, developmental level, and symptom presentation in autism. *Development and Psychopathology*, 6(3), 389–401.

O'Neill, D. K., & Gopnik, A. (1991). Young children's ability to identify the sources of their beliefs. *Developmental Psychology*, 27, 390–397.

Perner, J. (1991). *Understanding the Representational Mind*. Cambridge, MA: MIT Press.

Perner, J. (1995). The many faces of belief: Reflections on Fodor's and the child's theory of mind. *Cognition*, 57(3), 241–269.

Phillips, W., Baron-Cohen, S., & Rutter, M. (1998). Understanding intention in normal development and in autism. *British Journal of Developmental Psychology*, 16, 337–348.

Povinelli, D. J., & Eddy, T. J. (1996). What young chimpanzees know about seeing. *Monographs of the Society for Research in Child Development*, 61(3), 1–191.

Premack, D. (1990). The infant's theory of self-propelled objects. *Cognition*, 36, 1–16.

Premack, D., & Woodruff, G. (1978). Does the chimpanzee have a theory of mind? *Behavioral and Brain Sciences*, 1, 515–526.

Putnam, H. (1981). *Reason, Truth, History*. Cambridge: Cambridge University Press.

Repacholi, B. (1998). Infants' use of attentional cues to identify the referent of another person's emotional expression. *Developmental Psychology*, 34(5), 1017–1025.

Ristau, C. (1991). Aspects of the cognitive ethology of an injury-feigning bird, the piping plover. In C. Ristau (Ed.), *Cognitive Ethology: The Minds of Other Animals*. Hillsdale, NJ: Lawrence Erlbaum.

Russell, J. (Ed.). (1997). *Autism as an Executive Disorder*. Oxford: Oxford University Press.

Ryle, G. (1949/2002).*The Concept of Mind*. Chicago: University of Chicago Press.

Santer, R. D., Rind, F. C., Stafford, R., & Simmons, P. J. (2006). Role of an identified looming-sensitive neuron in triggering a flying locust's escape. *Journal of Neurophysiology*, 95(6), 3391–3400.

Schult, C. A. (2002). Children's understanding of the distinction between intentions and desires. *Child Development*, 73(6), 1727–1747.

Senju, A., Tojo, Y., Dairoku, H., & Hasegawa, T. (2003). Reflexive orienting in response to eye gaze and an arrow in children with and without autism. *Journal of Child Psychology and Psychiatry*, 44, 1–14.

Sigman, M., & Ruskin, E. (1999). Continuity and change in the social competence of children with autism, Down syndrome, and developmental delays. *Monographs of the Society for Research in Child Development*, 64(1).

Sorce, J., Emde, R., Campos, J., & Klinnert, M. (1985). Maternal emotional signaling: Its effect on the visual cliff behavior of 1-year-olds. *Developmental Psychology*, 21, 195–200.

Tomasello, M., Call, J., & Hare, B. (2003). Chimpanzees understand psychological states: The question is which ones and to what extent. *Trends in Cognitive Sciences*, 7, 153–156.

Tomasello, M., Carpenter, M., Call, J., Behne, T., & Moll, H. (2005). Understanding and sharing intentions: The origins of cultural cognition. *Behavioral & Brain Sciences*, 28, 675–735.

Tomasello, M., Carpenter, M., & Liszkowski, U. (forthcoming). A new look at infant pointing. *Child Development*.

Volkmar, F. R., & Klin, A. (2000). Diagnostic issues in Asperger syndrome. In A. Klin, F. R. Volkmar, & S. S. Sparrow (Eds.), *Asperger Syndrome* (pp. 25–71). New York: Guilford.

Weiner, N. (1948). *Cybernetics*. Wiley.

Wellman, H. M., Cross, D., & Watson, J. (2001). Meta-analysis of theory-of-mind development: The truth about false belief. *Child Development*, 72(3), 655–684.

Williams, D. (1998). *Like Colour to the Blind: Soul Searching and Soul Finding*. London: Jessica Kingsley Publishers.

Wimmer, H., & Perner, J. (1983). Beliefs about beliefs: Representation and constraining function of wrong beliefs in young children's understanding of deception. *Cognition*, 13, 103–128.

Wing, L., & Gould, J. (1979). Severe impairments of social interaction and associated abnormalities in children: Epidemiology and classification. *Journal of Autism and Developmental Disorders*, 9, 11–29.

Wittgenstein, L. (1953). *Philosophical Investigations*. Oxford: Blackwell.

Xu, F., Carey, S., & Quint, N. (2004). The emergence of kind-based object individuation in infancy. *Cognitive Psychology*, 49(2), 155–190.

Chapter 18

The Other End of the Spectrum? Social Cognition in Williams Syndrome

Jon Brock, Shiri Einav, and Deborah M. Riby

Introduction

In typical development, social-cognitive abilities are, by definition, predictable based on the child's chronological age. As a consequence, it is difficult to know whether associations between different social-cognitive skills and other capabilities reflect underlying causal relationships or mere maturational coincidence. In atypical development, this association between age and ability is disrupted, and, in many cases, social-cognitive functions appear to develop "out of synch" with one another or with the child's general developmental level. By looking at developmental disorders and trying to determine the reasons why specific skills may be relatively more impaired in one disorder (or individual) compared with another, it may be possible to tease apart hypothetical causal mechanisms and determine the factors that act as constraints upon development. The preceding chapters in this book have illustrated how the study of social-cognitive deficits in autism can illuminate the processes involved in typical social development. In this chapter, we review the social-cognitive capabilities of individuals with Williams syndrome – a rare genetic disorder that is often seen as representing the opposite of autism.

Williams syndrome is caused by the deletion of about twenty-five genes in the 7q11.23 region of chromosome seven (see Donnai & Karmiloff-Smith, 2000) and is associated with a number of medical and physical characteristics, including cardiac anomalies, excessive blood calcium levels, and an unusual "elfin" facial profile (see Morris, 2006). Although there is considerable individual variation, the overwhelming majority of people with Williams syndrome are characterized as having mild to moderate intellectual disability (see, e.g., Howlin, Davies, & Udwin, 1998). Crucially, however, the cognitive profile is somewhat uneven: visuo-spatial and number skills are particularly weak (e.g. Farran & Jarrold, 2003; Paterson, Girelli, Butterworth, & Karmiloff-Smith, 2006), whereas, by comparison, language and face-processing skills are considered to be much less severely affected.

Of particular relevance to this book and chapter, individuals with Williams syndrome are often described as having a characteristic "hypersociable" personality, behaving "as if everyone is their friend" (Jones et al., 2000). Parents of individuals with Williams syndrome rate their children as being more empathetic, sensitive, and gregarious than do parents of typically developing children or individuals with other developmental disorders such as Down syndrome, autism, or intellectual delay of mixed aetiology (Doyle, Bellugi, Korenberg, & Graham, 2004; Dykens & Rosner, 1999; Gosch & Pankau, 1997; Jones et al., 2000; Klein-Tasman & Mervis, 2003). Researchers have also reported increased use of social engagement devices and emotion inferences (Reilly, Harrison, & Klima, 1995; Reilly, Losh, Bellugi, & Wulfeck, 2004; see also Jones et al., 2000) and an increased tendency to react empathetically toward another person's distress (Tager-Flusberg & Sullivan, 2000). Moreover, in initial experimental cognitive studies, individuals with Williams syndrome were found to perform well on formal tests of theory of mind and emotion recognition that individuals with autism typically fail (Karmiloff-Smith, Klima, Bellugi, Grant, & Baron-Cohen, 1995; Tager-Flusberg, Boshart, & Baron-Cohen, 1998). Such findings led Bellugi and colleagues to conclude that individuals with Williams syndrome "exhibit a striking contrast to the social and language profiles of individuals with other disorders such as autism" (Bellugi, Lichtenberger, Mills, Galaburda, & Korenberg, 1999, p. 200; see also Bellugi, Wang & Jernigan, 1994). In a similar vein, Baron-Cohen and Hammer (1997) argued that, whereas individuals with autism have extreme "male brains," with better spatial skills than social skills, those with Williams syndrome show the reverse pattern and, as such, may be characterized as having extreme "female brains."

This view of Williams syndrome and autism as diametric opposites has, however, proven to be somewhat simplistic (Tager-Flusberg, Plesa-Skwerer, & Joseph, 2006). Despite their sociable and empathetic personalities, individuals with Williams syndrome are often reported as having high levels of social anxiety (Dykens, 2003; Udwin, Yule, & Martin, 1987). Children with Williams syndrome typically prefer adult company to mixing with their own age group, and have great difficulty making and sustaining friendships (Einfeld, Tonge, & Florio, 1997; Rosner, Hodapp, Fidler, Sagun, & Dykens, 2004; Udwin et al., 1987). The two disorders also overlap clinically. Leyfer, Woodruff-Borden, Klein-Tasman, Fricke, and Mervis (2006) reported that 7 percent of children with Williams syndrome met Diagnostic and Statistical Manual (DSM) criteria for autism spectrum disorders – considerably higher than in the general population. Similarly, Leekam, Burt, & Arnott (2006) noted that, although individuals with Williams syndrome were less impaired than those with autism on the socialization and repetitive behavior scales of the Diagnostic Interview for Social and Communication Disorders (Wing, Leekam, Libby, Gould, & Larcombe, 2002), ratings of communication skills were in fact comparable across the two groups.

Since the mid-1990s, experimental research on Williams syndrome has also moved on considerably, and this is the main focus of the present chapter. We aim to provide a comprehensive review of recent findings in relation to social cognition in Williams syndrome and, where possible, make direct comparisons between studies of Williams syndrome and studies that have employed similar methodologies to investigate autism. We begin by briefly reviewing the language capabilities of individuals with Williams syndrome, with particular reference to pragmatic skills. We then consider the performance of individuals with Williams syndrome on formal tests of theory of mind and its potential precursors in joint attention, before moving on to look at various aspects of face processing. Finally, we review recent evidence concerning the neural mechanisms that potentially underlie the hypersociable personalities of people with Williams syndrome.

Language Abilities in Williams Syndrome

Research on language in Williams syndrome has focused primarily on the structural aspects of language (syntax, phonology, and semantics). It has been widely claimed that language abilities in Williams syndrome are "intact" (e.g. Bellugi, Marks, Bihrle, & Sabo, 1988; Pinker, 1999), but this description appears to be well wide of the mark. Moreover, while few researchers would disagree that the language of individuals with Williams syndrome is relatively good when contrasted with their own visuo-spatial deficits (e.g. Mervis, Robinson, Rowe, Becerra, & Klein-Tasman, 2003), there is little evidence for a dissociation between language and other non-spatial abilities (Brock, 2007). One exception is that individuals with Williams syndrome do appear to perform relatively well on receptive vocabulary tests, in which they are required to match a spoken word to one of a number of pictures (e.g. Vicari et al., 2004). The reason for this is unclear, but it is notable that, on other measures of vocabulary knowledge, individuals with Williams syndrome tend not to show this advantage (e.g. Clahsen, Ring, & Temple, 2004).

A further issue concerns the extent to which language development in Williams syndrome, though clearly delayed, is subject to the same constraints as in typical development. Studies with young infants have indicated that joint attention (discussed in greater detail below), category concepts, and speech-segmentation skills are relatively weak when compared with the level of vocabulary knowledge obtained (e.g. Laing et al., 2002; Nazzi & Karmiloff-Smith, 2002; Nazzi, Paterson, & Karmiloff-Smith, 2003). In each case, the relevant skills resemble those of much younger typically developing children; however, given that these skills may all play an important role in vocabulary learning, relative delays in these areas may indicate that alternative mechanisms are involved in language acquisition. Researchers have argued that there may be "residual" abnormalities in the language of adolescents and adults with Williams syndrome that stem from early deviations from the normal developmental trajectory (see Thomas & Karmiloff-Smith, 2003), but attempts to replicate early findings supporting this view have almost universally failed (see Brock, 2007 for a review).

This focus on structural aspects of language in Williams syndrome has unfortunately meant that, at least until the mid-1990s, there was relatively little research on the pragmatic use of language as a social-communicative tool. Pragmatic skills are severely impaired in autism, even among high-functioning individuals (see, e.g., Tager-Flusberg, Paul, & Lord, 2005), but have often been described as a particular strength in Williams syndrome (Karmiloff-Smith et al., 1995; von Armin & Engel, 1964). Recent studies have, however, challenged such claims. For example, in quali- tative analyses of conversational interactions, individuals with Williams syndrome have been noted to display an over-familiar manner with the experimenter (Udwin & Yule, 1990) and show poor turntaking and topic maintenance (Meyerson & Frank, 1987; but see Stojanovik, 2006). Stojanovik and colleagues (Stojanovik, 2006; Stojanovik, Perkins, & Howard, 2001) have reported that individuals with Williams syndrome have difficulties interpreting the literal or inferential meaning of an experimenter's utterance and providing adequate information in responses: conversations involve little exchange of information and speech is often heavily parasitic on the experimenter's contributions.

Of particular note is a questionnaire study by Laws and Bishop (2004), who found that parents of individuals with Williams syndrome reported significant impairments in conversational coherence, appreciation of conversational context, and development of conversational rapport, as well as tendencies toward stereo- typed conversations and inappropriate initiation of conversations. In comparison with a group of younger typically developing children, those with Williams syn- drome were rated as having greater overall pragmatic difficulties despite equivalent syntactic abilities. Similarly, when compared with individuals with Down syndrome or specific language impairment, they showed significantly better syntax but signifi- cantly greater impairments on the stereotyped conversation and inappropriate initiation subscales.

To summarize, despite initial claims of "preserved" language abilities, formal testing of individuals with Williams syndrome reveal phonological, semantic, and grammatical skills that are broadly in line with overall mental age. In other words, the majority of people with Williams syndrome have significant language difficulties relative to their own typically developing peers. Given the importance of language for the development of social relationships and the difficulties with peer interaction that are often faced by children with more specific language impairments (see, e.g., Conti-Ramsden, Simkin, & Botting, 2006), this is important to bear in mind when considering the origin of social difficulties in Williams syndrome. Moreover, many tests of social competence involve verbal comprehension and production skills – researchers who assume that individuals with Williams syndrome do not have language difficulties run the risk of ignoring potentially important confounds in their studies.

Of greater direct relevance to this chapter, there is also growing evidence that pragmatic skills are not intact in Williams syndrome and may even be relatively impaired with respect to structural aspects of language development; however, further research is obviously required in this area. In particular, the extent to which the pragmatic difficulties associated with Williams syndrome are in any way comparable to those experienced by individuals with autism, or perhaps a subgroup of individuals on the autistic spectrum, is unclear. Research addressing this issue would have important practical consequences as well as being of considerable theoretical interest. Pragmatic deficits in autism are often attributed to impaired theory of mind (e.g. Baron-Cohen, 1988), and it is to this issue that we now turn.

Theory of Mind

"Theory of mind" refers to the ability to understand and predict behavior in terms of underlying mental states. Since the seminal work of Baron-Cohen, Leslie, and Frith (1985), researchers have been interested in the idea that individuals with autism lack a theory of mind and that this deficit may explain many of the social difficulties that they experience. As noted in the introduction to this chapter, Karmiloff-Smith et al. (1995) reported that, in contrast to those with autism, individuals with Williams syndrome performed well on a series of theory-of-mind tests; however, these findings may be misleading, because participants ranged in age from 9 to 23 years – much older than the age at which children typically pass such tasks. Tager-Flusberg and Sullivan therefore conducted a series of studies of theory-of-mind capabilities in younger individuals with Williams syndrome. Their performance was compared with that of age-matched children with either non-specific intellectual delay or Prader–Willi syndrome – a rare genetic disorder that, like Williams syndrome, is also associated with mild learning difficulties (see, e.g., Whittington et al., 2004).

First-order false-belief tasks require participants to discount their own knowledge of the true state of affairs and deduce the beliefs of another uninformed character. For example, in the classic false-location task, participants have to infer that a character who has not seen an object being moved will be under the misapprehension that the object is still in its original location. Such tasks are typically passed by the age of 4 or 5. However, Tager-Flusberg and Sullivan (2000; see also Tager-Flusberg, Sullivan, & Boshart, 1997) reported a pass rate of only 24–29 percent (depending on the question asked) among 4–9-year-old children with Williams syndrome. This was significantly lower than the pass rate for children in either of the two comparison groups, despite the fact that the children with Williams syndrome had somewhat higher verbal mental ages.

A similar picture emerges for "second-order" false-belief tasks, which require participants to reason about a character's false belief about another person's false belief (for example, Molly's father thinks that she does not know what her surprise present is, but in fact she has already seen it). Sullivan and Tager-Flusberg (1999) reported broadly equivalent performance on such tasks among 8–17-year-olds with Williams syndrome and those with Prader–Willi syndrome. Pass rates among children with unspecified intellectual delay were significantly lower than in the other two groups, but these individuals also had somewhat lower verbal mental ages. In a subsequent study with similar groups, Sullivan, Winner, and Tager-Flusberg

(2003) presented stories in which a child protagonist made a false statement and participants were required to decide whether the child was lying or joking. Children with Williams syndrome showed a trend toward poorer performance on second-order knowledge questions and, in attempting to justify their interpretations of the stories, made significantly fewer references to mental states than children in either of the other two groups (see Reilly et al., 2004, for similar results).

Together, the available evidence suggests that, although many individuals with Williams syndrome eventually acquire sophisticated theory of mind and understanding of false belief, the developmental process is delayed and is certainly no more advanced than general cognitive development. Tager-Flusberg and Sullivan (2000) argued, therefore, that Williams syndrome demonstrates the extent to which theory of mind is constrained by more general cognitive and linguistic delay. In a similar vein, De Villiers (2000) has proposed that, in typical development, a representational understanding of mind is closely connected with comprehension of sentential complements (for example, "John said that Mary went shopping"). A number of studies have hinted at particular difficulties in Williams syndrome with the comprehension and production of such complex grammatical structures (Grant, Valian, & Karmiloff-Smith, 2002; Zukowski, 2004), suggesting a potential common cause of theory-of-mind difficulties.

Tager-Flusberg and Sullivan (2000) further proposed that a distinction should be made between "the online immediate judgement of mental state" (termed "social *perception*") and what is traditionally considered to be "theory of mind" or social reasoning. Their suggestion was that in Williams syndrome (but not autism) social perception is relatively intact, but that theory of mind is constrained by more general reasoning abilities. Thus, despite being highly sociable and empathetic in nature, individuals with Williams syndrome have difficulties with more complex social reasoning and therefore struggle to maintain social relationships.

In support of their account, Tager-Flusberg and Sullivan (2000) cited evidence that individuals with Williams syndrome perform well in tests of emotion perception, and this is discussed below. However, it is fair to say that there have been no studies to date that have really addressed "on-line" social cognition in Williams syndrome. An example of the kind of approach that might be taken is provided by studies looking at children's eye movements as they complete variations of the false-location task. Young typically developing children tend to look toward the location in which the uninformed protagonist thinks the object remains, indicating an "implicit" awareness of false belief, even when they immediately then give the incorrect verbal response that the protagonist will look in the object's current location (Clements & Perner, 1994). Ruffman, Garnham, and Rideout (2001) suggested that individuals with autism demonstrate the opposite pattern, looking in the wrong location, even if they can subsequently reason their way to the correct verbal response. If Tager-Flusberg and Sullivan (2000) are correct, then we would predict that children with Williams syndrome would show the pattern evidenced by young typically developing children as opposed to that shown by children with autism.

Joint Attention

While it remains to be determined whether or not the relatively unimpressive performance of individuals with Williams syndrome on theory-of-mind tests is simply
a consequence of the tasks' cognitive and linguistic demands, researchers have also
explored the possibility that social-cognitive difficulties in Williams syndrome may
be related to earlier deficits in engaging in joint attention during infancy. Joint
attention refers to the three-way or "triadic" coordination of attention between an
infant, his or her caregiver, and an object of potential interest. It has been argued
that episodes of joint attention are early evidence of the infant's emerging understanding of others as intentional or mental agents (Tomasello, 1995) and that delays
in the emergence of joint attention in autism (see Charman, 2003) are the early
manifestation of impairment in this representational capacity (Baron-Cohen, 1995;
Leslie, 1987).

A number of studies have noted joint-attention difficulties in Williams syndrome. Using a standardized experimental procedure, Laing et al. (2002) found that
infants with Williams syndrome, aged between 17 months and 4 years 7 months,
were impaired at both initiating and responding to joint-attention bids in comparison to mental-age-matched typically developing children. Specifically, they were
poorer at using pointing to engage in a triadic interaction with their partner and a
toy object. This finding is consistent with an earlier study by Mervis and Bertrand
(1997), who reported that children with Williams syndrome did not respond appropriately to adults' pointing gestures.

One possibility is that, as postulated in the case of autism, deficits in joint attention in Williams syndrome are an early indicator of theory-of-mind difficulties.
However, there appear to be subtle differences in the joint-attention deficits associated with the two disorders. Individuals with autism are relatively unimpaired in
instrumental triadic interactions that function as a request (that is, to direct the
partner's behavior); but have severe difficulties in declarative triadic interactions,
which serve to share awareness, or the experience, of an event or object (Baron-
Cohen, 1989; Mundy & Sigman, 1989). By contrast, Laing et al. (2002) found that
children with Williams syndrome were impaired in their use of both instrumental
and declarative gesturing.

An alternative explanation, therefore, is that infants with Williams syndrome fail
to engage in triadic joint-attention episodes simply because they find objects far less
interesting than faces. Indeed, Mervis, Morris, et al. (2003) found that, compared
to typically developing infants and those with developmental delay, young infants
with Williams syndrome (aged 8 months–2 years 11 months) exhibited extended
looking behavior towards strangers' faces (see also Jones et al., 2000). A similar
point was recently made by Triesch, Teuscher, Deak, and Carlson (2006), who
proposed that infants learn to follow a caregiver's gaze because it predicts the location of interesting visual stimuli in the environment. According to their model,
infants with autism show little gaze-following behavior because they do not look at

the face in the first place (cf. Swettenham et al., 1998); by contrast, infants with Williams syndrome find the face much more rewarding than other objects and so have no motivation to follow the direction of gaze. It is important to point out that, thus far, research on infants with Williams syndrome has focused primarily on the production and comprehension of pointing as opposed to gaze following and that there is no evidence for gaze-following difficulties among older children and adults with Williams syndrome (Gyori, Lukacs, & Pleh, 2004). What remains to be determined is the extent to which the development of such capabilities is delayed and the consequences of this delay for social-cognitive development. Longitudinal research (cf. Charman, 2003; Charman et al., 2000) may help address this issue.

Recognition of Facial Identity

The fascination that individuals with Williams syndrome appear to have with faces could have further important consequences for their social development. The ability to recognize facial expressions of emotion is discussed in depth below; however, until recently, most of the research on face processing in Williams syndrome has focused on processing of facial identity and the claim that individuals with Williams syndrome have "intact" face-processing abilities. Such claims were based almost exclusively on studies using the Benton Faces task (Benton, VanAllen, Hamsher, & Levin, 1978) – a standardized assessment that involves the simultaneous matching of one or more exemplars of a face across different viewpoints or lighting conditions. Individuals with Williams syndrome typically perform better on this task than might be expected on the basis of their visuo-spatial skills or mental age, and performance is often described as being in "the normal range" (Bellugi, Lichtenberger et al., 1999; Bellugi et al., 1994; Gagliardi et al., 2003; Plesa-Skwerer, Verbalis, Schofield, Faja, & Tager-Flusberg, 2006). Critically, however, ceiling effects on this task make it difficult to evaluate claims of "age-appropriate" performance (Farran & Jarrold, 2003), and on other similar measures the performance of individuals with Williams syndrome is poorer than that of age-matched typically developing controls (Deruelle, Mancini, Livet, Casse-Perrot, & de Schonen, 1999; Karmiloff-Smith et al., 2004; Mills et al., 2000; Riby, Doherty-Sneddon, & Bruce, 2008; Tager-Flusberg, Plesa-Skwerer, Faja, & Joseph, 2003) and is typically no better than predicted by mental age (Deruelle et al., 1999; Riby et al., 2008; although see Udwin & Yule, 1991). Indeed, the Benton Faces test does not appear to be as sensitive to face-processing deficits (prosopagnosia) as other tasks and can be completed successfully by comparing individual features rather than processing the face as a whole (Duchaine & Nakayama, 2004; Duchaine and Weidenfeld, 2003).

Karmiloff-Smith (1997) suggested that individuals with Williams syndrome perform well on this task by adopting such a "piecemeal" strategy (see also Deruelle et al., 1999). A number of research groups have investigated this claim by comparing recognition of upright and inverted faces. Typically, adults' ability to discriminate between faces is severely disrupted when the faces are presented upside down, but the same manipulation is less disruptive when faces can be identified on the basis of individual features (e.g. Yin, 1969). It has been widely reported that individuals with Williams syndrome fail to show this inversion effect, indicating a reliance on featural processing (Deruelle et al., 1999; Karmiloff-Smith et al., 2004; Rossen, Jones, Wang, & Klima, 1995), although normal effects of inversion have been reported in several other studies (Mills et al., 2000; Rose et al., 2007; Tager-Flusberg et al., 2003).

In fact, the inversion effect can arise for a number of reasons, so its presence or absence is not necessarily diagnostic of face-processing strategy (Maurer, Grand, & Mondloch, 2002). An alternative research strategy, adopted in more recent studies, is to investigate the ability to discriminate between upright faces that have been manipulated in different ways. Tager-Flusberg et al. (2003) reported that, in contrast to those with autism (Joseph & Tanaka, 2003), individuals with Williams syndrome showed a normal advantage for discriminating between features in the context of a whole face as opposed to in isolation, indicating that they are affected by the facial gestalt when processing features.

Karmiloff-Smith and colleagues (2004) have argued, however, that individuals with Williams syndrome *are* relatively insensitive to the configural information in faces, specifically the distances between features. These authors reported that the participants had difficulties in detecting differences between photographs of faces that had been manipulated by changing the position of the features, although this finding may reflect a response bias rather than differences in accuracy and was not replicated by Riby, Doherty-Sneddon, and Bruce (forthcoming b). Karmiloff-Smith et al. (2004; see also Deruelle et al., 1999) also reported that individuals with Williams syndrome had particular difficulties detecting configural changes in schematic faces (that is, faces made up of geometric shapes), even when performance on the Benton Faces task was controlled for by covariation. This pattern of performance was apparent even among the oldest and most proficient performers in the Williams syndrome group, whereas typically developing children showed a gradual developmental progression toward a more configural approach.

The evidence, although far from conclusive, suggests that individuals with Williams syndrome may have an atypically immature strategy toward face processing (cf. Carey & Diamond, 1977). Given that, unlike children with autism, those with Williams syndrome appear to be fascinated by faces, this cannot be put down to a lack of experience with faces. So why do they fail to develop configural face-processing strategies? One possibility is that atypical face processing is related to more general visual-perceptual impairments associated with Williams syndrome.

This view is supported by studies looking at the neural basis of face perception in Williams syndrome. Mills et al. (2000) recorded event-related potentials (ERPs) while participants viewed pictures of faces. Early ERP components (N100 and P170) were smaller than normal in adults with Williams syndrome, and, unlike in typical adults, these components were not affected by orientation, even though individuals with Williams syndrome showed normal inversion effects in terms of their behavioral accuracy. The authors linked their findings to evidence for subtle structural abnormalities in brain regions involved in visual perception and reported prelimi-nary data showing similar group differences with non-social stimuli (cars).

Complementary results were reported by Mobbs and colleagues (2004) using functional magnetic resonance imaging (fMRI). Adults with Williams syndrome showed normal levels of activation in two regions, the fusiform gyrus (see also Meyer-Lindenberg et al., 2004) and the superior temporal sulcus, that have been linked to face processing in typical individuals (see, e.g., Haxby, Hoffman, & Gobbini, 2000). However, these individuals showed reduced activation of primary and secondary visual cortex and, conversely, increased activation within right pre-frontal, anterior cingulate cortex, thalamic, striatal areas, hippocampus, and middle temporal gyrus, perhaps reflecting compensatory activity related to the increased difficulty of the task for individuals with Williams syndrome.

If individuals with Williams syndrome do have difficulty processing configural information, then, by implication, they must rely heavily on featural information. A further issue, then, is whether they focus on the same features as typically developing children. Adults and children typically show a preference for looking at the eyes and mouths of human faces (Yarbus, 1967). There is some evidence to suggest that individuals with autism focus less on the eyes and perhaps more on the mouth region of faces (e.g. Klin, Jones, Schultz, Volkmar, & Cohen, 2002); however, findings are inconsistent and appear to vary depending on the specific paradigm used. Only two studies have investigated this issue in Williams syndrome, and both indicate that individuals with Williams syndrome recognize people from their eyes and mouths in much the same way as typically developing children. Tager-Flusberg et al. (2003) reported that, like typically developing individuals – and in contrast to individuals with autism (Joseph & Tanaka, 2003) – those with Williams syn-drome were better at detecting changes to the eyes region of the face than changes to the mouth region. Similar findings were reported by Riby et al. (forthcoming b), who also found that, like typically developing children and unlike children with autism (see also Langdell, 1978), those with Williams syndrome were better at matching faces using upper rather than lower facial features.

Recognition of Facial Expressions of Emotion

As noted above, faces provide important information about the emotions and mental states experienced by other people. Given reports of unusually empathetic responses in Williams syndrome, one might expect that individuals with Williams syndrome would perform relatively well on emotion recognition tasks. Indeed, as discussed earlier, Tager-Flusberg and Sullivan (2000) proposed that social *percep-tion* is a definite strength in Williams syndrome. This hypothesis was based in part on the findings of an earlier study by Tager-Flusberg et al. (1998), who presented participants with black-and-white photographs of the eye region and asked them to decide which of two labels best described the emotion in the eyes. Even high-functioning adults with autism find this task difficult (Baron-Cohen, Wheelwright,

& Jolliffe, 1997). In contrast, although adults with Williams syndrome performed worse than age-matched typically developing controls, they outperformed age-matched controls with Prader–Willi syndrome. Tager-Flusberg et al. (1998) concluded, therefore, that "adults with Williams syndrome are quite good at reading both simple and more complex mental state information from the eye region" (p. 635).

A potential concern with this study, however, is that, in the original version of the task, the correct answer was always paired with its semantic opposite. Consequently, individuals with Williams syndrome may have been able to deduce the correct answer on many trials simply on the basis of valence (that is, by determining whether the eyes were "happy" or "unhappy"). Indeed, Plesa-Skwerer, Faja, Schofield, Verbalis, and Tager-Flusberg (2006) found that, using a modified version of the eyes task that avoided this problem, children with Williams syndrome performed no better than a group of children with non-specific learning disabilities, despite being matched on age, vocabulary knowledge, and IQ, and performing significantly better than these controls on the Benton Faces task.

Other studies using whole face stimuli (rather than just the eye region) have similarly found that emotion "reading" in Williams syndrome is no better than that of comparison groups matched on mental age. Findings are consistent across a range of paradigms, including: matching a face to another face with the same emotion (Meyer-Lindenberg et al., 2005; Riby et al., 2008; Tager-Flusberg & Sullivan, 2000); choosing a face that matches a spoken emotion word (Riby et al., 2008); and choosing a word to describe the emotion expressed in a static face (Plesa-Skwerer et al., 2006), in a short video clip (Plesa-Skwerer et al., 2005), or in an image that morphs from a neutral face into an expressive face (Gagliardi et al., 2003). Plesa-Skwerer et al. (2006) further noted that all participants were generally better at recognizing happy faces compared with other emotions. This, the authors suggested, was because all other emotions were negative so were less discriminable. Thus, although individuals with Williams syndrome are able to categorize basic emotions by valence, they may have difficulties further differentiating between emotional expressions (cf. Adolphs, 2002).

Given these findings, we might question the idea that social perception is after all a relative strength in Williams syndrome. One possible mitigating factor is that performance on some of these tasks may be mediated by language abilities, thus disguising any Williams syndrome advantage (Tager-Flusberg & Sullivan, 2000). Alternatively, recognition of facial expressions may be impaired by more general difficulties in processing configural information, as discussed above. Contrary to this view, however, Plesa-Skwerer et al. (2006) recently found that individuals with Williams syndrome were also no better than mental age-matched controls at recognizing *vocal* expressions of emotion. Perhaps then individuals with Williams syndrome are just not especially good at differentiating between emotions. They may still be able to react empathetically in an appropriate way because they can pick up on whether someone is happy or sad even if they have greater difficulty interpreting more complex emotions. All we can say at present is that there is very little evidence to suggest that individuals with Williams syndrome have good emotion recognition skills.

Hypersociability and the Amygdala

In this final section, we consider studies of face processing that have attempted to uncover the origins of hypersociability in Williams syndrome. Bellugi, Adolphs, Cassidy, and Chiles (1999) noted that "social disinhibition" is characteristic, not only of individuals with Williams syndrome, but also of individuals with acquired lesions of the amygdala. These authors explored this similarity by asking individuals with Williams syndrome to rate black-and-white photographs of faces according to how much they would like to go up and begin a conversation with them. Like individuals with bilateral (but not unilateral) amygdala damage (cf. Adolphs, Tranel, & Damasio, 1998), those with Williams syndrome gave unusually high approach-ability ratings to all the faces. More recently, Frigerio et al. (2006) attempted to replicate this finding using face stimuli that were rated (by typically developing adults) as being of similar approachability to those used by Bellugi and colleagues, as well as faces that were considered much less approachable. Participants with Williams syndrome were more likely than typically developing controls to give extreme negative as well as positive ratings, perhaps, as the authors suggested, reflecting their sociable yet socially anxious personalities. However, given the diffi-culties that individuals with developmental disorders often have in using rating scales appropriately (cf. Hartley & Maclean, 2006), the findings from these two studies should be treated with caution. Having said that, recent fMRI and psycho-physical studies reviewed below do appear to support the idea that amygdala functioning is atypical in Williams syndrome.

Meyer-Lindenberg and colleagues (2005) conducted an fMRI study in which participants were presented with pictures of angry or afraid faces. Relative to typi-cally developing controls, individuals with Williams syndrome showed reduced amygdala activation; however, they showed a relative increase in amygdala activa-tion to non-social threatening stimuli (for example, spiders or car crashes). The authors suggested that this latter finding may be related to the high levels of non-social anxiety and phobias associated with the syndrome (see, e.g., Dykens, 2003; Leyfer et al., 2006). Meyer-Lindenberg and colleagues also noted that, whereas typi-cally developing controls showed increases in activation of various prefrontal regions (dorso-lateral and medial prefrontal cortex and orbitofrontal cortex) when viewing faces as compared to non-social scenes, this effect was not present in the Williams syndrome group. These prefrontal regions are highly interconnected with the amygdala and have been implicated in regulation of amygdala function (Adolphs, 2003). Path analysis of the fMRI data indicated atypical interactions between frontal regions and the amygdala in Williams syndrome, suggesting that the unusual social profile associated with Williams syndrome may be a reflection of a reduced modu-lating effect of prefrontal regions on amygdala function.

In typical individuals, amygdala activation is increased by direct eye contact. Unlike many children with autism, those with Williams syndrome do not appear to find eye contact aversive. Indeed, as noted above in relation to joint attention, infants with Williams syndrome appear to be transfixed by faces, and several authors have commented upon the unusual intensity of eye contact they exhibit (Jones et al., 2000; Mervis, Morris et al., 2003). Riby (2006) reported a relatively low level of autonomic arousal in children with Williams syndrome, as measured by galvanic skin responses. This suggests the possibility that, when individuals with Williams syndrome view faces, the resultant increase in arousal does not become uncomfortable and they are able to maintain fixation for longer than normal. These findings are only preliminary but provide an interesting contrast with studies of autism (e.g. Hutt, Hutt, Lee, & Ousted, 1964) and suggest a possible link between amygdala functioning and eye contact in Williams syndrome. It should be noted that Mobbs et al. (2004) reported normal activation of the amygdala when viewing faces with either direct or indirect gaze. Unfortunately, however, the design of the study was such that it was impossible to compare different trial types. Clearly, further research is needed in this area.

Conclusions

Williams syndrome has often been contrasted with autism, and there are certainly some interesting points of difference between the two disorders, as discussed below. However, it is clear that a straightforward dissociation between impaired social cognition in autism and "intact" functioning in Williams syndrome is untenable. In particular, there is very little evidence that any aspects of language, theory of mind, or face processing are in any sense "preserved" in Williams syndrome. Phonological, semantic, and grammatical language abilities are broadly in line with overall intelligence; pragmatic language skills are, if anything, poorer than structural language abilities; and the same can also be said of performance on theory-of-mind tests. Although individuals with Williams syndrome perform well on one specific face-matching measure, in general, their ability to match faces on either identity or emotional expression is no better than mental-age-based predictions.

Although social and linguistic skills in Williams syndrome are perhaps less impressive than one might be led to believe, the theoretical importance of the disorder remains. In particular, Williams syndrome provides a contrast with other disorders in which these abilities are severely and specifically impaired. Brock (2007) highlighted the contrast between language abilities in Williams syndrome and Down syndrome, arguing that there is clearly some factor (perhaps related to phonological processing) that prevents structural language development in Down syndrome reaching the level that is achieved by individuals with Williams syndrome of comparable non-verbal intelligence. In a similar vein, it is clear that there are some developmental constraints that prevent individuals with autism achieving the levels of social-cognitive competence one would predict on the basis of their overall intelligence. For most individuals with Williams syndrome, these additional constraints do not appear to be in operation – social-cognitive abilities are only constrained by more general verbal and non-verbal abilities (cf. Tager-Flusberg & Sullivan, 2000).

It is, nevertheless, important to make a distinction here between constraints on the process of social-cognitive development and confounding factors that might constrain performance on measures of social-cognitive functioning. For example, as noted earlier, language difficulties may impact upon theory-of-mind development in Williams syndrome but are also likely to make conventional theory-of-mind tasks difficult. Only by carefully designing studies to control for these difficulties or minimize their impact will this issue be resolved.

Further consideration should also be given to the more subtle patterns of similarities and differences between autism and Williams syndrome. For example, despite superficially similar impairments in joint attention, subsequent social capabilities are clearly less impaired in Williams syndrome than in autism. This suggests that subtle group differences in the pattern of joint-attention capabilities and their origins may illuminate the causal pathways leading from joint-attention to social-cognitive deficits. Similarly, when considering face processing, in some respects individuals with Williams syndrome resemble those with autism, despite clearly having extensive experience of processing faces. Again, direct comparison of the two disorders may prove instructive. Finally, both autism and Williams syndrome have been linked to abnormalities of the amygdala and its interaction with the prefrontal cortex. Comparing the neural basis of social functioning in autism and Williams syndrome should refine theories of both disorders.

In sum, the answer to the question posed in the title is that, no, Williams syndrome is not simply the "other end of the spectrum" to autism. While there is still much work to be done, it is clear that the differences between the disorders are far more subtle and, potentially, far more interesting.

Note

We are grateful to Annette Karmiloff-Smith for comments on an earlier draft of this chapter.

References

Adolphs, R. (2002). Neural systems for recognizing emotion. *Current Opinion in Neurobiology*, 12, 169–177.

Adolphs, R. (2003). Cognitive neuroscience of human social behaviour. *Nature Reviews Neuroscience*, 4, 165–178.

Adolphs, R., Tranel, D., & Damasio, A. R. (1998). The human amygdala in social judgement. *Nature*, 393, 470–475.

Baron-Cohen, S. (1988) Does the study of autism justify minimalist innate modularity? *Learning and Individual Differences*, 10, 179–191.

Baron-Cohen, S. (1989). Perceptual role-taking and proto-declarative pointing in autism. *British Journal of Developmental Psychology*, 7, 113–127.

Baron-Cohen, S. (1995). *Mindblindness: An Essay on Autism and Theory of Mind*. Cambridge, MA: MIT Press.

Baron-Cohen, S., & Hammer, J. (1997). Is autism an extreme form of the "male brain"? *Advances in Infancy Research*, 11, 193–217.

Baron-Cohen, S., Leslie, A. M., & Frith, U. (1985). Does the autistic child have a "theory of mind"? *Cognition*, 21, 37–46.

Baron-Cohen, S., Wheelwright, S., & Jolliffe, T. (1997). Is there a "language of the eyes"? Evidence from normal adults and adults with autism or Asperger syndrome. *Visual Cognition*, 4, 311–331.

Bellugi, U., Adolphs, R., Cassady, C., & Chiles, M. (1999). Towards the neural basis for hyper-sociability in a genetic syndrome, *Neuroreport*, 10, 1653–1657.

Bellugi, U., Lichtenberger, L., Mills, D., Galaburda, A., & Korenberg, J. R. (1999). Bridging cognition, the brain and molecular genetics: evidence from Williams syndrome. *Trends in Neurosciences*, 22, 197–207.

Bellugi, U., Marks, S., Bihrle, A., & Sabo, H. (1988). Dissociation between language and cognitive function in Williams Syndrome. In D. Bishop & K. Mogford (Eds.), *Language Development in Exceptional Circumstances*. Edinburgh: Churchill Livingstone.

Bellugi, U., Wang, P., & Jernigan, T. (1994). Williams syndrome: An unusual neuropsychological profile. In S. Broman & J. Grafman (Eds.), *Atypical Cognitive Deficits in Developmental Disorders: Implications for Brain Function*, Hillsdale, NJ: Lawrence Erlbaum.

Benton, A., VanAllen, M., Hamsher, K., & Levin, H. (1978). *Test of Facial Recognition Manual*. Iowa City, IA: Benton Laboratory of Neuropsychology.

Brock, J. (2007). Language abilities in Williams syndrome: A critical review. *Development and Psychopathology*, 19, 97–127.

Carey, S., & Diamond, R. (1977). From piecemeal to configurational representation of faces. *Science*, 195, 312–314.

Charman, T. (2003). Why is joint attention a pivotal skill in autism? *Philosophical Transactions of the Royal Society London, B*, 358, 315–324.

Charman, T., Baron-Cohen, S., Swettenham, J., Baird, G., Cox, A., & Drew, A. (2000). Testing joint attention, imitation, and play as infancy precursors to language and theory of mind. *Cognitive Development*, 15, 481–498.

Clahsen, H., Ring, M., & Temple, C. M. (2004). Lexical and morphological skills in English-speaking children with Williams syndrome. In S. Bartke & J. Siegmüller (Eds.), *Williams Syndrome across Languages* (pp. 222–244). Amsterdam: John Benjamins.

Clements, W. A., & Perner, J. (1994). Implicit understanding of belief. *Cognitive Development*, 9, 377–395.

Conti-Ramsden, G., Simkin, Z., & Botting, N. (2006). The prevalence of autistic spectrum disorders in adolescents with a history of specific language impairment (SLI). *Journal of Child Psychology and Psychiatry*, 47, 621–628.

Deruelle, C., Mancini, J., Livet, M. O., Casse-Perrot, C., & de Schonen, S. (1999). Configural and local processing of faces in children with Williams syndrome, *Brain and Cognition*, 41, 276–298.

De Villiers, J. (2000). Language and theory of mind: What are the developmental relationships? In S. Baron-Cohen, H. Tager-Flusberg, & D. J. Cohen (Eds.), *Understanding Other Minds: Perspectives from Developmental Cognitive Neuroscience*. 2nd edn. Oxford: Oxford University Press.

Donnai, D., & Karmiloff-Smith, A. (2000). Williams syndrome: From genotype through to the cognitive phenotype. *American Journal of Medical Genetics*, 97, 164–171.

Doyle, T. F., Bellugi, U., Korenberg, J. R., & Graham, J. (2004). "Everybody in the world is my friend" Hypersociability in young children with Williams syndrome. *American Journal of Medical Genetics*, 124A, 263–273.

Duchaine, B. C., & Nakayama, K. (2004). Developmental prosopagnosia and the Benton Facial Recognition Test. *Neurology*, 62, 1219–1220.

Duchaine, B. C., & Weidenfeld, A. (2003). An evalutaion of two commonly used tests of unfamiliar face recognition. *Neuropsychologia*, 41, 713–720.

Dykens, E. M. (2003). Anxiety, fears, and phobias in persons with Williams syndrome. *Developmental Neuropsychology*, 23, 291–316.

Dykens, E. M., & Rosner, B. (1999). Refining behavioural phenotypes: Personality-motivation in Williams and Pradar–Willi syndromes. *American Journal of Mental Retardation*, 104, 158–169.

Einfeld, S., Tonge, B., & Florio, T. (1997). Behavioural and emotional disturbance in individuals with Williams syndrome. *American Journal of Mental Retardation*, 102, 45–53.

Farran, E. K., & Jarrold, C. (2003). Visuo-spatial cognition in Williams syndrome: Reviewing and accounting for strengths and weaknesses in performance. *Developmental Neuropsychology*, 23, 173–200.

Frigerio, E., Burt, D. M., Gagliardi, C., Cioffi, G., Martelli, S., Perrett, D. I., & Borgatti, R. (2006). Is everybody always my friend? Perception of approachability in Williams syndrome. *Neuropsychologia*, 44, 254–259.

Gagliardi, C., Frigerio, E., Burt, D. M., Cazzaniga, I., Perrett, D. I., & Borgatti, R. (2003). Facial expression recognition in Williams syndrome, *Neuropsychologia*, 41, 733–738.

Gosch, A., & Pankau, R. (1997). Personality characteristics and behaviour problems in individuals of different ages with Williams syndrome. *Developmental Medicine and Child Neurology*, 39, 527–533.

Grant, J., Valian, V., & Karmiloff-Smith, A. (2002). A study of relative clauses in Williams syndrome. *Journal of Child Language*, 29, 403– 416.

Gyori, M., Lukacs, A., & Pleh, C. (2004). Towards the understanding of the neurogenesis of social cognition: Evidence from impaired populations. *Journal of Cultural and Evolutionary Psychology*, 2, 261–282.

Hartley, S. L., & Maclean, W. E. (2006). A review of the reliability and validity of Likert-type scales for people with intellectual disability. *Journal of Intellectual Disability Research*, 50, 813.

Haxby, J. V., Hoffman, E. A., & Gobbini, M. I. (2000). The distributed human neural system for face perception. *Trends in Cognitive Sciences*, 4, 223–233.

Howlin, P., Davies, M., & Udwin, O. (1998). Cognitive functioning in adults with Williams syndrome. *Journal of Child Psychology and Psychiatry*, 39, 183–189.

Hutt, C., Hutt, A. J., Lee, D., & Ousted, C. (1964). Arousal and childhood autism. *Nature*, 204, 908–909.

Jones, W., Bellugi, U., Lai, Z., Chiles, M., Reilly, J., Lincoln, A., & Adophs, R. (2000). Hypersociability in Williams syndrome. *Journal of Cognitive Neuroscience*, 12, 30–46.

Joseph, R. M., & Tanaka, J (2003). Holistic and part-based face recognition in children with autism. *Journal of Child Psychology and Psychiatry*, 44, 529–542.

Karmiloff-Smith, A. (1997). Crucial differences between developmental cognitive neuroscience and adult neuropsychology, *Developmental Neuropsychology*, 13, 513–524.

Karmiloff-Smith, A., Klima, E., Bellugi, U., Grant, J., & Baron-Cohen, S. (1995). Is there a social module? Language, face processing and theory of mind in individuals with Williams syndrome. *Journal of Cognitive Neuroscience*, 7, 196–208.

Karmiloff-Smith, A., Thomas, M., Annaz, D., Humphreys, K., Ewing, S., Brace, N., Duuren, M., Pike, G., Grice, S., & Campbell, R. (2004). Exploring the Williams syndrome face-processing debate: The importance of building developmental trajectories. *Journal of Child Psychology and Psychiatry*, 45, 1258–1274.

Klein-Tasman, B. P., & Mervis, C. B. (2003). Distinctive personality characteristics of 8-, 9-, and 10-year-olds with Williams syndrome. *Developmental Neuropsychology*, 23, 269–290.

Klin, A., Jones, W., Schultz, R., Volkmar, F., & Cohen, D. (2002). Visual fixation patterns during viewing of naturalistic social situations as predictors of social competence in individuals with autism. *Archives of General Psychiatry*, 59, 809–816.

Laing, E., Butterworth, G., Ansari, D., Gsödl, M., Longhi, E., Panagiotaki, G., Paterson, S., & Karmiloff-Smith, A. (2002). Atypical development of language and social communication in toddlers with Williams syndrome. *Developmental Science*, 5, 233–246.

Langdell, T. (1978). Recognition of faces: An approach to the study of autism. *Journal of Child Psychology and Psychiatry*, 19, 255–268.

Laws, G., & Bishop, D. V. M. (2004). Pragmatic language impairment and social deficits in Williams syndrome: A comparison with Down's syndrome and specific language impairment. *International Journal of Language and Communication Disorders*, 39, 45–64.

Leekam, S., Burt, M., & Arnott, B. (2006). Sensory symptoms and sociability in autism and Williams syndrome. Poster presented at International Meeting for Autism Research, Montreal, June.

Leslie, A. M. (1987). Pretence and representation: The origins of "theory of mind". *Psychological Review*, 94, 412–426.

Leyfer, O. T., Woodruff-Borden, J., Klein-Tasman, B. P., Fricke, J. S., & Mervis, C. B. (2006). Prevalence of psychiatric disorders in 4 to 16-year-olds with Williams syndrome. *American Journal of Medical Genetics B: Neuropsychiatric Genetics*, 141, 615–622.

Maurer, D., Grand, R. L., & Mondloch, C. J. (2002). The many faces of configural processing. *Trends in Cognitive Sciences*, 6, 255–260.

Mervis, C. B., & Bertrand, J. (1997). Developmental relations between cognition and language. In L. B. Adamson & M. A. Romski (Eds.), *Communication and Language Acquisition: Discoveries from Atypical Development*. Baltimore, MD: Paul Brookes Publishing.

Mervis, C. B., Morris, C. A., Klein, T., Bonita, P., Bertrand, J., Kwitny, S., Appelbaum, L. G., & Rice, C. E. (2003). Attentional characteristics of infants and toddlers with Williams syndrome during triadic interactions. *Developmental Neuropsychology*, 23, 243–268.

Mervis, C. B., Robinson, B. F., Rowe, M. L., Becerra, A. M., & Klein-Tasman, B. P. (2003). Language abilities of individuals with Williams syndrome. *International Review of Research in Mental Retardation*, 27, 35–81.

Meyer-Lindenberg, A., Hariri, A. R., Munoz, K. E., Mervis, C. B., Mattay, V. S., Morria, C. A., & Berman, K. F. (2005). Neural correlates of genetically abnormal social cognition in Williams syndrome. *Nature Neuroscience*, 8, 991–993.

Meyer-Lindenberg, A., Kohn, P., Mervis, C. B., Kippenhan, J. S., Olsen, R. K., Morris, C. A., & Berman, K. F. (2004). Neural basis of genetically determined visuospatial construction deficit in Williams syndrome. *Neuron*, 43, 623.

Meyerson, M. D., & Frank, R. A. (1987). Language, speech and hearing in Williams syndrome: Intervention approaches and research needs. *Developmental Medicine and Child Neurology*, 29, 258–270.

Mills, D. L., Alvarez, T. D., St George, M., Appelbaum, L. G., Bellugi, U., & Neville, H. (2000). Electrophysiological studies of face processing in Williams syndrome. *Journal of Cognitive Neuroscience*, 12, 47–64.

Mobbs, D., Garrett, A., Menon, V., Rose, F., Bellugi, U., & Reiss, L. (2004). Anomalous brain activation during face and gaze processing in Williams syndrome. *Neurology*, 62, 2070–2076.

Morris, C. A. (2006). The dysmorphology, genetics, and natural history of Williams–Beuren syndrome. In C. A. Morris, H. M. Lenhoff, & P. P. Wang (Eds.), *Williams–Beuren Syndrome: Research, Evaluation, and Treatment* (pp. 3–17). Baltimore, MD: Johns Hopkins University Press.

Mundy, P., & Sigman, P. (1989). Theoretical implications of joint attention deficits in autism. *Development and Psychopathology*, 1, 173–184.

Nazzi, T., & Karmiloff-Smith, A. (2002). Early categorization abilities in young children with Williams syndrome. *Neuroreport*, 13, 1259–1262.

Nazzi, T., Paterson, S., & Karmiloff-Smith, A. (2003). Word segmentation by infants with Williams syndrome. *Infancy*, 4, 251–271.

Paterson, S. J., Girelli, L., Butterworth, B., & Karmiloff-Smith, A. (2006). Are numerical impairments syndrome specific? Evidence from Williams syndrome and Down's syndrome. *Journal of Child Psychology and Psychiatry*, 47, 190–204.

Pinker, S. (1999). *Words and Rules*. London: Weidenfeld & Nicolson.

Plesa-Skwerer, D., Faja, S., Schofield, C., Verbalis, A., & Tager-Flusberg, H. (2006). Perceiving facial and vocal expressions of emotion in individuals with Williams syndrome. *American Journal of Mental Retardation*, 111, 15–26.

Plesa-Skwerer, D., Verbalis, A., Schofield, C., Faja, S., & Tager-Flusberg, H. (2005). Social-perceptual abilities in adolescents and adults with Williams syndrome. *Cognitive Neuropsychology*, 23, 1–12.

Reilly, J., Harrison, D., & Klima, E. S. (1995). Emotional talk and talk about emotions. *Genetic Counseling, Special Issue*, 6, 158–159.

Reilly, J., Losh, M., Bellugi, U., & Wulfeck, B. (2004). "Frog, where are you?" Narratives in children with specific language impairment, early focal brain injury, and Williams syndrome. *Brain and Language*, 88, 229–247.

Riby, D. M. (2006). Face processing in Williams syndrome and autism. Unpublished doctoral thesis. University of Stirling.

Riby, D. M., Doherty-Sneddon, G., & Bruce, V. (2008). Exploring face perception in disorders of development: Evidence from Williams syndrome and autism. *Journal of Neuropsychology*, 2, 47–64.

Riby, D. M., Doherty-Sneddon, G., & Bruce, V. (forthcoming). The eyes or the mouth? Feature salience and unfamiliar face processing in Williams syndrome and autism. *Quarterly Journal of Experimental Psychology*.

Rose, F. E., Lincoln, A. J., Lai, Z., Ene, M., Searcy, Y. M., & Bellugi, U. (2007). Orientation and affective expression effects on face recognition in Williams syndrome and autism. *Journal of Autism and Developmental Disorders*, 37, 513–522.

Rosner, B. A., Hodapp, R. M., Fidler, D. J., Sagun, J. N., & Dykens, E. M. (2004). Social competence in persons with Prader–Willi, Williams and Down's syndromes. *Journal of Applied Research in Intellectual Disabilities*, 17, 209–217.

Rossen, M. L., Jones, W., Wang, P. P., & Klima, E. S. (1995). Face processing: Remarkable sparing in Williams syndrome. *Genetic Counseling, Special Issue*, 6, 138–140.

Ruffman, T., Garnham, W., & Rideout, P. (2001). Social understanding in autism: Eye gaze as a measure of core insights. *Journal of Child Psychology and Psychiatry*, 42, 1083–1094.

Stojanovik, V. (2006). Social interaction deficits and conversational inadequacy in Williams syndrome. *Journal of Neurolinguistics*, 19, 157–173.

Stojanovik, V., Perkins, M., & Howard, S. (2001). Language and conversational abilities in Williams syndrome: How good is good? *International Journal of Language and Communication Disorders*, 36, 234–239.

Sullivan, K., & Tager-Flusberg, H. (1999). Second-order belief attribution in Williams syndrome: Intact or impaired? *American Journal of Mental Retardation*, 104, 523–532.

Sullivan, K., Winner, E., & Tager-Flusberg, H. (2003). Can adolescents with Williams syndrome tell the difference between lies and jokes? *Developmental Neuropsychology*, 23, 85–103.

Swettenham, J., Baron-Cohen, S., Charman, T., Cox, A., Baird, G., Drew, A., Rees, L., & Wheelwright, S. (1998). The frequency and distribution of spontaneous attention shifts between social and nonsocial stimuli in autistic, typically developing, and nonautistic developmentally delayed infants. *Journal of Child Psychology and Psychiatry*, 39, 747–753.

Tager-Flusberg, H., Boshart, J., & Baron-Cohen, S. (1998). Reading the windows to the soul: Evidence of domain-specific sparing in Williams syndrome. *Journal of Cognitive Neuroscience*, 10, 631–639.

Tager-Flusberg, H., Paul, R., & Lord, C. (2005). Language and communication in autism. In F. Volkmar, R. Paul, A. Klin, & D. J. Cohen (Eds.), *Handbook of Autism and Pervasive Developmental Disorder*. 3rd edn. (vol. 1, pp. 335–364). Wiley: New York.

Tager-Flusberg, H., Plesa-Skwerer, D., Faja, S., & Joseph, R. M. (2003). People with Williams syndrome process faces holistically. *Cognition*, 89, 11–24.

Tager-Flusberg, H., Plesa Skwerer, D., & Joseph, R. M. (2006). Model syndromes for investigating social cognitive and affective neuroscience: A comparison of autism and Williams syndrome. *Social Cognitive and Affective Neuroscience*, 1, 175–182.

Tager-Flusberg, H., & Sullivan, K. (2000). A componential view of theory of mind: Evidence from Williams syndrome. *Cognition*, 76, 59–90.

Tager-Flusberg, H., Sullivan, K., & Boshart, J. (1997). Executive functions and performance on false belief tasks. *Developmental Neuropsychology*, 13, 487–493.

Thomas, M. S. C., & Karmiloff-Smith, A. (2003). Modeling language acquisition in atypical phenotypes. *Psychological Review*, 110, 647–682.

Tomasello, M. (1995). Joint attention as social cognition. In C. Moore & P. Dunham (Eds.), *Joint Attention: Its Origins and Role in Development* (pp. 85–101). Hillsdale, NJ: Lawrence Erlbaum.

Triesch, J., Teuscher, C., Deak, G. O., & Carlson, E. (2006). Gaze following: Why (not) learn it? *Developmental Science*, 9, 125–157.

Udwin, O., & Yule, W. (1990). Expressive language of children with Williams syndrome. *American Journal of Medical Genetics Supplement*, 6, 108–114.

Udwin, O., & Yule, W. (1991). A cognitive and behavioural phenotype in Williams syndrome. *Journal of Clinical Experimental Neuropsychology*, 13, 232–244.

Udwin, O., Yule, W., & Martin, N. (1987). Cognitive abilities and behavioural characteristics of children with idiopathic infantile hypercalcemia. *Journal of Child Psychology and Psychiatry*, 28, 297–309.

Vicari, S., Bates, E., Caselli, M. C., Pasqualetti, P., Gagliardi, C., Tonucci, F., & Volterra, V. (2004). Neuropsychological profile of Italians with Williams syndrome: An example of a dissociation between language and cognition? *Journal of the International Neuropsychological Society*, 10, 862–876.

von Armin, G., & Engel, P. (1964). Mental retardation related to hypercalcaemia. *Developmental Medicine and Child Neurology*, 6, 366–377.

Whittington, J., Holland, A., Webb, T., Butler, J., Clarke, D., & Boer, H. (2004). Cognitive abilities and genotype in a population-based sample of people with Prader–Willi syndrome. *Journal of Intellectual Disability Research*, 48, 172–187.

Wing, L., Leekam, S. R., Libby, S. J., Gould, J., & Larcombe, M. (2002). The Diagnostic Interview for Social and Communication Disorders: Background, inter-rater reliability and clinical use. *Journal of Child Psychology and Psychiatry*, 43, 307–325.

Yarbus, A. L. (1967). *Eye Movements and Vision.* New York: Plenum Press.

Yin, R. K. (1969). Looking at upside down faces. *Journal of Experimental Psychology*, 81, 141–145.

Zukowski, A. (2004). Investigating knowledge of complex syntax: Insights from experimental studies of Williams syndrome. In M. L. Rice & S. F. Warren (Eds.), *Developmental Language Disorders: From Phenotypes to Etiologies.* Mahwah, NJ: Laurence Erlbaum.

Part Five
Commentaries

Chapter 19

Commentary: Mutual Recognition as a Foundation of Sociality and Social Comfort

Philippe Rochat

What makes us more or less understanding and feeling of each other? What does the experience of being connected or disconnected with one another actually mean psychologically? These questions are central to social cognition and require more than an engineering look at how we perceive and know people. Here I propose that social cognition is driven by the basic need to affiliate with others and that theories of mind are developmental by-products of this basic need. There is a primary affective and motivational context to the development of social cognition that deserves much more experimental scrutiny. At the core of this context, there is the need for mutual recognition and acknowledgment.

Social cognition is not an end in itself, but primarily a means to be connected and to "commune" with others, enjoying rather than dreading one another, overcoming tensions, gaining respect, building trust, getting our ways. We "cognize" and rationalize about other people as we show concern, try to help, cooperate, compete, or get even in revenge.

Most important is the fact that we expect similar treatment from others. We expect them to cognize and feel about us in the same way as we do toward them, expecting social payoffs or punishments from our actions, anticipating reciprocal understanding, validation, respect, prestige, or denigration in return. Viewed this way, social cognition is deeply embedded in a complex mirror game of reciprocation, mutual exchanges, and expectations. This is the view I present here.

In the complex mirror game, a context that characterizes human transactions, social cognition cannot simply be reduced to figuring and processing by inference what is hidden in the head of a particular individual. It is more relevant to consider social cognition as the process by which one builds and negotiates values such as respect and trust in relation to others, values that are shared and in which individuals can recognize themselves and be recognized by others as a measure of their social affiliation.

I will propose here that what underlies sociality and constitutes the experience of social comfort is individuals' sense of affiliation with others. The question of interest that derives from this proposition and should be at the core of social cognition is: what gives individuals the sense of their affiliation?

What is Sociality and What Constitutes Social Comfort?

Sociality and social comfort are of particular interest here. They are too often left to the exclusive consideration of clinicians and too rarely considered by developmental and experimental psychologists. They raise an issue that is all important to our daily existences, regardless of age and culture. This issue is what does it mean to feel more or less comfortable with others, to be socially "connected" as opposed to "disconnected," to pull toward and feel accepted, or, on the contrary, to pull away and feel socially rejected. My intention here is to address the question of what is sociality and what constitutes feelings of social comfort early in life and what these feelings mean in the course of the first years.

To do so, I propose to take a meta-step and consider social cognition in the perspective of early development, but for what it means in the life of the human child rather than how the child functions and grows as an information-processing capacity. My focus is on the affective and experiential aspects of social cognition early in life, a different take compared to most of the chapters assembled in this book.

In the context of the current debate on the origins of theories of mind and empathic feelings, my take is that social cognition encompasses much more than the two main views debated in the theory-of-mind literature, either the building of theories (e.g. Gopnick & Meltzoff, 1997) or the representational simulation of what is on the mind of others (e.g. Goldman & Sripada, 2005). This idea is not new, but I attempt to give it a new spin (see, e.g, Gallagher & Hutto, 2007; Hobson & Hobson, Chapter 15, this volume; Zahavi, 2006). In particular, I would like to make my case by discussing a common fact that is too often overlooked by cognitive psychologists, the fact that we are more or less sociable, more or less "inclined to associate with or be in the company of others."[1]

Beyond the "Engineering" Look at Social Cognition

We lose meaning by reducing the perception and understanding of people, including the self (i.e., social cognition[2]), to the issue of controlling and predicting behavior in the strict behaviorist and "engineering" sense. It is far more complex and challenging than just construing what others, including the self, are going to do next, what is on their mind, what kind of beliefs they hold, and whether their actions are intentional or not. Obviously, all these features are crucial parts of social cognition, but they are only the "cold" tip of the iceberg. They represent the engineering look at social cognition, what it takes "mechanically" to be socially adapted and functional in relation to others. What perceptual cues need to be picked up, what joint-attention capacities need to be in place, what degrees of executive functioning or representational abilities need to be operational for one to be able to learn, collaborate, and in general be productive when in contact with others. This is what cognitive psychologists mainly focus on, interested in the building of representations about the mind states of others: what their intentions are or what beliefs they hold. But this is only part of the story behind social cognition. It does not deal with what motivates us to relate socially the way we do. It does not tell us much about the nature of sociality.

By loose analogy, the meaning of cell phones and how they took over our lives are far more than what the analysis of how they are built and wired, and what function corresponds to what button, might reveal. The engineering power and configuration of the machine do not tell us why we use them in such an uncontrollable way, why it is so hard for most people to turn them off, and why they are so popular across generations and cultures. The engineering look does not inform us how the cell phone has changed the way we connect with one another, or the meaning this cultural artifact has in contemporary life. It misses the primal psychological reasons that lie behind what has ontological and developmental primacy: our basic need to be always faster in our transactions and continuously to be in touch with one another.

So, beyond the engineering look, the question is how and why do we engage in social cognition? How and why are we so compelled from a tender age to figure others' disposition, intention, and mental states? It is probably not just because we are wired to do so and have an early propensity to enact inherited potentials that are either there from the start or maturing, such as mirror neuron systems, theory building, or imitative capacities. Upstream, I shall contend, there is a major, foundational force that drives it all. This force is the basic need to affiliate with one another.

Motivational Roots of Social Cognition

Explicit social cognition such as theories of mind or the understanding of others' disposition is probably a by-product of a basic need to affiliate, the need to be and to feel inclusively recognized by others – the basic affiliative need (BAN) (see Rochat, forthcoming). In this perspective, social cognition is a special adaptation, possibly unique to our species, an adaptation to the basic need to connect and be part of others' life (Rochat, 2007).

This premiss dictates a different look at social cognition, a look that gives more explanatory power to the relational, affective, and emotional context of social cognition and what motivates our transactions with one another. From this premiss derives the general theoretical stance that social cognition does not occur or develop in the privacy of individuals' head. We do not experience others just by theorizing or simulating what is on their mind. On the contrary, social cognition is primarily rooted in relational transactions that are affective and emotional, driven by the need to affiliate and to be an integral part in the life of others. It operates at an interpersonal rather than an intrapersonal level, rooted in the fact that we essentially live through the eyes of others.

To be human is indeed not just having the ability to generate theories of mind or the capacity to take an intentional stance or to simulate the mental states of others by taking a "like-me-stance". It is primarily to care about how much empathy, hence acknowledgment and recognition of our own person, we generate in others – the fact that we care about our reputation as no other animal species does (Rochat, 2006a).

Honor, respectability, and social success – however one measures social prestige and recognition[3] – are universal values evolved across human cultures. We all develop our understanding of others in the context of these values. A primary motive for understanding others is to monitor our own social situation, how others perceive and represent our embodied person. The need to be recognized ultimately drives social cognition. It is a general motivation that determines much of what we understand about others, the social information that is processed, and what children develop in their social understanding. The concern about reputation does have a central place in the human psychic that cannot be overlooked. But how can we render operational and testable such a general theoretical construct?

Reputation as a value entails, in order to be represented, a differentiation between first- and third-person perspective, much of what theories of mind and other higher-order social-cognitive capacities entail. But it entails also something far more basic, an affective core around which social cognition is built. This affective core is the direct experience of being more or less *acknowledged* by others.

Uniqueness of Human Sociality

In order to make sense of others, rationalize about them, and eventually learn from them – goals of social cognition as it is typically researched and conceived (see the majority of chapters in this book) – you need to be attuned and psychologically "open" to them and have some "feelings" about them, rather than just processing them as information providers.

In this perspective, I assemble under the umbrella term of "sociality" the feeling experience of "relatedness," "attunement," or "connectedness", what is sometime described as "the critical connection with others" (Tronick, 2005). These feelings are the motivational core of social cognition and its development – they are what gives it its meanings and reasons to exist.

In comparison with other mammalian species, even close primate relatives, humans are born highly altricial (dependent on others) for their healthy growth, with a particularly late onset of basic autonomy in feeding or locomotion. In addition, human physiological and behavioral development is noticeably slower compared to the young of any other mammalian species – this in spite of a small litter, which typically correlates with precocity in all other species (Gould, 1977; see also Rochat, 2001).

From the outset and typically for the rest of our life (Robinson Crusoe(s) aside), we are highly dependent on others for food, comfort, and protection, but also for instruction, achievements, and, in general, for affective support and emotional well-being. Humans have the particularity to be born too soon. The first months of human life can be equated to some sort of "extero-gestation" (Montagu, 1961). The prolonged period of immaturity following human birth correlates with particular adaptations in the way we deal and understand each other, including unique care-giving and instruction practices (Bruner, 1972; Tomasello, 1999).

This is an evolutionary fact that should be factored in as the unique context of human sociality. This context is too often overlooked and not considered enough as a crucial variable and potential causal factor in the investigation of how and what we understand of others, but also how and why we connect with them, and what constitutes social comfort. Humans do have special social needs, one of which is the basic need to be *recognized* and *acknowledged*, to be validated of their own existence via others. I will argue here that this is a cardinal aspect of both human sociality and human experience of social comfort, or discomfort.

Human Critical Social Needs

The need for others, expressed in newborns, is not just physiological. It is from the start also emotional, affective, and cognitive. The devastating effects of early stays in crowded hospitals or orphanages, and the absence of early bonding between the infant and caring individual(s), are clear demonstrations that the psychological integrity of the young child rests on more than sufficient food (Bowlby, 1969/1982; Spitz, 1965).

Deprived of basic attention and "caring," children quickly slip within themselves. They withdraw from the social world, from which they cannot learn much any more. Social development is often arrested, drifting toward idling stereotypical actions, the kind reported by Spitz in what he labels as symptoms of "hospitalism," also expressed in low-functioning autistic children (Sigman & Capps, 1997). Affects become flat; emotional expressions and behaviors become erratic; learning or any kind of instruction becomes deeply problematic.

Whether the causes are environmental or genetic in origins, there is no need to expound the fact that whatever hinders early bonding will have significant, typically detrimental, consequences at all levels of psychic life. Healthy development, including the development of the ability to simulate others or to construct theories about the mental states of others, depends on the basic ability to "relate" to others, to be "connected" with others,

Mutual Recognition as a Cornerstone of Human Sociality

Understanding others is a complex business. It is infinitely more complex than, let us say, figuring the blooming of a tree, the behavior of fish, the migratory flight of birds, or the trajectory of stones falling off a cliff. This is not just due to the fact that others are far more complex entities in themselves, are far more open-ended systems than trees or stones; the fact that they belong to a higher cognitive order than fish or birds. It is, in addition – if not mainly – due to the fact that others are like me, are the same kind of entities as me, and that I am trying to figure them out. Here I submit, as a general framework, that the complexity of social cognition rests primarily on the equivalence in kind between me and others, on the paradoxical fact that others are like me, yet are differentiated entities that I depend upon and get selectively attached to.

Within this general framework, social cognition is inseparable from self-cognition. Social knowledge and self-knowledge are two sides of the same coin, in the same way that Gibson (1979), in his ecological approach to perception, suggested that perceiving the world always includes co-perceiving oneself as perceiver. What I know and predict of others reflects what I know and predict of myself, and vice versa. At the core of social cognition, there is mutual recognition. By analogy to Gibson, in the realm of perception, to cognize others always includes *co-cognizing* oneself as social knower.

To be sociable is thus much more than just rationalizing about others' disposition, intention, and mental states. It is primarily about being "connected" and "recognized." Sociality or the quality of being sociable is inseparable from the elusive feeling of being included and having a causal role or impact on the life of others. It is about being "connected," ultimately about being visible rather than invisible, recognized rather than ignored or ostracized (see Honneth, 1995, for an in-depth philosophical elaboration of the idea). In this view, sociality rests on *mutual recognition*. The dramatic experience of trying to engage and interact with a person suffering from a lack of sociality gives clinical support to such account.

Kanner (1943), in his description of what he is the first to have coined as "infantile autism," notes that these children appear to have "an innate inability to form the usual biologically provided affective contact with people, just as other children come into the world with innate physical and intellectual handicaps." Kanner goes on insisting on what he sees as the "extreme autistic aloneness" of these children, their social isolation. Interestingly, for novice, yet well-intended, healthy adults who might try to engage with a child diagnosed with autism, there is always a great deal of discomfort and frustration, and the sense of being "thwarted", of becoming unsettled and unsure of themselves (Greenspan & Wieder, 2006; Sigman & Capps, 1997). These children are difficult to figure, removed, unpredictable, unreachable. They look through or beside you, they behave as if you were transparent, invisible, nonexistent, nonconsequential – an experience that is a typical source of great discomfort for the well-intended parent or caregiver, and presumably a permanent discomfort for the autistic child withdrawn into his world.

The symptomatic trademark of autistic children is the depleted "sociality" experience by anybody trying to engage them and connect with them. The social current and co-creation of meanings that normally arise among communicating individuals are either hindered or plainly absent. It takes a great deal of expertise and exercises from parents, educators, and therapists to contact these children, a difficult and courageous enterprise that requires sometimes infinite patience (e.g. Greenspan & Wieder, 2006).

What makes the raising of an autistic child so much more difficult and exhausting compared to raising a healthy, even hyperactive child is the fact that there is no room for mutual recognition, no room for reciprocal acknowledgment of each other.

The love of parents might be inexhaustible; it consistently remains unmatched in its return. In this context, it is difficult for parents to recognize themselves in the impact they have on their child. Inversely, the child is impaired in recognizing himself in what he does to his parents. Autism causes *mutual* blindmindedness, mutual invisibility, and it is a source of great discomfort, obviously for the trying parents, but also for the disconnected child.

As a developmental, non-clinical psychologist, my point is that autism reveals the debilitating effect of a lack of sociality, the deep discomfort caused by the lack of mutual acknowledgment, and the hindered possibilities for reciprocal recognition in social exchanges. This appears to be a cardinal feature associated with this psychopathology and it is revealing of the point I am trying to make here.

The Social Mirror Game that Takes Place from the Outset

The sense of reciprocity is expressed very early in the life of the healthy child. By 2 months, infants start to engage in face-to-face proto-conversations, manifesting first signs of socially elicited smiles toward others (Rochat, 2001; Sroufe, 1996; Wolff, 1987). From this point on, infants express, in the context of interactive, typically face-to-face, plays, a new sense of shared experience with others, what Trevarthen (1979) first coined as primary intersubjectivity. When infants start to engage in proto-conversation, they are quick to pick up cues regarding what is to be expected next from the social partner. In general they are quick to expect that, following an emotional bid on their part, be it via a smile, a gaze, or a frown, the other will respond in return. Interestingly, adult caregivers in their response are typically inclined to reproduce, even exaggerate, the bid of the child. If the child smiles or frowns, we are inclined to smile or frown back at her with amplification and additional sound effects. There is some kind of irrepressible affective mirroring on the part of the adult (Gergely & Watson, 1999), almost as irrepressible as the opening of our own mouth while spoon-feeding someone else.

The complex mirror game underlying social cognition does manifest itself from approximately 2 months of age, and, from then on, infants develop expectations and representations as to what should happen next in this context. The still-face experimental paradigm that has been extensively used by infancy researchers since the 1970s provides good support for this assertion (see the original study by Tronick, Als, Adamson, Wise, & Brazelton, 1978).

From at least 2 months of age, infants are disturbed when the interactive partner suddenly freezes while starring at them (Rochat & Striano, 1999). They manifest unmistakable negative affects, frowning, suppressing bouts of smiling, looking away, and sometimes even starting to cry. In general, they become avoidant of the other person, presumably expecting him or her to behave in a different, more attuned way toward them.

This reliable phenomenon is not just due to the sudden stillness of the adult, as the infant's degree of negative responses varies depending on the kind of facial expression (that is, happy, neutral, or fearful) adopted by the adult while suddenly still (Rochat, Striano, & Blatt, 2002). Also, it appears that, beyond 7 months old, infants become increasingly active, rather than avoidant and unhappy, showing initiative in trying to re-engage the still-faced adult. Typically, they touch her, tap her, or clap hands to bring the still-faced adult back into the play, with an intense gaze toward her (Striano & Rochat, 1999).

The numerous studies based on the still-face paradigm, but also studies using the double video paradigm in which an infant interacts with his or her mother seen on a TV, either live or in a replay (Murray & Trevarthen, 1985; Nadel, Carchon, Kervella, Marcelli, & Réserbat-Plantey, 1999; Rochat, Neisser, & Marian, 1998), all show that, early on, infants develop social expectations as to what should happen next or what should happen while interacting with others. The difficult question is what do these expectations actually mean psychologically for the child? What does it mean for a 2-month-old infant to understand that, if he smiles toward an individual, this individual should "normally" smile back at him? What does it mean that he picks up the fact that amplified and synchronized mirroring from the adult is an invitation for more bouts of interaction?

From an engineering look perspective, one could interpret these expectations as being perceptual or "low level" in nature. Accordingly, face-to-face interactions could be information-rich events for which infants are innately wired to pick up information, attuned and prepared from birth to attend and eventually to recognize familiar voices and faces (e.g. De Casper & Fifer, 1980; Morton & Johnson, 1991). From birth, infants would be attuned to perceptual regularities and perceptual consequences of their own actions, wired to prefer faces, human voices, and contingent events as opposed to any other objects, any other noises, or any other random events. Accordingly, this would be enough for young infants to build social expectations and manifest apparent eagerness to be socially connected, as shown by studies using the still-face experimental paradigm or the double video system.

But I propose that there I more to this puzzle than can be discerned via an engineering look. It is more than just mechanical and requires another, richer look to capture its full psychological meaning. I base this proposal on evidence of major developmental changes in ways children appear to connect with others. I will briefly outline these changes, interpreting them at a more macroscopic level, linking them to changes in the way in which a child experiences others and ultimately figures them out, including the self. The point I am trying to get across is that there is a whole aspect of social cognition that needs to be specified and explored at this macro-level that the engineering look is missing.

Early Development of Social Connectedness as Co-Regulation

Among the multiple ways we are connected to the world, social connectedness is of a very special kind. My eyes and mind might be connected to my TV set or I might be actively connected to the object I am trying to reach and grasp, but I am not socially connected to them. We are not engaged in any kind of *co-regulation*.[4] My TV set will not shut off if I cry, and the object I am trying to reach will not come closer or present its most graspable side to get scooped up by me. I am the absolute agent and they are the blind patients of my action, not monitoring anything of what I do or feel. I am transparent and invisible to them.

Unless they are dead or comatose, connecting with animate things, particularly people, is a radically different matter. It entails co-regulation. All protagonists can, in turn, be agents or patients. Unless one ignores the other, as in some instances of autism, the connection is reciprocal and the exchange is open. The connection is transformed into a creative meaning-making system. Mutual feelings and understandings can be created in interaction and in the mutual monitoring by the individuals engaged in the exchange. What is going to be expressed and experienced next will refer to what is being expressed now and what has been expressed and experienced before. Each time, it is a new history that unfolds, which is memorized and entered as a new variable for future exchanges. It is, indeed, a complex open system defining a relationship among feeling and mutually experiencing persons (see Hobson & Hobson, Chapter 15, this volume).

Aside from particular "attraction states," such as the maintenance of an optimum flow in a joyful play, it is a self-organizing and for the most part non-deterministic process (see the dynamic system account of proto-conversational exchanges in Fogel & Thelen, 1987; Tronick, 2005).

Outcomes of social exchanges and what is going to happen next are hard to predict, as multiple variables interact simultaneously (mood, temperament, the familiarity and disposition of the protagonists, notwithstanding age, behavioral state such as hunger, fatigue, and so on). But, despite this highly unpredictable aspect, there is one major stable character in social connectedness. It is that the exchange is *mutual, cumulative, and creative*, as opposed to being purely unidirectional, causal, and non-creative, as in the case of a thermostat responding to temperature changes in a room (one-way regulation in a closed loop). The mutual, cumulative, and particularly the creative character of social connectedness as defined here does not apply to the imitation documented in newborns, which remains essentially rigid and responsive in character (Meltzoff & Moore, 1977; Rochat, 2006b). These responses become more flexible, attuned, and hence socially connected to the experimenter by 2 months. By 6 weeks, for example, infants show a deliberate effort in approximating an adult model moving his tongue either at the midline or to the side (Meltzoff & Moore, 1992).

In brief, it appears that, in development, from 2 months of age, infants become sensitive to the relative attunement that others express toward them, engaging in co-regulated exchanges, taking the role of agent and patient alternately in the interaction. In starting to do so, they become highly sensitive to how others respond to them and they themselves respond more or less "accordingly." The accord of their response is what makes them socially connected in the sense used here. In my view, this is indexed by what appears to be the universal emergence of socially elicited smiling at around 6 weeks of age (Rochat, 2001; Wolff, 1987).

If the onset of social connectedness as co-regulation emerges by 2 months, it develops rapidly and takes increasingly complex forms in the coming months and years. In general, these more complex forms correspond to the new ways in which young children co-regulate with others, first in the form of dyadic exchanges (primary intersubjectivity), and eventually, by 9 months in the form of triadic exchanges (secondary intersubjectivity), when children start to interact with others, in reference to and with the help of objects in the environment. (For more details, see Goubet, Rochat, Maire-Leblond & Poss, 2006; Rochat & Striano, 1999; Tomasello, 1995; Trevarthen & Hubley, 1978.) This development is now well documented, but I would like to end this chapter by accounting for its meaning at a more meta-level and in relation to what I view as important steps in the development of children's social connectedness.

Development of Mutual Recognition

In the light of what is developing next, I take it that the deeper psychological meaning of the still-face phenomenon that is observable from 2 months of age (a child's disengagement and unease when facing a suddenly frozen partner) is not just that the child is reacting to a violation of his or her social expectations. The deeper psychological meaning of this reaction is that the child has been unexpectedly "tricked" by the adult – that some kind of basic trust regarding what was unfolding between the child and the interacting partner is suddenly lost. In line with the idea that we are deep down driven by the need to affiliate with others, my interpretation is that the child is actually experiencing a loss, the unexpected loss of what he was enjoying, the pleasure of co-creating playful happenings, a pleasure literally "personified" in the engaging individual who is now frozen and starring at him for no obvious reasons.

In the still-face phenomenon, the infant expresses his experience of a transition from social comfort (the pleasure of co-creating and co-regulating with someone) to social discomfort (the sudden interruption of such pleasure). He also expresses what we could see as some sort of implicit mourning and "betrayal," in the fact that infants do not always recover their cheerfulness completely when the adult eventually snaps out of the still face and tries to re-engage the child (Muir & Hains, 1993; Rochat, Striano, & Blatt, 2002; Tronick et al., 1978). If mourning or betrayal might be too loaded as terms, still-face episodes appear nonetheless to affect future exchanges in the relationship. Early on, infants detect variations in interactive styles and become selective based on past exchanges. For example, there is evidence that infants from at least 4 months of age are attuned and seem to differentiate the particular interactive style and relative contingency of their mother as opposed to a female stranger (Bigelow & Rochat, 2006). This early sensitivity to familiar interactive styles gives more room for the experience of "betrayal", a sense of losing social connectedness and possibly experiencing rejection, a source of deep anxietiy when familiar persons change. Social connectedness suddenly vanishes because the other might be drunk, preoccupied, high, or in a rage. The child withdraws as his existence within the relationship vanishes. The new attitude of the other no longer reflects anything the child is used to. I would say that during this severance of social connectedness, the child is no longer acknowledged in his own existence.

What I propose is that, in fact, in the still-face phenomenon, the child manifests the loss of an alliance co-created in interaction with the now frozen other. Before the still-face episode, the child's own existence was acknowledged via affective mirroring and contingent responses from the adult. During the still-face episode, this acknowledgment was suddenly gone, pulled like a carpet from under his feet, and the child collapses by becoming suddenly transparent to the other. What ensues is profound *social discomfort* expressed in avoidance, agitation, and eventually crying.

The need for acknowledgment in relationships emerges with the onset of social connectedness at 2 months. From this time on, it becomes a major motive for the development of social cognition, both in form and in content. The child will learn how to please and what is pleasing or displeasing to others in order to capture their attention. The capturing of social attention becomes a major motive in the child's life. The child needs others' acknowledgment in order to exist. Attention toward them is the currency against which this acknowledgment is measured. This process becomes increasingly evident as children gain postural independence and autonomy by moving about on their own. From then on, one of the child's major social motives is typically to attract the attention of others in everything they do. When entering the infamous "terrible 2s," children will create social crises to assert their own social existence, running toward cliffs without turning back and despite the desperate calls from caregivers.

The control over the attention of others toward the self is a major drive for the development of social cognition. It is also what gives children, as well as adults, the sense of being recognized – ultimately the sense of an affiliation to others.

Conclusions

So what is sociality and what constitutes social comfort? I attempted to show that these two questions do not meet the prevalent "engineering look" at social cognition. What drives social cognition is primarily the basic need to be part of other people's lives, to communicate and affiliate with them. This need appears to be particularly exacerbated in our species. I have proposed that what underlies social cognition are first and foremost mechanisms by which others can be monitored in their relation to us – how they value and pay attention to us, and what place we have in their lives. In this general context and based on the developmental considerations outlined above, I conclude that sociality is the sense of mutual acknowledgment of each other's existence that is created in reciprocal exchanges with others. Social comfort thus consists in the experience of being recognized as much as we recognize the other. Inversely, social discomfort is the experience of being transparent or invisible for others, the experience of not being acknowledged, hence socially disconnected. I have proposed that sociality and the sense of social comfort begin to develop by the second month in the context of reciprocal exchanges, this development continuing through life. Social cognition is primarily a spin-off of such development.

My conclusion is that the perception and understanding of others should be considered primarily as the by-product of a basic need to be recognized, to partake in the life of others, a spin-off of the basic drive to be acknowledged in one's own existence through the eyes of others.

Notes

While writing this chapter, the author was supported by a John Simon Guggenheim fellowship. Much appreciation is expressed to Claudia Passos-Ferreira, Michel Heller, and Katrina Ebony White for their helpful comments and suggestions on an earlier draft.

1   This is the first definition of "sociability" offered by the *Unabridged Random House Dictionary* (2nd edn.). "Sociality" is defined as the state or quality of being sociable (third definition). This is the generic sense of these terms used here.
2   "essentially a blending of social and cognitive psychology which focuses on how individuals perceive, recall, think about and interpret information about the actions of themselves and others" (*The Penguin Dictionary of Psychology*, ed. A. Reber & E. Reber (3rd edn. Harmondsworth, Penguin, 2001)).
3   There is obviously great variability in how prestige and recognition can be accounted for. It varies across cultures but also across individuals and social-economical classes within a culture. These values of social recognition also change over historical time, particularly in changes in recent Western history that have led toward "modernity," "post-modernity," and now global "hypermodernity," which brings people closer faster, breaking barriers of space and time in the circulation of information and providing exploding opportunities for virtual experiences. These values can be measured as the accumulation of material wealth, acts of

courage, acts of devotion, learning achievements, or, more humbly, acts of obedience and submission. Obviously it is a complex issue and it all boils down to how individuals measure and represent their power situation in relation to particular others or to the group at large.

4 Artifacts such as computers or interactive video games represent interesting exceptions to the point I am trying to make. To some extent, these inanimate artifacts do co-regulate with us as we play with them. They track our actions and respond to them as we do to them. But these artifacts have been fabricated and designed for such purpose. As inanimate machines, they are not creative in themselves. They are just extensions of the intentions of the designers. In interacting with these machines, we are actually co-regulating with those who designed them. Machines are just inanimate intermediaries of their intentional designers. They are not creative in themselves.

References

Bigelow, A., & Rochat, P. (2006). Two-month-old infants' sensitivity to social contingency in mother–infant and stanger–infant interaction. *Infancy*, 9(3), 313–325.

Bowlby, J. (1969/1982). *Attachment and Loss* New York: Basic Books.

Bruner, J.S. (1972). Nature and uses of immaturity. *American Psychologist*, 27(8), 687–708.

DeCasper, A. J., & Fifer, W. P. (1980). Of human bonding: Newborns prefer their mother's voices. *Science*, 208, 1174–1176.

Fogel, A., & Thelen, E. (1987). Development of early expressive and communicative action: Reinterpreting the evidence from a dynamic systems perspective. *Developmental Psychology*, 23, 747–761.

Gallagher, S. and Hutto, D. (2007). Understanding others through primary interaction and narrative practice. In J. Zlatev, T. Racine, C. Sinha, and E. Itkonen (Eds.). *The Shared Mind: Perspectives on Intersubjectivity*. Amsterdam: John Benjamins.

Gergely, G., and Watson, J. S. (1999). Early social-emotional development: Contingency perception and the social-biofeedback model (pp. 101–136). In P. Rochat (Ed.) *Early Social Cognition*, Hillsdale, NJ: Lawrence Erlbaum.

Gibson, J. J. (1979). *The Ecological Approach to Visual Perception*. Boston: Houghton Mifflin.

Goldman, A., and Sripada, C. S. (2005). Simulationist models of face-based emotion recognition. *Cognition*, 94, 193–213.

Gopnick, A., & Meltzoff, A. (1997). *Words, Thoughts, and Theories*. Cambridge, MA: MIT Press.

Goubet, N., Rochat, P., Maire-Leblond, C., & Poss, S. (2006). Learning from others in 9–18-month-old infants. *Infant and Child Development*, 15(2), 161–177.

Gould, S. J. (1977). *Ontogeny and Phylogeny*. Cambridge, MA: Harvard University Press.

Greenspan, S., & Wieder, S. (2006). *Engaging Autism*. Cambridge, MA: Da Capo Press.

Honneth, A. (1995). *The Struggle for Recognition: The Moral Grammar of Social Conflicts*: Cambridge, MA: MIT Press.

Kanner, L. (1943). Autistic disturbances of affective contact. *The Nervous Child*, 2, 217–250.

Meltzoff, A. N. and Moore, M. K. (1977). Imitation of facial and manual gestures by human neonates. *Science*, 198, 75–78.

Meltzoff, A. N., & Moore, M. K. (1992). Early imitation within a functional framework: The importance of person identity, movement, and development. *Infant Behavior & Development*, 15(4), 479–505.

Montagu, A. (1961). Neonatal and infant immaturity in man. *Journal of the American Medical Association*, 178(23), 56–57.

Morton, J., & Johnson, M. H. (1991). CONSPEC and CONLERN: A two-process theory of infant face recognition. *Psychological Review*, 98(2), 164–181.

Muir, D., & Hains, S. M. J. (1993). Infant sensitivity to perturbations in adult facial, vocal, tactile, and contingent stimulation during face-to-face interactions. In B de Boysson-Bardies et al. (Eds.). *Developmental Neurocognition: Speech and Face Processing in the First Year of Life* (pp. 171–185). Amsterdam: Kluwer.

Murray, L., & Trevarthen, C. (1985). Emotional regulations of interactions between two-month-olds and their mothers. In T. M. Field & N. A. Fox (Eds.), *Social Perception in Infants* (pp. 177–197). Norwood, NJ: Ablex.

Nadel, J., Carchon, I. Kervella, C., Marcelli, D., & Réserbat-Plantey, D. (1999). Expectancies for social contingency in 2-month-olds. *Developmental Science*, 2, 164–173.

Rochat, P. (2001). *The Infant's World*. The Developing Child Series. Cambridge, MA: Harvard University Press.

Rochat, P. (2006a). Humans evolved to become *Homo Negotiatus* . . . the rest followed. *Behavioral and Brain Sciences*, 28, 714–715.

Rochat, P. (2006b). What does it mean to be human? *Anthropological Psychology*, 17, 100–108.

Rochat, P. (2007). Intentional action arises from early reciprocal exchanges. *Acta Psychologica*, 124, 1, 8–25.

Rochat, P. (forthcoming). *Others in Mind: Fear of Rejection and the Social Origins of Self-Consciousness*.

Rochat, P., Neisser, U., & Marian, V. (1998). Are young infants sensitive to interpersonal contingency? *Infant Behavior & Development*, 21(2), 355–366.

Rochat, P., & Striano, T. (1999). Social cognitive development in the first year. In P. Rochat (Ed.) *Early Social Cognition* (pp. 3–34). Hillsdale, NJ: Lawrence Erlbaum.

Rochat, P., Striano, T., & Blatt, L. (2002). Differential effects of happy, neutral, and sad still-faces on 2-, 4-, and 6-month-old infants. *Infant and Child Development*, 30, 289–303.

Sigman, M., & Capps, L. (1997). *Children with Autism: A Developmental Perspective*. Cambridge, MA: Harvard University Press.

Spitz, R. A. (1965). *The First Year of Life: A Psychoanalytic Study of Normal and Deviant Development of Object Relations*. New York: Basic Books.

Sroufe, L.A. (1996). *Emotional Development: The Organization of Emotional Life in the Early Years*. New York: Cambridge University Press.

Striano, T., & Rochat, P. (1999). Developmental link between dyadic and triadic social competence in infancy. *British Journal of Developmental Psychology*, 17, 551–562.

Tomasello, M. (1995). Joint attention as social cognition. In C. Moore & P. Dunham (Eds.), *Joint Attention: Its Origins and Role in Development* (pp. 103–130). Hillsdale, NJ: Lawrence Erlbaum.

Tomasello, M. (1999). *The Cultural Origins of Human Cognition*. Cambridge, MA: Harvard University Press.

Trevarthen, C. (1979). Communication and cooperation in early infancy: A description of primary intersubjectivity. In M. M. Bullowa (Ed.), *Before Speech: The Beginning of Interpersonal Communication* (pp. 321–347). New York: Cambridge University Press.

Trevarthen, C., & Hubley, P. (1978). Secondary intersubjectivity: Confidence, confiding and acts of meaning in the first year. In A. Lock (Ed.) *Action, Gesture and Symbol: The Emergence of Language* (pp. 183–229). London: Academic Press.

Tronick, E. Z. (2005). Why is connection with others so critical? The formation of dyadic states of consciousness and the expansion of individuals' states of consciousness: Coherence governed selection and the co-creation of meaning out of messy meaning making. In J. Nadel & D. Muir (Eds.). *Emotional Development* (pp. 293–315). Oxford: Oxford University Press.

Tronick, E. Z., Als, H., Adamson, L. Wise, S., & Brazelton, T. B. (1978). The infant's response to entrapment between contradictory messages in face-to-face interaction. *Journal of the American Academy of Child Psychiatry*, 17, 1–13.

Wolff, P. (1987). *The Development of Behavioral States and the Expression of Emotions in Early Infancy*. Chicago: University of Chicago Press.

Zahavi, D, (2006). *Subjectivity and Selfhood: Investigating the First-Person Perspective*. Cambridge, MA: MIT Press.

Chapter 20

Commentary on *Social Cognition: Development, Neuroscience, and Autism*

Charles A. Nelson

Striano and Reid have assembled a well-researched and timely volume on developmental social neuroscience. In the eighteen chapters and three commentaries that appear in the book, a wealth of information on both typical and atypical development (with a particular focus on autism) is presented. I have been asked to provide commentary on select aspects of the book. This is an enviable task, as it permits me to critique the work of others rather than have my own work critiqued. My dilemma in preparing this commentary was in deciding which chapters to focus on, given that I found so many attractive. In the end, I elected to discuss the chapter by Reid and Striano (Chapter 11, The Directed Attention Model of Infant Social Cognition: Further Evidence), as it offered an intriguing model that attempts to account for the development of many aspects of social cognition.

Critique of Reid and Striano, Chapter 11

The authors begin their chapter by introducing a number of perspectives designed to account for the development of social-cognitive capacities. Following this succinct précis, they go on to discuss their own information-processing account of how infants select which elements of their social environment to which to attend. They refer to this as a Directed Attention Model. Consistent with the long history in developmental psychology concerned with *stages* of development, the authors propose that infants proceed through hierarchically arranged stages of growth (five in all). Inherent in the authors' model is a strong bias toward early perceptual processes gradually being supplanted by increasingly sophisticated cognitive processes. In my opinion this is a wise course to adopt, as it recognizes that more sophisticated cognitive skills are probably built on a foundation of more basic perceptual biases and processes. In the sections that follow, I begin by providing a summary of each stage of the model, followed by commentary. I close this chapter with some overall comments.

Stage one. The detection of socially relevant organisms

The goal of this stage is for the infant to be able to identify conspecifics, not unlike Bowlby's early model of attachment (in which infants have an "inborn" bias to attend to the mother). They make the rather specific point that "the detection of biological motion is of high importance for detecting conspecifics and that this process is required in order for the identification of the specifics of the social inter-action" (p. 160).

Without Reid and Striano stating so specifically, this stage is reminiscent of Mark Johnson's conspec model of face processing. As Johnson has elegantly argued (e.g. Johnson, 2005; Johnson & Morton, 1991), very early in life (probably in the first 2 months), infants are involuntarily and perhaps reflexively attracted to face-like patterns. The putative mechanism underlying this preference is the superior colliculus, a midbrain structure heavily involved in tracking stimuli moving in the periphery. Similarly to Johnson, then, Reid and Striano posit that moving stimuli – faces in particular – are "inherently" attractive, which in turn leads the infant to attend (selectively?) to the faces of conspecifics (which again, implicitly, are predominant in the infant's world).

It is quite reasonable to propose that motion sensitivity leads to selective attention to the faces of conspecifics. However, focusing on motion sensitivity misses a few points that are worth noting. First, it disregards the voluminous literature on static faces, which collectively suggests that infants, *within the first few months of life*, are quite sensitive to non-moving faces; in other words, the authors must account for why faces are attended to selectively, rather than any object. Secondly, it fails to make clear what the neural circuitry is that underlies this stage (for example, area MT? superior colliculus?). This is important, as, if this stage involves face selectivity, then the putative neural architecture should be involved selectively in face processing. Thirdly, it disregards recent work by Simion and Macchi-Cassia suggesting that newborn preferences for faces over non-faces is driven by the arrangement of elements in the face – specifically, that infants are attracted to stimuli with more elements in the upper half of the face than in the lower half (see Macchi Cassia, Turati, & Simion, 2004; Simion, Macchi Cassia, Turati, & Valenza, 2001; Simion, Macchi Cassia, Turati, & Valenza, 2003; Simion, Valenza, Macchi Cassia, Turati, & Umiltà, 2002). These data, then, call into question whether it is faces qua faces that young infants find attractive, rather than any moving object. Finally, the authors fail to consider that most information early in life is multimodal (see Weikum et al., 2007). Thus, perhaps it is not the "attraction" to moving stimuli *per se* but the association infants acquire between voices and faces, with the former being responsible for the initial perceptual bias.

Stage two. The identification of socially relevant organisms

Here the authors are concerned with what is essentially the recognition of familiar people, such as a preference for a mother's face.

Needless to say, this is a crucial milestone in social-cognitive development, and clearly builds on previous perceptual abilities; indeed, one might reasonably posit that identification of an attachment figure results from a form of perceptual learning, as well as learning by association. However, this is very likely a multimodal experience, not simply visual. Thus, infants rarely see a caregiver's face without also hearing her voice, feeling her touch, and smelling her scent. These inputs probably combine very early in life to help the infant distinguish the socially relevant from irrelevant/nonessential figures. And, because this is probably a multimodal experience, the neural architecture that underlies its function will be more complex than if the experience were largely visual.

Stage three. Assessment of the locus of attention

The issue here concerns the focus of the observed organism's attention. For example, if the infant is looking at the mother's face, and the mother is looking to her right, at the father, does the infant show sensitivity to the mother's gaze and turn to look at the father (a behavior that might be considered a precursor to joint attention)? The functional significance of this stage is the infant's understanding of when a social signal is directed at the child and is "intended for the self" (to quote the authors).

Implicit in this milestone is the assumption that, once infants possess the ability to distinguish between information intended for themselves rather than for others, then they can progress to processing more complex forms of socially relevant information. This strikes me as quite reasonable, although one might ask how infants who are visually impaired, or who make little eye contact, negotiate this stage. Clinically, it would seem that this stage might prove to be a watershed in development for infants who may eventually develop autism. If this was the case, might an appropriate intervention be to train infants to attend to where others' intentional focus is directed?

Stage four. Detection of the location of another's attention

Here the goal is to use the gaze of an adult to facilitate attention to a location. Thus, again drawing on the joint-attention literature, do infants pay sufficient attention to the gaze of another to use that gaze information, in turn, to redirect their own attentional focus? The authors argue that this biases the infant toward attending to some objects more than others, which in turn will lead to attending to aspects of the environment that are more socially relevant. Such behaviors can be deeply complex, of course, and it would seem critical to disassemble this behavior into its component parts. For example, what is it about the eye region that draws infants to attend to direction of gaze? Is it eye position, contrast, movement, or something else? We have known for forty years that, after the age of 2 or 3 months, infants spend most time scanning the inner features of a face, and pay particular attention to the eyes. Presumably, though, what information is distilled from the eye region changes with age. My interpretation of the authors' proposal in this stage is that infants process gaze more deeply than its perceptual features. At the risk of over-interpreting the authors' intent, perhaps this stage reflects the emergence of infants' use of gaze information to monitor and/or modulate their own affective state, or to engage mirror neurons to assist them in knowing the intentions of others. Such speculation leads me to comment on the final stage in the authors' proposal.

Stage five. Inference of goals and/or preparation of response

Here the authors cite data that infants in the later half of the first year of life can (a) discern intentional from accidental action; (b) understand action in terms of future goals; and (c) focus on the goals of an action rather than other components (such as the direction of movement). They go on to suggest that one reason infants cannot do these things when they are younger is because of limited working memory capacity. Once again I find myself agreeing with the authors in arguing that these complex behaviors (a) build on earlier and simpler developmental milestones and (b) represent a very sophisticated set of behavioral function. That said, I would like to know more about the neural architecture that underlies this stage, and what forces drive the development of this architecture. For example, are the behaviors captured by this stage directed by maturation of a frontal-striatal system (as many goal-directed behaviors are), and, if so, what experiential or genetic (or more likely both) factors contribute to the development of this system?

Overall Summary

On the whole, I found myself intrigued by much of what the authors were proposing. As stated above, I would have liked to have seen more detail about the individual stages, and certainly some speculation about the neural mechanisms that underlie each stage. Presumably this "filling in" will come in time, as theory-inspired research is conducted.

It is worth noting, however, that the model proposed by Reid and Striano suffers from some of the same criticisms that afflicted Piaget's model. For example, do infants ascend through these stages in a strictly hierarchical fashion? Or is it possible to skip stages (or, in the case of developmental disorders, to arrest at a particular stage)? What is the engine that drives development – for example, is it experience viewing faces (and hearing voices, and being touched, and so on) that is chiefly responsible? If so, one might expect a broader range of individual differences than if there was some underlying genetic machinery that was driving development. Examining the progression through these five stages cross-culturally, and also in select clinical populations, might help address this issue. Finally, how does progression through these stages relate to other aspects of development (for example, language, object knowledge, and so on)?

In closing, the authors are to be applauded for undertaking such an ambitious attempt to explain key aspects of development. We should all look forward to the empirical elaboration of this story.

References

Johnson, M. H. (2005). Subcortical face processing. *Nature*, 6, 766–774.

Johnson, M. H., & Morton, J. (1991). *Biology and Cognitive Development. The Case of Face Recognition*. Oxford: Basil Blackwell.

Macchi Cassia, V., Turati, C., & Simion, F. (2004). Can a nonspecific bias toward top-heavy patterns explain newborns' face preference? *Psychological Science*, 15, 379–383.

Simion, F., Macchi Cassia, V., Turati, C., & Valenza, E. (2001). The origins of face perception: Specific versus non-specific mechanisms. *Infant and Child Development*, 10, 59–65.

Simion, F., Macchi Cassia, V., Turati, C., & Valenza, E. (2003). Non-specific perceptual biases at the origins of face processing. In O. Pascalis & A. Slater (Eds.), *The Development of Face Processing in Infancy and Early Childhood: Current Perspectives* (pp. 13–25). New York: Nova Science Publishers.

Simion, F., Valenza, E., Macchi Cassia, V., Turati, C., & Umiltà, C. (2002). Newborns' preference for up–down asymmetrical configurations. *Developmental Science*, 5, 427–434.

Weikum, W. M., Vouloumanos, A., Navarra, J., Soto-Faraco, S., Sebastián-Gallés, N., & Werker, J. F. (2007). Visual language discrimination in infancy. *Science*, 316, 1159.

Chapter 21

Commentary: How Social is Social Cognition?

Simon Baron-Cohen

It is a pleasure to be invited to write a commentary for this edited collection of essays. They converge on a question of fundamental importance to developmental cognitive neuroscience: are there special mechanisms in the typical brain that are dedicated to processing *social* information? In my own earlier work I postulated the existence of distinct neural mechanisms dedicated to "mindreading" or "empathizing" that we use for a specific aspect of social cognition: predicting agentive events (Baron-Cohen, 1995, 2003). In my later work I postulated a "systemizing mechanism" that we use for predicting non-agentive events (Baron-Cohen, 2006). In this commentary on the field of developmental social cognition (and its relevance to autism) I begin by summarizing these two mechanisms. I then consider whether there is any relationship between the social and non-social mechanisms.

Empathizing (or Mindreading) Mechanisms

If a change is perceived to be *self-generated* or *self-propelled* (that is, there is no apparent external cause), the brain interprets it as agentive: an agent with a *goal* (Baron-Cohen, 1994; Heider & Simmel, 1944; Perrett et al., 1985). Goal detection is one such basic mechanism we use to make sense of the social world. Humans have a suite of such specialized pieces of "hardware" for dealing with the complex social world. We can think of the "empathizing system" as comprising basic instruments that come compiled to help the normal infant make sense of the social world (Baron-Cohen 1995, 2003, 2005). The empathizing system is postulated to have six key components:

1   ID (the intentionality detector) automatically interprets or represents an agent's self-propelled movement as a goal-directed movement, a sign of its agency, or

an entity with *volition* (Premack, 1990), and is evident from at least 12 months of age (Gergeley, Nadasdy, Gergely, and Biro, 1995).

2 EDD (the eye-direction detector) automatically interprets eye-like stimuli as "*looking* at me" or "looking at something else." Cells in the superior temporal sulcus that respond to an averted or direct gaze have been identified via single-cell recording (Perrett et al., 1985). The EDD is active in early infancy (Connellan, Baron-Cohen, Wheelwright, Ba'tki, and Ahluwalia, 2001; Vecera & Johnson, 1995).

3 SAM (the shared attention mechanism) automatically represents whether the self and another agent are perceiving the *same* event, by building "triadic" representations. SAM is active from 9 months of age (Scaife & Bruner, 1975).

4 TOMM (the theory-of-mind mechanism) allows an *epistemic* mental state to be represented (Leslie, 1987), enabling understanding of false belief (Wimmer & Perner, 1983), and the relationships between mental states. TOMM is firmly established by 4 years of age (Wellman, 1990).

5 TED (the emotion detector) represents *affective* states (Baron-Cohen, 2005). Infants can represent affective states from as early as 3 months of age (Walker, 1982). TED allows the detection of the basic emotions (Ekman, Friesen, & Ellsworth, 1972).

6 TESS (the empathizing system) allows an empathic reaction to another's emotional state (Baron-Cohen, 2005).

The neural circuitry of empathizing has been investigated extensively (Baron-Cohen, Wheelwright, Stone, & Rutherford, 1999; Frith & Frith, 1999; Happé et al., 1996). Key brain areas involved in empathizing include the amygdala, the orbito and medial frontal cortex, and the superior temporal sulcus. Autism, one of the subjects of this book, has been shown to involve delays and deficits in empathizing (Baron-Cohen, 2002).

The Systemizing Mechanism

The above mechanisms would enable one to make sense of agentive change. But how do we make sense of non-agentive change? Non-agentive change is any change that is *not* self-propelled and where there is a *pattern* to the change. The brain therefore engages in pattern detection. Some change occurs with total (100 percent) regularity. Other change occurs with a lower frequency, but there is still a pattern to be discerned. Systemizing involves such pattern (or law) detection via observation of *input–operation–output* relationships (Baron-Cohen, 2002). Systemizing is the search for structure in data, to test whether the changing data are part of a system. Systems may be mechanical, natural, abstract, collectible, motoric, and even social (for example, the law).

Systems that are 100 percent lawful (for example, an electrical light switch, or a mathematical formula) have zero (or minimal) variance, and can therefore be predicted and controlled 100 percent. A computer might be an example of a 90 percent lawful system: the variance is wider, because the operating system may work differently depending on which other software is installed, and so on. The weather may be a system with only moderate lawfulness. While some aspects of agentive behavior are lawful (for example, ballroom dancing), most human behavior is low in lawfulness: the variance is maximal. For example, there is no one-to-one mapping between facial expression and the underlying mental state that might be causing such changes in the face (Baron-Cohen, Golan, Wheelwright, & Hill, 2004). Nor do situations predict the subtlety of emotions, since in the same situation different people react differently. Systemizing works only when the same patterns keep repeating with regularity.

Individual Differences in the Systemizing Mechanism (SM)

The systemizing theory proposes that we all have a systemizing mechanism (SM), and this is set at different levels in different individuals, for biological reasons. These different levels are broadly as follows:

1 *Below average*: those individuals who have little or no drive to systemize. For such individuals, their SM rarely looks for patterns, and thus rarely notices patterns and can cope with absence of pattern. We do not know much about people who systemize only at such an extremely low level, though they would be expected to avoid subjects like mathematics, science, and technology.

2 *Average*: those individuals who systemize at levels within the average range. The two sexes show subtle differences within the average range. Thus, males on average perform higher on tests of map reading (a navigational system) (Kimura, 1999), on the Systemizing Quotient (Baron-Cohen, Richler, Bisarya, Gurunathan, and Wheelwright, 2003), and "intuitive physics" (understanding mechanical systems) (Lawson, Baron-Cohen, & Wheelwright, 2004).

3 *Above average*: those individuals who systemize at more than average. These would be individuals who would be capable of working professionally in a systemizing field (an engineer, an accountant, and son on). People with Asperger syndrome (AS) (Asperger, 1944; Kanner, 1943) can be considered above average in systemizing in that they become "obsessed" with a particular system (Hermelin, 2002). They also score higher than average on the systemizing auotient (SQ) (Baron-Cohen et al., 2003), and on tests of intuitive physics and attention to detail (Baron-Cohen, Wheelwright, Scahill, Lawson, & Spong, 2001; Jolliffe and Baron-Cohen, 1997; Lawson et al., 2004; Shah & Frith, 1983). Indeed, some people with AS may achieve extremely high levels in systemizing domains such as mathematics, physics, or computer science (Baron-Cohen et al., 1999), or art (Myers, Baron-Cohen, & Wheelwright, 2004), showing superior attention to detail (O'Riordan, Plaisted, Driver, & Baron-Cohen, 2001; Plaisted, O'Riordan, & Baron-Cohen, 1998b).

4 *Extreme systemizing*: those individuals who are extreme at systemizing. Individuals with classic autism have been postulated to be extreme at systemizing, resulting in them coping only with highly predictable, patterned environments, producing highly repetitive behavior to produce predictability, and resisting any change to their system. On the picture-sequencing task their performance is above average on sequences that contain temporal or physical-causal (that is, systemizable) information (Baron-Cohen, Leslie, & Frith, 1986), and, in contrast to their difficulties on the false-belief task, their performance is normal or even above average on two equivalent systemizing tasks – the false-photograph task (Leslie & Thaiss, 1992) and the false-drawings task (Charman & Baron-Cohen, 1992). Their obsessions cluster in the domain of systems (Baron-Cohen & Wheelwright, 1999); and, given a set of colored counters, they show their hyper-systemizing as extreme "pattern imposition" (Frith, 1970).

It is well established that autism arises for genetic reasons (Bailey et al., 1995; Folstein & Rutter, 1988; Gillberg, 1991). There is some evidence for systemizing co-segregating with autism: thus, fathers and grandfathers of children with autism are twice as likely to work in the occupation of engineering (a clear example of a systemizing occupation) (Baron-Cohen, Wheelwright, Stott, Bolton, & Goodyer, 1997), and students in the natural sciences (engineering, mathematics, physics) have a higher number of relatives with autism than do students in the humanities (Baron-Cohen et al., 1998).

Questions for Future Research: How Do Empathizing and Systemizing Mechanisms Overlap?

The social deficits in autism could arise because of deficits in the empathizing mechanisms, and the non-social features of autism could arise from the systemizing mechanism being set too high. One question is whether having their SM set too high could explain not just why people with autism prefer either no change, or systems that change in highly lawful or predictable ways (such as mathematics, physics, repetition, objects that spin, routine, music, machines, collections), but also why they become disabled when faced with systems characterized by less lawful change (such as social behavior, conversation, people's emotions, or fiction). We need research to test whether there are two independent anomalies in autism (in the SM and in the empathizing mechanisms) or if there is a relationship between an individual's level of SM and the development of his or her empathy system.

Note

I am grateful for the support of the Medical Research Council during this work.

References

Asperger, H. (1944). "Die Autistischen Psychopathen" im Kindesalter. *Archiv fur Psychiatrie und Nervenkrankheiten,* 117, 76–136.

Bailey, A., Le Couteur, A., Gottesman, I., Bolton, P., Simmonoff, E., Yuzda, E., & Rutter, M. (1995). Autism as a strongly genetic disorder: Evidence from a British twin study. *Psychological Medicine,* 25, 63–77.

Baron-Cohen, S. (1994). How to build a baby that can read minds: Cognitive mechanisms in mindreading. *Cahiers de psychologie cognitive/Current Psychology of Cognition,* 13, 513–552.

Baron-Cohen, S. (1995). *Mindblindness: An Essay on Autism and Theory of Mind.* Boston, MIT Press/Bradford Books.

Baron-Cohen, S. (2002). The extreme male brain theory of autism. *Trends in Cognitive Sciences,* 6, 248–254.

Baron-Cohen, S. (2003). *The Essential Difference: Men, Women and the Extreme Male Brain.* London, Penguin.

Baron-Cohen, S. (2005). The Empathizing System: A revision of the 1994 model of the Mindreading System. In B. Ellis & D. Bjorklund (Eds.), *Origins of the Social Mind.* New York, Guilford Publications.

Baron-Cohen, S. (2006). Two new theories of autism: Hyper-systemising and assortative mating. *Archives of Disease in Childhood,* 91, 2–5.

Baron-Cohen, S., Bolton, P., Wheelwright, S., Short, L., Mead, G., Smith, A., & Scahill, V. (1998). Does autism occur more often in families of physicists, engineers, and mathematicians? *Autism,* 2, 296–301.

Baron-Cohen, S., Golan, O., Wheelwright, S., & Hill, J. J. (2004). *Mindreading: The Interactive Guide to Emotions.* London, Jessica Kingsley.

Baron-Cohen, S., Ring, H., Chitnis, X., Wheelwright, S., Gregory, L., Willams, S., Brammer, M. J., & Bullmore, E. T. (2006). fMRI of parents of children with Asperger ayndrome: A pilot study. *Brain and Cognition,* 61(1), 122–130.

Baron-Cohen, S., Leslie, A. M., & Frith, U. (1986). Mechanical, behavioural and intentional understanding of picture stories in autistic children. *British Journal of Developmental Psychology,* 4, 113–125.

Baron-Cohen, S., Richler, J., Bisarya, D., Gurunathan, N., & Wheelwright, S. (2003). The Systemising Quotient (SQ): An investigation of adults with Asperger syndrome or High Functioning Autism and normal sex differences. *Philosophical Transactions of the Royal Society, Series B, Special issue on "Autism: Mind and Brain",* 358, 361–374.

Baron-Cohen, S., Ring, H., Wheelwright, S., Bullmore, E. T., Brammer, M. J., Simmons, A., & Williams, S. (1999). Social intelligence in the normal and autistic brain: An fMRI study. *European Journal of Neuroscience,* 11, 1891–1898.

Baron-Cohen, S., & Wheelwright, S. (1999). Obsessions in children with autism or Asperger Syndrome: A content analysis in terms of core domains of cognition. *British Journal of Psychiatry,* 175, 484–490.

Baron-Cohen, S., Wheelwright, S., Scahill, V., Lawson, J., & Spong, A. (2001). Are intuitive physics and intuitive psychology independent? *Journal of Developmental and Learning Disorders,* 5, 47–78.

Baron-Cohen, S., Wheelwright, S., Stone, V., & Rutherford, M. (1999). A mathematician, a physicist, and a computer scientist with Asperger Syndrome: Performance on folk psychology and folk physics test. *Neurocase,* 5, 475–483.

Baron-Cohen, S., Wheelwright, S., Stott, C., Bolton, P., & Goodyer, I. (1997). Is there a link between engineering and autism? *Autism: An International Journal of Research and Practice*, 1, 153–163.

Charman, T., & Baron-Cohen, S. (1992). Understanding beliefs and drawings: A further test of the metarepresentation theory of autism. *Journal of Child Psychology and Psychiatry*, 33, 1105–1112.

Connellan, J., Baron-Cohen, S., Wheelwright, S., Ba'tki, A., & Ahluwalia, J. (2001). Sex differences in human neonatal social perception. *Infant Behavior and Development*, 23, 113–118.

Ekman, P., Friesen, W., & Ellsworth, P. (1972). *Emotion in the Human Face: Guidelines for Research and an Integration of Findings*. New York, Plenum Press.

Folstein, S., and Rutter, M. (1988). Autism: Familial aggregation and genetic implications. *Journal of Autism and Developmental Disorders*, 18, 3–30.

Frith, C., & Frith, U. (1999). Interacting minds: A biological basis. *Science*, 286, 1692–1695.

Frith, U. (1970). Studies in pattern detection in normal and autistic children. II. Reproduction and production of color sequences. *Journal of Experimental Child Psychology*, 10(1), 120–135.

Gergely, G., Nadasdy, Z., Gergely, C., & Biro, S. (1995). Taking the intentional stance at 12 months of age. *Cognition*, 56, 165–193.

Gillberg, C. (1991). Clinical and neurobiological aspects of Asperger syndrome in six family studies. In U. Frith (Ed.), *Autism and Asperger Syndrome*. Cambridge, Cambridge University Press.

Happé, F., Ehlers, S., Fletcher, P., Frith, U., Johansson, M., Gillberg, C., Dolan, R., Frackowiak, R., & Frith, C. (1996). Theory of mind in the brain. Evidence from a PET scan study of Asperger syndrome. *Neuroreport*, 8, 197–201.

Heider, F., & Simmel, M. (1944). An experimental study of apparent behavior. *American Journal of Psychology*, 57, 243–259.

Hermelin, B. (2002). *Bright Splinters of the Mind: A Personal Story of Research with Autistic Savants*. London, Jessica Kingsley.

Jolliffe, T., & Baron-Cohen, S. (1997). Are people with autism or Asperger's syndrome faster than normal on the Embedded Figures Task? *Journal of Child Psychology and Psychiatry*, 38, 527–534.

Kanner, L. (1943). Autistic disturbance of affective contact. *Nervous Child*, 2, 217–250.

Kimura, D. (1999). *Sex and Cognition*. Cambridge, MA, MIT Press.

Lawson, J., Baron-Cohen, S., & Wheelwright, S. (2004). Empathising and systemising in adults with and without Asperger syndrome. *Journal of Autism and Developmental Disorders*, 34, 301–310.

Leslie, A. M. (1987). Pretence and representation: The origins of "theory of mind". *Psychological Review*, 94, 412–426.

Leslie, A. M., & Thaiss, L. (1992). Domain specificity in conceptual development: Evidence from autism. *Cognition*, 43, 225–251.

Myers, P., Baron-Cohen, S., & Wheelwright, S. (2004). *An Exact Mind*. London, Jessica Kingsley.

O'Riordan, M., Plaisted, K., Driver, J., & Baron-Cohen, S. (2001). Superior visual search in autism. *Journal of Experimental Psychology: Human Perception and Performance*, 27, 719–730.

Perrett, D., Smith, P., Potter, D., Mistlin, A., Head, A., Milner, A., & Jeeves, M. (1985). Visual cells in the temporal cortex sensitive to face view and gaze direction. *Proceedings of the Royal Society of London*, B223, 293–317.

Plaisted, K., O'Riordan, M., & Baron-Cohen, S. (1998b). Enhanced discrimination of novel, highly similar stimuli by adults with autism during a perceptual learning task. *Journal of Child Psychology and Psychiatry*, 39, 765–775.

Premack, D. (1990). The infant's theory of self-propelled objects. *Cognition*, 36, 1–16.

Scaife, M., & Bruner, J. (1975). The capacity for joint visual attention in the infant. *Nature*, 253, 265–266.

Shah, A., & Frith, U. (1983). An islet of ability in autism: A research note. *Journal of Child Psychology and Psychiatry*, 24, 613–620.

Vecera, S. P., & Johnson, M. H. (1995). Gaze detection and the cortical processing of faces: Evidence from infants and adults. *Visual Cognition*, 2, 59–87.

Walker, A. S. (1982). Intermodal perception of expressive behaviours by human infants. *Journal of Experimental Child Psychology*, 33, 514–535.

Wellman, H. (1990). Children's theories of mind. Cambridge, MA, Bradford/MIT Press.

Wimmer, H., & Perner, J. (1983). Beliefs about beliefs: Representation and constraining function of wrong beliefs in young children's understanding of deception. *Cognition*, 13, 103–128.

Author Index

Subject Index